So what'

So what's a boy?

Addressing issues of masculinity and schooling

Wayne Martino and
Maria Pallotta-Chiarolli

Open University Press
Maidenhead · Philadelphia

Open University Press
McGraw-Hill Education
McGraw-Hill House
Shoppenhangers Road
Maidenhead
Berkshire
England
SL6 2QL

email: enquiries@openup.co.uk
world wide web: www.openup.co.uk

and

325 Chestnut Street
Philadelphia, PA 19106, USA

First published 2003

A catalogue record of this book is available from the British Library

ISBN 0 335 20381 7 (pb) 0 335 20382 5 (hb)

Library of Congress Cataloging-in-Publication Data
Martino, Wayne.
So what's a boy? : addressing issues of masculinity and schooling / Wayne Martino and Maria Pallotta-Chiarolli.
p. cm.
Includes bibliographical references and index.
ISBN 0–335–20382–5 – ISBN 0–335–20381–7 (pbk.)
1. Boys – Education – Social aspects. 2. Masculinity. 3. Sex differences in education – Social aspects. 4. Gender identity. I. Pallotta-Chiarolli, Maria, 1960–. II. Title.

LC1390 . M35 2003
371.823'41–dc21

2002042581

Typeset by RefineCatch Limited, Bungay, Suffolk
Printed in Great Britain by Biddles Limited, www.biddles.co.uk

Wayne would like to dedicate this book to his nephew, Hannes Kirchebner who lives in Vienna.

Maria would like to dedicate this book to Rob Chiarolli for his nurturing, loving and pro-feminist masculinity.

Wayne and Maria would also like to dedicate this book to all boys and young men living on the borders.

Contents

Acknowledgements

First of all, we wish to thank the interviewees for their time, insights, honesty, questions, good humour, inspiration and strength even while discussing very difficult and traumatic experiences. We have really appreciated and been strengthened by their encouragement of us and the work we are doing.

We also wish to thank the many teachers, principals, parents and youth workers around Australia who allowed us into their schools, homes and youth groups to conduct the interviews, distribute transcripts to boys, and ensure they were returned to us. Your support, patience and enthusiastic participation in this project was much appreciated.

We would like to thank Maria Baira and Indigenous educators who supported this project: Val Lenoy, Retz Oddy, Raba Solomon.

For transcribing 150 interviews: Pat Bentley and Geraldine Stack.

For technical support with taping/recording equipment: John Cooper, Alan Cosstick, Cameron, Janice and others at Audiovisual Learning Resources Services, Deakin University. We thank Tania Corbett, Secretary, Curriculum Section, Murdoch University; Susan Vukovic, Information Technology Services, Deakin Uni (Maria's computer whiz!).

We also wish to thank Shona Mullen, our publisher at Open University Press, for her patience as the research project kept unfolding and several unmet deadlines faded into the past.

We also wish to thank Dr Dawn Butler for her useful comments and editing. Our thanks also to Eleanor Hayes and Barker/Hilsdon for consulting with us in the development of the cover design, and Kevin Eaton from RefineCatch for his thoughtful and attentive liaison with us regarding the proofs.

We would also like to acknowledge the funding and support offered for this project by the School of Education, Murdoch University; and the Faculty of Health and Behavioural Sciences, Deakin University.

We would also like to thank friends, family, significant others and colleagues who supported us and the project, found contributors, provided sound advice and encouragement, put up with our regular updates, and loved us through it all.

We are grateful to our colleagues, friends and students in the School of Education, Murdoch University and the Faculty of Health and Behavioural Sciences, Deakin University who encouraged us, read drafts, directed us toward relevant literature, and mercifully left us alone or allowed us to skip a meeting or two when we were immersed in cross-continent telephone writing and editing sessions.

Other colleagues like Professors Blye Frank, Bob Lingard, Bob Meyenn, Annette Patterson, Pam Gilbert, Deborah Berrill, Dr Bronwyn Mellor, Dr Martin Mills, Kevin Davison, Shirley Dally, Dr Michael Crowhurst, Dr Lori Beckett, Shirley Dally, Ian Seal, are appreciated for their support of our work. In particular, we wish to acknowledge the pioneering work of Pam Gilbert which contributed in significant ways to the culmination of our research that is a legacy to her in many ways.

We thank: Rob Chiarolli (for feeding us during marathon writing and editing sessions in Melbourne); Steph Chiarolli (for love, for being a fabulous daughter, and providing us with welcome interludes of conversation and laughter); Alan Stafford (for his loving support and his own distinctive and disruptive masculinity, and for a Sydney home for Maria); Will Doherty, Jack and Diarmid, for providing a peaceful home of nurturing masculinities in San Francisco for two weeks in June 2001. The way that equity, diversity and social justice were not only discussed but modelled and socio-politically acted upon made for stimulating conversation and inspiration for Maria to draft several chapters. Matt Dury (Freedom Centre, Perth Western Australia); Rebecca Galvez (for her constant support and friendship to Wayne); Anthony Lambert (for his friendship, support and brilliant insights); Val Meyenn (for her support); Costa Rozakis (for his friendship and tremendous support); Dhara Stuart (for her significant support on this journey).

Preface

This is a book about boys, but it is also a book about schools and masculinities. It began with Wayne's doctoral research at one Catholic co-educational school in Western Australia and expanded to include collaborative work with Maria spanning the Australian continent from Western Australia to North Queensland. Over the past three years we have interviewed Indigenous and Anglo-Australian boys, boys from rural, regional and urban locations, boys with disabilities, boys from diverse socio-economic and cultural backgrounds, boys of diverse sexualities. Overall, 150 boys and young men were interviewed, ranging from 11 to 24 years of age.

Through semi-structured interviews the following questions were used to encourage boys and young men to tell their stories of what it means to be a boy in an Australian school:

- What does being a boy mean to you?
- What is school like for you? Do you experience any problems?
- What do you like about school?
- Can you talk to us about your friends, teachers, family and their influence on you?
- What subjects do you enjoy/dislike? Why?
- Are you experiencing any pressures in your life at school?

In order to include a diversity of boys' voices, specific schools and teachers in various locations in Australia were invited to participate in the research. We also approached youth/health organizations, Indigenous educators in schools, support networks for boys with disabilities and Parents and Friends of Lesbians and Gays (PFLAG). These groups put us in contact with boys and young men who may not have otherwise had the opportunity through mainstream schooling to tell their stories. For example, we interviewed a few young men in their early twenties who reflected upon their schooling experiences in ways that they had been unable to while at school for fear of reprisal from teachers and peers. A snowball method was also used with friends, parents and boys themselves introducing us to other research participants.

Throughout this book we, as researchers, with our own histories, values and social experiences of gender and borderland spaces, are not absent from the research we have conducted. In order to make our positions and positionings explicit, we have attempted to interweave our own subjectivities into the research through narratives provided at the beginning of most chapters (see Lather 1991). We have also deployed narrative as a tool to foreground and demystify the actual process of doing research. This is in keeping with what Game and Metcalfe (1996) call 'passionate sociology' which challenges modernist masculinist academic knowledge as 'something dispassionate and disembodied, a product of the mind rather than the heart, body or soul' (1996: 4). Narrative 'is a method of inquiry' and a way of knowing (Ely et al. 1997: 64). People 'lead storied lives and tell stories of those lives' (Connelly and Clandinin 1990: 146). In this book, we use narrative strategically to offer a 'complex sense of the lived' alongside and interwoven with 'the reported' (Ely et al. 1997: 88). The narratives also function to turn the reader's gaze onto him/herself to interrogate his/her own positions and positionings.

In this book our primary aim is to problematize the ways in which adolescent boys, from diverse backgrounds and locations in the Australian context, negotiate and perform their masculinities, both at school and in the wider society. This we believe is important, given the backlash politics driving a moral panic and concern about boys in Australia, the UK and the USA, which construct all boys as the 'new disadvantaged' (see Arnot et al. 1999; Lingard and Douglas 1999; Foster et al. 2001; Martino and Meyenn 2001; Skelton 2001). Within the context of these debates, boys are often categorized and homogenized as behaving, thinking and acting in similar or predetermined ways on the basis of their biological sex (see Gilbert and Gilbert 1998). In light of this politics, we take up a particular focus on those boys who are positioned on the margins in terms of their cultural backgrounds, sexuality, Indigeneity, disability, and socio-economic status. We explore how they negotiate social systems of identification that are often grounded in hierarchical and dichotomous classifications and how this impacts on their relationships and attitudes to schooling. However, in providing the perspectives of a diverse range of boys positioned on the margins, we are concerned to foreground the various ways in which some of these boys also invest in particular versions of dominant masculinity to compensate for their inferiorized positioning – at the bottom of the social hierarchy – by other boys at school.

There is also a focus in this book on white, Anglo-Australian, middle socio-economic status boys. We explore the various ways in which these boys negotiate their masculinities in an attempt to provide further insights into the intra-group dynamics governing their social practices of masculinity at school. Attention is drawn to those boys who challenge and question dominant versions of masculinity. This kind of analysis is important, given that social practices of masculinity are not consistent but fluid and indeed equally open to negotiation by those boys who position themselves and are positioned at the centre (see Martino 1999, 2001; Beckett 2001). In addition, we explore the role that schools play in legitimating certain normalized constructs of masculinity. We report what many boys say specifically about school, teachers and their engagement in learning to explore what the pedagogical implications might be for gender reform and whole school reform (see Kenway et al. 1997; Lingard et al. 2000).

Our investigation and approach to analysing the social practices of masculinity is informed theoretically by the work of Foucault (1984a, 1984b, 1985), whom we draw on to highlight how self-regulation and normalizing practices impact on boys' lives at school and in the broader society. We also use the metaphor of the borderland, in drawing on certain feminist and postcolonial theorists (Anzaldua 1987; Trinh 1989, 1990b; Bhabha 1990b), to elaborate how particular boys are positioned and position themselves in a border space that is not free of hierarchical and often dichotomous social systems of identification and categorization. In this sense, we offer some insight into how all the boys we interviewed negotiate, perpetuate and actively challenge such social systems and hierarchies in relation to how they fashion their masculinities.

An overview

In Part 1, Normalization and Schooling, we provide the theoretical framework for our research and begin a detailed investigation into the lives and experiences of diverse boys at school. We explore how boys come to understand themselves as particular kinds of 'normal' or 'abnormal' subjects and the role that the body plays in how they fashion their masculinities. An investigation into their friendships and regimes of bullying is also undertaken in this section.

In Part 2, Diverse Masculinities, we provide an analysis of specific groups of boys' social practices and negotiations of masculinity. Here we focus on boys of diverse sexualities, Indigenous boys, boys with disabilities and boys from diverse ethnic backgrounds. We are concerned to explore the ways in which hierarchical classifications inform these boys' understandings of themselves as gendered subjects and how they negotiate these social practices from within the borderland spaces in which they are positioned by a dominant Anglo, able-bodied, racialized and heteronormative culture.

In Part 3, Sites of Intervention, we explore boys' capacities for interrogating hegemonic or dominant social practices of masculinity and how they impact on their lives. Particular attention here is paid to the role that schools can play in encouraging these kinds of critical practices. We highlight how for many of the boys we interviewed, particularly those attending religious schools, there appeared to be a discrepancy between the rhetoric of pastoral care and how the boys saw themselves as being treated by those in authority. We look specifically at boys' perceptions of and experiences in English, physical education and health education as specific sites of intervention for interrogating hegemonic social practices of masculinity.

Wayne Martino
School of Education
Murdoch University
Perth, Western Australia

Maria Pallotta-Chiarolli
School of Health Sciences
Deakin University
Melbourne, Victoria

PART 1
Normalization and Schooling

1 'So what's a boy?'
Normalizing practices and borderland existences

Introduction

This chapter outlines the theoretical frames that inform our analysis of boys' experiences of schooling and social practices of masculinity in this book. We draw particularly on the work of Foucault (1978, 1984a, 1984b) and post-colonial mestiza feminists such as Anzaldua (1987) and Trinh (1989, 1990a, 1990b, 1991, 1992) to interrogate the ways in which masculinities are defined and negotiated in adolescent boys' lives at school. Our focus, therefore, is both on the ways in which boys come to understand and fashion themselves as particular kinds of subjects, and how they defy categorizations and binary classifications that are inscribed through certain normalizing tendencies and practices. We think it is helpful, therefore, to define these conceptual frames in two dimensions.

Normalizing regimes and practices of self-regulation

This focus draws attention to ways in which boys learn to police their masculinities and to place themselves (and other boys) under a particular kind of surveillance. In other words, we are interested in boys' understandings of what constitutes 'normal' or desirable masculinity and how they learn to fashion and embody this masculinity in socially acceptable ways. The application of the work of Foucault (1984a, 1984b, 1985) has been particularly useful in helping us to develop a greater understanding of the role that self-regulation and *normalizing practices* play in how boys learn to relate, behave and think as certain kinds of boys. We are concerned to highlight, therefore, how particular power relations are played out in their lives at school and, in this sense, pay attention to the pecking order of masculinities in boys' social experiences and relationships (see Walker 1988; Mac an Ghaill 1994b, 2000, Connell 1995; Epstein 1997; Martino, 1999, 2000a; Martino and Meyenn 2001; Skelton 2001).

Borderland and mestizaje existences and negotiations

We use the metaphor of the 'borderland' in drawing on mestiza feminist and postcolonial theories (Said 1979, 1990; Moraga and Anzaldua 1981; Anzaldua 1987, 1990; Bhabha 1988, 1990a, 1990b, 1990c, 1994; Trinh 1989, 1990a, 1990b, 1991, 1992; Lugones 1990, 1994) to elaborate a perspective on the ways in which boys from multiple, marginal, socio-cultural locations negotiate and fashion their masculinities. *Mestizaje* refers to people who negotiate being in-between, inhabiting a border space constructed by multiple, hierarchical and often dichotomous social systems of identification and categorization. In this sense, we are interested in those boys inhabiting such in-between spaces at school. We draw attention to their realities of negotiating identity and belonging between, within and beyond the expectations of multiple, socio-cultural locations, both dominant and marginal (Pallotta-Chiarolli 1995a, 1995c, 1999b, 1999c, 1999d). Thus we explore the ways in which disabled, sexually diverse, Indigenous and culturally diverse boys accept, negotiate, interweave and resist the divergent and convergent labels and regulations of masculinity from within their various communities.

In drawing on our research with diverse boys from a range of backgrounds, we also investigate the role that a range of socio-cultural, economic and pedagogical factors play in the way boys fashion their masculinities. We address the following questions:

1. How do boys fashion, interweave and negotiate for themselves particular forms of masculinity and how do these impact on their experiences of schooling?
2. What practices at school do boys engage in as forms of resistance to certain prescriptions of masculinity?
3. What role do schools play in enforcing particular dualistic and hierarchical classifications in terms of how boys are encouraged to fashion their masculinities?

The remainder of this chapter will explicate these theoretical frameworks before proceeding to apply them in later chapters.

Normalizing regimes of practice

> Boys have to face not looking like a fairy, not being too dumb, not being too smart, every pressure available, fitting in the right groups.
>
> (Grant, 16 years)

The concept of 'regimes of practice' is very useful and informs our thinking about the ways in which boys perform their masculinities at school (see Butler 1990). This idea of performativity is informed by Foucault's insights into the self-fashioning techniques and understandings of power involved in the production of the formation of identity or subjectivity (see Foucault 1978, 1980, 1988). For example, Foucault claims: 'What I wanted to know was how the subject constituted himself, in such and such a determined form, as a mad subject or as a normal subject, through a certain number of practices which were games of truth, applications of power, etc.' (Foucault 1987: 121).

Thus, different forms of the subject cannot be separated from a regime of practices through which power is channelled and particular truths established. In short, the formation of subjectivity or identity is understood in terms of the cultural techniques for working on and fashioning the gendered self. This, therefore, leads to an investigation of what Foucault (1978) terms 'polymorphous techniques of power' in relation to examining the formation of masculinities in various boys' lives at schools across a range of locations in the Australian context. Hence, the analytic focus is on how normalizing regimes permeate individual ways of behaving to incite particular forms of desire:

> My main concern will be to locate the forms of power, the channels, and the discourses it permeates in order to reach the most tenuous and individual modes of behaviour, the paths that give it access to the rare or scarcely perceivable forms of desire, how it penetrates and controls everyday pleasure – all this entailing effects that may be those of refusal, blockage, and invalidation, but also incitement and intensification: in short the 'polymorphous techniques of power'.
>
> (Foucault 1978: 11)

Thus particular forms of desire shape the way adolescent boys relate, not only to themselves as gendered subjects, but to one another. In this sense, sexuality is accorded a pivotal role in our work in terms of investigating the ways in which adolescent boys learn to police their masculinities within panopticonic regimes of self-surveillance (see Laskey and Beavis 1996; Beckett 1998; Epstein and Johnson 1998).

Foucault's theorizing can be used to illustrate how our understandings of sexual behaviour are tied to disciplines in which certain concepts, theories and rules are formed. These are governed by historically contingent norms for regulating the boundaries of acceptable and desirable forms of heteronormative masculinity (see Frank 1993; Redman 1996; Epstein 1997; Mac an Ghaill 2000). Foucault highlights how:

> a complex experience is constituted from and around certain forms of behaviour: an experience which conjoins a field of study (connaissance) (with its own concepts, theories, diverse disciplines), a collection of rules (which differentiate the permissible from the forbidden, natural from monstrous, normal from pathological, what is decent from what is not, etc.).
>
> (1984a: 333–4)

Versions of masculinity and their relationship with other factors – such as ethnicity, Indigeneity, socio-economic status, rurality, sexuality, disability – are understood, therefore, as a set of self-fashioning practices which are linked to normalizing judgements and techniques for producing culturally and historically specific forms of subjectivity (see Mangan and Walvin 1987; McMahon 1998; Shofield and Vaughan-Jackson 1913).

Technologies of the self

Foucault refers to regimes of social relations as 'technologies of the self' involving techniques of self-decipherment and normalizing practices. This framework helps us to think about the ways in which adolescent boys learn to monitor and police their sexuality in terms of proscribing the limits of desirable normative heterosexual masculinities (Frank 1987; Epstein 1998). We argue that individual boys learn to relate to themselves in particular ways through adopting certain techniques of self-decipherment and self-problematization which are governed by particular norms for policing their behaviour.

In fact, this perspective on the fashioning of subjectivity relates specifically to Foucault's notion of subjectification, which we apply in this book to a conceptualization of masculinities as the 'set of effects produced in bodies, behaviours, and social relations' (Foucault 1978: 127; 1988). It is in this sense that we direct attention to the normalizing practices and techniques that are deployed within particular 'technologies of the self' that enable adolescent boys to turn themselves into certain kinds of gendered subjects. Our research, therefore, involves an investigation of the practices by which adolescent boys learn to act on their own bodies, thoughts, conduct and 'ways of being' to enable them to achieve or acquire a desirable form of masculinity (see Butler 1990).

We are particularly interested in the effects of 'compulsory heterosexuality' (Rich, 1980) and how the requirements for boys to display themselves as appropriately heterosexual impacts on the way they fashion and police their masculinities. The role that homophobia plays as a specific technique of self-regulation and surveillance of other boys, therefore, is understood as linked to a particular 'technology of the self'. This involves practices of self-decipherment that are tied to certain normalizing regimes in which sexuality functions as a policing or gate-keeping mechanism. It also raises the important question of how curriculum material and pedagogical practices function as a policing or gate-keeping framework within a school, and its links to boys' practices of self-decipherment, and peer surveillance and harassment.

Foucault (1985), in fact, formulates a politics organized around inventing new subjectivities which applies to our research with boys in schools. For instance, he focuses on Bentham's panopticon and the confessional as localized instances of the historical use of specific techniques of power which encourage a particular practice of self-regulation and adjustment (Foucault 1978, 1979, 1985, 1986). Foucault demonstrates how the body is inscribed within a field of socio-political relations in which it is invested, marked, trained and, in short, deployed: '[individuals are] caught up in a system of subjectification (in which need is also a political instrument meticulously prepared, calculated and used); the body becomes a useful force only if it is both a productive and a subjected body' (Foucault 1979: 26).

This calls into play the strategic use of power/knowledge relations which converge around the body. Moreover, such a focus on technologies of power enables a particular theorization of masculinities to be elaborated. In short, it is within institutions, such as the school, that mechanisms of power are operationalized through specific administrative structures and pedagogical, social and disciplinary practices which are governed by particular norms. Our focus in this book then is to explore the effect of these normalizing regimes on boys' social practices of masculinity and how they are institutionalized at school (see Martino 2000a; Nayak and Kehily 1996; Dixon 1997; Epstein 1997). Hence, it is possible to analyse the role of specific rationalities or modes of thinking that are implicated in the political technologies which impinge on the lives of adolescent boys at school (see Foucault 1982: 210–11). This enables us to explore:

- the forms of power driving certain social practices and relations of masculinity with a focus on the context of schooling;
- the thinking behind adolescent boys' own understandings and interpretation of their social relationships and how this relates to their experiences of schooling;
- how adolescent boys articulate particular understandings of 'masculinity' and what the pedagogical implications of this might be (Salisbury and Jackson 1996; Martino 2000b; Mills 2001);

- how certain understandings or ways of thinking about 'masculinity' are institutionalized within the schooling context in relation to particular political technologies of the gendered self (see Haynes and McKenna 2001; Martino and Pallotta-Chiarolli 2001b).

This focus is important given our interest in exploring the social practices of masculinity of adolescent boys from a range of diverse backgrounds and locations. We investigate the influences impacting on those boys who engage in practices of masculinity considered to be alternative to dominant constructions. We do this with the view to exploring possibilities for encouraging boys to relate in ways which are not built on problematic hierarchical classifications and dualistic ways of thinking about gender (see Davies 1993). Moreover, we are concerned to investigate how normalization is effected through cultural, administrative and pedagogical routines at school and how these impact on the self-fashioning practices of boys' masculinities.

Borderland existences, mestizaje interweaving and a hierarchy of masculinities

> You got your popular people, then your sort of smart students, and your A-Grade students, and then probably at the bottom, your physically disabled guys and your mentally disabled guys and your physically disabled girls and your mentally disabled girls. The popular girls would be just below the popular guys, about half a step below the popular guys. And the Aboriginal guys would probably be above the disabled girls, I think, but sort of below the disabled guys, which is kind of sad. Basically, if you're disabled and white, that's fine, you're considered the least different, I think. But if you're black, you're considered different beyond recognition, I think.
>
> (Andrew, 16 years)

A postcolonial mestizaje feminist theoretical framework responds to and also promotes a critique of the kinds of normative and multiple hierarchies of gender, as illustrated by Andrew, a young man with a physical disability. This involves exploring how boys from multiple social locations negotiate and transgress certain norms, identity categories and group boundaries. We also investigate how dichotomous and hierarchical discourses have constructed a borderland within which many boys weave and live their multiple realities. In this sense, we elaborate the kinds of 'techniques of the self' involved in their negotiations and resistances within the context of shifting terrains of normalizing practices (Zerubavel 1991). Hence, mestizaje research – which is devoted to exploring borderland existences and interweavings – is applied to an investigation of masculinities in adolescent boys' lives at school.

The term *mestizaje* originally refers to the creation of Mexican culture through the mixing of the Spanish conquerors, the previously Indigenous tribes, and the African slaves brought by the Spaniards. What is now categorized as 'Mexican' is distinct from these contributing Spanish, Indigenous and African cultures, yet retains elements of each in both original and interwoven states. It also continues to become something new, and without any of these states necessarily becoming hegemonic (Anzaldua 1987; Lugones, 1994). As Bottomley writes: 'We have no polite word in English like the French *meteque* or the Spanish *mestizo*, but people who celebrate being in-between . . . have indeed begun to take up some of the space created by multiple identities' (1992: 136).

As illustrated by Latina/Chicana-American feminists, such as Anzaldua (1987, 1990) and Lugones (1990, 1994), mestizaje theory can be used to address issues of gender diversity, cultural diversity and sexual diversity in relation to dominant Anglo-centric, phallocentric and heteronormative ways of thinking (Pallotta-Chiarolli 1995a, 1995c, 1996; see also Moraga and Anzaldua 1981). Our research takes up the challenge of these theorists and researchers in exploring how boys from diverse ethnic and Indigenous backgrounds, and of diverse sexualities, fashion their borderland masculinities. We explore how the boys we interviewed deploy, resist, negotiate and interweave a range of discourses in order to make sense of their experiences as certain kinds of boys.

For many adolescent borderdwellers in Australia, identities and community allegiances are not fixed and dichotomous. Rather, they are hierarchical, fluid, transitory, fragmented, episodic. In mestizaje theory and research it is recognized that multiple-within identity is not necessarily and always a deficit for the individual. It can provide insights into how normative, multiple and hierarchical regimes of knowledge/power relations operate from both the centre and the margins (Burke 1999). Mestizaje theory, therefore, seeks to define identity as being in process, multi-placed and shifting. Many of the culturally and sexually diverse boys we interviewed position themselves and are positioned as being mestizaje. In other words, social, political and cultural forces locate boys within, outside and on the borders of hierarchical, binary classifications. The borderland experiences of many boys also exemplify how those positioned on the margins are struggling with their own internal systems of inclusion and exclusion, power and structural tensions. This is pointed out by Tony who has a disability, identifies as gay and is from a Greek background:

> My identity is something that is really confusing for me because I find myself switching between all these different identities . . . as I mix with other people who have disabilities and who are gay or bisexual, and

> who may also have a certain non-English speaking background, and I find that I have some aspects of myself that I can identify with each one of those, you know, Christians as well, and I'm sort of thinking, 'Oh, but who am I?' because I actually see aspects of myself in all these. Even with heterosexuals, sometimes I identify with them too.
>
> (Tony, 24 years)

We explore how boys' lives cannot be simply and neatly incorporated into binarily constructed hierarchical dualisms. However, at the same time, we also investigate how some boys may be caught within normalizing regimes of practice in which 'compulsory heterosexuality' and hegemonic masculinity interweave with ethnicity, disability, rurality and other marginal sites in hierarchical social relationships. Hence, to be Italian or Greek is better than being Chinese or Vietnamese, to be muscular and hairy is better than small bodied and hairless, to be heterosexual is better than homosexual. And hybrid and impure permutations of these categories such as being Italian and gay, or Catholic and Confucian, are borderzone realities that cannot adequately be theorized utilizing dichotomous logics. However, our focus is on how many boys are still confined within the limits of such ways of thinking, despite their attempts to challenge the stereotypes.

Mestizaje theory draws attention to how the process of determining one's identity or identities reveals the significance of three interwoven forces of socio-political structure and power as are apparent in schools:

1. *Social ascription:* the labels and categories (both affirming and negating) imposed on one by sites of power such as educational policies and programs based on dominant socio-political discourses.
2. *Community acknowledgement:* the labels and categories affirmed or disapproved of by significant others such as teachers and peers at school, as well as parents and friends outside the school.
3. *Personal agency:* strategies of active and passive resistance, negotiation and assimilation undertaken by boys in response to communal and societal ascription.

Our research also explores three modes of connection in the borderland existences of these boys:

- experiencing conflict between polarities resulting in an *either/or* position;
- synthesizing polarities resulting in a *both/and* intersecting position between the binaries;
- resisting polarities to interweave a mestizaje position which is multiple, fluid, beyond binaries.

We demonstrate that many boys experience and can articulate a clear understanding of factionalism and hierarchical differences. They may even use dichotomous categories for their own ends in competition for a slice of power allocated to the marginal by the central dominant group. These articulations and use of binary categories often appear to be an emulation of the factionalism and hierarchies used by dominant social groups. For example, some non-Anglo groups of boys assimilate Anglo norms in the ways they construct a hierarchy from the most dominant/superior to the most powerless/inferior ethnicity. Similarly, boys from a lower socio-economic group may not accept homosexual peers as this is seen to further diminish their status in relation to affluent heterosexual boys.

Thus, as we will demonstrate in our research, in order to counteract the classifications of one's 'oppressor', the 'oppressed' may devise an 'alternate' system of classification that then proceeds to 'regulate' and 'oppress' members of the 'oppressed' group (Memmi 1965; Freire 1972). In this sense, we also argue that it is important to examine how boys adopt certain norms and how particular versions of masculinity are played out in the borderlands. In fact, we argue that a particular virulent strain of hegemonic masculinity surfaces in terms of how some boys enact their subjectivities and how ethnicities, disabilities and non-heterosexual sexualities interweave in their lives at school.

We do acknowledge, however, that a minority group or community identity can provide security and support, and a location to plan and implement strategies of resistance to mainstream power. However, in its need to create a united, solid front against the external enemy, a minority community can devise its own systems of censorship and stricture of differences. Rigid conformity and uniformity become internally coercive as a means of resisting external social coercion (Anzaldua 1987; hooks 1990, 1994b; Udis-Kessler 1990; Pallotta-Chiarolli 1992). Thus, socio-culturally and sexually diverse boys are not outside or in transcendence of these identity and group belonging categories. Rather, they are located on the borderland of multiple possibilities in relation to these categories. They complicate and interrogate binary classifications, even as they require them in order to negotiate their masculinities. Instead of meaning deriving from dualistic difference, meaning derives from multiple difference where everything exists in wholeness in relation to everything else, as metaphorically described in the following: 'To think that red is red, no matter whether the red is that of blood or that of a rose, is to forget that there is no red without non-red elements, and no single essential red among reds' (Trinh 1991: 89; see also Burbules 1997).

We propose that some educational feminist, postcolonial and sexuality theory is still locked into framing boys into a dualistic paradigm rather than interrogating to what extent the binary paradigm misrepresents and constrains them (Pallotta-Chiarolli 1999e). For example, there are both inter- and intra-hierarchical social relations impacting on boys in dominant and marginal locations. We argue, therefore, that it is important for educational work to focus on equipping all boys with capacities for interrogating dualistic forms of rationality and how they are deployed in fashioning their masculinities. This also means encouraging boys to embrace diversity (see Giroux 1992a, 1992b, 1992c; McLaren 1993a, 1993b). As Bhabha argues: 'we find ourselves in the moment of transit where space and time cross to produce complex figures of difference and identity, past and present, inside and outside, inclusion and exclusion' (1994: 1).

Thus addressing diversity for boys in schools needs to involve a consideration of how factors such as Indigeneity, gender, class, sexuality and disability impact on boys' social practices of masculinity.

Interrogating masculinities in schools

The theoretical perspectives outlined in this chapter inform in very specific ways our articulation and framing of what we consider to be important implications for strategic intervention in schools (Martino 1995b; Pallotta-Chiarolli 1995b, 1995c, 1996, 1997; Martino and Pallotta-Chiarolli 2001c). We interweave Foucauldian and mestizaje theoretical frameworks, in order to investigate the ways in which boys fashion and negotiate their masculinities. However, we are also interested in exploring the possibilities and the obstacles that exist in schools which either promote or limit boys' capacities to interrogate the social practices of masculinity. The voices of the boys themselves are used to highlight how their existing capacities for self-problematization might be deployed as a basis for critical reflection on pedagogical and whole school reform (see Martino and Pallotta-Chiarolli 2001a; see also Pallotta-Chiarolli 1998a; Martino 2001). As Andrew argues below, schools need to recognize, embrace and celebrate diversity:

> Schools probably just need to be open minded about different people – that includes everybody and anybody who has got any sort of difference in ethnic background, or disability or colour or anything . . . Students also need to be more open minded about what they're feeling and about people.
>
> (Andrew, 16 years)

But as Hey points out: 'the formal pedagogy of schooling [has been about] denying questions of differences to their subjects . . . There was little official encouragement to engage school students in discussions of the divisions and relations of power' (1997: 130).

In this book we explore the conflict and tensions that arise for students as a result of the imposition and institutionalization of hierarchical power structures by using the voices of the boys themselves.

Conclusion

In this chapter we have outlined the interweaving theoretical perspectives that inform our approach to analysing adolescent boys' social practices of masculinity at school. As indicated, our aim is to investigate both the normalizing practices and the mestizaje existences and negotiations of masculinity for a diverse group of boys in Australian schools. This is important given that, in the Australian socio-political educational context, this mestizaje perspective in relation to boys' education has not been adequately explored and analysed. However, we have also included the voices of boys from white Anglo-Australian backgrounds to explore their negotiations of masculinity in relation to both resisting and perpetuating hierarchical systems of classification and dichotomization. Finally, we have indicated that we are using the voices of boys to explore the effects of certain pedagogical practices and the impact of curriculum and institutionalized regimes in school on boys' social fashioning of masculinity.

In the following chapters we will explore multiple masculinities in schools, the nexus between power and freedom in how boys negotiate, regulate and fashion their masculinities at school. We also consider strategies that students and teachers can implement in encouraging boys to interrogate dominant practices of masculinity and hierarchical power relationships.

2 'You have to be strong, big and muscular'

Boys, bodies and masculinities

The classroom door slams open against the wall, announcing his arrival. The rest of the class of boys become silent and watch, their bodies leaning forward in anticipation. The scene is set for another drama to unfold for their entertainment, to break the monotony of schooling, to do what 'normal' boys do.

I look up to see the boy. Like the others, he is both in and out of school uniform. Like the others, he is using his body to subvert the normalizing effect of the school uniform and in doing so, is fashioning and regulating himself as a particular kind of boy: the rebel-hero.

He is a living, moving text: his strutting and swaggering, his school backpack adorned with stickers and key rings, remnants of his other world, his real world, of ethnic national flags, soccer heroes, grunge musicians, the sports clothing logo on the t-shirt visible under his school shirt, like a framing backdrop, an impenetrable body shield the school shirt cannot permeate. His chin, mouth and nose push upward so that the first strands of facial hair greet anyone daring to challenge his gaze. The hair on his head, alternating between dark red and midnight black, is in tufts of spikes and shaved close to the scalp around his ears. His earlobes in band aids attesting to piercings and earrings, their absence fashioned into a loud presence.

I watch him as he swaggers toward me: deliberately slowly, deliberately reluctantly, deliberately ensuring his shoes screech along the linoleum. I am conscious of this boy's embodied masculinity. His embodied self is a collection of signifiers: the scuffed and muddy black shoes; the greyness of trousers disrupted by grass stains and mud on the knees testifying to a lunchtime of football on a damp and well-trodden oval; sleeves rolled up to display the biceps and the patches of green grass stains and streaks of mud strategically positioned on his arms; the blue and white striped shirt both tucked in and hanging out around his hips, the breast pocket ripped so that it lies gaping open, the school emblem embroidered on it now a lunchtime football war-hero's badge.

This is the image that is revived in my memory as I sit in this room interviewing boys who enter, some with a swagger or a shirt hanging out and unbuttoned, or with unruly hair, some who want to appear cool with a sense of bravado and masculine defiance masking other realities, anxieties, dimensions and vulnerabilities.

Introduction

> The postures, tensions and texture of a muscular body are one of the main ways in which the power of men is seen as part of the order of nature . . . A man's presence (fabricated or real) is dependent upon the promise of power he embodies.
>
> (Loeser 2002: 56)

In this chapter we investigate both the normalizing practices and mestizaje negotiations in how boys learn to embody their masculinities. We argue that how boys learn to relate to and use their bodies cannot be reduced to some order of nature, as Loeser illustrates above. Rather the uses of the body are inextricably tied to fashioning and negotiating social practices of masculinity within a space constructed by hierarchical and often dichotomous social systems of identification. Thus we argue that normalizing bodily practices and self-regulating techniques are interconnected in the boys' everyday lives at school. In light of this, we explore the following themes:

1. *The body as the site of normalizing practices and constructions of masculinity*: boys' understandings of the 'normal' body of masculinity, including muscularity, penis size, modes of walking and talking.
2. *Body fashioning/adornment as signifiers of 'normal' and 'abnormal' masculinity*: boys' understandings of how clothes, jewellery, make-up and other self-fashioning techniques define their masculinities.

'Mine's bigger than yours!'

Many boys talked about how their bodies became prime sites for defining and proving one's 'normal' masculinity or having one's masculinity called into question. The muscular or 'built' body 'has come to provide a dominant metaphor for the masculine virtues of strength, ability and control over one's environment' (Loeser 2002: 55; see also Dutton 1995). In Dyer's words: 'The built body is hard and contoured, often resembling armour . . . Only a hard, visibly bounded body can resist being submerged into the horror of femininity' (1997: 152–3).

In fact, our interviews highlight the kinds of inter-gender and intra-gendered embodied power relations that are implicated in boys' social practices of masculinity. A major bodily signifier of distinction from femininity is the penis. The peer group plays a major role in the policing of particular forms of phallic masculinity. For example, one boy, Brett recounted an incident during recess when his friends initiated talk about penis size. He indicated that this event was significant because, although the boys talked and joked a lot about sex, they had not discussed the penis in the way that he outlines below. Brett talked about feeling uncomfortable and the incident appeared to have provoked a great deal of anxiety for him which was linked to the normalizing surveillance of his peers. It appeared that their gaze was turned on the body as both a site and target for asserting their power and dominance over other boys. In response to our question about why he thought his friends wanted to talk about the size of their penises, Brett asserts that it was 'like the macho sort of thing, like they wanted to be seen as better':

> They were talking about measuring it, using a ruler. They passed it around the group and we all had to say how big it was. They gave me a ruler. I just gave it back and said, 'Get lost!'. They'd hold up the ruler and say about here [*holds up his hand*]. They didn't actually take them [their penises] out or go to the toilet. This was during recess and we went to class and my best friend at the time, he was really into talking about it. He goes, 'Oh it hangs to the right.' He just kept talking like trying to find out, so I just said anything, 'It's this big and hangs from the right.' Just to get him off my back. [They wanted] to see whose is bigger. I didn't really want to say, so I'd just say what was most common. I just stuck with what I thought was normal.
>
> (Brett, 16 years)

Brett was uncomfortable with being forced to regulate himself in this way under the normalizing gaze of his peers. He strongly indicates his rejection of such forms of power, but feels caught up in a normalizing practice from which he can find no escape. For example, he ends up by monitoring himself according to the measurements provided by the other boys. It seems that he did not want to risk being seen as 'abnormal' or become the object of derision, and hence, the brunt of his peers' demeaning humour as this would signify an assault on his masculinity. This is a very powerful instance of boys regulating themselves and feeling compelled to self-regulate so as to construct themselves as 'normal'. It is also a powerful account of embodied practices of masculinity and the kinds of hidden anxieties that are provoked for boys around issues of the 'normal body' in relation to penis size. Brett, however, is critical of such practices of normalization which he links to acting 'macho' and thus to a form of power designed to establish a hierarchy of masculinities on the basis of penis size. It is in this sense that he feels vulnerable and uncomfortable in being forced to engage in such an activity. This raises questions for educators about the ways in which boys' bodies are major sites for learning to understand themselves as 'normal', the kinds of power relations involved in these social practices at school, and the implications for interrogating what it means to be a 'normal' boy (see Britzman 1995).

'To be popular you have to be big and strong and good looking'

Other boys also highlighted how issues of physicality, muscularity and bodily posturing were implicated in the self-regulatory and policing practices of a normative masculinity. In fact, schools can be prime sites where the physical aggressive display of masculinity comes to signify a lack of safety for boys who do not physically 'measure up'. Daniel recalls the feeling of imminent harm when surrounded by the physically aggressive posturings of some boys at his school. His strategies for keeping himself safe involved trying not be noticed by these boys, while simultaneously strengthening his internal emotional resistance:

> The initial thing of course was my safety . . . and I suppose I did everything I could to be invisible. I did feel like I wasn't up there with the macho people, the toughest people were up the top and everyone else was sort of feeding down the bottom end.
>
> (Daniel, 23 years)

In the following, Daniel illustrates the complex pull toward normative physical masculinity. He wanted to be like his aggressors in the sense that he found their bodies desirable, but simultaneously feels alienated, repelled and anxious at not being able to live up to what was constructed as the physical, masculine ideal. He is positioned in a borderzone where there is a push/pull dynamic between desiring the 'athletic', 'good-looking' bodies of his aggressors and feeling shame around his own body, perceived as undesirable. This leads Daniel to engage in certain practices of self-surveillance and self-regulation:

> I wouldn't say I was fat but I was quite solid and I used to get called fat a lot. I remember in about Grade 5 I started dieting. I used to come home every night and do an exercise tape to try and get thinner. From about that time in my life, I suppose, admiring other boys, the ones who were slender, the ones who had the athletic bodies, the ones that were good looking, the ones that didn't have pimples – wishing with all my heart and soul that I could be them and that I could have their bodies and their looks. At some stage I noticed that I was attracted to them. I used to worry from about Year 7 going into the change rooms and taking off my

> top because of my stomach. Other boys were blissfully unaware and would whip off their tops. I used to think, well how come you're not embarrassed, how come you're not ashamed of your body and how can you not try to cover up or do it in the corner. So I was really aware of the difference between myself and others.
>
> (Daniel, 23 years)

However, physicality, muscularity and bodily deportment are implicated in broader socio-cultural regimes of normative heterosexual masculinity, thereby becoming major markers of boys' positions within hierarchies of masculinities at school (see Walker 1988; Mac an Ghaill 1994b; Connell 1995). This is highlighted by Michael who states how society pressures boys:

> To be masculine you have to be strong and big and muscular . . . you're sort of paranoid about your body image. To be popular in school you have to be big and strong and good looking, in a sense, so that all the girls think you're good and you'll be popular with them.
>
> (Michael, 13 years)

Indeed, achieving a particular 'normal' physicality grants permission to harass others who have not achieved that 'normal' boy's body, thus strengthening one's position in the hierarchy. Mario, for example, illuminates the issue of body image that plagues the lives of some boys: 'sometimes you might get kids who are chubby and they'll get paid out but most of the kids go to the gym just to keep fit but then they tell fatter kids that they're fat' (Mario, 16 years).

However, normative masculine physicality and muscularity are not only and always heterosexual. The fashioning of the body by some gay and bisexual identifying students is also indicative of the hierarchy and heteroeconomy of masculinity. As Glassner argues:

> A boy must prove decisively his commitment to masculinity . . . One irony, of course, is that for many years now it has not been much easier for a man to be nonathletic if he's gay than if he's straight. The ideal man within the gay world, as in the heterosexual, is powerfully built.
>
> (1992: 287–8)

Gay-identifying Luke, for instance, was aware of the extent to which physicality was used as a marker of masculinity. As a borderzone observer of the heterosexual boys around him at school, Luke provides an insight into how many boys experienced conflict as they attempted to self-regulate their behaviours and body according to normative codes, while simultaneously finding themselves transgressing these very codes:

> It was really interesting to watch because one minute they would be these strong masculine young men in that they would cling to the stereotypes that 'boys do this because they are boys'. The next minute they'd kind of drop their guards and act like themselves. And then realize that someone might see and they kind of jump back into this stereotype. There was always the debate about penis size and who has the best pecs and the general physique. The bigger the build and the more your muscles rippled, then the more of a man you were.
>
> (Luke, 19 years)

What emerges here is the powerful effect of self-surveillance and external ascription dictated by the norms of dominant masculinity. There were also some boys from non-Anglo-Australian backgrounds who spoke about 'measuring up' in physical ways to dominant white, heterosexist constructions of masculinity. For instance, Eric, 23, gay identifying and from Hong Kong states that he has a 'typical small Chinese build' and comments on racialized constructions of Chinese masculinities in the Australian context. He indicates the tendency for Anglo-Australians and Europeans to perceive Asian men as effeminate on the basis of their comparatively smaller build: 'they're effeminized. Some of them, they think that all Asian guys are just easy or just feminine, you know, small'. However, he mentions that while such normative constructions had framed his negotiations of masculinity in Hong Kong, it was acceptable there to be 'sissy' or 'effeminate' as long as one was 'chasing girls', getting married and generally displaying overt forms of heterosexuality:

> [In Hong Kong] you can sometimes see guys and guys putting arms around each other's shoulder, they're good mates or good friends. It's quite interesting that I thought that a country like Australia would be more open minded in physical contact between men. I mean, just physical contact between men immediately means they're gay. In Hong Kong, [they say] 'You might act a bit sissy, oh you have girlfriend, fine, you'll get married and have children anyway'. That's what they expect.
>
> (Eric, 23 years)

However, for some European and Anglo-Australian boys, muscularity is seen to be essential in order to initially attract girls. Johnny articulates that the pressure to conform to normative body fashioning is influenced by both the desire many boys have to attract girls and also representation of the male body in the popular media. He positions himself and his friends in the in-between space where they both desire and reject normative embodied masculinity:

> Some guys think that if they were well toned and had better bodies then girls would look at them more. Watching Baywatch you see a lot of guys with great bodies. A couple of friends of mine, they're rather podgy and when we go swimming at the beach we always pick on each other's belly flab. It's like a big joke, but I think beneath it we sort of say we'd better get rid of that before next summer. We don't talk about it in the sense that it's a really personal thing. We sort of say things about hairy legs and hairy body. Like a lot of my friends have only just started shaving. They'll say, 'Gee you've got a lot of hair around your belly, I haven't even got anything yet.' It's more like chat about it rather than talking about the issues and stuff behind it.
>
> (Johnny, 17 years)

Hence, while Johnny is aware of normative bodily expectations, he endeavours to adopt resistant strategies such as using humour to trivialize his and his friends' awareness of and anxieties about not measuring up to the ideal of embodied masculinity. This awareness of normative bodily expectations also emerged in the following comment about how walking in a particular way can become a signifier of 'abnormal' masculinity: 'Some people at this school they call boys that act like girls, they call them girls. They walk around like girls, even if they were born like that, and when they walk around everyone bags them out' (Peter, 14 years).

This focus on walking is significant because it highlights how those boys who are considered 'not to act like a guy' become visible targets in the eyes of other boys. They are either perceived to engage in practices associated with girls or as a result of bodily actions, gestures, posturings and tone of voice are identified as gay. Interestingly, while Peter appears to be rejecting this kind of policing, his comment about the boys being 'born like that' suggests that he subscribes to essentialist, dichotomous classifications of 'normal' and 'abnormal' masculinity. The rules governing the ways in which boys learn to embody a normative heterosexual masculinity are important issues for consideration when addressing the implications for learning at school (see Laskey and Beavis 1996; Epstein and Johnson 1998; Martino 2000a).

'Just feeling totally inadequate'

Many of the boys we interviewed who failed to measure up to embodied normative masculinity felt or were made to feel inadequate. The powerful role and effects of these social practices were particularly accentuated by many of the boys with disabilities. These boys were located within a borderland of having bodies that were simultaneously defined as 'not male' and 'normal male', replete with the contradictions and tensions occurring at the borders of these two definitions:

> To be a disabled male is to be subjugated to the realm of the abnormal, the 'feminine', the 'not-male' . . . Physically disabled men experience conflicting identities because as visibly disabled men, their exterior masculine identities are always relegated to the realm of the 'Other' since disability is defined in terms of 'abnormality' and 'lack'.
>
> (Loeser 2002: 56)

Often these boys who were unable to 'measure up' physically, felt compelled to compensate for this 'lack' by overt displays of heterosexuality. Marc, who often uses a wheelchair and crutches due to fracturing bones and weaknesses in his legs, was able to competitively fashion himself as popular and desirable due to his many girlfriends and his involvement in a rock band at local venues. He frames this fashioning of heterosexual masculinity in terms of acquiring the status of 'a stud'. When asked to explain what a stud looks like, he says:

> Just like, you know, look like a tank, rough, good looking, cool. I find that I don't even need that. The guys hate it because I had seven chicks after me all at once and that's because of all the music. I'm not ugly or anything, but I'm not like a full-on stud. If I wasn't able to have girlfriends, I would think, 'what's wrong with me?' At the moment I'm happy with what I look like because I feel and I know that I'm wanted, it just makes you feel more confident.
>
> (Marc, 18 years)

Other boys with physical disabilities were often marginalized further with homophobic labelling. This occurred when the lack of normative physical movement which prevented them from participating in hegemonic sports such as football was conflated with heteronormative constructions of homosexual physicality read as a specific form of feminized masculinity. Andrew attributed much of the homophobic harassment directly to his physical disability. Likewise, he found that students ascribed him with having an intellectual disability based on his physical disability. His right arm and hand movements were constructed as indicative of his 'gayness' and 'being spastic':

> I've got cerebral palsy and my right hand hangs limp, my right wrist hangs limp which is an easy target for that sort of [homophobic] comment. I'm soft compared to some guys. I'm called soft because I don't play football because I'm too embarrassed . . . that's probably

> where the gay label came from too because I don't play sport and I don't watch football.
>
> (Andrew, 16 years)

However, he does indicate that he probably would have been one of 'those football types' had it not been for cerebral palsy:

> I look at the stereotypes and I think, 'What would it be like to be in their brain?' I think they wouldn't know any different because they haven't been brought up that way with peer pressure, and I would probably have been one of those football types.
>
> (Andrew, 16 years)

Thus Andrew illustrates the multiple perspectives that a borderland location in relation to hegemonic masculinity makes available to him. In other words, he is critical of how powerful these hegemonic constructions of bodily use actually are for boys, while simultaneously concluding that if it was not for the physical disability, he would be following these hegemonic constructions of masculinity without any need for interrogation. He is aware of the viscous boundary (Douglas 1966) that has been constructed, based solely on how he moves or is unable to move his body, between what he would be as a 'normal' bodied boy and what he is due to his physical difference.

Tony in a wheelchair with minimal arm and head movement also recalls the admiration and internalization of the 'normal' body as the masculine ideal, perpetuated by the constant references to 'normal' physical development for boys both at school and in his home environment:

> [I remember] just feeling totally inadequate. Constantly. And admiring and feeling so envious of these dudes whose bodies were developing and because wanting a good body image is normal and wanting to be like other boys. Then you'd hear adults say to others, 'Oh look at you, you're growing, you're getting tall and strong' and on and on and on, and I felt really inadequate. I still do and that's something that stays and stays and I sometimes do battle with.
>
> (Tony, 24 years)

He also discusses his constant self-regulating vigilance to ensure that he resists and challenges these constructions. However, Tony articulates an awareness of how his borderland existence has allowed him a certain degree of agency to step out of heteronormative and hegemonic patterns of masculinist lifestyle. He links this to the privilege of having had 'an education' which enables him to critically interrogate the social 'system' rather than pathologize himself:

> On a more positive note, I know that this is all stuff that is constructed and it's been so powerful. I feel really privileged to have got an education because without that I would've felt like it was all my fault. And I know now that it's not . . . I know now that it's the system. I know that I'm in a very privileged position to be able to change. So that's really given me a lot of opportunities and given me a lot of motivation to actually continue to study. These guys who have all their muscles and these fantastic bodies. Now when I meet them again I say 'What are you up to?' half of them have gotten married and divorced and doing jobs they don't like. So now it's really not that bad.
>
> (Tony, 24 years)

Haseeb, also in a wheelchair, found that his masculinity was evaluated according to his physical capabilities. Many people assumed that because of his physical disability, he would be endeavouring to develop the muscularity of his upper body and regularly frequent a gym:

> Sometimes they [peers] pressure you like 'Oh, why don't you go to the gym?' Sometimes you think if you're in a wheelchair it's your duty to go to gym . . . you need to go and do something, make yourself a bit stronger. So that is a big problem. I believe that if you are strong from your heart that's what you need and not from your physical appearance.
>
> (Haseeb, 22 years)

Thus many boys in our research highlight how being positioned on the margins and inhabiting a borderland space, leads them to develop an awareness of the effects of the normalizing practices of embodied masculinity. From this borderland positioning, they acquire capacities to problematize the 'taken for grantedness' and naturalizating practices of embodied masculinity.

'It's what you wear and your hair and the number of earrings in each lobe'

What many boys said about body fashioning also tended to illuminate the various norms governing boys' policing of masculinity. Body adornment such as clothing, make-up, jewellery and hairstyles are key indicators of a 'normal' or borderland masculine positioning. For example, at one particular school, it was not only the study of home economics that could marginalize boys as 'girls', but the fact that doing home economics involved wearing an apron. Indeed, for Luke, the school perpetuated this marginalization by publicly drawing attention to the aprons:

> There were four boys in the Year 8 home economics class, myself included. We copped a lot of flack because of it and it was actually mentioned in the Yearbook. It said something like, 'The four boys wrestling with aprons', then listed our names. Considering that cooking is a skill that everyone should obtain, the 'gents' really couldn't look past the wife in the kitchen stereotype.
>
> (Luke, 19 years)

Other boys were also aware of how school systems perpetuate and construct inter-gender dualities and intra-gender hierarchies through uniforms and rules regarding hair, jewellery and make-up (see Symes and Meadmore 1996). This system is then manipulated by students to further accentuate the differences and use them as markers of power and marginality. Mike describes the concerns over his hair colour at his Catholic co-educational school which eventually led to his parents withdrawing him from the school:

> I couldn't even have an earring because I was a boy and if I did, I'd have to cover it up with a bandaid. I got suspended for having green hair. I think it's just plain sexism because we were boys. [The girls] are allowed to have one earring in each earlobe, and that's it. Also necklaces, you couldn't have necklaces unless it was a religious symbol. They're just power, power, power, rules, rules, rules. In the first five minutes of the first lesson this teacher sent me straight over to the front office to speak to the principal about my hair. He said that I was going to be suspended for three days. It's not as bad as discriminating against a race or anything like that but it's in the same sort of way.
>
> (Mike, 17 years)

Mike's act of dying his hair is regarded as defiance against a particular authoritarian system of discipline which is about enforcing inter-gender dualistic classifications and rules pertaining to gendered body adornment. In order to combat this system he strategically deploys the discourse of reverse sexism as an act of resistance. He sees such rules as irrelevant to learning and with this assertion highlights the limits of the social, moral and regulatory practices of schools (see Symes and Meadmore 1996).

Glenn is also aware of how transgressing gendernormative rules around body fashioning can be manipulated and displayed to support the constructions of a tough, 'cool' and resilient masculinity. He is able to draw the line between appropriate transgression or 'difference' that reinscribes a desirable masculinity, and inappropriate transgression that signifies effeminacy. For example, Glenn indicates that there is a 'difference' between wearing a girl's skirt and a girl's t-shirt. He talks about how wearing, displaying and performing with eyebrow rings, nipple rings and earrings can be deployed to assert a valorized normative construction of hegemonic masculinity. Body adornment for Glenn is not about signifying effeminacy inscribed on the body, but rather warding off any association with the feminine:

> If a male wears a skirt, well that's different. But you can have girls' t-shirts because there's not that much difference between clothing. It comes down to what you look like. If you have long curly blonde hair, you think, oh yeah, you're a female. But you can't dye your hair unless you're a female. You can't get earrings unless you're a female. I want to get a nipple ring, an eyebrow ring. I get called a female because I've about three or four earrings. I love them. You see someone and say, 'Oh wow, that looks really cool . . . I wouldn't mind getting one of those'. You see people with earrings in various places, like this rock climbing chap, he's a body piercer, he's got his nipples done and he joins two bits of rope and lifts bricks with them [his nipples] and I go, 'Oh wow, he's so cool'.
>
> (Glenn, 16 years)

However, Glenn is aware of how these body fashionings contravene traditional normative gender constructions within his Catholic school. But it is also about the school's role in the production and moral regulation of what is considered to be a respectable citizen. Glenn indicates that the public perception of young people with body piercing serves a major regulatory mechanism for policing, disciplining and demonizing the adolescent body in public institutions:

> I wouldn't be allowed to wear them [to school] because we're males. We're not allowed to wear earrings, and are not meant to have bleached or dyed hair, because of what the public would make of us. We're expected to dress neatly, like our uniforms tucked in, tie on, tie straight, but then what male dresses neatly? They like to be scruffy, hair scruffed up . . . and then on the way home, tie off, shirt out, undo the top buttons, scruff up my hair a bit, get out of school uniform.
>
> (Glenn, 16 years)

Glenn illustrates well how he shifts clothing styles as he traverses from one location to another. He subscribes to a naturalized construct of masculinity in his assertion that all boys 'like to be scruffy'. Interestingly he appears to be changing out of one uniform prescribed by the school and into another dictated by the norms of dominant masculinity.

Unlike Glenn, Danny, a circus performer, is sexualized and feminized by other boys for wearing tights. So rather than warding off effeminacy, he uses strategies of resistance which parody normative feminine responses to sexual objectification and harassment. He talks about pretending to like the attention which is how women are constructed as reacting in these kinds of situations:

> The boys mainly worry about tights. It's really a hassle, you get heaps of people just whistling at you. Guys trying to pay you out. But you just act it up if someone does that. You just pretend to like it. Just smile and just rub your chest or something like that.
>
> (Danny, 16 years)

This account of boys whistling at Danny when confronted with him wearing tights indicates that they have anxieties about dealing with those who transgress normative boundaries and expectations for acting, dressing and behaving suitably male. It is interesting how the male body in tights provokes such anxiety in other boys whose reactions indicate that they can only resort to sexualizing and objectifying him as the homosexual 'other' (Plummer 1999).

Bisexual-identifying Rowan is also aware that his transgression of normative masculine codes of dress and the wearing of make-up align him as non-heterosexual and thus he considers his body adornment to be a deliberate resistant signifier of his 'abnormal' sexuality. While he was prepared to deal with this at school and still does in the wider society, he finds it difficult 'keeping up the facade' that this incessant social scrutiny is not affecting him:

> I used to do things like wear nail polish or wear eyeliner. Not that anyone would be nasty to me about it, but they would comment on it and make an issue of it and my sexuality. I remember teachers treating me in the same way. Because I dress in a certain way which isn't traditionally a very masculine way to dress, people will feel that that's a bit of a freaky thing to do. I feel that I always have to have a facade up . . .
>
> (Rowan, 19 years)

Thus, deviance is marked and inscribed by others on the basis of body fashioning and adornment practices. However, the boys themselves have highlighted how conscious they are of the deliberate facade to fashion themselves in particular ways to contravene the dominant norms for what is considered to be suitably and traditionally masculine. In some cases, they are able to subvert these norms and escape an essentializing tendency which grounds gendered behaviour in biological sex differences. However, some boys simultaneously transgress and subscribe to normative embodied masculinity. But all boys are aware of certain forms of policing and surveillance driving institutionalized regimes of 'compulsory heterosexuality' and a form of moral regulation in schools which reinscribe conventional dualistic gender classifications (see Epstein and Johnson 1998).

'I'm a tomgirl'

There was one young person in our research who refuted the binary construction of gender duality outright. Stephen, 13 years, who attends an inner city state co-educational school, refuses to construct himself as a boy who could be pathologized as displaying symptoms of Gender Identity Dysphoria (GID), or as a transgendered girl who should undertake chemical, hormonal and surgical reconstruction in order to become a woman (Coates 1987; Zucker and Bradley 1995). Rather, Stephen appears to be comfortable dwelling in the mestizaje borderzone of gender diversity as a self-defined 'tomgirl' (see also Martino and Pallotta-Chiarolli 2001b). The interview with Stephen exemplifies how body performativity is about socially acquired bodily attributes and 'prestigious imitation' that have been developed through the child's involvement in a range of social practices (Mauss 1973; Butler 1990). S/he self-identifies as 'a tomgirl' due to experiencing four interactive processes: external classification by peers and teachers; external surveillance by peers and teachers; panopticonic self-fashioning; and transgressive agency in refusing to perform or pass as either girl or boy. S/he devises a new 'tomgirl' self based on imitation and manipulation of the available socio-cultural resources and discursive frameworks of masculinity and femininity.

During the interview, Stephen stood up several times to demonstrate to the interviewer how the walk and other bodily styles that were components of being a 'tomgirl' had been fashioned. Stephen explained these were based on the observation and imitation of girls at school and women in society, and on men performing femininity as 'drag queens' s/he had seen in magazines and on television:

> When I'm wearing girls' clothes I always walk around [*stands up gracefully*], strut, [*begins to walk slowly with hips forward*] like wiggling my butt [*does so*] and walk like that [*swinging arms and head slowly and sensually*], sort of curvy [*accentuating hip swaying*]. [As a boy] I just walk normally [*ceases all swaying and accentuated head, arm and hip movement*], like that [*walking straight ahead quickly*], walking up and down [*keeps body rigid, taking larger steps, louder stomping on the floor*], straight [*head forward slightly, shoulders hunched, hands as fists*]. I prefer bobbing up and down like that.
>
> (Stephen, 13 years)

This last walk was a mixture of both gendernormative masculine and feminine styles that Stephen had just performed as well as introducing a new up-and-down easygoing rhythm. Thus, we can see how Stephen has imitated and fashioned a self that can perform, indeed parody and imitate, a gender according to social context and individual desire, as well as devising a walk that transgresses both. Nevertheless, it is also interesting how Stephen labels the masculine walk as 'normal'.

As well as using bodily movements, Stephen also utilized clothing to distinguish between and perform various masculinities and femininities, based largely on styles in teen popular culture. For instance, despite ongoing verbal harassment from some male peers, Stephen had fashioned him/herself as Mel B from the Spice Girls for the week during his/her thirteenth birthday, including make-up worn to his/her 'Spice Girls Birthday Party'. More recently, Stephen was fashioning various forms of masculinity by adopting specific masculine dress codes. During the interview, Stephen was wearing what s/he described as 'surfie shirt, baggy shorts, and sneakers':

> Kids always pick on me when I wear something different, because I think it was last week I wanted to be a punk. I had the army pants, the jacket, the boots, the spiky hair . . . They were teasing me about it. And then I wanted to be a dance party guy. I've got the dance pants and the shirts, different coloured lights, and the pants glow . . . I had them on last week. Now I want to be a surfer and then . . . I don't know, I could change next week.
>
> (Stephen, 13 years)

When Stephen was asked to define a 'tomgirl's' gender during the interview, the response could easily be construed as a case of GID. S/he drew an imaginary line in the air in front of him/her with boys at one end and girls at the other, and s/he indicated 'right in the middle . . . because I'm different, I'm both, I dress up as a girl sometimes and a boy sometimes'.

Stephen's situation is an example of the possibilities that can be explored beyond diagnosis and treatment for GID. S/he had experienced severe harassment at his/her primary school before his/her parents had found a secondary school that was committed to accepting Stephen's cross-gender/transgender explorations and minimizing harassment. The school principal and teachers focused on Stephen's emotional well-being and educational achievements, while the young adolescent was given some latitude to explore various gender and sexual roles. This involved educating and monitoring other students in relation to their understandings of gender, sexuality and harassment of Stephen.

The theories of Foucault (1980), Mauss (1985) and Butler (1990), particularly their deconstruction of self-fashioning and panopticonic practices in relation to gender and sexuality, can be seen in the ongoing debates surrounding what psychiatry and psychotherapy have constructed as Gender Identity Dysphoria (GID) in children and adolescents. Practitioners and clinicians such as Coates (1987), Green (1987), Zucker and Bradley (1995) utilize gender normative and heteronormative constructs of identity to rationalize and justify psychiatric and other clinical interventions with children and adolescents who exhibit what is binarily constructed as 'cross-gender identification'. The focus of these therapeutic interventions is the reinstatement of a 'natural' gender duality by pathologizing the child and his/her lack of conformity to a panopticonic society's hegemonic norms for fashioning a feminine or masculine heterosexual self. The school is a major site of naturalizing gender duality via regulation and surveillance. The difficulties experienced by transgendered children and adolescents at school are often used to justify therapeutic intervention to modify the child rather than educational interventions to modify the school (Haynes and McKenna 2001; Martino and Pallotta-Chiarolli 2001b).

> We don't know how to change society, but we can change their gender identity problems so they can live in their peer group with less distress.
>
> (Bahlburg 1993, in Minter 1999: 18)

> The gender-disturbed child moving into adolescence is a sensitive individual with reduced tolerance to anxiety, a rather weak sense of himself or herself, and a degree of gender insecurity. These factors may make it very difficult for this individual to contemplate heterosexual involvement.
>
> (Bradley 1985, in Minter 1999: 21)

Rottnek poses the following questions in order to critique the above socio-cultural construction of GID; the pathologizing of children who do not conform to the gender duality imposed and normalized at school, and the treatment of Gender Identity Dysphoria:

> Is psychiatry, with the diagnosis of GID and diagnostic criterion of gender dysphoria, simply recreating a stigmatization that we experienced with homosexuality in the fifties and sixties? . . . If our conception of gender were more fluid, would not the very notion of gender 'nonconformity' be nonsensical? . . . Differently gendered lives – their individual variation, their difference from the majority – constitute a normal diversity of gendered experience.
>
> (Rottnek 1999: 5–6)

As Neisen argues: 'I was appalled . . . [that] research is still being conducted to differentiate between so called 'normal' and 'gender-disturbed' boys . . . the victim gets blamed while the perpetrator goes unchallenged. Implicit is that feminine behavior in itself is devalued . . . so too are there heterosexist overtones' (1992: 65–6).

Transgenderism and intersexuality (hermaphrodism) stand as glaring testimonies to the fact that the line between the sexes is not as rigid as binarily constructed theories of sex and gender propose (see Haynes and McKenna 2001). To date, Australian schools have not taken up this issue. Despite the increasing acknowledgement and activism in relation to gender diversity and sexual diversity, current debates, policies and programmes are still framed by notions of gender duality (Pallotta-Chiarolli 1999e; Martino and Pallotta-Chiarolli 2001b). Schools need to be involved in constructing 'gender multiculturalism – a postmodern multiplicity of acceptable ways of performing gender' (Lingard and Douglas 1999: 127; see also Connell 1995). The ultimate effect of such an approach would be to reconfigure the rigid heteronormative boundaries governing male/female and heterosexual/homosexual binary categorizations. These classifications are institutionalized within the social and educational contexts from which the subjects of this research speak. Davies refers to this disruption and reconfiguration of the 'male/female dualism' as what happens in 'the third space' where:

> Masculinity and femininity are removed from the equation, and both sides of what was once understood as part of a binary divide become something any person can and should have access to. . . . [and requires] an uncoupling of the concepts of masculinity/femininity and identity.
>
> (2000: 49)

In this way, ambiguity and the in-between categories of gender can be embraced as a strength rather than as symptomatic of a deviant or confused gender and sexual identity. This would mean embracing and affirming all ways of walking, all kinds of voices and body fashioning rather than perpetuating gendered hierarchical power relations.

Conclusion

In this chapter we have explored both normalizing and transgressive social practices of masculinity in boys' lives at school. We have highlighted how embodied masculinity (Connell 1995) in terms of muscularity, physicality and body deportment are implicated in panopticonic regimes of surveillance through which boys learn to regulate themselves and classify other boys. The voices of a number of boys who negotiate embodied practices of masculinity from within a border space are included. These negotiations are often being undertaken within multiple, hierarchical and dichotomous social systems of identification and categorization. Given the constraints imposed by such regimes we have stipulated the need for schools and educational policy to address these kinds of social practices of normalization and how they impact on boys' learning and social relationships. These are issues we address in greater detail in Part 3.

3 'That's what normal boys do'

Bullying and harassment in the lives of boys at school

What's it like doing an interview with a boy who's being bullied only to find that the interview has the potential to provoke further bullying for him?

He's walking quickly and anxiously toward the interview room. I can see him approach as the principal has given me a room off the library, three of its walls mainly glass, the 'fishbowl' effect. He's thin and small, glasses perched on his nose, his hair on end. His school jumper looks like it's been pulled and stretched.

I smile and welcome him in, gesturing toward a chair that faces away from the windows so that he won't be distracted by other students and teachers using the library even though we can still hear them. Instead, he takes a chair directly facing the windows and as I begin to explain the interview process, he is furtively and anxiously scanning the library, rarely looking at me. I find I need to repeat my first few interview questions and work hard to get him to provide more detail. He isn't there with me, he is preoccupied and terrified about what is going on out there beyond the glass walls.

At times, he pauses and attempts to shift his demeanour to one of nonchalance and casualness, and I follow his gaze to the windows where certain boys, tough-looking, tall, smirking boys, are sneering and laughing in at him. At one time, he freezes mid-sentence and stares out from a pale face. He struggles to smear a smile across his face, a smile totally incongruent to the bullying he is describing as part of his interview. Again, I follow his gaze to see a large boy glaring at him. When I rise to go to the door to ask the student to move, the boy looking in slowly swaggers away, but not before a final deathly look at the boy inside the glass room.

I turn back to him. 'You're being bullied right now aren't you?' I ask.

He nods and flushes, his eyes filling with tears, and averting them from my gaze as well as from the window. 'They're watching me, they're hassling me and they'll get me more later.'

I end the interview at that point and tell the student I'm going to request another room.

What's it like doing an interview on bullying with a boy who self-defines as a bully only to find that the interview has the potential to become another stage upon which to perform for the benefit of his spectators outside the glass windows?

His arrival in the library is announced in a loud voice, engaging in mocking and deprecating tones and asides to both library staff and students while letting them know he's about to 'star' in some 'crap uni shit interview.' I watch his heavy stride, the hands and arms sweeping along, dislodging a book here, shoving a chair there, pushing into a student with a mock apology, pointing his finger at the forehead of another as if shooting him.

He strides in, and even as I'm indicating the chair facing away from the windows, he is scraping another chair into position so that he is fully in sight of anyone in the library as well as being able to scrutinize me from a sideways angle.

Outside, there is a steady stream of fans grinning, pointing, waving, eyes shifting suggestively between him and me. He responds with exaggerated grins, hand and finger signals signifying 'Fuck off' and shooting a gun. Occasionally he doesn't respond to a question or loses concentration when he becomes immersed in the mutual displays and camaraderie.

I stop asking questions and sit quietly observing. The boys outside the window indicate to him that I'm watching. He turns to me. 'What's up?'

'What are you doing?'

'Just mucking around.'

'Why?'

'They're watching me. They're waiting for me to do it. Anyway, that's what normal boys do.'

I end that interview as well.

I meet with the principal and organize a more private room in the admin block.

What happens when bullied boys are interviewed about bullying in spaces that are safe and private? Boys cry, boys' bodies hunch over, boys' fingers tremble, boys' voices quiver, shoulders shrug in confusion and eyes stare into distances.

What happens when bullies are interviewed about bullying in spaces that are safe and private? Boys blush, boys' bodies fidget, boys' fingers rap on tables, boys' voices try to sound casual and carefree but break and go hoarse, shoulders shrug away hard questions and eyes avoid the interviewer's gaze.

What happens to the interviewer as stories of being bullied and bullying unfold? Faces work hard to hold back tears, mouths press shut to hold back anger, and one's own memories of schoolyard bullying take up residence in the interview room. And once the interviews are over, one staggers out in exhaustion, reeling from the density and intensity in the room.

Introduction

For many boys in our research, the interview was the only safe space to work through and reflect on many of these issues and concerns (see Martino, 1998, 2001). In this chapter we explore the extent to which bullying practices are implicated in wider regimes of masculinity. Boys who do not 'measure up' to the norms of what it means to be 'cool' or a 'normal' boy become targets, and life for them at school can become unbearable (see Frank 1993; Ward 1995; Collins et al. 1996; Laskey and Beavis 1996; Beckett 1998). It appears that for both boys and some teachers, such practices are normalized. These social relations are framed in terms of a gendered discourse in which particular put-downs and forms of humour are seen as an effect of 'boys just being boys' and thus leading to a non-interventionist or minimal interventionist approach (Fisher 1997). As we have already highlighted, the ways in which boys learn to relate are circumscribed by power relations governed by quite specific norms for fashioning hegemonic heterosexual masculinities (Frank 1987; Redman 1996; Kehily and Nayak 1997; Davison 2000). Furthermore, our research reveals that teachers and educational systems can indeed perpetuate these norms that actually inform and counteract the very policies and strategies they attempt to implement. These kinds of normalizing practices are often not explicated in the literature on bullying, as Gilbert and Gilbert (1998) point out (see Rigby 1996).

From our interviews, it appears that the following questions and themes need to be addressed in schools:

1. *Who are the bullies?* What do various boys say about peer group relations? We document their capacities to interrogate homophobic and other bullying practices from certain boys who position themselves and are positioned by others as policing the boundaries between appropriate and inappropriate masculinities.
2. *Who gets bullied?* What kinds of factors lead some boys to being classed as marginal or 'abnormal' by the 'normal' boys who are located in powerful positions as classifiers and boundary markers.
3. *What can boys do about bullying?* What do boys say about various strategies available to them to alleviate or minimize bullying, as well as diminish its painful and disruptive consequences.

'I'm just mucking around'

Who are the bullies?

Many boys understood that bullying was much more than physical intimidation – it involved emotional abuse. They talked at length about the abusive ways of relating and the role of the dominant group in perpetuating such bullying practices. Aaron, who was part of a 'footballer group', draws attention to what he terms 'emotional bullying.' This is perpetrated by his peers who police the boundaries of a desirable masculinity. Only certain boys are able to acquire a privileged status within this hierarchy of masculinities:

> This guy [a high achiever] used to come down to the oval and kick the footy. People used to constantly keep throwing dirt at him and calling him names until he went away. I couldn't understand why they'd do it. He hadn't done anything to them. He didn't have a lot of friends at that time and was sort of a loner, I s'pose. People just thought he was a 'loser.' It wasn't all of them [footballers], probably only about four or five. The others were sort of standing back, laughing though.
>
> (Aaron, 16 years)

For Aaron, hierarchical power relationships appear to be at the basis of how some boys learn to socialize with one another and to relate to other boys who somehow do not measure up in their eyes. He also provides an insight into the policing of geographical territories and boundaries in the school grounds, and how space and place within the school is used to signify exclusion and inclusion, and its related bullying practices (Nayak and Kehily 1996; Epstein 2001). Aaron indicates his disapproval of the abusive practices that are directed at those boys who are 'a bit different' and who try to gain acceptance from the 'footballers.' On one level, while he openly disapproves of the bullying, he does not see himself or others who stand around and laugh as colluding or perpetuating such harassment. It needs to be highlighted, however, that individual boys, like Aaron, feel helpless and are afraid to intervene for fear of being bullied themselves! What is often not provided at school are support structures and educational programmes designed to assist boys to develop the necessary skills for dealing with such emotionally charged situations. This raises crucial questions about the need for a whole school approach to bullying and harassment which adequately takes into consideration the gendered dimensions and effects of such power relations in boys' lives and peer group cultures (see Gilbert and Gilbert 1998; Alloway 2000).

Aaron discusses a particular abusive dynamic within the 'footballer' group with those boys who remain the silent observers perpetuating such harassment to avoid being the object of derision themselves:

> All the popular guys are loud mouths, they say what they want to say and all the other guys will just keep quiet, you know sensitive guys, they don't say anything. They do have their opinions but they don't voice them because they're afraid the group will rubbish them, give them crap.
>
> (Aaron, 16 years)

Another boy at this school, Steve, also discusses his involvement with the 'footballers' and comments on their bullying behaviour. What is interesting to note is that he had formerly been a member of this group and was the captain of the school football team:

> I got picked on by the group down on the oval [footballers]. So I just left 'em and found a new group. Like if we played footy I might mark it over the top of them and they just gave me shit as though they were jealous of me getting the ball. You had to sort of act the way everyone else wanted you to. If they'd pick on someone, you had to do that. If someone beat them at something, they'd pick on them because they didn't like being beaten.
>
> (Steve, 15 years)

Steve draws attention to the competitive dimension in the way the 'footballers' relate to one another and, since he has been the brunt of their abusive practices, he readily rejects these boys and joins another group where 'you can just be yourself'. He also elaborates on the sex-based harassment directed at other boys perpetrated by certain members of the 'footballer' group:

> They [football group] think they're all 'faggots.' They'll sit around with girls so they used to think these guys had a bit of feminine side to 'em, so they'd tell them they're 'poofters.' Ryan, he's got a sort of a 'poofter' voice which everyone picks up and gives him shit about. And then Friedman, there was a rumour going around that he got kicked out, or he left X school because he got caught wanking himself. So everyone labelled him as a 'faggot'. But I talk to him all the time, he's all right.
>
> (Steve, 15 years)

Ryan and Friedman are targeted and differentiated by the 'footballers' on the basis of their assumed homosexuality as ascribed primarily in terms of their association with girls as friends (Martino 1998) and bodily attributes or having a reputation from a previous school. This method of social prescription draws attention to homophobic strategies of surveillance that these boys use to police sex/gender boundaries in the school yard. Many boys' comments highlight that what counts as bullying does not relate only to physical acts of fighting, pushing and shoving. It involves an emotional dimension based on physical attributes which can be equally and even more traumatic for many boys. Furthermore, what is emphasized by many boys is how homophobia and 'acting cool' are implicated in the gendered dimensions of bullying at school and are the mechanism through which a hierarchy of masculinities becomes established in peer group cultures: 'They get a reputation, like if you fight and you win the fight, everyone reckons you're hard and you're cool' (Peter, 14 years).

Josh spoke about his earlier years as a school bully, likening his 'act' or performance to the dominant construct of hegemonic masculinity as conqueror and competitor, and yet disguising his insecurities about acceptance and social power:

> I used to think it was the cool thing to do, to be a bully. It was sort of an act because you wanted to prove yourself. I used to think, 'Yeah, I conquered him.' I guess it made me feel good, like I was trying to prove myself to other people, to be accepted. You just wake up one day and think, 'What am I doing? I've got to change.' I sort of looked at what it would be like for the other people, and you just think, 'Wow, it would be horrible.'
>
> (Josh, 15 years)

Later, he indicates that school anti-bullying strategies were ineffective as they would incite him to rebel and resist authority, thus being very much in line with dominant constructions of hegemonic masculinity as anti-authoritarian: 'A lot of the time with people, if they get told not to do something, they are usually more keen to do it' (Josh, 15 years).

Three major types of boys were seen as being bullies. First, boys involved in 'football' and other hegemonic sports were mainly seen as the bullies. Alongside them was a second group, boys who were not 'footballers' but attached themselves to that group and displayed the same 'attitude' in order to ensure that they were on the side of the border defined as bullying rather than bullied. In the following, Simon discusses the reasons behind why the 'jocks' need to bully other students. He is able to articulate the sense of insecurity behind the performances of security, the demeanour of power that is built on a fear of powerlessness:

> So you'll see the jocks, your sporty guys who aren't in touch with their feelings, the way they get around it is by violence or pushing people or calling them names. Some of those guys, they're insecure because they're good at sports, one of the only things that they have.
>
> (Simon, 16 years)

The third group identified as bullies were, as Josh labelled them, boys with 'problems' or those with 'disabilities':

> It's usually the people who have problems or have disabilities. Like they're not as good at reading or writing. They're usually the people who try to pick on other people. Maybe they're just trying to make up for what they don't have.
>
> (Josh, 15 years)

Here Josh identifies bullying behaviour as being driven by a compensatory masculinity. In other words, they engage in strategies of resistance in reaction to particular externally ascribed and self-defined inferiorities by performing an aggressive (supposedly superior) masculinity. Indeed, in the following Josh reflects upon the hierarchical binary of superior/inferior in relation to the differential power relationship between the former and the latter. However, he believes that the bully/bullied binary is actually an inversion of the superior/inferior hierarchy: 'The smarter people [get bullied], which if you look at it, it's the smarter people who are going to go better in life. It should probably be the other way round.'

Damien risked being bullied himself when he defended his best friend who was a high academic achiever. He used the discourses of getting ahead in life and economic status to counteract the bully:

> [The bully is] one that smokes out the front, he's not really intelligent. He picks on my best friend and so I go to him, 'He's going to be coming up to your petrol station and you're going to fill his car full of gas and just think, when he hands over the money all you'll get is 10 per cent of that.' And he kind of really stops and realizes that he won't get anywhere unless he stops what he's doing.
>
> (Damien, 14 years)

As well as drawing attention to the links between a 'cool' form of rebellious masculinity and bullying, Damien raises issues about its classed dimensions and how such practices relate to targeting those boys who are high achievers. These boys may be bullied because of their perceived inheritance of social and economic capital which will be denied to the bullies who do not publicly commit to or value school learning. However, Damien indicates that those who are bullied also retaliate with comments such as: ' "Oh you're a povvo, you can't even afford proper pants", and, "Look at yourself, you can't get a bike", and all this stuff.' Therefore, both advantage and disadvantage can be used to bully others. As Jason comments: 'I've been called the rich kid because we own our own house, we holiday around the world all the time. Guys will be really blunt. They go, "Oh, can I pinch some money?" I just give the money so they can quit hassling me' (Jason, 17 years).

Although boys who were bullied or who had been bullies were able to identify these three groups, many boys who belonged to the dominant popular groups appeared to be oblivious to the bullying occurring to other boys in their school. It is as if occupying a central socio-cultural location, or being positioned at the top of the hierarchy of masculinities, rendered invisible the experiences of those boys who were bullied. However, it is also possible that these boys may be deliberately denying the experiences of the latter so as to avoid being implicated in the bullying. For example, Brendon was a very sporty and popular boy who at first denies the existence of bullying at his school. However, with repeated questioning by the researcher, he shifts from a position of *personal* denial to one of acknowledging that bullying actually does exist, but then slips back into a zone of hesitancy where he both acknowledges the fact that bullying does happen, while simultaneously disavowing any *personal* knowledge of its existence. Yet, this was the school where many other boys discussed being bullied by the boys in Brendon's group:

> Maria: Do you notice that some guys are having a hard time at school?
> Brendon: Not to my according, I don't know as such.
> Maria: Do you notice any guys getting hassled in any way or not fitting in?
> Brendon: Not really. But the people who are pretty small always get hassled sometimes by bigger ones just because they're small.
> Maria: Do you notice that some guys do go out of their way to pick on others?
> Brendon: I haven't seen it happen but I suppose it does. But I haven't seen it happen in our school yet.
>
> (Brendon, 13 years)

Another response that some of the dominant boys gave was to legitimate bullying as a normal part of school life. Matthew, for example, considers bullying to be ritualized and, therefore, a harmless part of initiating younger boys into the single sex Catholic boarding school he attends:

> It can get a bit out of hand but a lot of it is just like getting you initiated, but not bad initiation. Once they hit Year 9 then it's over and then it's the next year's turn. It's not actually bullying where they get victimized and most of them actually don't mind. They enjoy the attention from the Year 12s.
>
> (Matthew, 16 years)

So for many boys like Matthew bullying becomes naturalized and an inevitable rite of passage into a particular stage of boyhood (Plummer 1999). One of the major issues that needs to be addressed in schools relates to what becomes naturalized and normalized for boys and teachers as harmless and apparently psychologically and emotionally inconsequential behaviour accompanying socially sanctioned rites of passage for boys in schools.

Shaun, who was also a member of a 'footballer' group, reiterated that the 'cool' boys were the ones who were skilled at 'giving crap' and 'getting a laugh' from their friends (see Kehily and Nayak 1997). This becomes a 'normal' part of the way boys learn to relate to one another:

> . . . how much crap you can give to someone else and kind of humiliate them. But it's like joking as well, and a lot of the 'cool' guys were good at giving crap. People could say something funny and everyone would laugh. And then the people who couldn't do it were kind of excluded from it. I suppose it's like a test, like you sit there and see who can come up with the funniest and the quickest joke. A lot of the guys will say something funny or do something funny and then go, 'Yeah, come on, where's your comeback? What are you doing?', and the person's sitting there and they're racking their brain over something. If they can't do anything then they end up taking it. They just have to be humiliated in front of this big group of guys.
>
> (Shaun, 16 years)

The dynamic involved in the way that these boys learn to relate involves almost a competition to prove who is the most powerful. Those who cannot retaliate and use verbal 'put-downs' are considered to be weak. Thus, through the use of 'put-downs' in the form of 'giving one another crap', a pecking order is established within the peer group in which each boy's masculinity is put to the test. Those boys who are not able to compete verbally with a quick 'comeback' resort to violence as a means of enforcing their masculinity:

> They will get up and they'll push you and they'll start scragging around, and it's all a big joke. But you know people still get kind of offended if they can't come up with something funny. They get angry or try to take it out on you by trying to humiliate you by pushing you over. It's pretty strange when you think about it, but you get a whole lot of laughs out of it as well.
>
> (Shaun, 16 years)

While on one level Shaun appears to be critical of such practices, on another he indicates that he derives a form of pleasure from engaging in this social dynamic. However, when asked to describe how boys act and behave in his peer group, he makes the following comment:

> I suppose that you could say that they act like a bunch of arseholes really. You stand back and you see this big group of people all gathered around the bench under that tree on the oval. I remember there was a dog shit lying there near the bench, but no one could see it. People who knew about it would sit there and they'd be drinking and sitting around and trying to get someone to walk into it. Finally, some poor bastard actually did step in it and everyone cracked up and just laughed at him. There's this poor person standing there with crap on his foot, and he was totally humiliated, and there's this big pack of guys around and they were just trying to humiliate him even more. And it's the way they relate, they like to work on other people's weaknesses.
>
> (Shaun, 16 years)

Shaun also indicates that on certain occasions boys follow particular rules because failure to do so will result in bullying. One of these rules is that 'guys are meant to have guys as best friends':

> People call him a 'faggot.' That's because he hangs around a bunch of girls and he hasn't got any guy friends really. There's a lot of stuff like if a guy doesn't follow the expectations then they'll give him crap. So it depends on what rule you're breaking and how you go about breaking the rule. I know one guy, he was new here and he didn't talk to anyone at all, only to me. I suppose that's one of the rules as well, getting along with other guys. One guy, it was his first day, he played footy with the guys down there. Someone said, 'He's got a really good kick', and then everyone went up and started talking to him. So there's a rule of doing stuff that other guys do, like playing sport, playing footy, you have to join in with them. So there's like a whole bunch of rules that you have to follow.
>
> (Shaun, 16 years)

Shaun highlights, therefore, how certain rules must be followed to be accepted by other boys, particularly in enacting an acceptable heterosexual masculinity (Epstein 1997; Steinberg et al. 1997). This involves doing things with other boys which constitute a 'normal' masculinity. These observations highlight how the rules for boys to relate in particular ways are framed within panopticonic regimes of regulatory and individualizing practices (Foucault 1982). This is highlighted later when Shaun mentions that 'guys don't really care about what girls think, they care more about what other guys think'.

'There's different and there's different'

Bullied masculinities

The perspectives of the bullied also provided considerable insight into the gendernormative hegemonic framework governing peer group social relationships. Many students believed that the bullied were 'mentally weaker ones' (Eddie, 11 years) as they were unable to handle the bullying in ways that could be respected according to masculinist norms such as fighting back, laughing it off, or attaching oneself to the group of bullies. Tim, 14 years, believes particular students bring the bullying repeatedly onto themselves by supposedly 'pretending' to be hurt and getting the bullies into trouble: 'There's a couple of real idiots, some of the squares, like one guy just pushes him or something, he acts like he's been knocked out, he gets people suspended and they get detention all the time.' Similarly, Aaron, 13 years, talks about the experience of a boy who gets bullied and will not retaliate: 'They bully him because he's smaller and never stands up for himself, so they think let's tease him, he won't do anything. It embarrasses him, he just falls to the ground because sometimes he's hurt bad and they just walk off and leave him.'

Thus, there seems to be a hierarchy of differences regarding which boys 'deserve' to be bullied because they are unable to respond in ways defined as 'appropriate'. In this sense their 'difference' was more deserving and inviting of bullying than other 'differences' which were less marked and defended by boys as reacting 'appropriately': 'If you just ignore it, it does tend to go away. But if you take offence to it and try and stick up for yourself, people sort of jump on you all the time. So it's a bit hard. I think it's just boys tend to prey on the weakness and go for the kill' (Scott, 17 years).

This hierarchy of differences usually involves a heteronormative framework wherein any hint of homosexuality within the boy or his life was a signifier of most deserving of bullying. Simon experienced constant bullying due to his mother being a lesbian: 'coming up to me and mucking around and punching . . . following me around, teasing, acting like an ape. And I was in a sport room, it was like a big room, so there's wasn't really anywhere to get away from it' (Simon, 13 years).

Likewise, Mark who lives with gay male foster parents found that he was a recipient of harassment due to his home life, but also because of his attempts to conceal these facts. Becoming informed about homosexuality and becoming confident about his home life led to his successful challenging of the teasing:

> [Having gay carers is] a real strong thing about me, that I really didn't want them to see. This kid said [to others], 'Ian and Brett, they're gay and they're his carers', and he teased me about that. He said, 'Your Carers are

> gay, they're poofs.' I began standing up for myself at the time and I was going, 'So what if they're gay, there's nothing wrong with being gay it's just another type of love' because Ian's told me a lot more about gay things. I said, 'You name one individual thing that is bad about gay' and he didn't say anything and he stopped then and he hasn't done anything since then, so I stood up for myself.
>
> (Mark, 12 years)

However, within a gendernormative framework, bullying also involved invoking insults against boys' mothers in an attempt to get them to react and to expose their vulnerabilities: 'A lot of times they just talk about paying people's mums for sex and all that sort of stuff' (John, 16 years). As Kehily and Nayak claim: "Mothers are invoked in insults to probe young men's associative links with femininity and expose their vulnerabilities' (1997: 73). The greater the emotional reaction, the more likely he is to be labelled 'a mummy's boy' and thereby considered an inappropriate male. 'Normal' boys are expected to cultivate or publicly perform a detached and misogynist relationship to their mothers and other women, including female teachers. This is significant considering the emphasis placed on the need for boys to detach from mothers, and mothers seen as effeminizing boys, by populist men's movement discourses (see Lingard and Douglas 1999).

Transgressing gendernormative boundaries also resulted in harassment for Jason. He was targeted for identifying as bisexual and for wearing his clothing in ways that displayed his playing with both gender and sexual dualities. However, the fact that he laughed back and constructed his refusal to fight back as being a sign of strength and self-control minimized the amount of harassment: 'I get hassles all the time, I come in with pink hair, two different coloured shoes. People have a go at me, but you have a smile, have a laugh, and that's it. I'm not that type of person, I'm just anti myself being in the violence, that's it' (Jason, 17 years).

Some of the border boys negotiating multiple marginalities or boundaries often found themselves trying to understand which facet about themselves brought on the bullying. In the following, Jonard, 18 years, discusses three issues that could be possibilities for himself; being openly gay, being Asian, not playing sport. Simplistic either/or understandings of bullying may prevent students and teachers from considering that it could be one or more factors simultaneously, progressively, and in constant shift and degree: 'Is it because he's a racist? I guess it's more because he's homophobic because he would hang around with other Filipino guys who play basketball, and why not me. Is it because I don't play basketball?'

The kind of 'being different' that could lead to bullying depended on the specific socio-cultural, economic and other contexts of the school: 'They're different, they like to smile a lot. Different culture, they've got problems, can't spell good or can't read' (Adam, 16 years). 'Being different' could mean being richer in a poorer school, or vice-versa; being from an ethnic background in a predominantly Anglo-Australian school or vice-versa; being an academic achiever in a school dominated by low achievers or vice-versa. These classifications of difference are all based on hierarchical dualisms of Centre and Margin, majority and minority. They exemplify the need to shift prevailing simplistic constructs of hierarchy to articulating difference according to diversity and multiplicity. In the following, Wayne, 16 years, can articulate the reasons why he is positioned as one of the majority and therefore avoids being targeted:

Wayne: They go down and down and down and become a reject in the school.

Maria: How does someone become a reject?

Wayne: They comb their hair different to everyone else. The way they dress, like on casual days, most people come with Nikes and stuff like this, he'll come with a Target [supermarket] brand.

Maria: So what makes you not get bullied?

Wayne: I'm into cars and sport but the guy that's getting paid out, he's not into it. He'll sit down with a book all day on a Sunday. But me, I'll be out playing sport or working on the car.

However, Ben reflects on how his borderzone existence makes him vulnerable to harassment as he was not willing to conform to the codes of any single group:

> I'm just a misfit, I don't fit in. I've watched other guys put on this big macho act and I don't do that. I can't. I look around my school and everyone is put into categories; there's the jocks, the pretty sets, the druggies and computer geeks . . . I look at these groups and there is not one that I fit into. It's been difficult because you need that sort of identity in order to make friends.
>
> (Ben, 17 years)

Boys who are unable to negotiate the public/school and private/home performances of masculinity may find themselves being bullied. Glenn, 16 years, discusses how being an academic achiever in the public sphere of school is considered inappropriate for boys. That is the site of performing a 'normal' masculinity displayed by mucking around and disrupting learning. Catching up with work in the privacy of the home is considered appropriate for boys of questionable 'reputation' because they are not subjected to the surveillance and policing of their peers: 'If you're really quiet and you get on with your work, you get called a nerd. All the people who muck around during the class then go home and do all their homework and keep up to date, they keep a good reputation.'

Those boys who attempted to defend or assist someone being bullied for publicly subscribing to school learning and achievement also risked being positioned as a target:

> There's a couple of people hanging out in the library because no one likes them in the playground because they read books for fun. Apparently it's cool to be dumb. I say, 'Leave him alone, he's all right, he's cool.' They turn on me, but I don't care.
>
> (Tim, 14 years)

Cultural differences were also the basis of harassment and bullying, as will be explored further in our chapters on ethnicity and Indigeneity. Racism was used by boys from a dominant group and also from a subordinated peer group as a means of establishing a power base denied to them by the dominant group (see Kessler et al. 1985; Walker 1988; Connell 1989; Mac an Ghaill 1994b). This practice appears to be born out of a compensatory mechanism which is driven by feelings of inferiority enforced through hegemonic power relations enacted by the dominant boys. In other words, the bullied learn to feel powerful by emulating the dominating and oppressive practices of the bullies (Memmi 1965; Freire 1972). Brian, 15 years, talks about the racist and bullying practices of his friends who are not part of the dominant 'footballer' group in their school and how they harassed younger boys to bolster their own masculinity and, hence, status with the 'footballer' group: 'He was calling him "nigger, nigger". He just likes to call people niggers.' However, such racist practices are also operationalized in a different register by the 'footballers' in this school and directed at one of their 'mates' who they refer to as 'boonga'. But, as Glen, 15 years, points out, this racist label is deployed apparently in humour and takes the form of a 'piss taking' practice which appears to help the boys to establish a particular form of male bonding (see Willis 1977; Walker 1988; Mac an Ghaill 1994b; Kehily and Nayak 1997): 'He's not actually hassled, they just call him "boonga". He's not Aboriginal, but he sort of looks like one. But he can take it . . . He just smiles . . . I don't think he really minds.'

It is important to note the differential ways in which racist practices are being deployed within two different peer groups at this particular school. In the 'footballer' group boys engage in such practices to establish a mode of male bonding, whereas in Brian's group they function apparently as a means by which two of the boys can establish some status with the footballers. However, both modes of socializing and relating are implicated in gendered regimes of bullying through which hegemonic white masculinity is enacted.

Indigenous boys also highlighted the racialized dimensions of bullying. Nic talks about the bullying behaviour of white boys whose embodied practices of masculinity (Connell 1995) are fashioned within a racist regime of asserting their power over Indigenous boys:

> [There are certain boys that make me angry] like if they tease me or if they give a dirty look or shoulder barge you . . . they'll knock you with their shoulders when they walk past you. At the tuckshop my friend Brendan . . . he is an Aboriginal boy, and that white fella, John, pushed him over and he fell. Then I walked up to him and asked him why he started on my friend Brendan. And he said, 'Oh, are you going to hit me, and then are all these other black fellas going to hit me?'
>
> (Nic, 13 years)

It appears that some white boys deliberately try to provoke confrontation to incite anger in the Indigenous boys. This emphasizes the extent to which enacting masculinity for some white boys on certain occasions is about asserting a particular racialized form of power. It becomes another means by which some white boys can assert their masculinity through racist practices deliberately deployed to incite Indigenous boys to violence. The effect of this is to ultimately demonize and pathologize the Indigenous 'other' as having a particular propensity for violent and aggressive behaviour (Dyer 1997).

'Slip into auto pilot'

Boys' strategies for dealing with harassment

Having examined the various dimensions of bullying and being bullied, we now turn to exploring the strategies deployed by boys to deflect or minimize bullying. Becoming invisible or becoming bullies themselves appear to be two prime responses: from attempts to hide oneself or stay away from the bullies' school territory, to aggressively retaliating and emulating the bullying tactics. Either strategy is fraught with the possibility that it will be considered an incitement to further bullying and harassment. Either strategy appears to be evaluated according to its positioning within normalizing practices regarding the expectations and regulations governing the performance of hegemonic masculinity.

Eddie, a circus performer, clearly articulates how the skills he acquired in handling audience heckling are very useful in dealing with harassment at school. He provides an example of how bullying is responded to with bullying, being mocked is followed by mocking. Thus the strategies of the oppressor are emulated by the oppressed as they are the models of how power functions.

Using the interrogation of the colonizer/colonized interactions in postcolonial theory, the subtle multiple layers and hierarchies of oppression inherent within and among the 'colonized' are evident in many of the boys we interviewed (Memmi 1965; Freire 1972; Said 1979, 1986, 1990). Not only do the 'colonizers'/bullies emulate as well as compete with one another, but so also do the 'colonized'/bullied. They often shift to methods and strategies that mimic, parody and replicate those of the 'colonizer'/bully, and then proceed to compete with each other in 'seeking sovereignty and independence' (Said 1990: 333–4; see also Freire 1972; Bhabha 1990a).

> Usually they [hecklers in the audience] stop when you get everyone else to laugh at them. I might cover their eyes and jump on them, shove them around and pull their hair, or touch their hair and look at my fingers and frown like 'Yuk, what have you got in your hair?' And if they [audience] laugh at them, then they'll just quit mucking around and do what you say. When other kids or someone at school might pay you out, that's just how you can handle it. You can take it as a joke and not care, or you can take it seriously and come back with something else and hurt their feelings.
>
> (Eddie, 11 years)

Another example was provided by Daniel who had been bullied for his problems in reading and writing and then he became a bully himself. In the following he describes his ascending the hierarchy and using bullying strategies in order to prevent himself from being bullied further:

> The more fights you're in, the bigger you get. There's one kid in my class, he's scared of me because we had a tiff last year. I threw a chair at him. It was like all the older kids had it out for me, so you had to be tough. Now they see I stick up for myself.
>
> (Daniel, 14 years)

The following boys illustrate the fine line (Zerubavel 1991) between being bullied and bullying, and how the latter response is validated by other boys and indeed from home. Boys negotiate, resist or surrender to what they believe to be a dichotomous and confining choice – to be bullied or be the bully: 'I don't take any shit from someone who pays me out. He cracks my head, I'll crack him back, that's what I've been taught from a young age, don't take any crap' (Wayne, 16 years). 'Being short, I used to get teased for that a lot. But now they don't because I usually get people to beat them up' (Lance, 15 years).

> I became really tough. There was this guy, he tried to stab me with a scalpel. I said 'Put it down.' He said 'No, I'll cut you' and I grabbed it out of

his hand and threw it at him. I was getting bullied so I thought 'Right, I'll get stronger, be stronger' and it was good. I wasn't a bully all the time. Only sometimes I'd bully people if they bully somebody that I knew.

(Adam, 13 years)

Some boys carve a position for themselves among the dominant boys in order to stop being bullied. They provide a service to the dominant boys who use them but still position them as inferior. Here, Tim talks about a bullied boy who constructed a site of safety and, to some degree, respect by dealing drugs for the popular boys and making money. This afforded him a respected higher economic status among the boys:

He's tremendously overweight, some people just hassled him. They don't really hassle him anymore because he hangs around with the lads, a local gang, became a drug dealer. He just gets heaps of money out of it. Most of the older guys that would be doing the bullying are all into drugs.

(Tim, 14 years)

Darren has also worked out strategies for preventing himself from being harassed. First, he has learned to construct as much teasing as possible as a joke, and thereby not feel as if he needs to retaliate or be affected by it. Second, although his skills and interest in computing could be easily used to categorize him as a 'geek', he has learned how to use these skills to gain a reputation as a 'hacker', thereby putting his 'good' computing skills to 'bad' and rebellious use. This makes him popular among the dominant boys who admire his 'rebelliousness' or 'badness' in virtual reality zones. Indeed, Darren's discussion reveals the tenuousness and blurring of the constructions of 'good' and 'bad' (Zerubavel 1991). He is 'good' at computers which would make other boys think he is 'bad' but because he puts the 'good' skills to 'bad' use, he is 'good'. Simultaneously, he has a 'bad' reputation of being a 'good' guy and friendly with everyone. Rather than create problems for him, it enables him to negotiate 'good/bad' relationships with the bullies by providing a hacking service:

Darren: I just hack into files and muck around. I'm doing something good as well as doing something bad. Hacking is bad, but doing actually proper computing is good. I could hack into the computer's network file, take proven files and muck around with them, or I could take the network folder and revise it and muck around with a virus. It's reputation basically, I have a good reputation so I never get copped out as much as everyone else does.

Maria: Can you tell us what your reputation is based on?

Darren: I'm friendly, kind, I help people, I'm always a good friend, I'm there. I still have fun though and muck around and do stupid things. I will muck around in class.

(Darren, 16 years)

Other boys talked about performing a loud and intimidating masculinity as a way of minimizing the bullying. Gay-identifying Luc knew he would inevitably be bullied when he came out at his Catholic single sex school and deployed strategies to minimize the bullying:

> I was physically abused on my way to the tram stop once. Yes, punched me in the stomach. And in the corridor I've been punched, but it didn't happen every day. Basically people would see that I was a strong sort of person, I wouldn't put up with that sort of stuff. The friends of mine who were gay and didn't come out, they had more of a shy introverted sort of personality. That personality was really nothing to do with their homosexuality. They were fine with that, it's just their natural personality. But I've always been the more outgoing, loud mouth, never stop talking sort of Italian boy. That kind of out there, loud attitude of mine intimidated a lot of people.
>
> (Luc, 18 years)

It is interesting to note how Luc, in his thinking about bullying, works with two generally held essentialist stereotypes, adopted by both dominant boys about marginal boys, and sometimes by marginal boys about themselves. While conforming to the stereotype of the 'loud' Italian boy in order to deflect a greater amount of bullying, he distances himself from being a shy, introverted, gay boy. However, he questions the essentializing tendency to align introversion with homosexuality, but still slips into invoking an essentialist discourse which reduces shyness to a 'natural personality' trait.

Another gay young man, Luke, also used what he calls 'personality' and an interrogative manner to strategically deflect any possible homophobic harassment. He plays upon the bullies' desire to be the centre of attention by slipping into 'autopilot', affirming the bullies in their 'little illusion' of coolness and machoism. He strikes up a 'normal' conversation with them, and while not outing himself, he turns the questions onto his potential attacker:

> I was just standing outside a shop and there were some guys from the year above me. One of them came up and said, 'Oh I see you're a faggot.' I turned the conversation around and was just talking to him like a normal human being. By the end of the conversation he said, 'Well have a really good day, I'll see you later.' If I'm put in that situation, I just kind of slip into auto pilot and talk to them. Just try not to be too direct. If they're

> being really big and macho, acknowledge that and don't try and break their little illusion straight away. The way you talk to someone, if you talk really aggressively to them, they're going to talk aggressively back and then you're not going to get anywhere. Most of the time they'll say something like, 'Oh I hear you're a faggot.' It's like, 'Oh yes, well who did you hear that from?' So be a little evasive, but it's more to get the conversation going. Whereas if you just go 'Oh yes', then it will prompt them. If you go 'Oh, no', if you come across too passive, then that could also prompt them into bullying you. You take hold of the conversation and turn it back around. If they ask a question, turn it back and ask them what they think about it before you just rattle off your answer.
>
> (Luke, 19 years)

Similarly, Paul, 16 years, talks about joking along with the harassers about himself as this performance of nonchalance will remove the bully's fun of watching him get upset over the teasing. This in turn may minimize the potential of the harassment being repeated: 'If anyone paid me out I would go along with them and then they don't pay me out as much because they see that it doesn't bother me.'

Another strategy that boys adopted to deal with bullies involved the strategic use of extreme niceness and 'perfection'. Damien was in awe of a boy who strategically used friendliness and being a 'perfect student' to deflect any harassment. Thus, his 'perfection' elicits curious and friendly responses due to its being constructed as 'freakish' and 'abnormal':

> He never gets picked on because he's so nice to people. He's like the perfect student. He does all his work, he's really smart, he never backchats, he's never had a warning, he's never had anything bad. He's just so perfect. Some boys try and make him swear, but he's never sworn at high school. He's kind of the role model because we want to be like him. It's like the whole school revolves around him. He's just so perfect. Everyone is just so nice to him, even the bullies. That's like god at school . . . he is nice to them [the bullies] and he doesn't want any trouble. He's the kind of person that really doesn't believe in violence. He's just so perfect.
>
> (Damien, 14 years)

Some students spoke about ignoring the bullying and hoping it would go away although this could lead to further bullying as refusal to fight back was seen as evidence of a boy's weakness and being gay. Bisexual-identifying Rowan remembers his frustration with this strategy: 'Adults would always say to you, ignore it and show people that it doesn't bother you and they'll stop. At the time that seemed ridiculous because I thought, Well, I am ignoring it all the time, and that just doesn't happen' (Rowan, 19 years).

Other students spoke about invisibilizing or 'passing' strategies, trying to avoid attention being attracted to themselves for something constructed as 'different'. 'Passing' is a strategy of assimilation to social ascriptions and avoiding harassment as 'different' (Memmi 1965; Trinh 1990a, 1991, 1992). This establishes hierarchies and tensions amongst those who are harassed as they attempt to deal with the either/or and both/and alternatives: either being the same as the bully and/or fashioning an Other that is acceptable to the bully:

> the worst aspect of passing – that you become what you imitate, and that disdain for your own kind, the member of your own kind who is too conspicuous or too courageous to try to pass, enters into your heart and you become a traitor . . . [and] stricken with terror at the idea that we would be taken for mice, that the us in us showed. In some cases, some of us became more ferocious toward mice than cats in order to show that there was no mouse in us.
>
> (Meigs 1983: 32–3)

Nevertheless, despite such overt or subtle strategies of passing, the boys who were trying to 'pass' – or invisibilize negotiated space and their occupation of it – were signals to other students that they were afraid of being harassed. This would often act as an incitement to further harassment for its display of effeminate or weak masculinity (Jackson 1998; Bergling 2001; Kendall 2001):

> You can pick out which ones are [being bullied] and [which ones] aren't. Just the way that they look or walk, like the people that are more confident usually walk in straight lines and the less confident people move out of their way, so they move to the side. I think it's just body language where you can see that if you make a sudden movement around them they'll flinch. They're sort of scared of you even though you may not be bullies, they sort of look up to you in a way.
>
> (Michael, 13 years)

Boys undertake self-regulating techniques based on panopticonic surveillance in relation to what their peers may be observing and thinking. Mario, a 16-year-old high achiever monitored his grades and academic achievement so as not to draw attention to himself: 'I'd be doing work and I'd say, Oh, I won't include this part because I'd probably get a really high mark.' Gay-identifying Daniel talks about how his whole day was monitored and mapped according to the likelihood of harassment. His explanations provide a powerful insight into the working of panopticonic self-regulation based on a few early incidents of harassment and perpetuated by a system that did not address homophobic harassment. In fact, the system promoted an environment where the danger of harassment was ever-present. Daniel talks about his negotiation of space, his sense of being scrutinized and confined, as well as his attempts at invisibilizing himself, and the effect the negotiation of this daily environment had on his physical stature and emotional well-being:

> It was a constant physical threat and throughout my entire high school life. There wasn't a day that I went to school thinking 'today there's no chance that physical harm could come to me', there was always that imminent threat for myself . . . being constantly scared for my own safety and just wanting to not stand out for any reason or to get into anyone's way. So I would do things like not answering in class, and I would sort of sit away from groups of boys, whether that meant sitting up the front. But then I was always paranoid because they might be behind me and throwing things and saying things behind me. I wouldn't go to secluded areas . . . I wouldn't go back to the lockers when they were there . . . just trying to be quiet and hide. I can remember quite clearly thinking, 'Okay, if there's males around it's going to be bad for me. I just don't want to be anywhere where there's going to be anymore than a couple of males.'
>
> (Daniel, 23 years)

The lengths to which boys who are bullied go to avoid being harassed are also documented by James, 17 years, who had been harassed on the basis of his imputed homosexuality. However, what is revealed in the following account of his daily experiences is that some boys are unable to invisibilize themselves or 'pass' within a context of the pervasive homophobic policing of masculinities. He recounts a series of experiences involving various groups of boys on the bus that he caught to and from school. On his way to school one morning, a group of boys at the back of the bus from one of the local high schools started calling him names. Initially, he was targeted as an 'art boy' because he was carrying an art file. But the harassment escalated and they began calling him 'fag boy'. Many of the boys in our research highlighted the extent to which participation in the curriculum was imbricated in a regime of gendered and sexualized bullying practices (see Martino 1997). The bullies also started throwing coins and bits of paper at him. Moreover, what exacerbated the harassment was the fact that one of his friends, Andrew, who always caught the bus with him, was a Year 9 boy aged 14: 'To me he is like my little brother because I don't have a little brother, he just comes over whenever he wants and does whatever he wants, he's good to be around.'

The homophobic harassment persisted, and Andrew also became implicated in the abuse that was directed at James, with implications of pedophilia being made. The socially dominant discursive meshing of pedophilia and homosexuality frames this kind of bullying. James indicates that he became very angry and at first tried to ignore the harassment. Eventually he ended up by catching another bus in an attempt to avoid being targeted. However, another group of Year 10 students from his own school started to harass him in much the same way as the previous group of boys from the local high school. James still persisted in avoiding fights and not standing up to them: 'I'm not the sort of person who wants to stand up to them and get physically involved. I'm pretty bloody thin . . . not exactly the biggest of builds. People see that, and I know it for a fact so I avoid fights. But I'm not saying I'm totally hopeless' (James, 17 years).

In order to avoid this kind of harassment, James and Andrew once again caught two different buses. But they could not seem to escape the homophobic abuse. As James was standing at the bus stop where he was waiting for another connection, the bus that he used to catch passed by:

> And this bus goes past almost every day of the year and every time I'd get 'art boy', 'faggie', 'you're going to die poofter', 'fuck you', hands out of windows, heads screaming . . . The thing that really irritates is the fact that the bus is full of all these students from other schools as well, and you can see them just look out for me and they just go, 'Yeah, those guys must be right!' or they just look at you blankly. They don't really give a shit and you think one of them might turn around and say, 'What the hell are you doing that for? You don't even know him.'
>
> (James, 17 years)

James highlights the collusion of other students in the bullying practices in their failure to support him in a situation in which he feels quite helpless and angry. He is unable to comprehend how other people could not intervene. This is reiterated in the following where he stresses the need for adults such as bus drivers to address the problem, even though there may be negative repercussions for him: 'You think the bus driver might have done something like stop the bus and say "Don't do that, don't hang your heads out of the window" . . . one driver did once and I thought, Oh, shit, they're going to big mouth me and say, "It's your fault, fag boy."'

The effects of such long-term, sex-based harassment on boys are clearly documented by James:

> It sort of gets to you. It's like I've got a chip on my shoulder. When I walk home from the bus stop and a group of people walk towards me and I'm walking their way, I feel intimidated so that I have to look at the ground or just look the other way. I don't want to look them in the eye.
>
> (James, 17 years)

Conclusion

In this chapter we have highlighted the implication of heteronormative and gendernormative masculinities in the bullying and harassing practices of boys at school. Bullying needs to be understood in terms which acknowledge the regime of normalizing practices in which sex/gender boundaries are policed for adolescent boys (see Laskey and Beavis 1996; Steinberg et al. 1997; Beckett 1998; Epstein and Johnson 1998; Letts and Sears 1999). Those boys who failed to measure up to rules and regulations for behaving as 'proper boys' were targeted. We have interrogated the dualistic categorization of bully versus bullied to explore how the latter may take on the strategies of the former to regain some sense of power as a means of dealing with being inferiorized by dominant boys at school. The boys highlighted the need for schools to address the gender- and sex-based dimensions of bullying. Practices of normalization are implicated in the way that many boys learn to negotiate their position in a social hierarchy of masculinities and the interconnections with hierarchies of harassment. This calls for more attention in schools to assist both the boys who bully and those who are bullied to develop specific conflict resolution skills and capacities for interrogating and reflecting on the abusive effects and uses of power. From many of the boys' perspectives, schools were not adequately able to address bullying and these dimensions of it in their lives. However, this work can only be undertaken within a policy and pedagogical framework that names the effects of hierarchies and affirms the diversity of masculinity.

4 'Getting into the cool group is like passing an exam'

Boys talk about friendships at school

I remember the cool group of 'footballer-surfie' boys, as they were called, when I was a teacher. There were about 30 boys in this group and they would all stand around at the bottom of the oval during lunchtime, kicking the footy, talking and joking around. They had such a presence just because of the sheer number of boys in the group. They had a reputation. They were the rebel tough guys that teachers on duty were meant to keep their eye on! I would always wonder about the public side of their performance because privately they revealed other facets to me – their more sensitive, honest and often vulnerable sides.

I remember watching them on many occasions 'scrag' on the oval – this involved about six or seven boys jumping on top of – or falling on top of – one boy to create a mountain of bodies. I was always worried about them hurting themselves, particularly the boy at the bottom – they were screaming and shouting and having a great time. Just boys being 'normal' boys, testosterone overload? But I was never convinced that this performance was just another example of a 'natural' way of relating as friends. This kind of behaviour always fascinated me – the kind of body contact that was permissible under the guise of rough and tumble play.

Another incident that I relive as I am interviewing boys about their friendships also relates to this group. I remember standing there one lunchtime talking to some of the boys when an 'outsider' to their group approached me. He said he needed to talk to me. His name was Leon and he was one year older than these boys, but had been classified and stigmatized as gay. As he approached the whole group disbanded immediately, making homophobic comments. I'll never forget the instantaneous reaction and repulsion of those boys, the scorn on their faces, the fear that any association or respectful contact with Leon would render their status as heterosexual boys questionable. They moved right away as if they feared contamination or infection. I don't know to this day whether Leon identified as gay or straight. It didn't matter really because the footballer-surfie boys had already ascribed him a deviant sexuality, regardless of what his actual sexual orientation was. They had already classified him according to the fact that he didn't play sport, preferred the company of girls and talked in a particular way. Was this just another example of boys just naturally being boys?

Introduction

In any school, there are different kinds of friendship groups amongst boys. This has been documented well in the research that has explored the ways in which boys tend to relate at school. Kessler et al. (1985), Walker (1988) Connell (1989), and Mac an Ghaill (1994b), for example, all draw attention to how a pecking order of masculinities is negotiated and established in boys' lives at school and how this, in turn, impacts on their social experiences and relationships. In this chapter we explore further how these hierarchical relationships get played out in boys' peer group cultures. We focus on:

1. *Exclusion and inclusion:* how boys gain or are refused membership to certain friendship groups.
2. *Classifications used by boys to define and negotiate friendship boundaries:* how normative masculinity demarcates the limits and possibilities for forming particular kinds of friendships.
3. *The difference between friendship and 'mateship':* how homophobic constructions impact on intimacy between boys.
4. *Boys' friendships with girls:* how relationships with girls appear to function as compensating for the lack of intimacy in their friendships with other boys.

'Who's in? Who's out?'

Boys commented on how certain membership classifications involving who is excluded and who is included, who is rejected and who is accepted, informed the ways in which many boys negotiated their friendships. Bryce, for instance, talks about gaining acceptance into the 'cool' group and draws an analogy to passing an exam: 'Some people get into the cool group . . . it's like an exam and you've got to pass it . . . like being cool and going out with good girls, not doing as much work and saying some stuff about other kids' (Bryce, 13 years).

Bryce draws attention to the pressures placed on boys to continually prove themselves and to demonstrate that they are 'cool'. The pressure does not end with passing the test, but continues with boys having to continually demonstrate that they are maintaining and performing their 'coolness'.

The 'cool' boys in other schools also functioned as prime boundary markers and hierarchy maintainers. They played a major role in assigning and policing the inclusion and exclusion of other boys' membership into groups according to whether they assimilated to or transgressed hegemonic masculinist norms. Apart from gendernormativity, students often spoke of other criteria that were used to delineate boundaries and hierarchies which resulted in asserting uniformity and conformity among the boys. Many of these criteria were classified into neat hierarchical binaries such as being thin or fat, being 'sporty' or 'nerdy', having a 'big dick' or 'small dick', being seen with popular girls or unpopular girls. Simon reflects on the exclusionary practices and classifications that led him to be rejected by the 'cool boys':

> They always say I'm fat. To the cools, the 'in' group, you're supposed to play football and be really rough and talk about the size of your dick. I stay away from the people who I don't get on with and hang around with the people who are friends and don't try to be one of the popular ones. At times I've found myself trying to blend in with them, but it doesn't work. [To blend in, I] just hang around in certain areas, and talk about certain things, like how much they smoke . . . and dislike certain girls, some of them which are fairly good friends of mine so that's a bit weird. They go like, 'Oh why would you choose this girl or that girl.'
>
> (Simon, 13 years)

Simon provides insight into how the norms and prescriptions for behaving in certain ways appear to be heavily policed by the boys themselves who have gained membership to the 'cool' group. For instance, 'cool boys' cannot just like or 'hang around' with any girl – only certain kinds of girls are deemed acceptable. Moreover, for boys who desire inclusion into the cool group, there is a tension between desiring to conform to the norms in order to be accepted, while simultaneously questioning those very norms. For example, Simon is caught between the expectation to dislike certain girls and to approve of others, while still liking the girls he is expected to dislike. This highlights the level of anxiety and pressure informing the social practices of masculinity to which some boys may feel compelled to subscribe in order to maintain and enhance their cool status.

Several boys interrogated the classifications informing the social hierarchies of boys' peer group cultures at school. Matthew comments critically on the 'splitting' of boys into groups:

> They can split themselves up, so that they can say this is me because I'm following everyone else. You can see it at lunchtime, if you stand above the school you can see all the different groups of people and you can see just by their hair colour what group they're in because you'll see either a whole lot of people with either blonde or bleached blonde hair, and the darker hair. It's just the way it is, it's so cliquey.
>
> (Matthew, 16 years)

Matthew rejects the social cliques and associative norms governing boys' conformity to certain body-fashioning practices. In the following, Jarrod, 16 years, like Matthew, was also very aware of the peer pressure to conform to the behavioural and attitudinal codes of a friendship group such as 'doing drugs'. However, in a contradictory fashion, he was also conscious of how he was implicated in maintaining these normalizing practices and policing techniques: 'There are guys like me . . . that want to impress people.'

Mario also pointed to the connection between being accepted into a popular group and behaviours such as partying and drinking (Martino 1999). He relates how one of his friends began to perform this identity which 'wasn't him' in order to avoid constant interrogations by other boys:

> I know one friend who was quiet, but the people he mixes with – now he's like them. I'd say before he wouldn't really talk about those things like getting drunk. That was not his scene, that wasn't him, but he has gradually got like that . . . peer pressure. He might have friends who all say 'Why don't you want to come?' and 'Oh your parents won't let you', just stuff like that, so he goes, 'Oh well, I'll do what they do and follow them.'
>
> (Mario, 16 years)

In reaction to the exclusionary practices from the dominant group and yet replicating its normalizing practices, some students spoke about establishing their own groups within which they were able to gain support. For example, gay-identifying Luke talks about the group called 'the misfits'. However, within this label were gathered a 'diverse' group of people classified together as Other to the central group:

> Within my little circle of friends at school we were all kind of misfits, each in our own way. But we acknowledged that and if something was happening we would actually sit down and talk about it instead of just pretending that the world is wonderful. We would sit down and help each other through these situations. We didn't fit into the other norms [of] the sheer number of people who conformed to the ideals set down by the way the school was set up, and activities you did if you were male or female. Or in class, if you were discussing someone, it would always be a very heterosexual base, so therefore anything that didn't quite fit into that was not the norm.
>
> (Luke, 19 years)

In the above, Luke draws attention to the school system as framing these exclusionary practices by classifying students in heteronormative and gender-normative ways. This is also emphasized by bisexual-identifying Rowan, who had very similar experiences of being involved with a group of boys who were not part of the two polarized dominant groups: the sporty guys and the intellectuals. In opposition to the hegemony of these two groups, Rowan was part of a 'strange' group where supposedly polarized subordinate groups met on the border: the non-heterosexual guys and the guys in 'resistance to authority' who were getting into trouble at school:

> Well, it was quite a strange group that I hung around with because it was mainly the people that didn't fit in with the accepted groups like the intellectuals and the jocks. They were the kind of groups that were accepted, the groups that everyone expects to be a group, and I use group very loosely, not like your friends but a group of people. On the one hand it was people like me and my friends who were gay who didn't fit in for those reasons, and on the other hand it was people whose attitudes were I think really bad but who didn't fit in because of a general kind of resistance to authority. So it was a really strange mixture.
>
> (Rowan, 19 years)

Several students identified themselves as borderdwellers, bordering the boundaries of several groups and playing with the identity-markers of each. Josh inhabits this space, belonging and not belonging to several groups. From this position he is able to evaluate fixed and stereotypical identity labels such as 'geek' which are attributed to others by the 'cool' group. He is also able to scrutinize, as an outsider/insider/no-sider, the workings of the 'cool' group and undermine the validity of their friendship by pointing to the superficial connections between the boys who do not 'even know each other':

> They don't really even know each other, but if you're friends with him or wear this then you're part of a group. And that's how you recognize them. I've got a really wide group of friends, I don't really stick to one group of people. [But] people say 'Why do you hang around with him because he's gay or he's a geek?' So I probably come out with something like, 'Do you actually know them? Have you actually gone up and had a conversation with him?'
>
> (Josh, 15 years)

The following is an interrogation of the 'cool' group by Ben who, in positioning himself as an outsider, explores the performance of friendship and interrogates the strategic workings of the group as well as its shifting and expanding boundaries:

> You wouldn't call them friends, though. These people stick by each other as a way to not be the person getting picked on. They would never stand

> up against this guy [the main bully within their group] because that would mean jeopardizing the protective circle they had. Most groups are formed under that one criteria. I don't think they have 'deep and meaningfuls' . . . they are not what I'd call close. All they talk about is their imaginary sex lives. . . . and it's so boring . . . even among my friends of guys and girls. I wish we could talk about something else and at first I felt stupid, but then I realized that I had no reason to feel that way. Maybe they are just threatened. They are just as insecure as I am. I wish we could all just come together and be friends.
>
> (Ben, 17 years)

Here Ben draws attention to how friendship amongst the 'cool' boys is based on maintaining a 'protective circle' to ensure that its members avoid becoming the target of the main bully of the group. He finds the level of their interaction superficial and dishonest, particularly in his reference to how these 'cool' boys only seem to talk about their 'imaginary sex lives'. In this sense, he draws attention to the performative dimensions of masculinity which are dictated by the norms of compulsory heterosexuality (see Redman 1996; Steinberg et al. 1997; Epstein and Johnson 1998).

Bisexual-identifying Jason also positioned himself as an outsider and yet his very status as being outside the domains of any particular group assigned him a certain reputation and popularity. Others would confide in him about members of their groups. Again, this exposes the tensions and tenuousness of maintaining friendships and allegiances within the peer group where hierarchical power relations are at play. This necessitates a constant jockeying for positions of power both within and between certain friendship groups which is often driven by a deep-seated anxiety to avoid being pushed:

> What gets to me is that everyone does it behind everyone's back and because I stay out of it, everyone will come to me and say, 'Oh, this, this and this happened', or 'I'm sleeping with this person, don't tell anyone', or 'Is this person sleeping with this one?' I'm like, 'No, I ain't saying anything to you.'
>
> (Jason, 17 years)

John also appeared to shift and move between dichotomous and contradictory labels of 'cool bad reputation' and 'loner bad reputation'. He monitored his interactions with 'loner' boys in order to prevent being externally ascribed as one of them even though seeing himself as 'leaning' toward that category anyway:

> There's two [bad reputations]. There's the naughty reputation which is a bad reputation but that's cool. And there's the bad reputation as in a

> loner. I prefer to have the cool one. They're the ones who don't care about the rules and don't really care about work and some of them are rude to the teachers. I'm the sort of the silent person here, no one pays a great deal of attention to me, but I'm not sort of a cool bad reputation but I'm not a loner bad reputation, I'm somewhere in the middle, maybe leaning more towards the loner bad reputation.
>
> (John, 16 years)

Michael located himself as a border boy between and on the borders of the oppositional binary of the 'sporty' guys and the 'geeks' (Walker 1988; Mac an Ghaill 1994b). This was despite his assertion that having separate groups was actually beneficial for all boys. He used the example of differing body sizes and physical expressions of puberty to justify this assertion as it prevented boys from experiencing unnecessary discomfort with boys different from themselves. Nevertheless, Michael saw himself as 'feeling comfortable' and able to negotiate and manage the expectations and regulations of both groups:

> The geeks would feel more comfortable with other geeks, like having a shower with other geeks than they would with the sport males because the guys that are into sport usually reach puberty first and grow faster. They're all bigger while the geeks are quite small and wiry. So they may not feel comfortable because they're not the same size as the other guys and they might feel sort of ashamed if their bits aren't as big as the other guys. I would sort of place myself in all of them because I got an award earlier this year for a good report, like an excelled report, so I'm sort of put into the bit of the geek category there, but I play sport and I'm big and solid so I fit into virtually all of those categories. I would say that they [other boys] actually might be jealous that someone that's good at sport can be good in other areas and I feel comfortable being smart and playing sport, or being smarter than them and playing sport. I don't think that they would be comfortable if they had a role change, I don't think they would be comfortable being a geek than being a sport player.
>
> (Michael, 13 years)

This illustrates the cultural and social capital assigned to boys who are 'sporty' and physically 'big' which allows them to negotiate the boundaries between different groups of boys without being targeted.

Other boys were unable to experience the multiple and interrogative allegiances of borderdwelling but remained clearly on the outside of all group boundaries:

> There were jocks . . . there were music people . . . everyone was separated into different groups. It was all really divided and it was really hard to fit

> into any one of those groups if you didn't solely commit yourself to what they stood for. If you were a jock you would love sport completely and be really good at everything. Music, you knew four or five instruments. That's how you would be accepted into each particular group and you always had friends.
>
> (Jordan, 16 years)

Some students expressed the frustration that the constant manufacturing of a self that was sociable and popular was very restricting. It was seen as preventing the expansion of one's awareness and connections with others, as well as stifling one's understandings of one's fluid and multiple self: 'you're constantly surrounded, and if you are unable to detach yourself from those people that you're with, then you don't give yourself the chance to open up or just become yourself. You're not able to move forward.' (Christian, 22 years)

'Boys have mates, not friends'

Negotiating tensions between mateship and intimate friendships

Having explored the classifications used by boys to define and negotiate friendship boundaries, in this section we will examine how the distinction between friendship and mateship for boys provides further insights into the policing and regulation of their social relationships. The term 'mateship' has a specifically Australian nationalist history. It is used to define the camaraderie (including being anti-authoritarian, drinking, smoking, gambling and chasing women) and friendship between men, particularly in times of hardship such as during wars and pioneering in the harsh Australian outback (see Ward, 1985; Garton 1998; Murrie 1998; Rickard 1998). It rests on shared understandings and discourses of loyalty, trust, and support, as well as on the premise that it is strictly a homosocial bonding between men which denies any sexual intimacy. Without necessarily undermining these meanings of 'mateship', this section will explore how the word 'mate' has come to signify for many boys in our research something quite distinct from 'friend'.

According to Andrew: 'Friends talk to each other and relate to each other their experiences because it's all about sharing and being trustworthy and having someone there for you. I think they're very caring and they genuinely care for you' (Andrew, 16 years). This can be quite distinct from being a 'mate' which has come to connote the 'normal' relationship of conformity and uniformity between boys with its focus on shared activities, nonchalance, rebelliousness, and having fun. 'Friend' is constructed as Other because, as Andrew explains above, it involves a deeper sharing of emotions, support and a level of intimacy. Boys who had migrated to Australia such as Eric, who was Hong

Kong Chinese, were particularly aware of what they saw as a specifically Australian kind of friendship between men:

> I felt very excluded. I guess it might be the whole sort of mateship thing. The only way that they can really belong is to get the people that they call mate together, exclude the people who they think are different from them. In my case it's because I was more serious. I seemed to have such a good relationship with all of my teachers. I'm such a 'nerd' for them. Maybe for them they just see me as someone who just studies all the time and pleases the teachers.
>
> (Eric, 22 years)

Thus, from his borderland positioning, Eric interrogates the culture of mateship from which he is excluded and classified as a 'nerd'.

When speaking about the kind of intimate experiences the boys in his Catholic single-sex school had while on Retreat, Scott clearly traces a shift from a narrow and exclusionary 'mateship' with which they had gone on Retreat, to a deeper and inclusive level of 'friendship' by the time it was over:

> Near the end after everyone's really talked a lot and found out things about each other, you find new friendships and guys seem to be hanging around with different guys all the time. Before they go on a Retreat, they've got a group of mates and towards the end it seems that they make friends with different groups they never thought they would.
>
> (Scott, 17 years)

'Mateship' involves loyalty, sharing interests and activities that are dictated by what may be termed a heterosexually masculine camaraderie including drinking, smoking, taking drugs and a certain kind of 'yobbo' or 'laddish' behaviour:

> Kieran's a really good mate . . . he's a derro like me. We get drunk way too often, and smoke too much dope. He's good and he knows where his loyalties lie. About a week ago, when I got really, really drunk, I kissed his girlfriend and I just said, 'Sorry, I kissed your girlfriend', he just said nothing.
>
> (Stephen, 15 years)

Stephen then proceeded to mention how boys sometimes feel the need to boast about sex but adds that '90 per cent of what they say is bullshit, they bullshit that they've got more experience than they have, I've done that sometimes, it's just trying to feel superior'. Mateship for boys like Tim and Wayne in the following is often about a public display of a hegemonic masculinity which involves an avoidance of emotional intimacy – sharing secrets, talking about problems, and offering support carry the risk of being exposed as vulnerable and hence questionable:

> Most of me mates stick up for me out on the street [but] we don't really open up like girls. If we've got a problem we don't really talk about it, just deal with it. Because if you're going, 'Oh, I got really hurt by this person', they think you're weak and stupid.
>
> (Tim, 14 years)

> Go out at the weekend, get pissed. I don't get too personal, I don't tell them secrets, not family problems or anything like that. I don't say anything.
>
> (Wayne, 16 years)

For boys like Stephen, Tim and Wayne, mateship involves being 'a bit of a larrikin' or a bloke who indulges in a certain recklessness with their mates but they do not 'really get personal' (see Rickard 1998). It involves certain power relationships as Stephen indicates in his reference to his mates 'talking bull-shit', particularly with regards to boasting about their sexual experiences with girls. This is evident when he comments that such practices are tied to boys needing to 'feel superior'. Another aspect of being a mate, as Tim points out, is built around a collective and protective masculinity which involves 'sticking up' for your friends, particularly if there is a threat of violence or a fight. In fact, Tim and Wayne mention that talking openly about problems is not something that mates do, 'they just deal with it'.

Boys with disabilities, however, spoke highly of the need for trustworthy friends they could depend upon for help. This was very different from non-disabled boys who rarely spoke about friendship in terms of dependence, a trait traditionally constructed as feminine: 'He's a good friend, he cares about my disability' (Nick, 16 years). 'He helps me. There's no one that can help me in the classroom if it wasn't for him' (Bryce, 13 years).

While 'mates' joke and tease about puberty, the body and sex, 'friends' sit and 'discuss what was going on':

> What male friends that I did have . . . we all sat down and were discussing puberty and what was happening with us, who was at what stage and what they'd experienced and what they actually thought about it all. I don't see that as being a regular conversation between most 14-year-old males. But we just all had this closeness where we could actually sit down and discuss what was going on.
>
> (Luke, 19 years)

Friendships are formed between boys who had 'opinions' and are interested in personal and social issues while the 'jocks' who were sport and action focused were not seen as having close friends:

> There are a lot of guys who just don't really think about personal issues all that deeply. I would say that the jocks, the sporting guys, generally, don't have close friends because a lot of the sports orientated guys just don't think very much. And it's the guys who think and talk about social issues and things that concern them and who voice their opinions that have close friends.
>
> (Simon, 16 years)

Some boys displayed a tension within themselves in regard to their friendships. On the one hand, they were proud of their intimate friendships with other boys, but would then proceed to disparage this very relationship by considering the gendernormative manner with which it would be denigrated: 'I was on the phone to my friend and sort of deep and meaningful, when we're real close we can talk about anything together. It's probably bullshit that we talk about, girlfriends, we probably sound like little girls' (Nick, 16 years). Nick has internalized a particular misogynistic denigration of the feminine which kicks in once the threshold between what are socially acceptable levels of intimacy for boys and girls run the danger of being crossed.

However, some students believed that boys were far more open with each other than girls were. There appeared to be two conditions that facilitated this: the talk had to be about sex, and it had to be about heterosexual sex (Holland et al. 1993; Kehily and Nayak 1997).

> I think guys can speak about it [sex] more openly with each other from what I've seen from the girls in my school. They usually keep to themselves about it instead of talking about it, whereas guys can talk about it and be open with it. We talk about girls and wet dreams. I barely ever hear the girls saying, 'Oh, I had my period last night.' With the guys you can just say, 'Oh, I saw this really good looking chick on TV and I cracked a boner' . . . [But] I've got a friend of mine whose mum died a few years ago and he never brought it up in school and even now he rarely talks about it. I've got another friend of mine whose dad is in hospital with a disease and he never ever talks about that.
>
> (Michael, 13 years)

It is interesting to note the distinction between what can be voiced and what must remain silent, which corresponds to a public advocacy of a heterosexual masculinity versus the suppression of a potentially effeminizing masculinity associated with the expression of grief and vulnerability.

'We're boy friends, not boyfriends'

Heteronormative and homophobic regulations of boys' friendships

Some boys spoke specifically about how heteronormative and homophobic regimes led to boys policing the development of intimate friendships: 'Well, there's this one guy that I tell everything, we don't care what it is we just tell each other everything. It sounds like we have a [gay] relationship but we tell each other everything' (Paul, 16 years).

For many boys, a major barrier to the establishment of more intimate friendships with other boys was the heteronormative policing and labelling coming mainly from boys in the 'cool' or 'matey' groups. Luc discusses how his sexuality impacted on his friendship with two heterosexual boys:

> I used to have my two very best friends at school, they were both straight. They went through a lot, they got hassled for hanging around me. They got identified as being gay just because they were hanging around me and I really admired the way they handled it. They just didn't care. There were rumours going around that we were having threesomes at recess. I felt guilty that they had to experience that sort of thing from these other people just because they were being friends with me. Once it was so bad that I said to them, 'You don't have to hang around me any more, this is bad for you.' They didn't like to be too emotional about it 'Oh no, no it's fine, whatever happens it doesn't matter'. Like they didn't want to say 'We're here right behind you or anything', they just said, 'Oh no don't be stupid'.
>
> (Luc, 17 years)

Luc constructs his friends as being caught within a heteronormative bind where they experienced difficulty in expressing what they really felt for him while wanting to remain very supportive.

Luke, who was also an openly gay student at school, reflects on the heteronormative bind informing his friendship with a straight boy who was targeted by other boys. His friend's response to this was to behave aggressively toward him which created temporary tension within the friendship. The tension was resolved as both boys refused to comply with the imposition of norms governed by the external homophobic surveillance and harassment from other boys:

> I actually had a male friend who started being really aggressive towards me, and I got really sick of it and I pulled him aside and I said, 'Look what is the problem? What is going on?' He said that other people had started assuming he was a homosexual because he talked to me and he was

> starting to get harassed about it. I said, 'Look I'm really sorry but it's not my fault. They're going to say whatever they want to say regardless of whether you talk to me or not.' So we had a big long chat about it and he was fine after that, he would tell them all to go and get stuffed. He went back to how he was before.
>
> (Luke, 19 years)

Various heterosexual-identifying boys talked about self-regulation and external policing in regard to their sexuality if their friendships were seen to cross an invisible but rigid line (Zerubavel 1991). Darren spoke about how he was labelled gay for having close friendships at school. His discomfort, perplexity and inability to articulate his concerns and feelings are clear, and this exemplifies the need to provide a language and discourse with which boys can interrogate and explain the workings of heteronormativity and homophobia on their relationships:

> Maria: How do you feel about that [being labelled gay for having close friendships with other boys]?
>
> Darren: It's weird but I wouldn't know how to explain it. It gives you a shock.
>
> Maria: And do you find that you change the way you talk to some guys?
>
> Darren: Yes, exactly. I wouldn't bring up some subjects, I would just try and keep away from it.
>
> (Darren, 16 years)

Paul explained how heteronormative policing within his school led him to categorize his friendships into two groups that he keeps apart: the 'mates' at school and the 'friend' outside of school:

> I'd say most people wouldn't have friends like that [very close and intimate] in school. Because if their other friends find out about it, then the gay thing would come out and once it gets around one person it will go around the whole school. I wouldn't have anyone at this school that I would trust enough anyway because this bloke [outside of school] that I tell everything he has not told a soul. I don't tell anyone anything about him.
>
> (Paul, 16 years)

Heteronormative panopticonic policing also creates discomfort, perplexity and silencing between gay-identifying boys who are unable to negotiate a 'coming out' to each other and, instead, border ambiguously around each other's unspoken but silently understood sexualities, even as they face harassment together from other boys:

> I had one best friend, and he turned out to be gay. It wasn't until Year 11 we ended up coming out to each other. And it wasn't until then that we even acknowledged some of that stuff but a lot of that had been a silent understanding between the both of us. Like it was just a sort of look and you knew how the other was feeling about it and knowing that we were going through similar things. For example, my friend was really good at saying, 'Daniel, let's get out of this situation' or 'Let's not go there because this situation could happen' and it was a sort of unspoken communication that happened between us. We just knew that certain things were bad or, gee, that was a bad experience, let's not think about it, let's talk about something else.
>
> (Daniel, 23 years)

Research participants such as Daniel illustrate how boys learn to regulate various levels of intimacy in their relationships with one another, and highlight both the homophobic and heteronormative dimensions of these social practices. An Indigenous boy, Neil, highlights how his friend, James, defies such homophobic practices, involving a policing of masculinity, in the way that he openly displays affection for his friends by hugging them:

> Like James, he's all open, he's in the group, and he goes, 'Oh, I love you man' like that, and hugs us in front of everyone. They [other boys] look at us like funny way . . . They know that James is an open person and we're all close mates and I say, 'Yeah, we do love each other.'
>
> (Neil, 16 years)

Neil talks quite explicitly about how he perceives friendships in his peer group as being governed by alternative norms of masculinity:

> We're more open to each other in our group. I think it's because we don't keep things underneath and we just say things straight out. I trust them. If something really embarrassing happened to you and you told that person, well you know that it's not going to get out. But you wouldn't tell the others if you think, 'Oh, they might accidentally tell someone.' It's all got to do with trust.
>
> (Neil, 16 years)

But Neil does talk at length about the impact of regimes of homophobia and how they relate to boys acting cool which are based on differentiating between various acceptable and unacceptable social practices of masculinity:

> If a boy is not macho, if he was academic and not into sport like the other boys were, well that's just the same as being gay. If you're not macho and

> you hang around with a lot of girls and don't have any male friends, well you're classed as an outsider to all the males. It's pathetic when you think about it. A guy at the school is like that. The first time he got to the school everyone looked at him a weird way because he walked like dainty. He hanged around girls, so he was only the boy in the group. And people would think 'Oh he's a girl, he's like a girl'. And when he first got to the school he was really aggressive. But when we got to know him after a while he turned out to be a really good fella. Like he's a really kind fella . . . At the start they didn't treat him very well, calling him gay, pansy. Everyone used to have a little laugh about that. After a while when we got to know him, he was just Craig.
>
> (Neil, 16 years)

This highlights how marginalized boys sometimes tend to gravitate to girls who are often constructed as being more supportive and nurturing.

'You need girls as friends'

The role of friendships with girls

For many boys, friendships with girls were considered to be important as social spaces within which they could legitimately express a form of intimacy denied to them in their relationships with boys. It appears that girls can play compensatory roles for boys in mainly three binarily constructed ways. First, they provide access to 'deep and meaningful' friendships which are absent in many boys' friendships with each other:

> I just think I can relate better to girls. I just think sometimes it's easier to talk to a girl than another guy. Sometimes when I'm talking to another male, things that they say easily agitate you. If I'm speaking to a girl, it just seems always to be a normal, fine conversation.
>
> (Mike, 17 years)

> I generally hang around with a whole heap of girls. They're really easygoing. They act like themselves and I respect that. With guys I don't think I would actually speak to them in a heart-to-heart way. Girls really understand, they immediately know that what you're talking about is serious and quite secretive, and they immediately change their attitude.
>
> (Johnny, 17 years)

Second, girls are seen to provide access to knowledge about the supposedly distinctive and mysterious world of femininity and girls' perspectives: 'It's good to get to know the other sex really, just physically and mentally . . .

things that girls hate you doing and you don't really know why they hate it or something, then being around them you actually realize why' (Eddie, 11 years).

And third, girls are seen to provide access to friendship for boys who are ostracized or alienated from other boys. Jordan was harassed at school by other boys but found he could establish a mutually supportive relationship with girls, some of whom were also experiencing exploitation and abuse from these boys:

> They accepted me for who I was. They didn't care that I was a guy, that I was a bit chubby, that I didn't look like everybody else, they didn't give a shit. We'd have fun, we'd make jokes, we'd laugh and it was a really enjoyable experience. If any one of us had a trouble we would meet. Whenever one of us needed the others we would always be there. These girls were my best friends, we could trust each other. Whenever I was in a class I would always have somebody to talk to, they all had a different frame of mind, they didn't belittle you or anything like that.
>
> (Jordan, 16 years)

Jordan's positioning on the borderland as insider/outsider is further explicated in the way he is both still marginal in relation to other boys and yet central in their navigation of paths to the girls. Their attempts at manipulating him also afford Jordan some degree of power in his knowledge of the girls' intimate social relationships with other boys:

> [The boys] always came to me saying, 'Oh, what's this one like, you know her, don't you?', and I would go, 'Yeah.' Then they would get really chummy with me and say, 'Oh, do you want a packet of chips or drink or can I get you something, Jordan' and I thought, 'Piss off.' Because I knew exactly what they wanted. They felt I had a lot of influence with their girlfriends, so in a way they wanted to keep me happy.
>
> (Jordan, 16 years)

Often the girls with whom marginal boys become close friends are not the popular girls or they are marginalized in some way themselves. Tony labels the girls who were his friends at school as 'nerdy' and also articulates his own ambiguous border position to them, being part of and yet not part of their group because of his physical disability:

> I didn't have many friends at school, and basically I hanged around with the nerdy girls. They didn't have boyfriends. They didn't go out. They didn't do drugs. They didn't smoke. They did their homework. They got good marks. [But it was] ambiguous. I think there was this constant

> sense of 'What's Tony in this group for?' I think there was a bit of uncomfortableness while also tolerating me and valuing me. I was really funny. I had them in stitches. They had me around because I was fun to be with, but I didn't have group rights necessarily, you know what I mean? They'd do stuff and didn't include me, but they hung around with me at school.
>
> (Tony, 24 years)

Here Tony suggests that these girls' border positioning in relation to other groups of heterosexual girls at school was a basis for the formation of the friendship that he developed with them as a boy with a disability. However, his ambivalent feelings about their response to him vacillates between the poles of tolerating and valuing him. The valuing appears to be built on his capacity to entertain them, but this was not sufficient to gain full membership to their group and to be included in their perhaps gender specific social practices outside of school. Thus, this account draws attention to how multiple marginalities and border positionings within peer group cultures at school can draw certain groups of students together, while still enforcing certain gendernormative boundaries for relating as friends.

Conclusion

In this chapter we have highlighted how hierarchical and dualistic categorizations are negotiated in boys' social relationships and friendships at school. We also found that many boys' friendships were influenced by the need to police particular forms of masculinity which are dictated by the norms of 'compulsory heterosexuality' (see Epstein 1994; Steinberg et al. 1997; Plummer 1999). Driving the way that many boys learnt to self-regulate and to place other boys under a particular kind of surveillance was also a notion of what it meant to be 'cool'. This too was framed within gendernormative and heteronormative boundaries for policing masculinities in terms of who gained membership to such a 'status' peer group positioned at the top of the hierarchical social ladder (Walker 1988; Frank 1993; Mac an Ghaill 1994b; Connell 1995; Gilbert and Gilbert 1998; Martino, 1999). In this sense, we have explicated how such versions of masculinity and hierarchical classifications governing membership to a particular peer group of masculinities are influenced and nuanced by a range of border positionings (Steinberg et al. 1997) related to self-identification on the basis of non-normative sexuality, ethnicity, disability and Indigeneity.

PART 2

Diverse Masculinities

5 'It was never openly talked about'

The experiences of sexually diverse boys at school

'Passing as straight', 'straight acting' or what Kendall (2001) terms, in relation to gay men, 'mimicking masculinity' – these are the ideas that go through my head as I read the transcripts of interviews. I am confronted by the need for many boys to work at presenting themselves as 'normal' – it is about assimilation. Failing to assimilate has its costs and consequences. Homophobia is still alive and well, despite the discourse of tolerance and acceptance from many apparently straight people. The interviews confront me with effects of the straight gaze that is continually directed to those who dare to name their non-normative sexuality or to appear different in their bodily enactment of masculinity. And yet in writing about sexually diverse boys, we want to shift this normalizing gaze away from the Other and to fix it firmly on those who have the power to classify and objectify. Homophobia after all is about regimes of heterosexuality and those who have the officially sanctioned power to inferiorize and pathologize the other. Homophobia is about heterosexuality and normalization – it is about compulsory heterosexuality. How do we get those in schools to understand that this is not about 'promotion' and 'recruitment'? Often when I mention the word 'homophobia' in presentations, it is equated with 'promoting' homosexuality, the effect of which is to divert attention away from 'heterosexual privilege'. Within this frame of reference, it immediately gets caught up in discourses of recruitment – another strategy to divert attention away from the powerful Centre.

I remember giving a keynote address at a teachers' conference. I was asked to talk about issues of masculinity and homophobia and how to address them in schools. There was another male speaker at this conference who also spoke about these issues in his keynote. The conference organizer mentioned to me that one male in the audience had said that while they thought the presentations were excellent, it would have been better if a straight man could have been invited to speak about boys and masculinities. No mention is made of my sexuality in these presentations and yet, interestingly – on the basis of body performativity and voice cues – it is so easy to read everything I say through the homosexual lens. Do I choose to be positioned in this way? Do I always want to be positioned and essentialized in this way? I often get constructed as having 'an agenda' which somehow prevents me from presenting a more balanced perspective. And yet, I always make it explicit that homophobia is about heterosexual privilege and how this relates to gender policing.

These thoughts and questions are going through my mind as I read interview transcripts where boys talk about their experiences of being delegitimated on the basis of how they perform their masculinities. 'Passing as straight?' 'Straight acting?' Is this the only alternative for boys who want to avoid being belittled, dismissed or essentialized?

And –

'Heterosexual privilege' and 'straight-acting femininity' – these are the ideas that go through my head as I read the transcripts of interviews. I am confronted by the way I am constructed as 'normal' by students and by teachers and parents when I challenge homophobia and support sexual diversity. I am a 'wife' and a 'mother' and although I may do my feminist heterosexuality in a non-heteronormative way, I am saved the costs and consequences of 'being a lesbian'. Wearing a frock and a wedding ring does wonders when you are doing anti-homophobic work. Since the early 1990s, I have been able to write, speak and get into schools and other spaces actively promoting social justice in relation to sexual diversity in ways and places that I would not be able to if I were lesbian.

The straight gaze smiles on the me it sees. As I perform and embody my femininity in ways that are seen as gendernormative, I have been able to cross borders still set in concrete for women who wear a different uniform, for they are all uniforms of some sort after all. Discourses of 'recruitment' and 'having an agenda' are less likely to be used to silence me. As if I am detached or sanitized from having a responsibility and accountability that comes with heteroprivilege to do something about the homophobia that heteroprivilege constructs. As if gay, lesbian and bisexual people are removed from me, only research objects rather than family, friends and significant others. On the basis of body performativity and visual cues I am immediately positioned as the sexualized heterosexual Centre, albeit a woman, albeit an 'ethnic'. Do I choose to be positioned in this way? Do I always want to be positioned and essentialized in this way?

For there is a tension, a disruption once I begin to speak, challenges that are seen as not fitting how a heterosexual and ethnic woman should perform her femininity. How often do I hear 'You don't look like an academic' and 'you don't look like a feminist', and these also come from other academics and feminists, usually Anglocentric ones, doing their own kinds of performativity and uniformity. Why is it presumed that fashioning a sexual feminine self erases intellectuality and political engagement? So I sit on the borders, negotiate the tensions, between my heterocentric privileged self and my ethnic working-class 'wog-chick' self as Other, strategically using my partnering and parenting cues to gain access, to open dialogue, to create spaces that 'recruit' and 'promote'. Yes, I do have a blatantly obvious 'agenda': to affirm, support and encourage the health and well-being of a gender diverse and sexually diverse society.

These thoughts and questions are going through my mind as I read the interview transcripts. The focus should be on the heteronormative anti-feminist straight men and boys who need to assert their heterosexuality. Why do they try to regulate and separate out my feminist-feminine, sexual-intellectual-political self? Desiring/dismissing me? Legitimating/delegitimating me? Who, me confused? Not so. Only your binaries frame me, trap you!

Introduction

In this chapter, we focus on interviews with boys and young men who self-identify as same-sex attracted so that a greater understanding of the issues they face at school can be acquired (see Harris, 1997). This is important in the context of the literature and research which highlights the pervasive role of homophobia in schools and the wider society (see Kimmel 1994; Collins et al. 1996; Mason and Tomsen 1997; Kendall 1998). We examine the following:

1. *How gendernormativity and heteronormativity intersect in boys' lives, particularly with regard to the fashioning and performance of 'straight-acting' masculinities.* We draw attention to the impact of what we term to be the effects of 'femiphobia' or fear of the feminine, which is also very much a part of how some gay men and many boys learn to define their masculinities and how this relates to straight-acting (see Bailey, 1995). The issue is not so much straight-acting in and of itself but how straight-acting behaviour is valorized within a hierarchical system of differentiated masculinities. In other words, we argue that it is often appropriated and defined in opposition to other forms of denigrated masculinity, particularly those considered to be associated with the feminine or effeminacy (see Connell 1992; Kimmel 1994; Burfit 1998; Bergling 2001). We examine how gendernormative behaviours are linked to 'passing as straight' or acting straight and how these behaviours are appropriated or adopted by some gay students as a means to avoid homophobic harassment and policing and/or in a compensatory fashion to assert a particular form of masculinity and normalization over other masculinities considered to be subordinate and denigrated. Thus, we explore the tensions, meshings and negotiations between 'being straight', 'acting straight', 'being gay', 'acting gay', and the power of the heteronormative framework and homophobic policing.
2. *How same-sex attraction is problematized in boys rather than situating*

the problems within the heteronormative framework of school policies, structures and pedagogies. We focus on the experiences of gay, bisexual, queer and same-sex attracted boys at school where their sexuality is constructed as the problem. However, we explore how these boys' experiences, perceptions and recommendations demonstrate that 'the problem' is outside their sexual identification and located within and impacting upon all students as a result of hegemonic constructions of heteronormativity. In other words, the problem is the regime of 'compulsory heterosexuality' and how it impacts on these boys' lives at school (Rich 1980; Epstein 1994; Martino 2000b; Pallotta-Chiarolli 2000).

Either 'acting straight' or 'acting gay'

Several boys talked at length about what it was like being gay at school. Vince links his sense of alienation at school – the feeling that he did not belong – to the issue of his self-identification as gay. For instance, he talks about being a member of the 'out crowd', but even within this group he felt compelled to deny his sexuality:

> It was kind of like the 'in crowd' and the 'out crowd'. The 'in crowd' would be the ones that would go to parties and drink alcohol and smoke, and the 'out crowd' would be the ones who didn't. I was with the 'out crowd' at that time, me and my friends used to sit outside the library and talk. Up until I told them about me we'd just sort of sit there and comment on the girls that walked past, she's got a nice arse, that sort of thing. There was one boy there that I really liked and he used to walk past every now and then and I'd look.
>
> (Vince, 17 years)

This draws attention to the 'category boundary maintenance' work of which Davies (1993) speaks, and which for Vince is also linked to same-sex desire. He later talks about the general or pervasive teasing about being 'faggot' and 'a poofter' in his school community which did not necessarily have anything to do with actually being gay:

> You usually get the teasing about, oh faggot, poofter, that sort of thing, but I don't think they knew. It was just general teasing . . . [but] there was one boy but we don't know whether he was actually gay or not, but he was very effeminate. They used to call him gay all the time. He just used to get fed up with it, eventually he left the school.
>
> (Vince, 17 years)

So once a boy is classified as having what are considered to be feminine characteristics, he becomes a visible target for homophobic abuse despite, apparently, whether he is gay or not! This raises important issues about normalization and how non-heterosexual identifying boys/men may take on what we identify as a form of straight-acting masculinity (Burfit 1998; Signorile 1997; Martino and Pallotta-Chiarolli 2001b). Such a form of masculinity which is about acting like a 'straight man', confers power on those boys who would otherwise be stigmatized as gay on the basis of the equation that effeminacy is an indicator of being gay and, hence, of deviant sexuality. To assume a straight-acting masculinity, therefore – which involves talking, acting and behaving like a 'normal' man, like a 'straight' man – can be a means of appropriating a heteronormative form of power, often denied to non-heterosexual men/boys on the basis of their alternative or non-normative sexualities. Such a currency of heteronormative masculinity is often grounded in regimes of misogyny in which the denigration of the feminine is built into a hierarchical set of power relations that also impact on those men/boys who identify as non-heterosexual (see Connell 1992).

This kind of dynamics is evident with Andrew, gay-identifying, who reflects back on his experiences of growing up at school. He talks about his dissatisfaction with school and how he just wanted to leave – a desire which he links to his need to explore his sexuality outside of the constraints of a rural school and community:

> I just feel freer, more responsible, and that's something I always wanted when I was in school. I mean when you're at school it's like you can't really choose your friends. I felt I couldn't come out while I was at school, so that was limiting in a way. And it was partly being isolated in a small town. They were very restricting in a lot of ways. I certainly knew I was gay all through high school and the end of primary school. But there was no way I was going to tell anyone, and I wasn't bothered by it, I just knew. Again I think that was part of wanting to get out of school because I just felt that while I was there I couldn't tell anyone, but I felt once I got to Uni and to the city I could just be all different. So that's certainly what happened. I wasn't really interested in Uni, it was sort of a ticket out of the country to the city. I just knew that I had to move away and then I could be who I wanted to be.
>
> (Andrew, 21 years)

This is particularly significant given the influence of the rural community and the kinds of homophobic and racist attitudes which prevailed in this community. Andrew made decisions to keep quiet about his sexuality, not so much because of fear or shame, but on the basis of his understanding of the consequences of such an act of disclosure in a closed-minded community:

> It was just a small country town where so many people know so many other people . . . it would have been particularly difficult [to come out]. Maybe I could have told a friend. I think they knew anyway, it wouldn't have been a huge thing, but to have been sort of a raging queen running round school would not have really been possible, not in that sort of place. At school it was relatively racially harmonious among the students but a lot of white parents had very backward attitudes towards race. I sort of just assumed that it would be the same with sexuality. I mean just listening to some of my parents' friends talk when they came for dinner or something, about issues. A good friend is a policeman and he used to be in charge up there, some of his attitudes were just incredible about the police and Aboriginals – quite scary. When you listen to that you sort of associate intolerance as a general thing and it would apply to me as well.
>
> (Andrew, 21 years)

However, Andrew is in a position of power in the sense that he is able to choose not to disclose his sexuality, while other boys do not appear to readily have this choice due to the fact that they embody masculinity in non-normative ways. What emerges in the interview is the extent to which passing as straight ensures that he can escape from the homophobia that is directed at those boys who are visibly perceived to be gay. Contravening dominant norms for behaving appropriately masculine leads to sex-based harassment for many boys – as demonstrated by Vince – regardless of whether they identify as gay or not (see McMahon 1998; Rickard 1998). Andrew, for example, comments on one English boy who was targeted because of his 'posh' English accent: 'The English guy, someone accused him of being gay because of his posh English accent, and he's sort of tall and slim. Just a stereotype, people with posh English accents are gay. But they probably didn't think I was, so you can never quite tell' (Andrew, 21 years).

The issue here is one of 'straight-acting' masculinities (Bergling 2001). If a boy does not fit the gay stereotype and appears to act like a straight boy, he is able to escape the regimes of homophobia that are implicated in the policing of a powerful form of heteronormative masculinity. However, if he is effeminate, or considered to exhibit characteristics or traits of a stereotypical gay person, he becomes a visible target. There is no way that such a boy can pass as straight in the same way that Andrew can. There is no way that he can escape the homophobia in the way that Andrew, and other straight-acting boys, can. In the following comment, 'no one was really gay', refers to the issue of visibility: 'No one was really gay, I don't remember any teachers who sort of matched the stereotype of who you might have thought were gay' (Andrew, 21 years).

In his eyes, no one really conformed to the stereotype to warrant such an attribution being made. This becomes clear when Andrew is asked about life after school and whether he has encountered any forms of homophobia:

> I'm out to people who ask but I don't sort of wear stereotyped clothes and have a limp wrist and all that. So I think a lot of homophobia is directed towards people who look gay, I mean these guys may not even be gay. Whereas I've never been in that position, not because I'm trying not to be, it's not straight-acting, I mean I'm not deliberately trying to act straight. So I guess I'm not in a position where I might experience that as much. If I go into a shop that's full of strangers they don't think, 'Oh he's gay'. But certain staff members do and I've never had any problems dealing with them. But maybe Uni is more of an accepting place.
>
> (Andrew, 21 years)

The issue that emerges here is that Andrew is in a position where he is able to make certain decisions – he can choose on any occasion not to be out:

> It's just about being visible in some way as being gay. The silly thing is I guess that a lot of people have images. For example there's the art student image and often that merges with a kind of gay image and you think, they look gay . . . whereas a lot of my friends who are gay are what you'd call straight-acting, you just would not know they're gay. But I think you don't suffer as much if you're straight-acting, because you're just not visible. It's like if a black person could look white, they wouldn't get the hassle of the blacks. It's how you dress, and it's your actions. You don't put it around that you're gay or anything. I mean that sounds silly, it sounds like non-straight-acting people do try and be flamboyant or something, they probably don't, it's just how they are. I think it's just being masculine.
>
> (Andrew, 21 years)

In appropriating certain versions of masculinity – either consciously or unconsciously – what is accrued is a certain form of power and a decision-making capacity to disclose one's sexual orientation on particular occasions, which is not available to those boys who are immediately identified as gay or are perceived to be:

> I think it's how you talk, it's bodily movements. That's how I've always sort of thought of me as being straight-acting. I don't like the term, it sort of suggests you're acting, you're not like you are. Every now and then you'll see someone will make a point about it, often a very non-straight-acting person. They're saying you're not being who you are, and it's ridiculous. As if they are being who they are, and I'm not. I mean I think

> gay people have got all these stereotypes in their head just like straight people, about what it is to be gay, or straight. And we use them probably just as much.
>
> (Andrew, 21 years)

Thus the problem for Andrew is to reconcile the fact that he is not acting in the strictest sense of the word – that he is not deliberately trying to be somebody he's not! He is just acting in a way that is 'natural' to him – he's just being who he is! While this claim might also be made by and about those boys who adopt a non-straight-acting version of masculinity, Andrew does acknowledge the power differentials that exist in assuming a straight-acting version of masculinity. Moreover the hierarchical power relations and devaluation of the feminine that is implicated in these relational dynamics of ascendant and subordinated masculinities are not acknowledged.

While Andrew appears to imply that straight-acting masculinity is something which comes naturally to him, the effects of the homophobia are so highlighted for Vince that he attempts to actively fashion his masculinity as straight-acting in order to escape the sex-based harassment and violence perpetrated by other boys:

> I just tried to protect myself by acting heterosexual. Like going around saying 'Oh yes she's nice, blah, blah, blah . . .' Everyone seems to believe that sort of thing. I hate it, it's the most uncomfortable feeling ever because you just want to be yourself. You feel like you're living a lie. I just wanted to let everyone know, get up at full school assembly, tell everyone so I could just be myself. But I thought, no, to be safe just don't give too much away. I've been frightened by gay bashers, because if they find out you're gay they don't like it, they'll beat the crap out of you. And I'm not a very strong person so I'm liable to get the shit beaten out of me. Like I don't even like going into the city just in case my walk or my hands or something just give it away and someone just decides to beat the crap out of me.
>
> (Vince, 17 years)

So Vince is careful to regulate himself for fear of having 'the crap beaten out of him'. This mode of self-regulation is not something that Andrew has to endure because acting straight appears to come 'naturally' to him. However, 'just being yourself' is something which is important to both young men but what 'being yourself' means is circumscribed by culturally specific norms and practices of negotiation which involve protecting oneself from the effects of institutionalized regimes of 'compulsory heterosexuality' through which particular forms of discrimination are inscribed. When asked to discuss what masculinity means to him, and the kinds of expectations that are placed on boys, Vince is quite articulate about the social norms governing the requirement to fashion a particular straight-acting form of masculinity: 'Some heterosexual people may walk a bit feminine and they might get targeted because people might think they're gay just because they walk like a woman, or talk like a woman, or not have a low voice, a high voice. They might get picked on for that' (Vince, 17 years).

Vince also makes the point that growing up as a gay boy was scary for him in a homophobic society:

> It's hard and it's scary in a way. You feel nervous, sometimes you get depressed – Why can't I be normal? For me in the beginning it was easier to respect myself because I thought that was normal. When you're young you don't know the difference. But as you get older and you find out what's happening. There's just so many restrictions, it's just so hard . . . what you can and can't do, what you can and can't say, where you can go, where you can't go, what you can wear, what you can't wear, what you can watch on TV, what you can't, what you can listen to, what you can't. Sometimes I'm conscious of the way I walk. I think, no, walk like this, there's people coming.
>
> (Vince, 17 years)

What is interesting is the extent to which both Vince and Andrew regulate and monitor their behaviour. Vince, in particular, is afraid that if he does not behave in a particular way, his safety is at risk. He also highlights that being 'normal' is something which is imposed by societal norms because when he was a child he never really considered the issue of normality – it was only as he was growing up, apparently, that he was made aware that he was different.

Another interviewee, Byron, gay-identifying, also highlights how gender non-conforming behaviours for boys at school in terms of dress and appearance accounted for why they were classified as gay and hence became homophobic targets. This leads on to a discussion about straight-acting masculinities, how normalized constructions of masculinity are appropriated by boys regardless of their sexuality, and how this appears to be governed by femiphobia which then feeds into homophobia:

> I made that distinction between someone who straight acts in that they go about their lives saying that they're heterosexual, even though they're not. And straight-acting as in not being perceived as a stereotypical homosexual who behaves like a woman. People expect gay men to be effeminate because I guess that's what they see. I have friends who say, 'I can't believe you're gay, you're so straight.' 'What do you mean by that?' 'Well, you don't do this, you don't do that'. 'Well, should I necessarily do

> those things?' People who don't know me, from first impressions say 'I thought you were straight'. I think it's because I don't do what they normally expect for a gay person like being camp and effeminate, being like 'darling', over the top that kind of persona. Rather than just being much like anyone else.
>
> (Byron, 22 years)

This repudiation of the stereotype of the effeminate gay appears to be driving the fashioning of and investment in straight-acting masculinities for many sexually diverse boys at school. This is understandable given the role that gender non-conformity plays in the regimes of bullying that lead to certain kinds of boys being identified in homophobic ways as deviant. This also points to the need for anti-homophobic work in schools not to lapse into perpetuating a new hierarchy – the upholding of straight-acting masculinities and the continued denigration of gay men who display non-normative masculinities.

Between 'acting gay' and 'acting straight'

Luc, from an Italian background, also raises issues about stereotypes of gay men which are associated with effeminacy and how his own fashioning and understanding of masculinity is differentiated in dissociation from such stereotypes. The effects of normalization are noted in his assertion that despite the fact that he identifies as gay, he is still a man:

> I really like dressing as a boy, that stereotypical sort of boyish image. I think it's just a part of me. The fact that I identify as homosexual doesn't have anything to do with the fact that I'm a boy. It's kind of weird to explain. Just because I'm gay doesn't mean I don't like to be a man. I still have my traditional male views.
>
> (Luc, 18 years)

Through his dress code Luc fashions a particular form of normalized masculinity which enables him to assert that identifying as gay does not somehow detract from the fact that he is a man. Being a certain kind of boy is desirable for him and has a particular social capital (see Burfit 1998; Bergling 2001). For Luc who has been positioned as inferior, both on the basis of his cultural background and sexuality, appropriating such desirable masculinity may be his way of gaining some form of power. Moreover, being able to assert that he is a man may be a means by which he is able to repudiate attributions of deviancy and, hence, the notion of gay men as somehow not 'real' men in the sense that they represent failed masculinity. His investment in fashioning what appears to be a straight-acting form of masculinity, therefore, may be read as a response to being positioned as socially inferior on the basis of both his ethnicity and sexuality.

This is emphasized further when Luc links such understandings about what it means to be a man to his ethnic upbringing which he believes is governed by norms dictating differential social practices for men and women in terms of their participation in gendered forms of labour:

> I've been brought up in that Italian family where my mum goes to work and my mum comes back and does the cooking and the cleaning and the ironing. And so in that respect I've always had a woman look after me. I mean my dad works hard, but when he comes home he doesn't do much work around the house. That's just the way he is and nobody complains about it, it just is. So that's probably why I still retain that traditional male.
>
> (Luc, 18 years)

So, for Luc, enacting masculinity is tied to traditional patriarchal views about what it means to be a man. In this sense there is no discontinuity between being a certain kind of boy and identifying as gay. However, Luc is also able to play around with his gender in subversive and powerful ways to challenge what he considers to be other boys' narrow conceptualization of gay masculinity. In the following, he talks about the way he manipulated his externally ascribed and self-acknowledged outsiderhood status to construct a position of centrality from where he was able to undertake political actions in the school. Through this hierarchical inversion or strategic use of carnivalesque (Bakhtin 1965, 1981), or what Memmi (1965) and Fanon (1967) refer to as the strategic mimicry and mockery of the oppressor, Luc was able to gain the support of straight-identifying friends, many of whom considered him to be 'cool'. They framed his homosexuality as a rebellion against their Catholic single-sex school and religious authorities and it allowed them to assume the traditional male role of protector. Luc was also able to situate himself centrally with English faculty teachers as his non-masculinist expressiveness in English was recognized. Finally, he was able to act as a mediator and agent on behalf of other gay students who were less willing or able to identify themselves:

> There were lots of guys who identified as straight that really liked me. They thought it was cool that I was gay and I was their gay friend, they protected me and took me under their wing. That was very nice. I suppose I had a lot of attention at high school. I suppose I kind of liked getting the attention. Like when I was in Year 12 there would be new Year 7 or 8 boys that would come up to me and say, 'Are you the gay boy?' So in that respect I think I achieved something in making my presence felt. In the English faculty I was teachers' pet. There I wrote about my

> experiences as a homosexual male in my assignments . . . [I had gay friends at school] but they weren't out so I took them under my wing, and I spoke up for a lot of them.
>
> (Luc, 18 years)

As the interview progressed, Luc continued to explore how he used clothing, performance and humour to interrogate, mock and mimic the assumptions and prescriptions – the normalizing practices – of the hegemonic heterosexual masculinist Centre. In this way, he went from being an outsider who was a passive victim of harassment to being a borderdweller. He positioned himself on the Outside of external ascriptions and performances of straight-acting and gay-acting as polarized and simplistic dualisms. In this way, he positioned himself and was positioned by others as an insider/outsider/no-sider, both regulated and regulating, both under surveillance and surveillant, at times assimilating, at times resisting (Anzaldua 1987; Trinh 1990b, 1992). In this way, he fulfilled his aim at school which was to gain recognition of gay students and gay rights, and carve out public spaces of safety and acknowledgement for himself from other students, the curriculum and the teachers:

> I got verbal abuse, 'poofter', 'faggot' and they used to say it with this tone of voice of hatred, like 'I really hate your guts'. I used to cry. By about mid Year 11 when it was just common knowledge, if someone was giving me shit about being gay I'd tell them to just get over it, I just don't care. Sometimes I used to give shit back to them, but in a joking way. Sometimes actually I would put my arm around one or two of the guys and go 'darling', which is a bit stirring. Then they just started to see that it was no point making fun of me because I really didn't care. Some of them had this smile on their face. How do I explain that kind of smile, that 'Oh my god I've got a poofter hanging round my neck' kind of discomfort. Some of them would just put their arms back around me and go 'Oh darling, let's go now'. A lot of them would be pushing me away and saying, 'Don't fucking touch me, you dirty homosexual'. If I was seen with my shirt out they'd all look at me. Whereas they'd all have their shirts out and nobody would look at them. And I found that weird because they were all dressed like that, but because I was, it was weird to them.
>
> (Luc, 18 years)

In the following, Luc identifies the stereotype of the effeminate gay male and uses it in a parodied exaggerated performance to subvert the power of the hegemonic boys at school. The idea of having nice manners and being the dainty fop sipping tea with the little finger lifted is the stereotype that Luc is also working against in his performance. This is about educating the other boys that these behaviours are not what being gay entails for all men. While Luc was describing his performance, he was gesturing and performing for the interviewer:

> I used to have fun with claiming 'homosexual men have manners, we all sit with our legs crossed and with our hands like this [*hands folded in his lap*] and use big words and read the dictionary, and we all lift our little finger when we drink [*pretends to raise a tea cup in one hand, little finger out, and hold a saucer with the other*] and we are all very polite'. I'd be sitting in class going, 'hmmm', being very snobby. I'd be sitting there going 'Tuck your shirt in, darling' . . . trying to keep everyone on the straight and narrow. Some of them really loved it, some of them made fun of me in a joking kind of way. One morning I got to school and this group of boys all had their socks up which I thought was strange because they usually don't. They came down the corridor and their shirts were tucked in and I just looked and said, 'What drugs are you on?' They're trying to be all neat and tidy and this is the Luciano Fan Club, they're all so mannered. So basically a lot of them have had this notion that gay males were always the cleanest people, and always so well dressed. That was a big thing, I don't know why but I was known to always be well dressed on casual clothes days. I was always the one that wore nice clothes.
>
> (Luc, 18 years)

But this clean-cut and tidy look is something which Luc attributes to the fashionable way in which Italian boys like to dress:

> A lot of the Italian boys came to school very well dressed. But I think there is that notion that gay men are like that, so you kind of take that on and exploit that particular part – very effeminate. But when I started to quieten down, they used to make comments. Like one particular time it was a casual clothes day and I was just wearing this checked shirt and these boots and a cap. They're all stunned and like, 'You look like a boy, you're wearing your cap on backwards, you're wearing a checked shirt and a pair of boots. Where's your tight pants and your velvet shirt?' So very stereotypical.
>
> (Luc, 18 years)

So fashioning a particular ethnic masculinity in terms of dress code becomes conflated with being gay in many boys' eyes. But it is also about conforming to acceptable dress codes at school which lead to the denigration and feminization of those boys who don't measure up to norms of desirable hegemonic heterosexual masculinities (see Epstein 1998).

Luc highlights the complex ways in which ethnicity, masculinity and sexuality get played out in one boy's life at school. While on the one hand he claims that he is still a man despite his sexuality, he also performs gender strategically and in highly politicized ways to challenge the dualistic and fallacious logic of the dominant boys at his school.

'I thought I was abnormal'

Heteronormative boundaries at school

Our research draws attention to how heteronormativity and homophobia in schools construct boundaries and hierarchies in regard to sexual identity and gendered classifications that impact upon self-ascription for boys. In fact, Plummer traces the development of homophobia as a boundary marker: from its broad asexual designations of difference and subordination in early childhood; to a 'presexual' classification of 'boyhood/gendered/unmasculine difference'; to homophobic labelling used by peers to designate and marginalize children who would later be homosexual, sometimes before their so-classified peers knew they were gay themselves (1999: 210). In the following, Daniel traces his progression from the external ascription of the label gay to the self-ascription:

> I had my first sexual experience at the start of Year 7 and at the time I realized that I wanted it to happen but I didn't identify it as anything. I knew it was wrong but I didn't relate it to my sexuality. I clearly remember the way that people used it [the word gay] . . . in a very nasty and vicious way. It wasn't really something that I can remember ever being said in the household, although it might have been. I just knew that that was something that I didn't want happening to myself. It wasn't until Year 7 when one day someone said, gay, poofter and faggot and all of a sudden it was like a cold feeling rushed over me. It was like a sledge hammer in the stomach and my first reaction was, how did they know what I'd done with another guy? How can they see that I had this sexual experience? I can clearly remember that I was attracted to males and I started to form that identity. I think at the time I thought it was possible that I was gay but I was still thinking that at some stage I might like girls as well and that I would be, at the very least, bisexual. But I pretty much ruled that out around Year 9 or Year 10 and from then on I identified as gay to myself.
>
> (Daniel, 23 years)

Straight-identifying Marc talks about 'knowing' that some students are gay before they do, again supporting Plummer's notion of external ascription being extremely powerful: 'I'm not homophobic, I've got a couple of friends that I know are gay but they don't know they are, or they know they are but they're not coming out yet' (Marc, 18 years).

As research participants illustrate, boys who do not observe boundaries and construct a gendered identity accordingly can become defined by their 'transgressions' and thus targets for homophobia, regardless of their sexual orientation. By orchestrating the successive restriction of behaviours that are acceptably masculine and by stigmatizing fluidity as perverse and in opposition to hegemonic masculinity, it would appear that homophobia polarizes male sexuality and drives a wedge between what is homosexual and heterosexual (Plummer 1999: 219). Plummer thus labels the interweaving and oppressive domination of hegemonic masculinity and heteronormative sexuality 'hegemonic homophobia' (1999: 220). The following account by Rowan, bisexual-identifying, is an example of the workings of this interweaving where gay-identifying boys acknowledge their attraction to straight-identifying boys who conform to hegemonic masculinist images, and the power of societal and familial normalizing practices to partake of and participate in the Centre even when one is not of the Centre:

> I do remember discussing [with gay friends] being attracted to straight guys because we were always discussing how straight guys were really quite attractive and that a lot of my friends wouldn't actually be attracted to more feminine guys. I guess especially if you grow up in a less accepting family, being gay you tend to be identified as a woman in your sexuality, and so in that context a very straight guy, a very masculine man, is what seems to be attractive by society, in general, and that perception is hammered home quite a lot.
>
> (Rowan, 19 years)

As Plummer argues, there are 'elaborate homophobic codes and repetitive practices' which permeate everyday life at school, radically influencing boys' relationships; 'how it shapes self-concept; and how the self is styled and presented to others in response':

> The way men walk, how they use their eyes, how they apply sunscreen and use other cosmetics, how they move their wrists, how they talk, what clothes they wear, where they wear their earrings, who they mix with, what games they play, and their hairstyles are all prescribed in boyhood homophobic codes and rites.
>
> (Plummer 1999: 304)

Many boys who identified as gay or bisexual spoke at length about feeling displaced at school with two common resultant responses: enforced placement utilizing strategies of concealment and camouflage; or self-placement, 'coming out' and gaining strength as borderdwellers. Strategies of 'camouflage and concealment', 'protective facades and dual lives' were deployed to reinvent or fashion a self that could survive the heteronormativity of the school (Plummer 1999: 187). The power of normalizing practices and heteronormativity is acknowledged by some gay students in their internalization of boundary-markers which positioned them on the outside such as in the following by disabled student, Tony:

> I look at myself in old videos and I think 'What a poofter!' I have this squeaky voice – it sounded like a girl. And I did lots of arm movements and I hated listening to myself on tape because, I'd think, 'You sound a bit camp there, Tony, work on that.' I internalized all the crap.
>
> (Tony, 24 years)

Rowan, bisexual-identifying, is also aware of how normalizing practices and heteronormativity meant that non-heterosexual boys could be both oppressed and oppressor (Memmi 1965; Freire 1972; hooks 1990):

> I found at school in my later years, gays apologized to me for teasing me about my sexuality . . . like those guys were gay and one of them said to me, 'I'm really, really sorry about hassling you about your sexuality.' I think it was their own sexuality they realized, and felt guilty.
>
> (Rowan, 19 years)

Gay students also provided many examples of defiance or agency in resisting and interrogating the heteronormative school-ground orthodoxy. In the following, straight-identifying Paul recalls how a gay student's coming out and undertaking curriculum studies around homosexuality led to a decrease in homophobic harassment in his Catholic single-sex school:

> There was one guy that was gay, and he admitted it and funnily enough, he didn't get much crap from everyone. We couldn't pay him out because when people used to go, 'We know you're gay', no more was he getting offended. Guys normally really get offended by it. He did this project on gays and he came in and he said, 'Who thinks gays should be locked up?' Everyone just put their hands up and he called us bastards and he ran out of the class. That was really funny . . . he was just joking around. He came back later and did it again, and we did it seriously.
>
> (Paul, 16 years)

Thus, gay students can be provocative and uphold their position of marginality as a powerful site of scrutiny and deconstruction of taken-for-granted prescriptions regarding sexuality and masculinity. This is related to borderland theory's construction of borderdwellers and outsiders being less restrained and blinded by convention (Anzaldua 1987; Lugones 1990; Trinh 1991). In the following, Rob reflects on what he has gained by coming out to himself about being gay, as well as acknowledging the ongoing dilemmas. For example, although he wants children, his schooling experiences have made him reluctant to put his own children through the difficulties:

> I just know that experiences that I've gone through have made me into a stronger person. Like stuff with losing friends, gaining new ones, watching other people go through different things. I think this whole gay thing has been a growing experience for me. When it first came about I thought I was abnormal, I was disgusted at myself and all I could think of was how much of a problem it is going to be for my life in the future. I've always wanted to have kids and now I can't . . . I'm starting to see things differently. I think after talking to friends about how I feel, they show me a different side of it. I know things are still going to be hard but I've kind of learnt that I can get over them. But I just think, from what I've gone through at school, if someone at our school had two dads, that kid would get so much shit and I don't want that to happen with my kid.
>
> (Rob, 16 years)

A heteronormative and gendernormative framework can also justify and encourage an interest and voyeurism in relation to homosexuality, as well as legitimating the straight gaze. For example, Michael illustrates finding lesbians desirable is a proper boundary-marker of heterosexuality as it is promulgated in pornography as an acceptable practice of masculinity: 'We wish that the girls were lesos! . . . [*confident strong laughter*] . . . It's all teenage guys' fantasy . . . [*nonchalant and matter of fact attitude*] . . . Guys see things in porn magazines and stuff like that' (Michael, 13 years). It is also a marker of boys' gendered power over girls, as Michael indicates later in his interview, that the reversal of the fantasy of girls desiring boys having sex together and requesting this of boys is constructed as unthinkable and 'deviant'.

Rowan was also aware of this gendered discrepancy in his school where bisexuality in girls was encouraged for the pleasure of the 'straight male gaze' whilst his own bisexuality was rendered invisible or silenced:

> It was much, much more accepted for girls to be bisexual. I would go to parties and people would play spin the bottle and girls were always expected to kiss other girls but guys never ever would. I think bisexuality has come to be more accepted among girls probably because it's straight male fantasy.
>
> (Rowan, 19 years)

'You're not just one or the other'

Multicultural and multisexual realities in schools

Same-sex attracted young people, no matter what their cultural background, experience institutional and interpersonal heteronormativity and homophobia in their schools. For example, students from an ethnic background may position a same-sex attracted peer as not belonging to their shared ethnic grouping: 'Other Asian students think "Oh no, it must be that western thing, you know, invaded you"' (Eric, 22 years).

> It was like 'Oh well, you can't be gay if you're Italian'. No Italian male is gay, that's just not possible. No, no, I wasn't Italian, even though I was the only one that was actually born in Italy, actually lived in Italy, actually really properly Italian.
>
> (Luc, 18 years)

However, what appears to be operating in Luc's situation is the apparent inability to reconcile a heteronormative form of ethnic masculinity with Anglocentric stereotypes of gay males held by other Italian boys. Even boys from other ethnic groups targeted him for harassment:

> I got harassed by some of the Asian boys for being gay. Like, I'm in a low minority group but so are you, so what are you talking about? They were kind of startled when I said that. I was also kind of abused by this one group of very, very woggy boys, Greeks.
>
> (Luc, 18 years)

Jonard, a young man whose Filipino family accepted him as gay and who had been openly gay in his Catholic boys' school in the Philippines, changed schools three times due to the homophobic harassment he refused to endure. Even though the principal of his final school encouraged him to enrol due to its anti-homophobic policies, he found the school did not adequately support him against harassment. In much of Jonard's self-analysis and the analysis of the shifting geographical and cultural sites, we see his interweavings and negotiations of a range of factors in his borderland existence. These include multiple religious influences (Catholic and Confucian), multiple cultural influences (Anglo and Filipino), and multiple educational experiences. Throughout, he is aware of divergent and convergent constructions around masculinity and sexuality. He attributes the way he was treated at his former school in the Philippines to cultural and socio-economic factors (see Ratti 1993):

> I think it's because of cultural difference. Like the Philippines is an Asian country and Asian people value other people. I'm not saying that Western culture does not value other people, but Western culture is very individual. I guess Philippines is a very poor country and not a welfare society, and we have to help other people because we want to see them survive. For example, there were 20 openly gay people in my school. One person who was gay even became the Year 9 representative for my school, and that was just really great. It was so open in the Philippines. Some young gay Australians are just unfortunate because they don't have the support of their parents and the school. I guess it's not the Catholic but the Filipino belief that if you do good to other people then other people will do good to you. We follow the Golden Rule of Confucianism. It's just ingrained in our minds. I was brought up as a Catholic [but] Confucianism is a part of Asia, so I guess it's just because of that.
>
> (Jonard, 18 years)

Thus, anti-racism, anti-sexism and anti-homophobic policies, programmes and practices need to be equally addressed and reflect the way these issues are being lived as interconnected by many students.

The growing awareness of sexual diversity rather than sexual duality in schools was also evident among several boys in our research who identified as bisexual. Heterosexism 'formalizes a societal dichotomy of heterosexuality versus homosexuality with little room for bisexuals' (Owens 1998: 55). Bisexual students often find themselves being forced into either the heterosexual or homosexual category. In our research they spoke of the need to acknowledge a broader and more flexible system of sexual classification that moves beyond either/or categorization and classification of sexuality. Jason, bisexual-identifying, for example, is aware of how he needs to 'work with people' to gain their respect and thus positions himself as an agent within a heteronormative and indeed sexually dualistic society:

> A lot of people know that I'm bi, and I haven't copped much for it. But I know that I've earned their respect. A couple of years ago, I was probably on the fence, one day I'd be gay, one day I would be straight, one day I'd start on one side and then during the day switch teams, so now it doesn't bother me. I've actually told most of my girlfriends that I'm bi, and most of them have been cool. I find females are more accepting. A lot of my older male friends are accepting. But bisexuality in society is really considered on the bench, you make a decision sooner or later, you don't be bi forever. Who knows, maybe that's the case for me but right now I'm content.
>
> (Jason, 17 years)

Jason fashions a visual self that symbolizes his bisexuality. On the day of the interview, he had bright pink shoulder-length hair and was wearing one red shoe and one blue shoe. He believed that his weekend activity as a football umpire had given him skills that stand him in good stead when dealing with homophobia. Again, the school is not referenced as a place where this skill learning has occurred. Rather, it is a major site where he needs to utilize these skills in order to protect himself by engaging with and earning the respect of other students:

> There's this really homophobic guy here who will talk about how he really hates poofs. He'll put on the really deep male accent and they'll talk about how they kick the shit out of everyone. I say to everyone, 'You can kick the shit out of me but I'll win in the long run because I'll go to the police. I'll have you up on charges. That'll create a criminal record which will always be there, which will make it harder for you to find a job and blah, blah.' But as an umpire, I've been taught how to handle situations and I'm quite good at it, I can usually talk myself out of a situation that's why I'm hardly ever in a fight. I'm educating people more.
>
> (Jason, 17 years)

Another bisexual-identifying student, Rowan, also spoke about his shifting self-ascribed multiple positioning, while others try to locate and fix him into the heterosexual/homosexual duality. This need to fix and detach often led to the invisibilizing of Rowan's specific situation. He was also aware that if he was positioned by peers within the heterosexual category, this afforded him protection:

> Well, I don't say bisexual. I think of myself more as a kind of artistic person, a logic based person. I don't really know if these are valid kinds of categories to put people into. If someone asked about it, it wasn't something that I would try to hide. But on the other hand, I didn't try to make an issue out of it either. I think that with most of them it came as quite a surprise, but I think that's because being bisexual, people generally assume that you're heterosexual because that's the way their minds work. Apart from people who had those issues themselves – whether they were gay, which quite a few of my friends there were – they kind of ignored it generally. There weren't very many gay guys there who actually identified and who were relatively out about being gay. I was the only person there who actually identified as bisexual, although there were people who behaved bisexually but at that stage most identified as gay or straight. At school people who were straight thought of me as straight, and people who were gay thought of me as gay. I don't even think that the word

> bisexual was ever, ever used while I was at school . . . you're either gay or you're straight.
>
> (Rowan, 19 years)

Simon, who self-labelled as a 'tomgirl', talks about the dilemmas heteronormative and gendernormative structures and practices construct for young people wishing to explore sexual diversity beyond sexual duality. At the time of the interview, Simon was hoping to find a girlfriend to 'find out if I'm gay'. Within a normative framework of sexual duality, homosexuality shifts into the zone of 'normality' for Simon, as opposed to the 'abnormality' of bisexuality:

> There's no gay kids in this school. I don't think so. It would be pretty hard, I'll probably have to have a girlfriend. Actually I've felt sad about that but, yeah, I thought I might be bisexual. It would be a bit hard to cope with. I want to be myself like every other kid, be normal and not like both guys and girls. It's normal being gay, but it's going to be really hard if I am [bisexual].
>
> (Simon, 13 years)

Here we see an example of the use of panopticonic silence that prevents any other option for Simon to explore in order to situate him/her self as gay, heterosexual or bisexual. The options and strategies are severely limited within the heteronormative context of the school and the homophobia of other male students.

The 'three-parent syndrome'

Parental surveillance in schools

Some students were aware of how quickly anti-homophobic programmes and teaching strategies are either not initiated or ceased as soon as a few parents complain to the administration. As Luc, 18 years, from a single-sex Catholic school stated: 'They suffer from TPS, the three-parent syndrome.' Some boys refused to accept that the complaints of a few parents justified inaction or the cessation of action by school authorities. Rob talks about the unwritten hidden codes that are constructed as universal and unchanging in relation to homophobia. He reflects upon the power of parents in his Catholic coeducational school:

> You can't say those things at school . . . it's like there's a strict sort of code of conduct . . . it's not actually written but you can't. If a teacher would say that then the principal would have to talk to them and the

> school board would get involved. Especially parent committees would get involved, a teacher shouldn't be talking about that stuff because it might influence kids. Like if a teacher was gay, then the parent committee would get onto it straight away and they'd get rid of the teacher. Because they'd think that it's a bad influence for the school, and the kids are in danger.
>
> (Rob, 16 years)

However, Rob also draws attention to how panopticonic surveillance and policing constructs borderzones within which multiple realities are lived and negotiated. The same principal, whom Rob sees as preventing anti-homophobic work in his school because of parental surveillance, is himself the parent of a lesbian daughter. Thus, this principal/parent splits his life into detached compartments, the loving father at home who has come to accept his lesbian daughter, the school principal with whom another gay student has confided, and the leader of a Catholic school who publicly refuses to allow anti-homophobic strategies into his school. Likewise, Rob 'acts straight' with both the principal at school and at the principal's home when he visits his best friend who knows he's gay and where his best friend's lesbian sister also lives:

> The principal who has a gay daughter, they talk about it all the time [at home]. The principal actually is my friend's dad and out of school he's just a normal person [with her] because I talk to him at my friend's house. [He doesn't know I'm gay] . . . He'd be totally ashamed and embarrassed [if it became known at school that his daughter is a lesbian]. She went to the school, you'd think that he'd do something about it [homophobia at school] like encourage awareness.
>
> (Rob, 16 years)

Jordan also explores the positioning of parents as rhetorical regulators, utilized by school counsellors, teachers and administrators to avoid anything other than reproductive, heterosexual sex and sexuality education. Of particular poignancy is the fact that even the school counsellor who should be prioritizing the welfare of students makes it known that his/her work and actions are under the surveillance and approval/disapproval of vocal parents and couched within a rhetoric of what may 'distress' students:

> The school counsellor and most of the people on the school board thought that it would be upsetting for the children and the PTA thought it would be a bad thing. They thought that most of the parents would react and object to things like that being taught in the school so that's not part of the school curriculum. Whenever we did have sex education, it was sex between a man and a woman, never anything else.
>
> (Jordan, 16 years)

The discourse of pedophilia may also be used as a rhetorical regulator to avoid addressing the issue of homophobia in schools. However, in the following, Mathew spoke about how his Catholic single-sex school decided to undertake anti-homophobic strategies, despite the likely resistance from some parents and the reality that there had been convicted pedophiles in the school's history. Rather than this being used to silence and deter the school from actually addressing homophobia, the links between pedophilia and homophobia are foregrounded rather than reinscribing the heteronormative conflation of pedophilia and homosexuality:

> Over the past 50 years there's been two convicted pedophiles that have come through my school. It's something that everyone at the school seems to talk about or snigger about behind the Brothers' backs. We've got a particular Brother . . . he gets called Brother Faggoty and he's retired, but he still helps out with the younger classes. He is definitely looked upon as a pedophile. I reckon most definitely because of the past, there is quite a lot of homophobia at this school. We've only just recently had a gay person from a community youth service at this school and he was doing a unit with the Year 9s. Some of the bosses up in the higher ranks don't like it because we're addressing homosexuality which isn't accepted in the Catholic Church. But a lot of parents have written to the school praising it, and others have come back negative saying it shouldn't happen because it's Catholic. But the deputy principal, he won't tolerate it [homophobia] one bit. He just put his foot down and decided no matter what the religion says, it's time to get rid of it.
>
> (Matthew, 16 years)

'Immunizing against homophobia'

Students taking action

Several boys talked about two main ways of challenging heteronormativity in schools: student activism as opposed to adultcentric intervention; and calling for the problematization of the harassers, not the victim. They talked about supporting and initiating anti-homophobic activism in their schools and demanded that they be listened to. When Jonard approached his principal, who had positioned himself as proactively anti-homophobic, to set up a student-run support group for same-sex attracted students, he refused to allow it and said there was no need for such a group in his school. This led Jonard to undertake his own individual actions by conducting a survey as part of a school assignment to see what other students felt about a support group:

> It's ridiculous because they [teachers] have to censor. My topic is the only topic that they have to censor. I had to submit my survey, at first it's a four-page survey and they reduce it to a two-page survey. They don't want me to ask them [students] about sexuality issues, so instead of talking about sexuality I have to talk about homophobia. Like not offensive but rational, non-political words. I cannot give it to people from Year 7 to Year 9. That's really funny. So I don't have their view, so I have to give it to the students from Year 10 to Year 12. They think that there is a homophobia problem and they think that the school should act about that. I told the principal that we should talk about the survey in a more public way but he doesn't agree with me. He read the end results, so that's really good.
>
> (Jonard, 18 years)

Hence, Jonard illustrates how the 'adultcentric' focus of the school may stifle students' initiatives in exploring strategies for addressing homophobia. In fact, he illustrates the extent to which the principal was merely paying lip-service to his attempts to address homophobia in the school.

Heteronormative, adultcentric constructions of sexuality may also lead to the problematization and pathologization of same-sex attraction in schools. Some gay-identifying and bisexual-identifying boys in our research refused to be subsumed into the discourse of 'the problem' of being gay and requiring support: 'I never actually sought out any support. It seemed irrelevant, I was there to study and to get my grades up and do what I had to do. My sexuality should have nothing to do with it' (Luke, 19 years).

For those students who are experiencing homophobic harassment, it is also important that they do not become constructed as 'having a problem'. Special training for counsellors is required so that their strategies and perspectives do not perpetuate the problematization and pathologization of same-sex attracted young people. 'It is our society that clearly owns this problem, not lesbians, gays, and bisexuals' (Owens 1998: 163).

Some boys indicated that their schools 'still don't get it' when it comes to who is causing the problem. Problematizing and pathologizing the recipient of homophobic harassment leads to normalizing and justifying the actions of the perpetuator and thus maintaining the heteronormative framework (Pallotta-Chiarolli 2000). Matthew, for example, was advised by the deputy principal not to 'come out' as this would endanger him. Matthew agreed and explains his position, again revealing how the problematization of the victim is another form of potential victimization that a gay student has to contend with. Ultimately, he would be the one to disrupt his education such as changing schools:

> It's not worth it because you can get yourself in trouble and if you like the school then you won't want to leave. When someone comes out, it's the

> extreme minority of one against practically the whole school. They don't have to leave, they can stay there but they'll get verbal abuse every day and it just won't be worth it to them. If they want to fight the system they can, if they want to fight the people then they can, but I personally wouldn't.
>
> (Matthew, 16 years)

Jonard uses the metaphor of immunization and claims that he wishes to immunize gay students against homophobic students. Thus, he specifically locates the disease, illness or pathological condition to rest with the homophobes rather than the targets of homophobia. This is an interesting reversal of the heteronormative mythology of homosexuality being contagious and pathological. Jonard also reverses the mainstream religious dogma by saying how he strives to love the diseased, the homophobes, despite what they do, a significant co-option, appropriation and subversion of the love the sinner/hate the sin dichotomy as it is applied to homosexual persons by homophobic persons:

> I use the word immunize, I want to immunize young gay and lesbian people against homophobia. Immunization meaning that they have to know that they would probably suffer homophobia if they don't act in a normal way, but they have to realize that the most important thing is for them to survive. Immunization meaning they have an internalized feeling about positive thinking, about being courageous, about helping themselves. With me it helped me to read stuff about positive thinking because sometimes I'm isolated in school and it helps me be more tolerant about other people. The Christian church teaches you to love your enemies as you love yourself, and that's what I do. I don't hate them because of what they do to me and I hope that other young gay and lesbian people would do the same, that they would love their enemies as they love themselves.
>
> (Jonard, 18 years)

However, he still believes that if gay students 'act in a normal way', they will be able to avoid catching the disease of homophobic harassment. This highlights the extent to which boys on the borders are still implicated in normalizing regimes which lead them to discursively construct their sexuality in dualistic terms as either 'normal' or 'deviant'.

Conclusion

In this chapter we have raised important issues about the role that homophobia plays in boys' lives at school. In drawing attention to the role that femiphobia and straight-acting masculinities play in the way that hierarchical classifications and dualistic categories inform some boys' understandings about what it means to be a 'normal' boy, we have highlighted the impact of normalization on the lives of same-sex attracted students. Moreover, one of the central issues to emerge in our research with these boys was that of silence around discussing diverse sexualities in schools. This silence contributes to creating cultures of isolation and alienation for these students. Furthermore, the refusal to address homophobia constitutes a fundamental abnegation of responsibility on behalf of staff to ensure that schools are safe spaces and free of harassment for all students (see Nickson 1996). Ironically, it is many Catholic schools, which supposedly have a strong commitment to pastoral care policies, that are refusing to address the impact and effects of homophobia on students' lives at school. In this regard, we have also attempted to illustrate how there is much to learn from the students in our schools, not only in terms of explaining why homophobia is still an issue among student populations, but also in finding out what insights students can provide into: what kind of anti-homophobic strategies work; what strategies and approaches are required; and what they believe their role as students to be in a whole school approach to homophobia and heterosexism (see also Perrotti and Westheimer 2001). As one young student indicates, 'They don't say all the truth at school, but I know it anyway' (Pallotta-Chiarolli 1999a: 180). But a number of students are increasingly taking their 'truths' to school and challenging the silences and lies. These students need to be supported.

6 'If you're a wog you're cool, but if you're Asian you get picked on'

Multiple masculinities and cultural diversity

They call themselves the wog boys. They also call themselves Italian. They never call themselves Australian. On weekends and school holidays we shared the same home cultures, did the same festas, weddings and funerals. I shopped and ate in their parents' shops and restaurants, and it was their parents who did my plumbing and electrical work. It was their parents and grandparents who talked to my parents about making wine and raising children in Australia.

At school the teacher–student relationship carved a chasm between us as did the way they did their school masculinity, often quite different from their Italian community masculinity, and one which my Italian feminist-femininity could not relate to. Only sometimes did we acknowledge in this Anglo-school world that we shared a different home reality. But they knew I knew, and I knew they knew, and the knowing was always there connecting us in an unspoken and unclassifiable way. And it served to prevent them from performing the extremes of ethno-macho-chauvinism on me, for I knew otherwise about them.

They had their own uniform – black jeans, black t-shirts, black hair greased back. They had their own walk – a slow swagger – and they had their own talk – Italo-English spoken with inflections, accents and hand gestures that mimicked those of our parents and grandparents. They addressed each other as 'paesan' or 'cumpar' and slapped each other's backs or hugged each other roughly. They were loud and loudly proclaimed they 'dig soccer, cars and chicks'. But not all Italian boys could belong just by the fact of an Italian heritage: if you were a nerd, a geek or a fag, you were not a wog boy. If you didn't have muscles, facial hair or hairy chests, you weren't a wog boy.

I felt myself bordering, my loyalties and multiple selves straddling the 'home' world I shared with the students, and my professional teacher–school world I shared with these other adults who would make comments like, 'That's the way Italian boys are. It's their culture.' Meanwhile, I am standing there, and it's my culture they're talking about, the same culture they exoticize and fetishize as an object of entertainment: particularly Hollywood's Italian stallions and mafia men. Meanwhile, the wog boys got louder and more disruptive. They put up soccer club posters in the classroom and used them to start fights over soccer clubs with the Croatian and Greek boys, and to undermine the predominance of Anglo-Australian football in the school. But the wog boys of various backgrounds would come together to hassle the Asian students, who took to working in tight groups in the computer labs.

And what was I doing? I held discussions about the links between sport, nationalism and masculinity. I set up activities exploring cross-cultural and historical gender roles. I engaged them in oral history projects where boys interviewed family members on the impact of culture, migration and war on gender roles. In my yard duty journeys across the oval and asphalt, I made a point of treating the boys individually rather than constantly referring to and addressing them as a group. I talked to them about racism and stereotyping, about their 'wog-boy' masculinity and my 'wog-chick' femininity.

They'd get uncomfortable, ashamed and angry with this 'knowing otherwise' insider I was with them. 'But the teachers, they believe it. They want to believe it. And the skip [Aussie] students who think they're better than us, coming into my Dad's shop with their rich snooty parents and snickering at me. Or they catch me with my little sister and call me an Italian mama. They think we're dumb wog trash. I have to be different here at school because I'm different at home.'

And I'd tell them about my friends and myself being labelled as loud, ignorant, unladylike Italian girls when I was at school and so we became more so and made life hell for those teachers. But we also nearly did ourselves out of useful schooling and just perpetuated their ignorance. That even as a teacher my looks, my mannerisms, my background, my Italian female self, were sometimes used to position me as Other.

Introduction

In this chapter we focus on ethnic boys, or boys from culturally diverse backgrounds, and how they negotiate and fashion their masculinities as specifically articulated through the following hierarchical dualities: Anglo/ethnic; male/female; heterosexual/homosexual. There is still relatively sparse educational research into the social practices of ethnic boys with regards to how issues of masculinity and sexuality impact on their lives. Masculinity and ethnicity 'abrade, inflame, amplify, twist, negate, dampen and complicate each other' (Poynting et al. 1998: 81). Schools are cultural constituents of 'diaspora-space', being 'a point of confluence of economic, political, cultural and psychic processes . . . where multiple subject positions are juxtaposed, contested, proclaimed or disavowed' (Brah 1996: 208). Yet, as Tsolidis says, 'there persist strong commonsense understandings among Australian educationists that the two areas of gender and ethnicity are separate and incompatible' (2001a: 55; see also Tsolidis 2001b). We explore the complexities of the interweaving categories that inform ethnic boys' ways of thinking about the social worlds and borderland existences they inhabit in how they come to understand themselves as particular kinds of boys. In this sense, we draw attention to the normalizing practices through which these boys learn to relate and how particular discourses pertaining to family, culture, nationalism, schooling, class and sexuality intersect in their 'borderland existence' (Anzaldua 1987; Giroux 1992a, 1992b, 1992c; McLaren 1993a, 1993b; Guerra and White 1995).

The following themes were very evident in the interviews with boys from culturally diverse backgrounds:

1 *Ethnic masculinity as a distinct category distinguished from Anglo-masculinity:* how the former is constructed as a protest or site of resistance to the latter in an attempt to reverse the hierarchical dualism of Anglo/ethnic.
2 *The significance of other interweaving factors:* how socio-economic status, family background, ramifications of migration, sexuality and constructs of ethno-nationalism and Australian nationalism impact on the ways ethnic boys articulate their masculinities.
3 *The multiple-within hierarchies and multiple forms of racism:* how hierarchies and racist harassment exist both between Anglo and ethnic groups and among ethnic groups of boys.

'They played up to the stereotypes'

Embodiment and fashioning of ethnic masculinities

Through manipulating and subverting dominant constructions of ethnicized masculinities, many boys are able to build their own hierarchy of masculinities within which the Anglo boys appear to be lower on the social scale. For example, the fashioning of a 'tough' body, as well as other cultural practices, enable ethnic boys to establish some measure of superiority (see Francis 1995). Stereotypes of ethnic youth related to group unity, violence and muscularity can be utilized by the ethnic group to compensate for the absence of socio-economic and socio-cultural power and, hence, to ameliorate the humiliation of racism (Poynting et al. 1998, 1999). The young men in Poynting et al.'s study were critical of the racism in being labelled 'dumb Lebs'. But within certain contexts, they operated with this very concept themselves, ethnicizing their 'macho toughness' as being inconsistent with and dissociated from 'bookish smartness' which they saw as belonging to certain Asian groups (1998: 85). In the following, high academic achiever and school captain, Johnny, speaks about the way other ethnic boys played up to cultural essentialist stereotypes, based on masculinist body performativity and heternormativity. Johnny is himself of Italian-Peruvian background, but had positioned himself as removed from the other ethnic boys due to his academic and leadership achievements in school:

> I think the bullies were generally bigger than everyone else so they could literally push their force on everyone. They were mostly Greek or Lebanese or from European background. They may have felt threatened as they were a minority in the school. Like they had to state their presence. They played up to the stereotypes and really sexualized themselves. They thought they were really sexy, suave. They'd say they're Greek or Italian and make it a known fact. They're loud people . . . they had a totally different way of speaking English. Would always want to build up their bodies.
>
> (Johnny, 17 years)

When asked how the Italian and Greek boys can get away with bullying, Bora from Turkish background accredited it to their body weight – which he attributes to essentialist notions of 'the way they are' as a result of their cultural background – rather than having anything to do with their participation in sport, weight training and muscle building:

> Their bodies are massive and they can get away with it [bullying] real easy. It's just the way they are. 'Hey you, shut up', one punch from them I'm out the window, that's it. I know this. I've copped it. It's like a few Italians and a few Greeks taking on all of Australia, that's it. The Australians are weak. Maybe they don't even know what a gym is, but some people are just built like that, some people have a lot of weight and they get away with everything.
>
> (Bora, 16 years)

Racist harassment was therefore based on embodied performances and built around particular subcultures and national groupings. In our research, the category 'Australian' was owned by and applied to boys from Anglo backgrounds, even if boys from non-Anglo backgrounds were actually Australian-born. In the following, Peco describes a range of physical attributes and performances, linguistic and subcultural practices used to distinguish himself as a 'wog', and in opposition to the category 'Australian' even though he was Australian-born:

> Some of us aren't the same colour, we have different colour eyes and hair. We are more into cars than them. We don't surf. [I'm] Macedonian. My parents are from Macedonia [and] I was born here. Just the way I walk and look [is different]. To them it's a bit funny and they say 'That's

> the wog's walk'. That's just the way I walk. Just the way I swing around when I walk. I do up my hair, put gel in it, when I come to school they reckon 'Oh my God, look at that wog'. [But the way they walk] that's perfectly normal for them. They walk like they're big and tough. They are always racist toward us and we retaliate sometimes. We just call them 'dumb skips'. I start swearing at them in my language and they don't understand. Gives me a bit of a boost because they don't know what I'm talking about.
>
> (Peco, 14 years)

There was also the idea of certain 'standards' existing for boys of ethnic backgrounds that they have to live up to based on cultural pride, physical strength, body fashioning and displays of wealth, whatever the socioeconomic reality:

> They [Maoris and Pacific Islanders] have to act tough and look good because of their background. In their country they have to go fishing in these humongous boats and they come over here and they have to live up to a standard. They wear the Fila and Nike brands. They just have to be cool boys . . . expensive watches, and cars. [Even if they do not come from wealthier families] like the Greek background, they [Maoris] have to have the Commodore and the cool clothes and the big chunky gold ring.
>
> (Murray, 15 years)

'They stick together'

Ethnic gangs or ethnic support?

Our research shows that ethnic identity can be a powerful form of intra-group affiliation and association (Pettman 1992; Vasta 1993). Sewell uses Fordham's (1998) notion of 'fictive kinship' to describe the way ethnic boys will group together for the blanket of security a shared ethnic community gives in a hostile or hierarchical schooling context (1998: 114). Discourses regarding family structure, unity and cohesion are often evoked that are not necessarily about ethnic chauvinism but seen by both ethnic and Anglo-Australian boys as an obvious result of the familial/communal networks these boys come from outside the school: 'They probably know each other, all cousins' (Darren, 16 years). Michael explains why he thinks certain boys from specific shared cultural backgrounds may wish to stay together. He does not perceive this segregation as a problematic indicator of exclusionary and hierarchical practices from the dominant Anglo boys but rather as positive and supportive in-group responses to the 'unquestioned and unquestionable' (Schutz 1944) cultural hierarchy in the school:

> They [Indians and Asians] just stick to their own little groups. I think because maybe they can talk the same language that they feel they're more comfortable with people from their own country. We don't mind at all, we just stick to our groups.
>
> (Michael, 13 years)

However, research shows that these ethnic groupings may also encourage a descent into 'ethnic chauvinism' that often parallels Anglo-chauvinism (Patterson 1983: 42). As we have seen in regard to body fashioning and gendered performativity, ethnic boys may accept prevailing notions of cultural essentialism and turn that into forms of resistance and hierarchical inversion (Sewell 1998; Poynting et al. 1998, 1999). Thus, external prescriptions of labels such as 'tough wogs' become internalized, self-ascribed and utilized against the external definer. Glenn considers himself an Australian with a Mum who is Maltese, and thus he talks about ethnic gangs and rivalries from his self-ascribed insider-outsider positioning. He points out how some ethnic boys may feel coerced or threatened to belong to those gangs by the virtue of a shared ethnicity even if they do not wish to:

> We get a big clash of the Lebanese people, the Asians, the Greeks and Italians and they all walk in gangs. They'll stick up for their own cousins and friends and know a whole lot of people outside the school so if you say something to one person, you go outside the school they'll all be after you. Like a wog can't turn around and say, 'No, I'm not going with the wogs', that's their background and they feel like they have got to go with them. You've got some people who don't really care, like Donato who's Italian but he won't go and join in the wog gang. But he does single out some of them as friends.
>
> (Glenn, 16 years)

Marc attributes the growing segregations in his school to the increasing number of 'wogs'. Yet he can give reasons for why these students may 'cut themselves from other people'. These reasons are about not having the popularity or status accorded the 'sportos', even though they may wear designer clothing of an oppositional sport and as a symbol of their socio-economic superiority. Status is thus gained quantitatively by the numbers in a gang as they are not able to gain status by quality. Likewise, having a huge group is seen as preventing harassment from other boys:

> They're not accepted for what their image is by other people, especially the sportos. The wogs have made themselves in a huge group . . . they all dress the same with their soccer tops and their Adidas clothes and their greasy hair. They do it purposely. They could look Aussie if they wanted to

> but they want to look like wogs because it makes them feel tougher, because they've got a big group of friends and they stick together like brothers. They don't cause fights or start fights, they just hang around in their groups because they know they can be accepted in that group no matter who they are, as long as they're a wog. [But] if there was a big argument and a fight broke out between the wogs and the sportos and the musos, the sportos and musos would get together because they're Australian.
>
> (Marc, 18 years)

Marc highlights the workings of oppositional competing masculinities in his labelling of two types of masculine toughness apparent at his school:

> They're tough but not like Aussie tough, they're like wog tough and that's not right. You ask any guy at school between Aussie tough and wog tough and they'll know even though I can't explain. Because of the way they dress and the way they act, the wogs, it's different to the way the Aussies act.
>
> (Marc, 18 years)

Marc's perspectives about the way 'wog boys' deliberately fashion themselves as a means by which to assert their 'toughness', signals an attempt to position themselves as powerful within the pecking order of masculinities at school. They are conscious of mounting a direct challenge to the power base secured by the Australian 'sporto' boys. In many cases boys adopt a political or nationalist position to explain their rejection of school and resistance to teachers and students of particular cultural backgrounds. In relation to why soccer became the site for macho-ethno-nationalism, Hughson discusses how his young Croatian interviewees 'expressed the clear belief that they had experienced a form of discrimination during school years that resulted in their exclusion from Australian sports such as rugby league and cricket . . . related to an ethnocentric "sporting culture" within schools' (1997: 171). The more they felt ostracized from the dominant sporting culture, the more inclined they were to band together with other Croatians and 'wogs' to play soccer. Poynting et al. (1998, 1999) explored Connell's notion of 'protest masculinity' (Connell 1995: 109–19) among groups of Lebanese young men subordinated by class relations and by racism. They identified the call among these young men of 'wogs rule' as a hierarchical inversion of the wider Australian reality of Anglo domination. The carving out of some sort of power and territory in the school was a claiming of space in a zone of contestation framed by the wider power of an Anglo Centre. Inferiorization of masculinity via class and ethnicity can lead to attempts at establishing superiority and accentuation of a heteronormative masculinity via the deployment and performance of aggression, sexism and homophobia.

'From strong values and strong traditions'

Ethno-nationalist masculine identities

Many boys from migrant and refugee backgrounds in our research displayed and strategically utilized what Skrbis (1999) calls 'long-distance nationalism': the construction and sustenance of ethno-nationalist hegemonic narratives, a strong awareness of the impact of contemporary nationalist conflicts on migrant groups living in Australia, and the interactions between diasporas and homelands (see Said 1990; Safran 1991; Hesse 2000). Questions need to be asked in relation to boys from diasporic backgrounds in schools:

- To what extent do the cultural and other dichotomies between country of origin and host country explain particular macho-ethno-nationalist attitudes, behaviours, concerns of these boys?
- What are the connections between boys' perceptions of discrimination, actual oppression, and diaspora sentiments within a host society?
- What are the connections of the boys' ethno-nationalism to class, gender, urbanization, industrialization, education, familial and generational factors?
- How and to what extent should a school encourage/discourage cultural, political and organizational expressions in its diasporic students?

Chris, for example, considered having an 'ethnic' background to be advantageous over who he defined as 'normal' or 'typical' people. We see here the power of normalizing practices in the way that Anglo-Australians are still positioned as 'the normal people' and yet resistance to these practices is established by boys from ethnic backgrounds asserting themselves as being culturally superior:

> I'm Greek, both of my parents were born in Greece. I was born in Australia. I know Greek, it's just something over the top of the normal people. The Australian people just know English. I think in the long run it will probably help me get a job. I'm pretty proud of my [Greek Orthodox] religion, I'm not scared to hide it. The typical Australian people, they don't have the same values as an ethnic. They go out every night, they muck around a lot, they use Australian slang. I just don't like those words. They're allowed to do a lot more things than what I am. I'm not really

> allowed to stay out late, or drink alcohol. With an ethnic person, especially with my parents they would expect me to do good at school or to be good at sport and good at something else. There would be more expectations maybe on an ethnic person than an Australian person who only has to do good in one thing.
>
> (Chris, 16 years)

When the conversation turns to other ethnic students, Chris situates his derision of the performance of 'ethnic toughness' of 'other' ethnic groups alongside his pride in ethnic affluent practices and the way some Anglo-Australians aspire to be like them:

> The Lebanese, they think they rule the school. They act like they're superior to everyone else. When we play soccer they kick our ball over the fence, they try to pick fights. A lot of us just turn around and pay them out. The ethnic people they try to be really cool to females. [We do it] by dressing up and getting parents to buy hotted up cars. I know a few of them [Australian guys] have tried to be like an ethnic, they try to get a hotted up car which they pretty much can't. It might be the money or if they do have the money they ended up getting the lower range of something, whereas an ethnic would probably get the higher range. For ethnics, it's pushed upon us that everything has to be a good standard. We've got a lot more money, we flash around the money, we'll be wearing gold chains . . . because I think we want to show that we've got cash, and think we're tough because we've got cash.
>
> (Chris, 16 years)

Thus Chris highlights how class becomes another important marker for some ethnic people to acquire a particular differentiated and valued status. Daniel, however, was aware of how the links between rigid masculinity and the maintenance of strong cultural values were much more intensified. He is also able to interrogate his own idealization of a German heritage:

> I felt that those particularly of Yugoslav backgrounds were quite rigid, a lot more rigid than the Australian boys. Definitely they would come across thinking of themselves as powerful and confident, and they had really come from strong values and strong traditions. I believe that made them very confident in their actions. They would be so strong in their convictions and even more macho if their beliefs were challenged. I wanted to be fully German and to have that cultural thing. I felt strong and proud and I looked at things like the German athletes and always thought, 'Well, gee, these are really strong people, they're smart and strong and

> confident and good looking.' These were always attributes that I wanted for myself.
>
> (Daniel, 23 years)

Boys often equated their cultural background with hegemonic masculine traits: 'I see myself as Turkish. It's bravery, like when I think of Turks it's about when the war was won' (Mustafa, 15 years). Other boys also were able to reflect upon their homeland histories and links to their self-ascriptive essentialist ethno-nationalist identities in Australia (Nagel 1994): 'I've been a Turk for 16 years and I don't want to change that, I don't want to be Australian. It's like the blood that runs inside me is Turkish, I'm Turkish, that's it' (Bora, 16 years).

These responses highlight how many boys embraced 'a respect for the culture and ethnic tradition to which they feel an allegiance, an ethnic solidarity' (Poynting et al. 1998: 87; Hughson 1997). Ethnic nationality for many boys in our study appeared to be grounded in essentializing discourses which were then interwoven with essentialist understandings of masculinity, and used to establish some degree of power and superiority in a school.

'I know all about my family past'

Embracing and exploring a familial/cultural heritage

Many ethnic boys talked about the familial values and cultural beliefs they had inherited as supporting and indeed determining their understandings of themselves as 'Australian ethnic boys': 'My gran teach me how to behave in class, your attitude, you have to be good. If you not concentrate on your work, like your attitude, you won't be concentrating to achieve your goal' (Huen, 16 years). Thus, it is because of his particular history and cultural/familial background that Huen learns to fashion his masculinity according to norms organized around the valuing of hard work and achievement. He is driven to study hard because he sees school as a gateway to a better life than the one he could have had in Vietnam: 'When you in Vietnam you see people around you really poor.' However, according to Huen, for many Vietnamese boys, particularly those who are born and who grow up in Australia, they become subjected to toxic cultural influences which he identifies in the Anglo-Australian boys' anti-school and anti-social behaviour.

In the following, Chris identified aspects of his cultural heritage that he was proud of. Indeed, his masculinity is linked to this cultural pride. However, he also reveals a cultural insularity in regard to knowledge of other cultural heritages, implying his inferiorization of other boys' masculinities:

> Some of the heritage that we have in Greece, like the oldest buildings. We invented a lot of things as well like sports and religion. In a way you feel

> more superior because you've come from a background that has done more things. To be Greek and male to me is someone that would be proud of themselves and they would stick up for themselves if anyone paid them out.
>
> (Chris, 16 years)

Here is another student, Mario, 16 years, who appreciates his cultural and linguistic heritage. He volunteers to do community service at a local aged care facility for ageing Italians and speaks very positively of this experience, particularly in listening to the elderly Italian men talking about their lives: 'Some of them were talking about the war, how they lived and everything, they were like the bread winner, they talk about how they had to survive on their own and they're the strong sort of Italian character.' This experience also presents Mario with opportunities to reflect upon shifting constructs of Italian masculinity:

> I think that I am probably different, you know how the Italians are kind of rough and I wouldn't classify myself as that . . . probably a gentler sort of person. [Being] Italian it's sort of like something inside, like your character. I suppose the culture, Italian background, your beliefs, what you eat. Like your family, you have your nonna and nonno and it makes your Italian beliefs. I hear a lot of stories like when they came to Australia they had to struggle . . . my nonno went and got a job working for the council laying bitumen on the roads. They just talk about that, and you get the realization of how they came here.
>
> (Mario, 16 years)

Peco's sense of pride in his cultural identity is conveyed when he talks about his self-ascription as Macedonian, despite the fact that his family history and cultural heritage is rarely discussed at home. Constructs of 'real Australian' and 'full blood Macedonian' point to essentialist and binarily constructed categories of ethnic identification, as well as a set of values and attitudes that are claimed as 'Macedonian'. His reclamation of cultural identity may also be a protest against and an honouring of the 'hard time' his parents experienced. For instance, he identifies 'working hard' as a particular value or ideal associated with his cultural heritage, despite the fact that he does not have specific knowledge about his cultural background because it is not spoken about at home:

> I call myself Macedonian 'cos I'm full blood Macedonian. So just 'cos I was born in Australia doesn't mean I'm a real Australian. I don't know much [about Macedonian culture], we don't talk about it much at home because it was a hard time when they first came out, getting hassled.
>
> (Peco, 14 years)

Many boys could also link a cultural and religious heritage with understandings and expectations of gendered relations, as Muslim student, Haseeb, does in relation to attending school with girls. The gendered relationships that he had taken for granted as 'normal' in Pakistan are now re-evaluated as 'strange' in an Australian setting:

> In Pakistan, the girls and boys are separated and also they usually don't talk if they are together. I know it's very strange. In the countryside, if you talk to someone's daughter, they get offended. When I came here and I saw the girls going out when they're 16 or 17 I was always thinking, 'How different!' 'How do they feel?' These things were a mystery about women but now I'm beginning to understand. The situation came when we got a project, girls and boys together. I was not very good because I was unnecessarily too much shy and I didn't say anything or I typed my report very quietly. I think I treated them [girls] very badly. If they sit with me many times, come in and talk to me I couldn't answer them properly and I don't know whether they understood it or not.
>
> (Haseeb, 22 years)

Thus, many boys point to the need for schools to situate gendered behaviours, harassment and learning practices within specific ethnic, nationalist and religious contexts.

'Going through a western phase'

The interweavings of ethnicity, masculinity and sexuality and the way these relations are deployed in Western schools has also received minimal attention (Pallotta-Chiarolli 1995a, 1999b, 1999c, 1999d, 2000). Overall, these diverse and intricate permutations involve the negotiation of identities and codes of belonging to at least three socio-cultural groups: the ethnic family and community; the gay community; and the wider Australian society. For example, ethnic same-sex attracted boys may experience regulation, exclusion and omission in ethnic families, in the wider society, in various communities to which they belong such as the gay community, and in various environments as in the school. They may also experience acceptance, mediation and active support in these communities (Ratti 1993; Pallotta-Chiarolli and Skrbis 1994; Pallotta-Chiarolli 1998b).

Two other major factors are also interwoven with the above identity formation and community location negotiations: the specific socio-cultural constructions of masculinity within each social group; and the value systems and structural boundaries operating within schools. Constructions of masculinity, and their interconnectedness with sexual behaviour, identity and expression, vary according to socio-cultural, historical and other factors (Williams 1997; Cheng 1999). Being sexually marginal to an ethnic community that may itself be marginal and misunderstood in the wider Australian society is problematic for young gay and bisexual-identifying boys in constructing feelings of divided loyalties and betrayal. Change is equated with assimilating to the host culture's norms and losing one's own cultural self, of losing the remnants of the 'home' that was left behind in the migration or refugee process. Machismo, chauvinism, misogyny and homophobia may form the basis of male identity based on the desire to publicly present the qualities of strength, pride, virility and honour (Hughson 1997). Therefore, our research posits that ethnic same-sex attracted boys may be constructed as symbolic of ethnic and indeed nationalist weakness, shame, effeminacy, lack of patriotism and lack of heterosexual virility. It also supports evidence of the common ethnic contention that homosexuality or its manifestation as a gay identity is a Westernized corruption or Australian influence (Pallotta-Chiarolli 1998b). We posit that a shared cross-cultural homophobia constructs some form of alliance or indeed superior positioning of ethnic heterosexual boys with the boys from the dominant Anglo group. Homophobia prevents being further positioned even lower on the social hierarchy as not-male next to possibly existing negations such as not-Anglo, not-English speaking, not-middle class.

The constraints of oppositionally constructed categories of ethnicity and gay masculinity are evident in the way that Luc makes a 'choice' between identities, and indeed a hierarchical one, where the identification is not only between labels but assigns one of the identity categories as less significant: 'I'd rather them label me as Luc, the Italian guy, not Luc the gay guy. I think the homosexuality side of it is only really a minor thing' (Luc, 18 years). The links between nationalism or patriotism and heterosexual masculinity are also evident in Luc's father's response to his 'coming out', and is similar to the common notion of homosexuality as a product of a Western or Anglo decadent culture migrants have come into. The 'homeland' then becomes a symbol not only of cultural security and the known but also of appropriate gendered and heteronormative sexual relations: 'It was the first time I'd ever seen my dad cry. He said, "I'll send you to Italy, maybe you'll meet a nice girl." My dad is an accepting man, he's got gay friends. But it was just weird . . . like go to Italy and you might change' (Luc, 18 years).

Rob spoke of feelings of exclusion from his Italian cultural group due to his sexuality:

> I get depressed at weddings because I feel like I'm not going to be able to get married. And just the whole thing of getting married and having kids, my parents would think that it's a beautiful special thing, but they'd think it is gross because it's two guys.
>
> (Rob, 16 years)

Another gay-identifying borderland student was Eric, who is Hong Kong Chinese. He arrived in Australia at the beginning of Year 11 and became an Australian citizen. The geographical shifts from Hong Kong to Australia provided Eric with interesting insights into different schooling systems and knowledges of homosexuality (Pallotta-Chiarolli et al. 1999). He recalls the silences he experienced as a child in Hong Kong and concludes that coming to an Australian school created major shifts in 'coming out' as this was a prevalent discourse of the gay communities here in Australia: 'I'm not sure whether I would have the courage to come out [in Hong Kong] like what I did [in the Australian school]. I remember when I was a kid I didn't even know what homosexuality is' (Eric, 23 years).

However, although Eric was able to utilize the wider Australian societal recognitions and understandings of sexuality to locate himself as gay within a secondary school setting, the same Australian societal/racist presumptions about his ethnicity created confusion for him. This was eventually resolved by a disclaiming of a specific ethnicity for a more cosmopolitan citizenship or adoption of an Anglocentric generic category of 'Asian', and a synthesizing of two supposedly disparate and oppositional cultural identities – Western and Chinese:

> I can proudly say I'm an Asian Australian. Now I speak more English and I haven't forgotten Chinese. So I think I'm a bit of a mixture, of this so-called Western culture and Chinese culture. I feel that I'm one of the persons who is in the borderline all the time.
>
> (Eric, 23 years)

The extent to which his gay identity led Eric to incorporate 'Western' into his cultural identity can be debated, as in the following he explains how homosexuality is considered to be a Western construction by Asian peoples:

> Asian people in my country think that homosexuality is something from Western culture. Other Asian students think, 'Oh no, it must be that western thing, you know, invaded you.' I overheard my mum tell my stepfather, 'Oh, I think Eric is gay, but going through a phase – Western influences.' At some stage this Chinese guy and I got on quite well [at school] but everyone started to say we were a couple and he got really pissed off with them and also with me. Whereas I didn't give a shit because it wasn't true. I was gay, he wasn't. He was saying that this was the end of our friendship because of that.
>
> (Eric, 23 years)

While an Australian school setting made it apparently easier for Eric to 'come out', he believed European and Anglo-Australian heteronormative masculinity had no place for him: 'They don't want to have anything to do with me. I don't really have any Anglo or even European straight male friends. As a matter of fact I don't make many male friends here.' Before arriving at a position of cultural interweaving rather than Anglo assimilation or Chinese ghettoization, Eric was aware of the journeys between polarities he had undertaken, and indeed the need to perform a dominant version of masculinity that would assist in his efforts to assimilate. Thus, again we see the interconnectedness of dominant cultural, heteronormative and gendered constructions framing the kinds of negotiations and strategies some recently arrived students may undertake in order to determine a location for themselves in an Australian school setting:

> When initially I came here I got this sense of not fitting in. Me and another Chinese guy, we had this cultural shock and we tried to fit in. I got this feeling that he did a much better job than I did because he was straight. With his other friends he could start learning about football, talking about girls. I decided maybe I should just stop thinking about fitting in the so-called mainstream society or the Anglo culture, and I joined a Hong Kong student association. I didn't go to their functions because they're a whole bunch of straights and talked about girls, and the girls seemed to have crushes on me. I felt a little bit devastated. 'Oh what happened to me, I don't fit in here, I don't fit in there, I'm not in the gay community, I'm not in the Chinese community, I'm just an isolated boring student who studies all the time.' I felt like I'm in the borderline.
>
> (Eric, 23 years)

Several heterosexual-identifying boys commented on the implications and concerns they had with acknowledging that other boys from their cultures may be gay. Some students spoke about their anger and discomfort if aspersions about having same-sex attracted people in their communities were made. If these comments were made by Anglo-Australian boys, they were considered to be a form of inferiorization of their masculinity. In the following, Chris attempts to own the reality of gay Greek men and yet utilizes geographical distancing and numerical evaluation to minimize the impact or reality of homosexuality within his Greek community:

> I got really angry when one of them [an Anglo male student] turned around and said that all Greeks are gay. OK, some of them are, especially in Melbourne, there might be a couple. But it's not true, not every Greek is gay. I think it's just one person, but it's changed the look for everyone. My uncle in Melbourne was telling me a story about a Greek gay guy there, and because of him the other Greeks in that street got paid out for

> it, their kids as well. It's like an Australian person thinks you're a lower standard to what he is.
>
> (Chris, 16 years)

Adam makes an interesting distinction between the way he reacts to being called gay and the way he reacts when being called wog:

> It didn't really bother me [being called a wog] because I said, 'I'm more intelligent than you because I can speak another language.' So they used to walk off and leave me alone. I was proud that I was a 'wog'. They called me 'fag' and that's really annoying to hear.
>
> (Adam, 13 years)

In the following, Haseeb talks about differing or absent notions of sexual identity according to culture and class. Interestingly, homophobia was learned when he arrived in Australia:

> I was brought up in a very different culture where such concepts do not exist. In fact, I wasn't aware of such things. But from friends [in Australia], they don't like it mostly. Also, I found my language teacher [at English language school for migrants] who was Australian also disliked this concept. She once said that the church should try to stop homosexuality.
>
> (Haseeb, 22 years)

Other heterosexual-identifying boys were supportive of sexual diversity and yet found their efforts to counteract homophobia were not necessarily supported by the school. The following is a thought-provoking example of how some boys will attempt to negotiate the limitations of language and definition that the school imposes in order to articulate broader far-reaching societal concerns. Because his school has no clear and specific articulation or policy naming homophobia, Glenn incorporates it under the umbrella of racism. In this way, he is also suggesting that the word 'culture' is not only applicable to those of specific ethnic or national backgrounds. He is also expressing his understanding of the multi-dimensionality of identity and the dilemmas with school policies and societal perspectives that dichotomize identity by positioning various aspects of the self as opposed or detached from each other:

> Racism [education] covers gays, lesbians and straight people. A black person might be straight and a black person may be gay. What's the difference? You might not like blacks, full stop. But then you might like blacks, and 'That black's all right because he's straight'. Then the other guy

> is gay, is that racism? You're discriminating against someone because of their image and their sexuality, like racism covers from sexuality through to what they look like and what colour they are.
>
> (Glenn, 16 years)

The boys we interviewed illustrate how socio-economic, religious, educational, migrational and other specificities interweave with culture, gender and sexuality and create a complex and intricate world within which the individual has to navigate a comfortable, or at least safe, course (Moraga and Anzaldua 1981; Walker 1988; hooks 1990). For students, the school and its official and unofficial panopticonic systems of regulations and belongings, is a major site requiring strategies of negotiation and manoeuvring within and between the categories of ethnicity, masculinity and sexuality.

Neither 'torn between two worlds' nor 'the best of both worlds'

Our research illustrates how ethnicity is both externally ascribed and self-prescribed, a product of actions undertaken by both the individual and their communities of significant others, in locations such as at school and the wider society. Ethnic identity is 'both optional and mandatory', as individual choices are circumscribed by the ethnic categories available at a particular time and place and have 'varying degrees of stigma or advantage attached to them' (Nagel 1994: 156). In some ethnic groups, the second and third generations have become the 'cultural brokers', utilizing their 'double cultural competences' to represent their communities in a variety of ways, for they are the ones who know how to negotiate Australian institutions such as schools (Patterson 1983: 220).

The cultural conflict either/or model has been traditionally used to metaphorically position second generation individuals or individuals living within and between a cultural Centre and a cultural Margin as 'torn between two worlds', the one 'ethnic' and the other Anglocentric (Child 1945 in 1970; see also Vasta 1975). Later sociological understandings have considered how operating in two or more cultural contexts can afford opportunities and choices of 'the best of both worlds' (both/and) (Tsolidis 1986; Gucciardo 1987; Pallotta-Chiarolli 1989, 1990a, 1992). More recently, there has been an acknowledgement and understanding of 'borderdwelling' or mestizaje, whereby a coherent set of multiple meanings can emerge from several rather than two diverging sources of cultural reality or 'lifeworlds' (Bottomley 1992; Cope and Kalantzis 1995; Pallotta-Chiarolli 1995a, 1999d). Australia's cultural diversity can no longer be defined according to binarily constructed models of 'two worlds' or 'home' and 'Australia', as there are many mestizaje individuals living in, moving away from and returning to Australia who are the products of years of cultural interweavings.

Several boys considered themselves to be multiple-within borderdwellers, negotiating two or more inherited cultural backgrounds that set them beyond the assimilation to one fixed community and its codes. Of mixed Italian father–English mother background, Christian drew direct links between being raised to negotiate two different cultural codes and his awareness of and acceptance of cultural, gendered and sexual diversity: 'I'm willing to participate in or have a look at different cultures and the way that they operate. Whether it be gay and lesbian, or whether it be Moroccan. I'm really interested in the way that other people live their lives' (Christian, 23 years).

When asked to describe how he dealt with the other boys' responses to sexual diversity, Christian was again able to connect his own culturally hybrid background and his interest and skills in negotiating cultural conflicts to the way he approached issues of sexual diversity and performed his masculinity:

> I think because of what I saw at home in the fact that there were two different cultures and they really clashed. I saw that if you fight, if you don't give someone their time to explain themselves, or to argue for what they live for, then it only causes arguments. I would rather see people get along harmoniously. Then they would give me the chance to explain things back.
>
> (Christian, 23 years)

Border boys talked about the harassment and isolation they experienced if they did not fit into the styles of masculinity and gendered behaviours of the cultural group they were biologically part of and yet did not exhibit any allegiance to. Kieran had left his old school due to racial fights that he did not want to be drawn into:

> I'm half Greek, but I don't mix well with the Greeks and Lebanese. I don't speak Greek and I wasn't brought up as a Greek. Some of them [students] actually said to me I was Greek because I was in a Greek class. My parents were both born in Australia. I think Irish is her [mother's] background.
>
> (Kieran, 16 years)

Andrew inhabited a borderland insider/outsider/no-sider space in relation to other boys from his own Italian cultural background. From this position, he was able to critically analyse what he called 'acting woggy', a performance based on an external 'image'. This was something he refused to do. He linked his refusal to the way his Australian-born parents were also not immersed in the traditional Italian culture. However, he does acknowledge the power and sense of superiority that comes from this performance, such as hierarchical inversion, whereby boys from dominant cultural groups are cowered and become targets of harassment due to the overt display of hegemonic masculinity:

> They try to act more woggy, just to live up to the image I think. I just don't see myself as one of them. I just don't see myself hanging around in a certain group. I just see myself as a neutral person. I think it comes from your family. My dad and my mum aren't like that, they're not involved in any groups. Their [other Italian boys] parents have got an attitude like 'I'm Italian and I'm better than you'. I know my heritage, where I've come from, even though I wasn't born there, but I'm proud that I've come from Italian and I'm learning Italian. I would call myself Australian because I wasn't born in Italy, so I wouldn't call myself an Italian.
>
> (Andrew, 16 years)

Haseeb's notions of nationalism, patriotism and cultural identity are also mestizaje or cosmopolitan: 'I don't believe in nationalism. I even don't believe I'm a Pakistani, nor I believe I'm Australian.' Ben also shows an awareness of intra-cultural heterogeneity:

> In the final analysis race is irrelevant to me. I prefer to take people on as individuals. When I have become friends with someone who is of Italian, Greek or Polish descent I learn interesting facts about their family traditions and culture. But I don't then go and generalize, expecting all Italians, or Greeks, or Polish to be that way.
>
> (Ben, 17 years)

Thus, many boys displayed multiple and fluid identities and group bordering rather than group belonging. They questioned singular fixed notions of ethnicity and nationalism and the performance of an ethnic masculinity:

> [Being an Australian] it's not anything in particular. It's about recognizing that different people come from different places, we're all different, I mean I really enjoy hanging around my Greek friends and talking like a wog, doing the whole sort of, 'Oh my God' [*changes tone of voice to sound more stereotypically Greek-Australian male*]. It's fun, and it's fun to hear about parents that are really possessive and won't let their 25-year-old son move out of home. We have a good laugh about it. But it's not the only thing for me.
>
> (Tony, 23 years)

'There are naughty Vietnamese boys and good Vietnamese boys'

Intra-ethnic hierarchies of masculinity

Many members of marginalized groups 'perform hegemonic masculinity in order to gain patriarchal privileges within their group, if not the larger society. Performing hegemonic masculinity by a marginalized person is seen as passing behaviour that distracts from her/his stigma' (Cheng 1999: 299; see also Chua and Fujino 1999). Many research participants offered insights into the kinds of intra-ethnic dualities and hierarchies constructed by ethnic boys in schools. Huen is a Vietnamese boy who has been in Australia for four years, having fled from Vietnam with his family in a small boat. Like many migrant and refugee boys, the family has a major influence in his life. It influences his attitude to his school and the way he fashions his masculinity which is differentiated from the masculinity enacted by the 'cool' naughty boys at school (see Willis 1977). He explains how difficult he found school at first because he could not speak English and how he was teased by 'naughty boys' of Anglo-Australian, European-Australian and Australian-born Vietnamese backgrounds. This last group of 'bad' Vietnamese boys utilize their linguistic and birthplace criteria to project themselves as superior to refugee boys like Huen, and in line with normalizing binary practices, they position themselves as resistant to their parents' culture:

> When they're growing up in here [Australia] they are really bad because the parents don't know English, and they can talk English because they learn it at school. So they can go out with their friends and they do really naughty things. But there are some Vietnamese boys that are good, like good boys, but they don't make friends much in this school. The good ones go on with the work and not talk too much. The naughty ones hang around with other boys, take drugs and smoke at lunchtime. So they have friends, but they're not good friends either. So it's like the old saying in my language, if you stay near the light you get brighter; if you go near the ink you get darker. If you go hang around with naughty people you become one of them.
>
> (Huen, 16 years)

This powerful discourse about the 'naughty boys' at school is very significant in terms of how Huen positions himself in relation to the latter. He reiterates that the 'naughty boys' engage in culturally specific Australian practices which have toxic effects, and, for this reason, he chooses not to associate with them. In fact, he has no desire to identify with them: 'I don't like friends that's naughty, swearing all the time, and talk rude, smoke, take drugs. They just making you bad every time, so I like to hang around with the quiet ones.' Huen also talks about another Vietnamese boy at the school who used to be his friend but now associates with the 'naughty boys':

> Because when they come here from Vietnam, it's like their parents don't teach them how to do properly because their parent doesn't know English. They don't know the Vietnamese language and their parents do. So it's two languages, can't communicate with each other. So they got out of hand. The parents have to work, because you have to really work here, you can't stay home. No one to stay home to teach them how to live properly.
>
> (Huen, 16 years)

Here Huen talks specifically about the impact of family, cultural values, and the ramifications of migration on family and employment practices, and how these in turn affect Vietnamese boys. He believes that those Vietnamese boys, who are born and grow up in Australia learning English, are more prone to the toxic influences of Australian culture. Moreover, these influences appear to be related to a particular macho masculinity organized around defying institutional authority and engaging in criminal activity. However, Huen highlights that the parents of these boys, due to their class location and thus having to work long hours, are not adequately available and present in their lives so that they can learn the 'right' sort of values:

> We still learn how to be good because we were born in Vietnam. So people there is really nice, they listen to their parent . . . teach them how to be good in school and to respect everyone as well. So mostly the one who born in Vietnam when they come here they're really good and really smart and learning really well in school. But those who born here, or born somewhere else rather than Vietnam, because they don't see around them the people who is nice, they see around them it's all naughty, so they become naughty. So they become like everyone else . . . they want to be the coolest.
>
> (Huen, 16 years)

Huen also identifies how the norms of 'compulsory heterosexuality' appear to be at the basis of how these 'naughty boys' learn to perform a 'cool' masculinity which involves 'showing off' to gain the girls' attention:

> They think I'll just have girlfriend and having sex early is good because everyone else has done it. Most of the Vietnamese boys doesn't want to be like that, but they kind of got into it because there's like a

> group thing. They think they can be tough. They want to be like normal people because around them is people like that, so they want to be normal.
>
> (Huen, 16 years)

His comment that these boys 'want to be like normal people' highlights how the 'naughty boys' social practices of heterosexual masculinity are tied to establishing intra-ethnic hierarchies which in turn may be explained in terms of creating a particular power base to assert their superiority over conformist Vietnamese boys. Huen, however, is also positioned within normalizing regimes of practice in which 'compulsory heterosexuality' operates in the way that he defines his masculinity. When asked about homophobia at school he mentions at first that boys just call other boys names like 'faggot', as a 'put down', without really making any direct reference to that person's sexuality, and then explains: 'I don't really care because I'm not one anyway. It doesn't worry me, as long as they stay away from me. I don't like them anyway.' Here, Huen clearly demarcates his masculinity by declaring that he is definitely not gay. He does not want to be marked as the deviant 'other' through any association or identification with gay sexuality. In this sense another form of intra-ethnic hierarchy is also established in the way that Huen positions himself on the social ladder of the pecking order of masculinities.

Luc identified as gay and talked at length about how both ethnicity and sexuality impacted on his experiences of schooling. At first he tends to speak of these two influences as almost operating independently in terms of how he positions himself as a particular kind of boy. For example, he emphasizes the importance of family values and ethnic background in identifying as a 'wog': 'I come from a very Italian family and I like to identify with my family . . . I have very strong family values, I think most families do but especially Mediterranean families.' Here Luc acknowledges his allegiance to a particular ethnic identity, one which is implicated in the mobilization of certain discourses about family values defined as distinctively Mediterranean. This particular ethnic positioning is strengthened through his experience in the Australian schooling system at the age of nine when he first arrived. Because he did not understand the language, he immediately experienced himself as different in that he 'didn't fit in'. Identifying as 'wog' for Luc, therefore, may be read as functioning as a form of resistance to the wider Australian reality of Anglo-domination:

> It [Australian schooling system] was very different from the Italian schooling system. I didn't understand the language. I had a bit of a tough time, I always found that I didn't fit in with the main group of people. So I was always like on the fringe, like the less popular people.

> I remember trying to play football when I first came to Australia and trying to fit in with the boys' crowd and it didn't work. So I think I used to hang around with the girls a lot. I just found I related to them a bit more because I liked doing the quieter things like standing around chatting rather than getting myself drenched in mud from head to toe.
>
> (Luc, 18 years)

Luc's sense of difference is accentuated through his refusal to actively position himself within the normalizing regimes of masculinity through which the status of a proper boy is conferred. He was aware of being a very different kind of boy due to his refusal to do masculinity with other boys in culturally acceptable ways at school (see Martino 1999, 2000a). Discourses of gender here intersect with those of ethnicity in how he comes to differentiate himself from other boys at school. He rejects the dominant Australian sporting practices of football, of rough and dirty play – through which a particular hegemonic Australian heterosexual masculinity is inscribed – and opts for the 'quieter things'. Thus, while embracing his ethnicity he rejects other norms governing the performance of hegemonic heterosexual masculinities (Frank 1987; Walker 1988; Mac an Ghaill 1994a, 1994b; Redman 1996; Epstein 1997).

The intersection of ethnicity and masculinity is made explicit when Luc proceeded to talk about how his Australian-born Italian friends also rejected him when he started associating with girls instead of playing football. It is the rejection and denigration of the feminine within a particular gender system (Connell 1994) which appears to be operating here in terms of how Luc becomes positioned. Masculinity is defined in relation to femininity, cutting across ethnic affiliations and boundaries. The interplay of various masculinities, in terms of their intersection with class, race, ethnicity and sexuality, appeared to be governed by norms for fashioning and regulating an ascendant form of hegemonic heterosexual masculinity that is grounded in a misogynist and homophobic denigration of the feminine (Epstein 1998; Jackson 1998). For example, Luc talks about how other Italian boys felt threatened. They were unable to reconcile a particular form of ethnic masculinity with stereotypical constructs of gay males. This highlights the intra-ethnic hierarchies of masculinities:

> I was abused by this one group of very, very woggy boys, Greeks and Italian students. They'd have their hair slicked back and they'd be wearing their jewellery and their chains. I was harassed by them. I kind of belong to their community as well in that I am Italian . . . even though I was the only one that was actually born in Italy, actually lived in Italy, actually

> really properly Italian. But I wasn't Italian because no Italian male was gay. I remember one student saying to me, 'You're either not Italian or you're not a faggot.'
>
> (Luc, 18 years)

Thus, Luc highlights that a gay ethnic boy may be constructed by heterosexual ethnic boys as disrupting unity and homogeneity in the group, based on a particular version of hegemonic masculinity. This is achieved by introducing a socially defined inferior masculinity and 'deviant' sexuality that plays into the hands of the powerful group of boys who are already positioning the ethnic boys as marginal, deviant, inferior. Hence, differences in sexualities cannot be afforded when differences in ethnicity already mean that the group has been stigmatized.

'There was a lot of racism'

Multicultural and multidirectional power relations at school

Inter-ethnic relations are implicated in a wider set of hierarchical social practices involving 'race-specific elements' and particular sex/gender regimes (Mac an Ghaill 1994a, 1994b). Our research shows that both overt and covert forms of racism are rife in schools, not only between the binarily constructed Anglo/non-Anglo duality, but also within and between ethnic groups based on a hierarchical factionalism whereby certain ethnicities are deemed more inferior than others. Hence, again we see the need to situate racism and other specific forms of harassment within the broader structural and social contexts of the school which is a location of multiple and competing groups and identities for superiority. For example, some boys identified cultural hierarchies and responding harassment within the category of 'Anglo': 'I'm Scottish myself and I'm supposed to hate English people' (Paul, 16 years).

Luc draws attention to the pecking order of ethnicities at the single-sex Catholic boys' school where the Asian boys were at the bottom of the social ladder:

> There's a kind of notion that if you're a wog, you're cool. People from Asian backgrounds, they got very much picked on. There was one particular boy. He was very, very Asian and people would walk past him and slit back their eyes, because he has very, very narrow kind of eyes. Teachers just treated it as a big joke. I remember the public-speaking competition in Year 11. One boy who came from Cambodia spoke about the racism in school and he actually won, because he genuinely cried during his speech. You could actually feel his emotions and the way he'd

> been beaten up so badly one time by a bunch of Australian boys. They [Asian students] hung around together, you got no choice but to annex yourself off because you have to be in that comfort zone . . . but there's people walking past making fun of their languages.
>
> (Luc, 18 years)

Eric also presents how the impact of stereotypes and cultural dichotomies, promulgated in the wider society, can frame racist competing masculinities at school:

> They're saying how Asian students seem to get all the top HSC marks . . . it's just bad journalism. Why can't they see these are Australians as well, these are Asian-Australian. They are born here or immigrant here but they are accepted to be citizens here. Students in my high school think that I was such a smart arse. People who never talked to me in class all of a sudden would be interested in talking to me just once because they want to know what mark I got. I feel sad you know, almost as if they turn me into this sort of competition object because I'm from an Asian country. But I don't think I'm smarter than they are, I just try harder. I had to spend like double, triple hours of their reading time because it wasn't my first language.
>
> (Eric, 22 years)

Racism could also be used to subvert and reverse the dominant socio-cultural order in society, the oppressed using the tactics and forms of power of the oppressor (Memmi 1965; Freire 1972). Some research participants, like Anglo-Australian student Stephen, talked about the multiple directions and manifestations of racism, indicating that it is not linear and only a binarily constructed white-to-black situation, but cuts across various interlocked trajectories between cultural groups. He also highlights how anti-racism policies, pedagogy and pastoral care may be missing the diverse manifestations of racism within a school. Nevertheless, while acknowledging the diverse forms of racism, he could understand some of the reasons for these ethnic boys being racist. He stresses that it is not a culturally essentialist factor to be racist, but something that emanates from the wider society's expectations and inferiorization of a culture, and connected to the way some ethnic masculinities are performed:

> White people were seriously in the minority and we got picked on and called skips. I didn't care. I'm not going to be ashamed of the colour of my skin. But a lot of racism on one side goes on so I suppose you've got to expect some on both sides. Pretty much everyone would try and pick fights. 'My race is better and I'm here to prove it.' I don't think it affects white people as much, I think there's a lot of expectations of

> people of other races. A lot of Greek guys they're expected to be really strong and not too bright and in some cases it's true and in a lot of cases it's not.
>
> (Stephen, 16 years)

In the following, Jason reveals the unsettling contradictions and hierarchical inversions that become apparent when racism and national identity are defined and responded to as fixed and singular notions, and interwoven with aggressive masculinist performativity:

> The school I was at was a very anti-Australian school. There was 50 per cent Asian, 35 per cent Lebanese, 5 per cent Australian. I turned into a really big racist because I was hassled for being Australian. I was thinking at the time, 'Hey, I'm in Australia, why should I be hassled by other races.' So I went through my whole stage of Hitler was a god and I wanted to join the Ku-Klux-Klan . . . I think they knew at the back of their mind that they weren't superior and I think that's why they lashed out. They tend to have a strong love for it [their culture], as everyone does for their nation, I can respect that. I hung out with all the Australian boys but if the Australian boys had banded together we could have formed a gang and they would have left us alone, but that wasn't the case. I mean you get all that Asian stuff, pulling out their flick knives, I'd have more respect for them if they want to fight fist to fist. I did have a punch-up with an Australian because we were both angry and after we kicked the living shit out of each other, we shook hands and I thought that was very Australian.
>
> (Jason, 17 years)

Here Jason asserts a pride in his own Australian masculinity constructed as superior and honourable, which he demonstrates in a 'fist to fist' fight with another Australian boy, and which he differentiates from the kinds of fights involving Asian boys that he implies are more cowardly or less of a manifestation of 'appropriate' masculinity. This is substantiated by further comments he makes about the leaders of ethnic gangs:

> Gutless, very, very gutless, and once you knock the leader, you knock the whole heap of them. Australians will fight with their fists and they look after their mates. The Lebanese and Asians will bring their knives, if they don't have them they can't defend themselves.
>
> (Jason, 17 years)

However, he is able to reflect on his own racist behaviour and attitudes, positioning them within the broader political and national frameworks. This reflection is partly due to having participated in this interview:

> Actually, after this interview I'll probably realize that I'm still more racist than ever. Yes, I think that everyone is a product of their environment and I've been in an environment where I've been hassled for being an Australian. So, yes, I am going to be a racist. You have to consider that Australia is a very young country and any country needs migrants to build it up, etc., etc. Because it's such a young country we're still learning to mix in and that's why everyone's sticking to their own culture. I'd say it's because we're starting off on a new generation.
>
> (Jason, 17 years)

Lance also speaks about the racial tensions between the boys from Aboriginal background such as himself and the Asians. He explains that he is not targeted as much for racial harassment as other Aboriginal boys because of the lightness of his skin. The lightness/darkness of skin becomes a major signifier of the degree of racial harassment an Aboriginal boy may receive from other lighter skinned boys, whether they be Anglo or ethnic or Aboriginal (Francis 1995):

> I know of one time where a kid got mobbed and stabbed over in the lunch area. He got mobbed by about five Asians. It has been mainly the Asians that have started stuff. It's not all of them, like I'm a friend with a few Asians. I don't get it that much because I'm not that dark a skin, but my friend does.
>
> (Lance, 15 years)

Max, 16 years, was also aware of what he calls the 'double standard' at work in victims of racism being racist themselves. This once again highlights the power dynamic involved in terms of the impact and effects of inferiorization on the basis of one's ethnicity or race. Performing a 'cool' ethnic masculinity involves styling the body in aggressive and fashionable ways, having pride in one's country and picking on others while not tolerating anything negative being said about one's own culture. These technologies are used to reverse and subvert the dominant hierarchy:

> A lot of them [Italians] are racist. It's really kind of stupid, like they'll go off if anyone says 'wog', but they'll turn around and say hundreds of Aboriginal jokes, and so it's a double standard. Also a lot of Italian and Lebanese people are really strong and have a pride in their country, so it's really cool to be real proud about who you are. We have Japanese overseas students every year, they just treat them terribly, really shocking. Just because they're different and easy targets because they can't speak English, so it's just really easy to pay them out. I said a joke once that was pretty pathetic, it was an Italian joke and for the next three days I was

> getting threatened by all these Italian people. I had these big Italians coming up and they just wanted to kill me. Yes, it's pretty scary sometimes, like they get all their cousins.
>
> (Max, 16 years)

In the following, Matthew believes the constant references to having sex by some of the ethnic boys may be biologically determined, and thus an innate element of their culture. However, he is aware of the performative nature of their other hegemonic masculinist behaviours that become conflated with the way the boys do their ethnicities. They use elements of their ethnicity such as language and body fashioning, perceived by Matthew as Other to the Anglo 'everyday type' of boy, to assert a superiority and the power of in-group exclusive understandings and membership:

> especially the Italians, Croatians, they might have a higher sex drive than the more western people. You can hear the conversations, it always centres around how many women they've been with, or what their latest girlfriend is like in bed. And when they're in a group they're all the same. They're all very heavy into swearing and smoking, and in class they're talking back to the teachers, and basically showing off to each other. But when they're on their own, most of them aren't like that. They're more everyday type. If they want to say something about someone, they'll speak in their own tongue. They'll have a word for a certain staff member, and then they'll all just laugh and joke about that person behind their back and in front of them. It's kind of like I suppose a thrill or something, like they're bagging the crap out of a particular person right in front of them, as they're speaking to them.
>
> (Matthew, 16 years)

It is interesting how Matthew is able to interrogate ethnic boys' strategies of asserting superiority as a form of resistance, while resorting to deploying, in an unreflective way, the taken for granted discourse of the 'everyday type' of boy. There is an assumption that the white Anglo-Australian masculinity is the 'normal', 'everyday type' to which all other boys either react or assimilate.

Students who experienced feeling culturally isolated in predominantly monocultural rural schools spoke about the need for cultural support in small towns which lacked exposure to cultural diversity. Having experienced racist harassment and bullying in several rural schools, Adam was relieved to be back in a city school. He discusses how moving into a rural town from the city was a reason for being targeted as a cultural outsider. The few boys from Italian background who had grown up in the town and were thus insider-outsiders, such as in possibly speaking in the same 'slang' and not 'proper' like Adam, did not receive the same harassment. Nevertheless, despite interrogating the presence of harassment based on difference, Adam is still positioning himself within a hierarchy whereby a 'normal' boy is an Australian boy:

> [In rural schools] they were all Australians. Definitely you can tell they're from the country. They thought they were really good and strong and tough. They used to call me 'wog'. I remember the first day of school we'd sit in a circle and we'd tell each other our names, and if we've got a language. That's how they found out [I was Italian]. Because I had never lived in the country before I always used to get 'City slicker' because of how they always used to speak with slang words and I spoke proper. They used to always go 'You are a city slicker, you don't speak properly'. [Other Italian boys at the school] did not get picked on because they had lived there all their life. [In the first city school] there was Greeks and Italians and Vietnamese and Chinese gangs. We sometimes used to stand up for each other, against the Australians, because the Australians all thought they were good because this is their homeland. [At the current school] because I'm Italian and I've got some very close Australian friends, they don't say or do anything, they just muck around like I'm a normal guy, just a normal Australian.
>
> (Adam, 13 years)

This is an example of how ethnic boys do not appear to be able to extricate themselves from the production and reinforcement of a discursive framework which sets the white, Anglo-Australian male as the benchmark against which they must evaluate and validate their masculinities. Daniel divides the 'wogs' into 'cool' and 'uncool', thus highlighting how the dominant Anglo culture differentiates and hierarchically sorts boys within their own ethnic groups into particular categories, dependent upon their insider 'allies' status with the Anglo-Australian boys:

> There was what you would call the cool wogs and the uncool wogs. The cool wogs had come through primary school with a lot of Australian kids. If you went to primary school together they were like your allies in high school and they would recruit others.
>
> (Daniel, 23 years)

Tony, disabled and from Greek background, also spoke of experiences of racism in the 'special school' he attended, another example of the hierarchies within minority groups of boys. He makes an insightful comment about individuals from one marginal group not always being able or willing to support or empathize with someone else from another marginal group, and acknowledges his complicity within this hierarchy of marginalities:

> You know how they say if you're in a minority group, you'll support other minority groups? I don't believe that. I think you need a lot of self-confidence to be able to befriend someone else from another minority group. I was marginalized enough on my own, why would I want to start associating with Asians or other marginalized groups?
>
> (Tony, 23 years)

Conclusion

In this chapter we have examined the complexities and intersections of masculinity, sexuality, class, geographical location and ethnicity in boys' lives from culturally diverse backgrounds in the Australian context. Given that there is relatively little research which explores the perspectives of culturally diverse students in Australian schools, we have attempted to include the voices of boys from diverse cultural backgrounds and to demonstrate the limitations of essentializing, homogenizing and normalizing boys on the basis of their ethnicity. One of the major emphases in this chapter has been on the intra-group hierarchical social relations and practices of masculinity for culturally diverse boys. This often entailed examining the factionalism and inter-ethnic competitiveness of many ethnic boys in their attempts to assimilate to dominant norms of masculinity. We found that hegemonic heterosexual masculinity (Frank, 1987) played a major role in driving this factionalism and those exclusionary practices adopted by many ethnic boys in their attempts to claim a position of power over other ethnic boys considered to be less 'cool' or less masculine and, hence, inferior. Such hierarchies of masculinity warrant further interrogation in schools, particularly within the context of anti-racist and anti-homophobic education that needs to address the multidirectional forms of racism in culturally diverse schools.

7 'One of the main problems at school would be racism'[1]

Indigenous boys, masculinities and schooling

I was afraid at first and acutely aware of my own whiteness and its history. How would I be received and perceived? Would the boys be willing to speak with me? These are fears that white researchers in my position must have, but which rarely seem to be acknowledged as impacting significantly on the ways we conduct research and come to understand ourselves as particular kinds of researchers producing knowledge. I realized that I would be meeting the boys on the borders where I would negotiate and name my whiteness as privilege in ways I had never before imagined or understood.

I explained to the boys I was interviewing that being white and, given my white history, meant that I was limited in terms of my understandings of Indigenous cultures. I wanted them to feel comfortable about challenging me and my assumptions and at the same time I realized that, being able to ask questions in the first place put me in a very powerful position. I continued to be plagued by the power relationship between researcher as the 'producer of knowledge' and researched 'as object of the researcher's gaze' in ways that I had never had to consider previously.

One boy I interviewed would often stop and ask me the same questions. I found myself being asked to move out of my powerful position as researcher asking the questions to answering the same questions I was asking him! After responding to one of his questions about my experiences at school, he said, 'You have a gift. Not many people have that gift. You're different. I can see that you understand and see things. My friend, he has the gift too.' And so what unfolded was a meaningful exchange based on establishing trust and mutual respect because we had both come to the interview with our colonizer/colonized histories laid out

[1] We would like to thank Val Lenoy and Raba Solomon (Indigenous educators in schools) who read this chapter and talked with us about its content. They emphasized the importance of providing access to the perspectives and experiences of Indigenous boys and indicated that their reading highlighted the powerful influence of white culture and its often detrimental impact on Indigenous boys' lives. We would also like to thank Christine Ross (Lecturer/Support Officer for Aboriginal Students, School of Education, Murdoch University) for reading this chapter and for her feedback.

on the table. This was amazing because I had only just met the student. Afterwards, apparently he went back to his friends and talked very positively about his experience of the interview. As a result, all of his six friends wanted to be interviewed as well. They talked openly and at length about their experiences at school and as Indigenous boys.

I was overwhelmed by this experience and I decided to focus a lot of the writing on an exploration of the kinds of relationships and friendships that these boys had developed and continued to actively nurture in their peer group. This experience also highlighted for me how important it is to create spaces for students to talk and to present what they really think and feel. But they have to know that they are really valued and that there is a genuine concern and desire to learn about their worlds. The power relations also need to be named: researcher/researched, colonizer/colonized.

Introduction

In this chapter we focus on Indigenous boys and their experiences of schooling. We are particularly interested in exploring how issues of masculinity impact on these boys' lives because this is something that has not been foregrounded in the literature dealing with the experiences of Aboriginal/Torres Strait Islander students in the Australian context (see Groome 1995; Partington 1998; Bourke et al. 2000; Purdie et al. 2000). We focus on the following:

1. *Indigenous boys' experiences of racism*: how the prevalence of racial hierarchies impacted on Indigenous boy's learning and social relations with white boys.
2. *The impact and interrogation of normative constructions of masculinity on Indigenous boys*: how particular Indigenous boys either complied with or rejected masculinist hierarchical and abusive power relations.
3. *The interconnected borderland experiences of some Indigenous and white boys*: how a shared understanding of various marginalities led to the development of supportive social relationships.

In undertaking this kind of research, we acknowledge the problematics of white researchers interviewing Indigenous students within the racialized context of a history of colonization of Indigenous people in Australia (Graham 1989; Morris 1990; Dodson 1994; Longley 1995; Holland 1996; Dyer 1997). The dilemma was how to provide access to the perspectives of Indigenous boys – alongside the perspectives of Anglo and culturally diverse boys – while still rejecting the colonizing tendency to present a deficit view of Aboriginal/Torres Strait Islander boys. As Aveling argues:

> In education, as in other fields, the 'problem' largely continues to be conceptualized as residing with the Other and the 'cultural gaze of surveillance' – whether it be a gaze of pity, blame or liberal hope' (Fine 1997: 64), has remained squarely focused on people of colour. Thus in Australia, Aboriginal youth have been constructed either as deviant, culturally impoverished and as powerless victims (cf. Palmer and Collard 1993) or have been 'stereotyped, iconised and mythologised' (Langton 1993: 34).
>
> (1998: 301)

The impact of colonialist and racist regimes of practice, through which social relations between Aboriginal/Torres Islander boys and their white peers at school are enacted and negotiated, cannot be ignored. These power relations must be situated within the broader socio-cultural context of neo-conservative politics around race relations in Australia. We worked closely with Aboriginal/ Torres Strait Islander educators who liaised with the boys' parents to ensure that our interpretation of the data was culturally sensitive in addressing the issues we identified as impacting on the boys' lives at school. In this sense, we were conscious of our whiteness as 'a social marker of power and privilege' (Levine-Raskey 1998; see also Dyer 1997) and were careful to avoid classifying Aboriginal/Torres Strait Islander boys as culturally impoverished victims of racialized practices and regimes. As Memmi argues: 'the Other is always seen as Not, as a lack, a void, as deficient in the valued qualities of the society, whatever those qualities may be' (1965: 83). In colonial research and writing, the Others are not seen as fellow individual members of the human community, but rather are constructed and represented as homogeneous. This is a way of dividing up the world that puts an omnipotent white subject at the Centre (colonizer) and constructs marginal Others (colonized) as sets of negative qualities, ahistorical and fixed (Dyer 1997).

Hence, this research with Indigenous boys is undertaken with a scrutinizing awareness of the silencings and other oppressive workings of the colonizer/colonized hierarchy. Our research also illustrates that this simplistic binary is itself problematic. It does not take into account the subtle multiple layers and hierarchies of oppression inherent within and among the colonized, such as in relation to gender, sexuality, class and notions of 'pure' and 'miscegenated' Indigeneity; and the subtle and multiple levels and hierarchies of dominance, marginality and resistance within and among the colonizer (Memmi 1965; Fanon 1967; Said 1979, 1986, 1990; Bhabha 1990a, 1994).

'You got to have a strong heart'

Being Indigenous

Being an Indigenous boy involves the analysis of several factors such as the impact of racism, family and history, community and peers. Purdie et al., in their research into Indigenous students and schooling, highlight that there are 'multiple influences on the development of self-identity', but that 'positive aspects of self-identity mostly evolved from home community and school influences'. (2000: 9) They also indicate that some students remained uncertain or confused about their self-identity as Indigenous students, indicating that conflict arose for those who were rejected by Indigenous peers because they were too white, either in terms of their appearance or in terms of their life style. So Indigenous students whose parents were educated or affluent also risked being rejected by their Indigenous peers. This highlights the point made by Langton (1993) and Holland (1996) regarding the essentializing tendencies within Indigenous communities that are framed by the oppressor's strategies of gaining power and domination (Freire 1972), the effects of which are to fix self-identity within a normalizing regime of practices. Racism also featured as a frequent experience for Indigenous students at school in Purdie et al.'s study and highlighted that this was a significant factor impacting negatively on the formation of self-identity for Indigenous students. However, they also comment:

> It does not appear that most Indigenous young people dwell on their identities; in some respects they do not perceive themselves to be different from non-Indigenous people – they listen to the same music, eat KFC, barrack for this football team or that, have future aspirations, and so on. But when pressured, many appear to think that other (non-Indigenous) people think they are different. This difference is often interpreted as being inferior.
>
> (2000: 9)

While our research with Indigenous students tended to support the above claim, it highlighted the multiple and often fragmentary ways in which they fashioned and negotiated their identities within a context of racialized and gender-specific regimes of practice. This is supported by Boyd who spoke about what it means to be an Indigenous boy:

> You got to have a strong heart when you're growing up because if you have a strong heart you know right from wrong. If you have a weak heart, you just sort of take whatever your friends are doing and do that. Because usually what I do when people call me names, I make them real shamed

> and then they know not to do that again, because boys don't like to be shamed. I don't like to be shamed. So I like to teach people, it changes the community. It just used to be me and my friend, and then everyone who didn't smoke drugs and drink started hanging around us because we didn't and they thought we were cool. We talk to people, we ask about their weekends, what they doing and they say, 'Oh, we just smoked drugs' and we usually ask, 'Why do you do it? It's not good for you'.
>
> (Boyd, 16 years)

For Boyd, being an Indigenous boy is about having a 'strong heart'. He articulates a view of being strong that is not prescribed by a normative masculinity which requires boys to assert physical strength and power over subordinated others (see Herbert 1995; Epstein and Johnson 1998; Gilbert and Gilbert 1998). His notion of being strong is associated with matters of the heart and involves being able to stand up to peer pressure and having the willpower not to be influenced by other boys' practices of smoking and doing drugs in order to be accepted. This alternative practice of masculinity also involves an instructional dimension of problematizing other boys' investment in acting 'cool'. However, for boys like Colin, being an Indigenous boy involves dealing with the issue of racial differentiation on the basis of skin colour and, therefore, racism:

> It's just that we just want to get treated like everyone else. Like we're not different it's just the skin colour, but there's nothing different. Like underneath the skin we're all the same, so you just want to get treated the same.
>
> (Colin, 16 years)

Within a liberal humanist framework that does not address the structural, social and economic inequities that construct a hierarchy of difference, Colin is able to assert that 'we're all the same', thereby drawing upon an individualist, assimilationist discourse in response to the racism he experiences. This draws attention to the need for schools to provide spaces for interrogating the historically specific regimes of racialized hierarchies that go beyond the reductionist tendency to perceive difference as 'just the skin colour'. This would involve disrupting the 'sameness/difference' binary within an alternative critical pedagogical framework that draws attention to multiplicity, diversity and interrogation of hierarchical power relationships (Giroux 1992a, 1992b, 1992c; McLaren 1993a, 1993b; Burbules 1997).

Some Torres Strait Islander boys had strong links with and had maintained aspects of their traditional lifestyle/culture as illustrated also by the Torres Strait Islander boys in Purdie et al.'s (2000) study. Some of the students in our research challenge the socially ascribed either/or constructions of 'traditional home' and 'modern school', illustrating that rather than being 'torn between two worlds' they are living in, bordering and negotiating 'both worlds' (Anzaldua 1987; Harp 1994). What emerges is the need to avoid essentializing Aboriginality as a static or fixed attribute within a culturalist framework which invokes a notion of cultural identity as linked to a pre-invasion romanticized traditional past (Crowley 1993; Harp 1994). Indigenous boys experience and know that the very 'worlds' of home and school are not fixed, homogeneous and unified, and that their place is on the borders not only between these 'worlds' but within them and beyond them. For example, Chris, who had come from one of the islands to 'get a better education' was living with his grandmother, but would frequently return to his home island. He speaks about his culture with a great sense of pride and interweaves the need to maintain a traditional Torres Strait culture with the need to 'get to know white people':

> Being a Torres Strait Islander is a good thing. Yes, it's a bit confusing when you talk to us and we can't understand. My father says, 'You have to get to know white people and the white people can get to know you so you can get the attention of the white people and they can get attention of you.' [It's also about] our culture, we can [keep] the culture alive, and not let it flow away, just keep the culture going higher.
>
> (Chris, 13 years)

Chris proceeds to talk about those traditional practices, which are tied to the land and the sea, even if he may be unfamiliar with some of them as they were not taught to him as part of his early education. Thus, the constructs of what is defined as 'traditional culture' are also acknowledged as shifting due to its not being handed down through the education system:

> In our culture you have to get to know weaving and Island dance. You have to get coconut leaves and you just keep on weaving. You can make a coconut leaf bowl with coconut leaves to put fruits in it. My mother can [make it but] I don't know how to. Only some men and women do. I was getting to know the culture but down at pre-school . . . the teacher didn't come up to us and say it.
>
> (Chris, 13 years)

Chris describes the traditional dance that he has learnt and, in his description of needing to wear shorts, again illustrates his borderzone comfort with shifting aspects of 'tradition'. The adornment of the male body in order to undertake this traditional dance involves the deployment and meshing of various cultural resources to fashion a situationally specific form of masculinity which does not appear to be defined in opposition to femininity. Lace can be worn with cloth, flowers can be worn with shorts in a dance undertaken by both mothers and fathers:

> You got the drums and this thing, it's got a hole in it and you grab two sticks and the boys wear a luva luva . . . it's like a piece of cloth with lace on top, you tie that around your waist. You can wear Island shorts too, just plain white, we've got a flower here [*indicating the genital area*]. You wear it, underneath the shorts, and if you got jocks on and it came out then all the people just laugh. We got coconut leaves, we put them around [the hips] and a piece of cloth tied under our legs. Got a headdress thing, we call it Dari. We got feathers coming on top and all around it. You put it on your head, you tie it there and you dance. The meaning is we just have to dance, dance to get people to just join in, have fun. When I was little I saw my parents do dancing. They taught me to dance till I got used to it.
>
> (Chris, 13 years)

Chris also illustrates the diversity within the colonial homogenizing category of Indigeneity by pointing to specific regional cultural differences as well as interwoven linguistics:

> [Some Indigenous boys] don't dance like us, they dance with a bow and arrow, spears and all that. They're a different kind of culture to us, they're like dancing with things . . . They have different language than us. We talk Creole/English. Creole is half English, and half Torres Strait Islander's language . . . and second language is Miria, that's another Torres Strait language we use, and the third one is English.
>
> (Chris, 13 years)

This supports Purdie et al.'s point that 'the identity of young Indigenous people [is] very much linked to the communities in which they live'. They further add: 'Pan Aboriginality (Price and Price 1998) is not usually recognized in these remote communities because *'people of mixed ancestry are seen as being culturally different'* (Elder, remote community) (2000: 5).

Darren also mentions his love for the Islands and the cultural significance of his life there. As a boy growing up, he talks about not being concerned about the presence of sharks when he would go swimming with his cousins. He also talks about the annual moving back and forth between 'home' and 'school' which illustrates his border positioning:

> All my cousins [taught me to fish], I just hang around them . . . We go diving, we're just all small boys from Grade 1 to Grade 7, and we just went and take the dinghy out ourselves. Swim, jump in, we didn't care if a shark was in the water, we'd still swim. And it's really, really deep. I had to go right down, swim right down to the coral. I had to spear the crayfish and bring five crayfish, take it back to Uncle Reece's house, give them to him . . . I want to go back . . . I'll spend my whole Christmas holiday there, just

> going diving, making money and then I'm just going to catch the plane back to X High and do Grade 9 again, and then I'll go back up for Christmas.
>
> (Darren, 13 years)

These perspectives on growing up as a Torres Strait Islander boy concur with those presented by Purdie et al. who claim:

> Some communities have maintained aspects of their traditional lifestyles, and links with the land and the sea, such as a strong link with the sea in the Torres Strait Islands where fishing and related activities are still of major importance. This is in keeping with the observation made by Synott and Whatman (1998) that the islands and waters of the Torres Strait unite the Islanders through spiritual bonds. In the current study, young Torres Strait Islander students spoke with great pride about this aspect of their culture.
>
> (2000: 17)

However, Purdie et al. also make the point that in some urban schools 'young Indigenous people were not always clear in the knowledge of who they were and they struggled to understand their relationship to their Aboriginal or Torres Strait Islander backgrounds' (2000: 6). Thus, the modernist dualist construction of 'homeland' and 'traditional culture' for Indigenous students bordering multiple worlds may create a sense of falling between the gaps, of not belonging anywhere (Fanon 1967; Harp 1994; hooks 1994b). However, some students such as Neil, within the context of this struggle, spoke with great pride about his self-identification as an Aboriginal boy after witnessing the traditional culture of another tribe. Likewise, his decisions regarding his spiritual beliefs were made after reflecting upon Christian and non-Christian Indigenous belief systems, as well as his deep connection with his family:

> I'm really proud to be an Aboriginal boy. We went on a camp and there was this Aboriginal tribe, and they were singing the song 'I'm proud to be an Aborigine', and my hand just went up all by itself, and everyone was looking at me. Then I noticed right deep down I'm really proud, I'm so proud to be an Aborigine and believe stuff that my family believes. When I went to primary school I used to believe in God and Jesus. I stopped believing in them because I heard that if you believe in God and Jesus you're going to heaven, if you don't you're going to hell. My family don't believe in God and Jesus and I'm thinking, 'They're going to hell.' See it ain't heaven to me if my family is not there. If my family is going to a river, a burning river to die or they're going to be in this cage all

> their life, I want to be in that river to burn with my family, I want to be in that cage. I just want to be wherever they are. If I'm in this golden castle with everything, all the food you can eat and never make mistakes, that's still not heaven to me. And that's why I've stopped believing in God and Jesus. I said to mum, 'Where are you going to go when you die?' She said, 'I don't know, son, I just want to go with Uncle Y who passed away and mum.' I said, 'Mum I'll come with you, I don't care where it is I'm coming.'
>
> (Neil, 16 years)

Similarly John, while fashioning a positive self-identity as an Indigenous boy, particularly in relation to family, highlights to a far greater degree the context of the struggle involved in this process for him, as well as many of his peers, such as the problem of Indigenous boys dropping out of school (Simpson et al. 2001):

> I'm proud of being an Indigenous Islander. I think when you're Torres Strait Islander or Aboriginal it's sort of a feel you get into your family. My uncle was just saying that all of us cousins and uncles and aunties and grandfathers and grandmothers getting together, it's a sad thing that we all have to get together because of a funeral. One thing I hate is that [Indigenous boys] drop out of school early. And then you see them working and after a while you don't see them working at all. They should have a real think because education today is really vital, you need it. I think the main thing why they probably drop out is because they get into fights. They just hate the school system and they say, 'No way, I don't want no part of this, I'm going, I'm not hanging around.'
>
> (John, 18 years)

John highlights the crucial influence of family on both boys' rejection of schooling and their fashioning of a positive self-identity as an Indigenous person. He constructs the family as playing a crucial educational role in imparting life skills but also passing on the culture and knowledge of one's positioning within a historical and familial context. This involves inheriting responsibility and taking a 'stand':

> They are dropping out because of family problems. I reckon the main thing for Indigenous people is family . . . you should always be there for your family. My uncle says he's getting old now, we're the one with the black hair and he's the one with the grey hair now, and we have to stand up. We've learned what to do in situations, how to make stuff like traditional foods. When we were young, we were standing next to the table and watching them how to cut up a turtle, how to fillet a fish, stuff

> like that. We learn like that . . . most Indigenous people probably suicide because of something happening in the family.
>
> (John, 18 years)

John elaborates further about what it means to 'stand up' which involves the need and the responsibility to pass on 'the real story' after the elders have died of colonial invasion and the destruction of his ancestors:

> because if no one stands up nothing will get done. No one would probably hear about us, wouldn't want to know about us. Would other people care about what happened in Australia, the real story about Aboriginals. They should know the real story because maybe when they were small their fathers or grandfathers told them what happened about those people in Australia . . . that they were monsters, that they were bad. The Europeans wanted to make them extinct by killing them off but really Aboriginals are smart people. They knew the land and so when the white people formed the thing called the black line in Tasmania, where they all walked in a line about a metre apart and covered the whole of Tasmania [to massacre the Aboriginals], they couldn't find any because the Aboriginals were all hiding in the trees and caves. I think that people should know that Aboriginals endured a lot of suffering.
>
> (John, 18 years)

For John, learning about the story of colonialist invasion and its impact on Indigenous people plays a very important part in the fashioning of a politicized self-identity as an Indigenous boy. In the following, he advocates the need for a discourse and practice of equality with regards to the racist treatment of Indigenous people in contemporary white society. He talks about how his cousin was discriminated against in applying for a job, highlighting the persistence of racist and colonialist attitudes and practices in society today (Longley 1995):

> Well it happened to my cousin, he went for a job. He had all these references and all his certificates and they were talking real good on the phone, they were talking for a long time. Then the fella said 'Okay come down for an interview' and when he went down there the fella just got a shock because he was a bit prejudiced. He didn't get the job because the fellow was racist, because he saw the colour of his skin. When he rang up to see if he had the job he said 'No I'm sorry, the job has been taken'. So he didn't worry about it. Maybe a couple of weeks after, he looked in the paper again, there was the same job for the same position. He just felt disgusted that someone could be so cunning.
>
> (John, 18 years)

This leads him to assert the need to connect and interweave the present with the past so that important lessons can be learnt about the ways in which Indigenous people were treated and continue to be treated. The effects of this can then form the basis, he adds, for relating to Indigenous people in more respectful ways:

> I think still you can't really get over the fact that what they've done to Aboriginal people, that the whiteys killed them, raped their women, taken their children away from their family and shown them to worship God. To dress like the white people, to go to church on Sundays and to forget about their culture when you are communicating with each other, to use English not your language. I think Aboriginals are the main ones who have been humiliated . . . they have endured a long time of suffering. Maybe Torres Strait Islanders could be the same story, but I haven't really heard anything so disgusting. When we read an article, on the front page, it had all the Aboriginal kids and they were all crying. They were sitting at the back of this truck and it said the children were crying, and mums were beating their heads with rocks. I think the main thing is family because you don't want to see a little child taken away from you. And they were also told that your mum left you on the truck and she didn't want you no more. A lot of bad things happened. Even today I don't think some people stop and think of what happened. If they thought about it they'd probably say 'I'm sorry, maybe I'll change what I do. How I relate to people.'
>
> (John, 18 years)

John also mentions the issues of Indigenous boys not being able to really sit down and talk about what they are feeling, which highlights how normative constructions of masculinity impact detrimentally on all boys. He makes the point that it would be different for Indigenous boys in terms of being able to communicate better if the 'stuff in the past didn't happen'. This highlights that practices of masculinity cannot be adequately understood outside of specific racialized historical and cultural formations which impact significantly on the processes involved in negotiating and fashioning gendered subjectivities. In this sense, understanding what it means to be an Indigenous boy for John involves the development of a politicized consciousness about the treatment of Aboriginal and Torres Strait Islander people: 'I think our history is the main thing. We should tell the young generation about what happened, not what they assumed happened. Tell them the real story of what happened so that they can do something about it.' (John, 13 years)

'When they get fired up, they don't know what they're saying'

Experiences of racism at school

While schools could be a site where 'the real story' gets told, for almost every Aboriginal and Torres Strait Islander boys, school was a prime site where racist practices persisted. Indigenous boys spoke at length about how some white boys often incited them to anger as a result of their racist behaviour and attitudes. This provoked Indigenous boys and fights often resulted, with Indigenous boys being constructed and demonized as the aggressors. The racist behaviour of some white boys, however, was often manifested in subtle or implicit ways. It appears that this behaviour is directly related to the effects of certain hierarchical practices of masculinity deployed by dominant white boys. These social practices are deployed to assert a particular form of masculinity that is enacted through a racialized discourse of inferiorizing students of colour. In this sense, the racist practices of the white boys are understood as another means by which they are able to assert their position of power at the top of a social hierarchy of masculinities in the schooling context (see Mac an Ghaill 1994a; Dyer 1997; Sewell 1997). However, Indigenous boys such as Boyd actively challenged the racist practices of the white boys:

> Racism is a problem . . . like white boys and how they talk about Indigenous boys, 'I don't really like them dark boys because they start too much trouble'. But it's not really us, we just get aggravated real easy. They say, 'Oh I don't really like dark people'. It's just little things that I hear when I'm walking past. I don't mean to hear it but, if I hear that type of stuff, I chuck my ear in a bit. I think it is because of their culture and the way they're taught at home . . . for Indigenous people respect is the biggest thing you could ever have.
>
> (Boyd, 16 years)

Here, Boyd talks about how he becomes the object of the racist white boys' gaze through which Indigenous boys are constructed as the *real* aggressors. However, he relates this racist positioning and surveillance of Indigenous boys to wider socio-cultural practices pertaining to 'the way you're taught at home'. Thus, for Boyd, the racist behaviour of white boys is about a fundamental lack of respect for Indigenous people which he links to family upbringing and attitudes. Neil also links the racist attitudes of the white boys to their upbringing:

> I reckon if your parents bring you up always hating blacks and not mixing with blacks, of course it's going to be a problem when they're at the same

> school and trying to work together in the same class. That's where it all breaks down from the start. It's all about the kids' parents. When there's black against white, there's a fight right there. I even get angry too when they call someone 'a black cunt' . . . they get fired up and then the truth comes out.
>
> (Neil, 16 years)

Thus, Neil comments on how 'the reproduction of racism in everyday speech' (Morris 1990: 63) impinges on the lives of Indigenous boys at school, leading to racial tensions often resulting in fighting. Also of significance and not remarked upon by Neil is the conflation of racialized, sexualized and gendered speech which interweaves the specificities of marginality. This leads to establishing the hierarchical power of being a white male and fixing Indigenous males as subordinate in relation to their 'other' culture and othering their masculinity further by equating and referring to it with language naming/abusing a woman's genitals and sexual behaviour. This colonizer/colonized conflict emerged as a major problem for almost all of the Indigenous boys we interviewed who provide a perspective on how the social practices of masculinity for some white boys are enacted through what becomes for Indigenous boys an intensification of racialized power relations (Dyer 1997).

Neil then proceeds to draw attention to the gendered dimensions of Indigenous boys' response to racism. They tend to respond, he argues, by resorting to physical violence, which he claims is considered to be more 'macho' in their eyes. Again, the verbal harassment is structured around references weaving derogatory and violent images of black femininity, in this case, their mothers, with allusions to broader international historical and social events marking racial power struggles. This is evidenced in his reference to global systems of communication such as the internet, police shootings of black people, and the politically endorsed systems of segregation and apartheid:

> You just don't see girls fighting about racism. They do have fights, but it's more boys because boys are more macho. That's the way boys prove themselves for being popular. After discos, you see boys fighting and you can hear them talking like they own the town. It's just all got to do with reputation, and seriously they got no reason to fight. I'm not saying that I'm an angel but I have never been in a serious fight. The only one I might be in is when they call my mum something, or they call me something . . . even if they just joke around and say something, it just gets you fired up. They just get if off TV, they get heaps of stuff off the internet, for example, 'Your mum is so black that when the police shot her in the dark, the bullets had to come back looking for directions.' And 'Your mum is so black that she had to sit up the back of the bus', blah, blah, blah. And it

> just all builds up. When they call your mum something, that's when they'll just snap and go off. They're [white boys] just trying to be funny. They don't realize that's hurting other people deep down inside when they say jokes like that.
>
> (Neil, 16 years)

While Neil seems to be suggesting that many Indigenous boys engage in fighting to bolster their masculine status, he does indicate that white boys deliberately provoke and incite them to violence through engaging in racist and misogynist humour which targets their mothers (see Kehily and Nayak 1997). This humour is also about an assertion of a particular version of dominant white heterosexual masculinity used to mobilize a form of power intended to intimidate and humiliate Indigenous boys. As discussed in Chapter 3, sexist and misogynist humour can be used as a specific technique for fashioning hyper-heterosexual masculinity which works to 'consolidate the bonds of an in-group' through mutual hostility against an 'out-group' (Kehily and Nayak 1997: 73). However, while Kehily and Nayak claim that the deployment of insults against boys' mothers is 'to probe young men's associative links with femininity and expose their vulnerabilities', the effect is to produce sexual hierarchies (Kehily and Nayak 1997: 73). Our research with Indigenous boys highlights a further racialized dimension to these practices.

In the following, there appear to be tensions and contradictions informing the discursive frameworks which Neil draws on to explain his response to fighting. On the one hand, he perceives boys' toughness in essentialist terms as a natural expression of the way boys are, while rejecting the social practice of fighting as a means of bolstering one's hyper-masculinist status: 'Guys feel they have to be tough. It's just the way things are. I never went into a serious fight ever in my whole entire life. I don't see it as being macho, [but if I did fight] I'd just see it as a way of releasing tension' (Neil).

Thus, Neil does indicate that if he did get into a fight, he would not be practising his masculinity, but it would be a response of anger and hence a release of tension ignited by the racist practices of the white boys. He refuses to be implicated in the dominant practices of macho masculinity because he does not subscribe to the norm of 'guys' having 'to be tough'. This is important because he has a significant influence on other boys in his peer group at school in terms of encouraging them to reflect on how they relate and treat one another. He argues that boys need to find alternative ways of dealing with their anger:

> You got to try to get through to their heads, and tell them you're not a little wussy if you don't hit a guy. Somehow you just got to get them to believe that fighting is not cool, [that] it's cool to walk away . . . [that]

> you're not a gig, you're not scared, chicken shit . . . that it is stronger and harder to walk away than to swing a punch.
>
> (Neil, 16 years)

In asserting that fighting is not 'cool' and that in fact it is harder to walk away from a fight, Neil is advocating the need for alternative versions of masculinity to be encouraged and advocated. This raises the question of how schools might create spaces for this kind of reflection and work with all boys (see Salisbury and Jackson 1996).

Simon also talks about the issue of fighting. Like Neil, he discusses the need to resist the tendency to fight when provoked by the racist comments of white boys. In fact, he talks about how the racist behaviour of the white students has created a kind of cross-age bonding between Indigenous boys, with the older boys protecting and supporting the younger boys. Once again the wider regime of racist practices enacted by white boys produces a kind of solidarity amongst the Indigenous boys, in this case extending beyond same age year groupings:

> We're all friends with each other. We all stick together. It's like family . . . we try to teach younger people not to muck around in class. We look after the younger students and make sure they don't get into any trouble. We go help them out. If they get in a fight because they're called black c's [cunts] or something, we just tell them, 'Hold back and settle down'. We've got to look after them while they're here. We try to stop the fights.
>
> (Simon, 17 years)

Simon here is highlighting how the prevalence of widespread racism in school has led to more nurturing and supportive ways of relating to younger boys. What is illuminated here is how Indigenous boys like Simon are engaging in alternative practices of masculinity.

'You can't get the past out of your head'

Interrogating racism at school

Through undertaking Aboriginal/Torres Strait Islander Studies at school, many boys were able to contextualize the racism they experienced in their immediate social localities within the broader historical context of the impact of colonialist and colonizing practices. Some of the boys indicated that they had gained a lot through studying this subject at school, thus reinforcing the point made by Holland that 're/membering the past is important because the past has shaped our present':

> Re/membering is a form of resistance; it is a life-affirming and self-defining act. Re/membering is a cry of defiance in the face of that which steal our past, predetermine our future, cut short our present, challenge our humanity, render our lives meaningless, and make us invisible. It is our refusal to be silent, our rejection of oppression.
>
> (1996: 99)

John, for instance, appears to be engaging in this practice of re/membering the past through the learning he has done in Aboriginal and Torres Strait Islander Studies at school:

> Well you can learn a lot from Aboriginal, Torres Strait Islander Studies. Like when you have interviews with other Indigenous people, they can really tell you what it was like. [It's] from them, not from what newspapers say. You really get the true meaning of it. It's a good class, I would recommend it to anybody who wants to learn about our culture, customs, what we do, stuff like that.
>
> (John, 18 years)

John also talks about how useful it has been for the white students studying the course in terms of presenting alternative perspectives to the racist and colonialist representations of Indigenous culture:

> There are a couple [of white students] in my class. They've also been very good . . . they've said what they think. We don't argue about it. I don't mind them being in the class. [It's] just learning what's true and what's not, what's a lie. Because maybe they were told a different story about what happened to the Aboriginals. About maybe the old Dreamtime stories, they were told that Aborigines eat their children or they're monsters. But when they come to Aboriginal and Torres Strait Islander Studies, it tells the real story. But I think the most affected was the Aboriginals, even in this century today like what they did to the Aboriginals, made them slaves . . . some of the stuff is still going on today. Aboriginals are still getting abused. When is it going to stop?
>
> (John, 18 years)

For John knowledge about the past leads him to reassess the present in terms of the persistence of racism and its effects on Indigenous people.

Brian also provides an important politicized perspective on the impact and effect of practices of 're/membering' which he gained through undertaking Aboriginal/Torres Strait Islander Studies:

> It feels that we're important . . . You just pretty much couldn't forget about the past, like the genocide of Aboriginal, Torres Strait Islander people . . . racism, just Australian history, black history . . . you couldn't get the past or whatever happened in the history out of your head. Today it still goes on and it hurts a lot of people and you think you're still in the past. Even though you keep trying and trying, something happens again and just pulls you down . . . [It's] like all the past is just coming back to you and little by little just growing again.
>
> (Brian, 16 years)

Brian's perspective is one which resonates with that of Holland who in claiming that 'racism is alive and well in Australia today' (1996: 110) reiterates how re/membering constitutes a 'self-defining act' as well as 'a cry of defiance' (1996: 99). Aboriginal/Torres Strait Islander Studies created a space for boys to explore the interweaving of past and present practices of racialized power relations and their manifestations in their lives. This is important for both white and Indigenous students, given the essentializing and homogenizing tendencies in the way the latter are constructed or reacted to on the basis of their race. Moreover, it is important to emphasize that not all Indigenous boys are alike, nor do they have the same access to knowledge about the historical and racialized practices of colonization. In this sense it is necessary, as Crowley argues, to interrogate 'the taken for granted superiority of the observer's cultural identity and gaze' and thereby avoid the tendency to 'universalise Aboriginal cultural histories' (1993: 35–6). In other words, it is important not to invoke a fundamental culturalism which informs the way in which many people think about cultural difference and Indigeneity as 'linked almost exclusively to culture as traditional and pre-invasion heritage' (Crowley 1993: 34). As Langton argues:

> There is a naive belief that Aboriginal people will make 'better' representations of us, simply because being Aboriginal gives 'greater' understanding. This belief is based on an ancient and universal feature of racism: the assumption of the undifferentiated Other. More specifically, the assumption is that all Aborigines are alike and equally understand each other, without regard to cultural variation, history, gender, sexual preference and so on.
>
> (1993: 27)

Therefore, Aboriginal/Torres Strait Islander Studies can be a strategic site for engaging both Indigenous and white students in reflecting on the colonial and racialized discourses that suffuse their social relations at school.

'I sort of learned that it was all right to be black'

The impact of skin colour and miscegenation on Indigenous boys

The need to interrogate the effects of constructing Indigenous boys as the 'undifferentiated other' is highlighted by those miscegenated boys inhabiting borderland spaces within Indigenous cultures. Through the scientific racism of the nineteenth century, the notion of many distinct 'races' within humanity was popularized in order to construct a hierarchy from Caucasian (White) as superior to Negroid (Black) as inferior. Hybridization and miscegenation became coded as negative categories. White colonialist science constructed the identity of the 'pure race'. Monogenists and polygenists alike claimed that hybridity and miscegenation led to a 'degeneration', a monstrosity, a sterility, a decadence (Lionnet 1989; Spickard 1992; see also Douglas 1966).

Recently more multivalent and multidimensional responses have been constructed that articulate the complexity and diversity of black practices and interrogate the otherness of blackness/whiteness. This is based on a rejection of essence, origin, purity or homogeneity and recognition of a necessary heterogeneity and diversity within and between these categories (Hall 1990; Trinh 1991; Lugones 1994; Dyer 1997). However, Harp explores the divisive effects of colonialism in relation to Indigenous people such as Native Americans who find themselves constructing internal hierarchies based on the lightness/darkness of skin colour and notions of purity/miscegenation:

> '*Who is a real Indian?*': if there is one question which essentially captures the way in which Native identity is shaped by the forces of colonialism, this would be it . . . at no point have enough of us stopped long enough to realize who is responsible for posing the question in the first place, never mind pondering whether or not an answer to it actually exists.
>
> (1994: 47)

This emerged in our research with some Indigenous boys talking about the effects of this practice in their lives and communities. It is important to emphasize that miscegenated children are border dwellers for they not only challenge white power by their 'corruption' and 'pollution' (Douglas 1966) of it, but also symbolically undermine the emerging polarized black purist movements. Studies show that such children in Britain have a positive view of their miscegenated position and tend to think of themselves as belonging to a separate, mixed cultural group. For many of the children in Wilson's (1987) study, for example, being of mixed cultural background had a reality and an importance that could not be seen purely in black/white terms. They believed they have a certain amount of *choice* about their cultural identity and ability to juggle with any number of secondary identification categories. Within this white/non-white distinction, some younger children see cultural categorizations as a series of skin colour gradations ranging from very dark to very light (see also Tizard and Phoenix 1993).

While wanting to avoid constructing all Indigenous boys as the same or as the 'undifferentiated Other', what did emerge in our research was a commonality in how they described the ways in which racism impacted and impinged on their lives at school. In the following, Darren talks about denying his Indigenous heritage by not associating with black people as he thinks he is able to 'pass' as white. These decisions are made within a schooling framework where racism is rife, and he lacks a support group of peers and teachers that would positively affirm and share his Indigenous heritage. Nevertheless, despite his attempts to ignore his Indigenous background, other students externally ascribe him an Indigenous classification and bully him. It isn't until he goes to a new school where there are more Indigenous students and teachers and less racist bullying, that he feels more secure and able to acknowledge he has lost his black culture:

> I didn't hang around with a lot of black people because I was a light-skinned boy, so no one ever used to call me names. I was afraid of people calling me black, and 'coon', and 'boong' all the time. I had an incident where I was in Year 6, I was walking home and there was this bunch of white teenagers, Year 9s, and they came after me and tried to bash me up. They caught me and beat into me, they were just being racist pigs. That was just terrible, man, they were just laying the swear words down and calling me 'boong'. I told my mum. My dad went and spoke to one of their parents, because my dad is white too, and his dad started up at my dad, telling him, 'You shouldn't be cross-breeding.' So that was pretty terrible for me because at X school, there wasn't a lot of black kids . . . I tended to hang around the white kids so I finally lost my culture. Then I came over to Y school and there are a lot more black kids there, and I sort of learned that it was all right to be black. At Y school, I felt more safe, secure having more black people around.
>
> (Darren, 16 years)

However, for another borderdweller, Simon, the problem of growing up as an Indigenous boy is that while he self-ascribes as Indigenous, people refuse to acknowledge his Aboriginality because he looks white:

> [Growing up has] been all right but sort of hard as well, because I'm white but I identify as Australian Aboriginal. Most people don't believe that I am. I've got a pale complexion and blonde hair. It's been real hard

> making new friends because you're saying you've got Aboriginal in you and they don't want to know you. One teacher didn't realize I had Aboriginal blood in me and she goes, 'But you're white and you've got blond hair and fair complexion.' I said, 'Yes, it doesn't change anything, I've still got Aboriginal blood in me.'
>
> (Simon, 17 years)

This resonates with Holland's experiences who claims that while she cannot deny the privileges accrued to her on the basis of being 'mis/taken as white', she is still subjected to a certain form of racism: 'Living in a white body and identifying as a murri means that my experience of racism has always been different to that of a murri living in a black body' (1996: 97). This leads Holland to problematize 'essentializing notions of aboriginality [which] restrict us from acknowledging and celebrating the diversity within our own families and communities' (1996: 98).

'We're not into the same sort of things'

Diversity amongst Indigenous boys

In a report published on youth sexuality and suicide in Western Australia, this issue of essentializing Aboriginality and the realities of bordering several communities is highlighted by the perspective provided by a gay Indigenous youth, Simon, 17 years, who would visit a drop-in centre for queer young people. As he became more involved with the centre, he spoke more to the volunteer staff about issues he was facing. These included dealing with stereotypes of both Indigenous communities and gay communities; trying to reconcile the way he felt about guys with his own Indigenous culture and family that was very important to him; and trying to make links to the gay community. He said a few members of his family who know about his sexuality refused to ever talk about it, saying it was a 'white' thing (Goldflam et al. 2000: 31).

Johnson argues that we need to challenge 'monocultural belief structures' and to avoid an 'emphasis on the exotic and on Aboriginal cultures in the past' to present 'a more realistic view of the complexities of Aboriginal cultures, histories and contemporary circumstances' (1993: 9). In this sense, Don provides another perspective on diversity amongst Indigenous boys when reflecting on his own peer group which he differentiates from the 'big bunch of black kids' at school:

> Like you'll notice if you walked around the school you'll see a big bunch of black kids from seniors to first year kids, they're all together. The only boys at this school outside of that black group there would be us mob, me and

> my five friends. And that's because we're not into the same sort of things that they're into. Like they're all more into the social side of school and none of them will jump into their schoolwork. Like us mob, we're always into our schoolwork, always want to do well.
>
> (Don, 16 years)

Don differentiates his group of friends from other Indigenous boys in terms of their attitude to and commitment to study (Gilbert and Gilbert 1998). He reiterates that he wants to achieve and mentions a seminar he attended which had an impact on his desire to succeed:

> I want to achieve. We went to a Year 11 seminar and they had motivational speakers. It made me think I've got to plan, I've got to plan to succeed. So I try my best. I messed around from about Year 8 to starting Year 10 and then I realized that messing around is not going to get me anywhere. So I thought this year now, I'll just buck up and do as good as I could. So far I've done that.
>
> (Don, 16 years)

Don and his group of friends do not appear to engage in practices of masculinity that typify the way he perceives the majority of other Indigenous boys relating to one another. The basis for this differentiation is that he constructs them as investing more in the social side of school whereas he and his friends are more interested in achieving. This becomes particularly pertinent for him in light of what he perceives to be a changing labour market which requires a level of credentialing not considered necessary in the past:

> I reckon kids around our era have got more of a responsibility than kids back when old man Jimmy was young, and they could just quit school and go get a job, work in industry. It's not like that anymore. You can't possibly do that. You look in the paper for jobs, it says 'Year 12 Certificate'. You've got to finish Year 12 in order to get away with life in the mines now, I reckon. So all my kids are definitely going to finish their Year 12. It will be important.
>
> (Don, 16 years)

This concurs with the perspective on changing labour markets articulated by Mac an Ghaill who cogently argues that 'the cumulative effects of globalization of capital' has resulted in:

> new patterns in the international division of labour, the changing nature of the nation state and the associated crisis in Anglo ethnicity, new labour processes and local labour markets, new school and

> work technologies, increased state surveillance, and regulation of young people, diverse family forms, complex consumption patterns, advanced global communication systems.
>
> (1996: 172)

This highlights how Don's comments about entering the prospective post-school labour market cannot be adequately understood outside of this context of the globalized market economy, and how this impacts on the learning experiences of lower socio-economic status and Indigenous students. For instance, Don talks about this class and race issue in relation to his early experiences of schooling. He indicates that he felt different from all the spoilt, white kids at the new school he had moved to:

> It was a good school because there were a lot of black teachers and black upbringings. More people related to how I was brought up and not to how all the other spoilt white kids were. When we were young there was a fair few of us kids so I didn't really want to ask my mum for a lot of money. We didn't get a lot of things. My mum was unemployed and my dad had a crap job. Around that time it was pretty hard.
>
> (Don, 16 years)

However, as Mac an Ghaill illustrates, with the rise of the New Right agenda with its 'projected atavistic representations of a consumer based acquisitive individualism' (1996: 165) within the context of the emergence of globalized market economies, issues of social class are erased or marginalized:

> This hegemonic managerialist perspective is uninterested in how complex sets of power relations may distort the learning experiences of large numbers of working class students faced with institutionalised processes of cultural exclusion, marginalization and subordination.
>
> (1996: 169)

This is why it is important to situate Don's racialized experiences of schooling and his response to the labour market within a broader socio-cultural context which pays heed to the demands of post-industrial capitalism.

'I always stick up for him'

Indigenous boys' friendships with each other and with white boys

Several Indigenous boys, perhaps because of their own experiences of racism and, hence, inferiorization, showed an awareness of the ways in which marginalized boys who were white were ostracized by the dominant group and made an effort to relate to and include them. Darren discusses his friendship with a marginalized white boy:

> There's my white friend, Joel in my class, he always gets teased because he's got big ears and all them other boys call him fruit bat. I always stick up for him, I say they better leave him alone or else I'll come after them. Then they go, 'Oh we'll get our big brothers', and I go, 'I've got plenty of family' . . . [I stick up for him] because he's the only one in the class who doesn't have any friends, and he's just lonely. If everyone didn't want to be my friend because of my skin colour, I'd feel bad too. So I thought, same way it feels bad for him because he's got big ears and the way he looks, no one likes him . . . that's why I stick up for him. I got tired of them teasing him.
>
> (Darren, 14 years)

Darren has developed a strong empathy for other marginalized boys because of his own experiences of being bullied and ostracized by dominant boys on the basis of his race. However, rather than appropriating the practices of the bullies to compensate for his own abusive treatment, as demonstrated by other boys in our research, he has developed certain capacities for empathizing and supporting other marginalized boys, even those who are white. This tends to support the claim made by McLean who argues:

> Getting boys ... or indeed men to recognize the injustice they have experienced themselves can be the first step in enabling them to empathise with other people's experiences of injustice, and to recognise the ways in which they have themselves participated in perpetrating injustice.
>
> (1995: 23)

Boyd who is a member of Darren's friendship group, has also developed similar capacities for relating to those students who 'don't really fit in' at school and are excluded:

> There's this one kid, he's Greek, he doesn't really fit in well. I think he's a pretty quiet person and he's soft hearted. In class, he had to do an oral and he was a bit scared because he thought everyone would laugh at him. He always sits by himself. But a couple of times actually, me and my friends asked him if he wanted to sit with us, so he did. He's not a talking person so we asked him questions. We asked a bit about him so he could ask us questions or something about us. Thought he might feel more freer then. [And] he did actually, he had a bit of a smile on his face more than usual.
>
> (Boyd, 16 years)

What needs to be emphasized about the way these boys relate to white marginalized boys at school is that it is a collective practice embraced by the entire peer group, of racially different boys meeting on the borders. Boyd makes a point of saying that it is 'he and his friends' who decide to talk to the Greek boy. This constitutes an alternative practice of masculinity embraced by the boys in this peer group and is highlighted by Boyd himself when he talks about the other boys laughing at the Greek boy in class when he did his oral presentation. In the following, these boys are constructed as doing this to 'act cool' in front of their mates, which is a practice of doing masculinity that appears to be actively repudiated by Boyd and his group of friends:

> I reckon they laughed because they were trying to be cool in front of their friends . . . they would have just been egging each other on, 'I bet you can't make him cry' or something like that. They're trying to be big. I just thought they were idiots for doing that.
>
> (Boyd, 16 years)

The extent to which this peer group is based on non-hierarchical, respectful and nurturing practices of masculinity is highlighted by Neil who talks at length about his friends, how they relate and what they mean to him:

> I believe in all my mates. They're really smart. They might not be getting really high grades in class but if you look at every single one of them, they are smart in their different way. James, he's really unconfident, he says, 'I'm dumb.' I give him examples, 'Who gave us the idea of what would be the quickest way to go somewhere?', and he'd be the one that came up with it. I said, 'See, man, you thought of that before any of us, how could you say that you were dumber than all of us?' It's just we're all different in different ways, not everyone is smart at everything, you're smart at a particular thing. Then they really realize. They do the exact same to me, like sometimes I feel down as well and sometimes they pick me up when I'm falling.
>
> (Neil, 16 years)

Neil appears to play a key role in the group as a leader in modelling supportive ways of relating and in helping his friends to develop a positive self-concept. In the following, he talks openly about issues, particularly if they involve the possibility that one of his friends might be offended by what someone else in the group has said or done. For example, one of the Indigenous boys, James, makes a comment about not wanting to look white. However, Neil is aware of and sensitive to what their white friend might be feeling, and addresses what he perceives to be the possible exclusionary effects of James's comment. Thus, the following is another example of boys from differing racial groups meeting on the borders and interweaving their lives and cultures through friendship. They are endeavouring to maintain equal relationships rather than reversing the hierarchy to black is better than white:

> Like James, he's light coloured skin but he's black, and he goes, 'See, I am white, man, I don't want to be white, man, I want to be black like you.' When he said it in front of Ben [the white friend] the first time I looked at Ben and he looked offended. So when we were all together again I said, 'Look, James, do you realize what you're saying in front of Ben?' I said, 'Look Ben, there's nothing wrong with being white.' James goes, 'Oh no, bros', and I've realized he didn't mean to say it, and he sees Ben as a brother as well, like all of us do. And Ben realized that. I didn't say anything. I'm not going to say 'See Ben, he even called you brother'. We didn't make out as if it was a big thing . . . it's just something you've got to talk about. It was just that I was supportive. I think that's something we can do, and that's what keeps us close.
>
> (Neil, 16 years)

Neil models a mode of relating which is based on care, respect and support for his friends. This is reiterated by Boyd, who is also a member of this peer group: 'I feel more comfortable at school because I've got all my friends here and they stick up for me. All my friends respect me and I respect them. I give back what I'm given. If something happens to me, they're always there for me' (Boyd, 16 years).

Boyd also highlights the significant support that Neil provides as a friend and indicates that 'we claim each other as brothers'. He also acknowledges the influence of his peer group in his response to a boy at school who is perceived to be gay and who associates with girls as friends (Martino 1998):

> Boys don't really like the idea of boys liking other boys. They seem to think, 'Oh well, if you like a boy, you're not hanging around me', that type of stuff, and they start calling him names. But if they want to be gay they can be, I am not going to hit them for it. [My attitude is different] probably because of the people who I've hung around with, so I sort of think like that as well. And Neil thinks like that as well.
>
> (Boyd, 16 years)

So the peer group plays a significant role in shaping Boyd's attitude to gay people and in his capacity to acknowledge and embrace diversity.

'They're too cool, too macho'

Indigenous boys negotiating hegemonic/homophobic masculinity

Neil also provides a perspective on the dominant social practices of masculinity of other boys, but he and his friends invest in and value different social relationships. He suggests that there are particular gender regimes and a form of racialization of Indigenous students that are institutionalized – boys are praised officially for certain achievements and not others, and Indigenous students are acknowledged specifically for their achievement in Aboriginal and Torres Strait Islander Studies. He identifies the valuing of sport for boys and the role of the educational institution in valuing certain achievements for specific groups of boys. Neil appears to be suggesting that the school is tokenistic in its acknowledgement of Indigenous students:

> If we [Indigenous boys] are praised, it wouldn't usually be for something like academic achievement. If it's academic it would be something to do with Aboriginal, Torres Strait Islander Studies . . . it wouldn't be like within the whole general school. You'd only get one or two Aboriginal or Islander people who'd go up there for general stuff. [A boy who wasn't into sport] wouldn't be as popular as the other boys, he wouldn't be as cool as the other boys.
>
> (Neil, 16 years)

However, despite the investment of many boys in such 'cool' versions of masculinity enacted and negotiated through their involvement in sport, Neil and his friends do not appear to subscribe to such practices of masculinity:

> ['Cool' boys] they're too macho, too cool [to talk about feeling close to one another]. I just can't imagine another group talking like that to each other. They'd be all embarrassed, they'd be like 'Oh you're gay, you love me, you love my arse'. They'd say stuff like that, and make the other guy shamed so he wouldn't say it again. They think gay people are outside of the society and they don't want to be like that.
>
> (Neil, 16 years)

This highlights the extent to which homophobia, in Neil's eyes, appears to dictate the limits of boys' emotional engagement and attachment with one another:

> They try being open. They'd be thinking 'Oh no, you're gay'. But they don't say it in those words, they say it in their own little words. Some

> Islanders, I listened to them and they were saying stuff like, 'Chooch', it's hard to explain. When they say something, for example, 'Oh, he's got nice legs', or 'He's got a tattoo on his hip', they'll go 'Chooch', like you've been looking at his hip. They say stuff like that to make them shamed in front of everyone else. Like if you say to a guy, 'You got a nice bum', they go, 'Chooch, don't look this way'. They find it a bit uncomfortable, they get shamed in front of everyone else.
>
> (Neil, 16 years)

Neil reiterates the point that this regime of homophobia acts as a means by which many Indigenous men and boys police their relationships with one another. In fact, Neil's account highlights the ways in which 'compulsory heterosexuality' operates to constrain how Indigenous men and boys relate. Humour is used through the use of the word 'chooch' as a homophobic means of warding off the open acknowledgement of any intimate association with another male. Neil's difficulty in explaining 'chooch' points to the pertinence and specificity of 'culturally shaped attitudes towards homosexuality' and homophobia, 'cultural variations in homosexual conceptualization, identity, and expression' and homophobic resistances (Tran 1999: xviii; see also Jackson and Sullivan 1999). As Duruz points out, confronting homophobic 'prohibitions in their own cultures against being homosexual' is difficult enough, but 'challenging these views in addition to Anglo-Australian homophobia and racism takes a great deal of strength and commitment' (1999: 177).

Neil's interview draws attention to the questions raised by Langton (1993) and Holland (1996) who talk about the need to move beyond essentialist notions of Aboriginality and to interrogate hierarchical identity formations. Indigenous boys who defy the norms of acceptable 'masculine' behaviour also risk being subjected to a form of policing and harassment that is driven by regimes of homophobia.

Conclusion

In this chapter, we have tried to avoid the normalizing 'cultural gaze of surveillance' (Fine 1997: 64; see also Dyer 1997) in providing the perspectives of Indigenous boys. Our objective has been to illuminate the ways in which many of the Indigenous boys we interviewed were actively challenging and negotiating dominant practices of masculinity. We have also provided their perspective on and construction of schooling in order to foreground issues of whiteness. Many Indigenous boys documented the interweaving of racialized, sexualized and gendered hierarchies impacting on their social practices of masculinity. Several boys actively resisted the tendency to fight in response to being provoked and racially positioned as aggressors. Other Indigenous boys also rejected the kinds of hierarchical power relations that seem to pervade peer group social relations for white boys (Walker 1998; Martino 1999). We have suggested that the positioning of the Indigenous subject as the inferiorized Other within the broader social context of racialized discourses perhaps accounts for the Indigenous boys' conscious attempts to equalize power relations amongst their Indigenous peers and, hence, engage in alternative practices of masculinity. This is not to deny that Indigenous boys do engage in an active process of negotiation which also involves other aspects of dominant heterosexual masculinity remaining intact (see Davies 1995). However, we have illustrated how some Indigenous boys feel compelled to deploy a particular form of power, typical of aggressive macho masculinity (Jackson 1998), in response to the ways in which they are provoked by white boys and inferiorized on the basis of their race. In telling their stories, the Indigenous boys also highlighted that it is not really possible to discuss their social practices of masculinity outside the impact of historically specific and racialized power relations.

8 'You're not a real boy if you're disabled'

Boys negotiating physical disability and masculinity in schools

Interviewing boys with physical disabilities highlighted my inabilities. I had to visualize the geographic terrain differently, move within the familiar world as if it was unknown – which it became as I set out to remap, relocate, rethink the meanings and logistics of time and space and place.

How to get to the interviewee, how to physically position the interviewee's mouth, arms, legs, wheelchair, laptop in order to be clearly audio-taped, printed, written. How to get the interviewee from his locality to the researcher's office. Assumptions and taken-for-granted notions of motion, travel, time and space were disrupted and demanded immediate reinscription.

In what I thought was the known and easily traversed geographical, temporal and spatial terrain of my university grounds and university office, of footpaths and other public spaces on streets and in schools, I discovered a parallel world, one that had always been there but rendered invisible through my able-bodied impairment. In this world, lift buttons were unreachable, footpaths were potholed and treacherous, sheltering from the rain was not just a matter of opening an umbrella. New paths to my office needed to be found, my own office furniture needed to be shifted.

Boys and young men needed to be assisted into my car, wheelchairs dismantled while my fingers trembled in fear of breaking such vital equipment while struggling to understand the boy's polite and patient directions. Familiar lines and bumps in the palms of my hands being remapped by wheelchair tyre grease and dirt. The knees of my jeans dirty from gravel and mud where I had knelt to figure out how to take a wheelchair apart.

What was it like to be a young man being lifted, moved, pushed by a woman? What was it like to have to ask for everyday materials to be taken out of your bag slung unreachably behind you on the chair? What was it like to request a straw for the glass of water naively placed on the wheelchair tray by the researcher, to have to request the glass be brought closer to the mouth, to have to request that a cushion under one's neck be adjusted? These questions took up residence within me.

Introduction

In this chapter, we analyse the interweaving of physical disability and masculinity. There has been an absence of educational research on the multiple intersections of disability and gender in schools. Those who have undertaken research into disability in the wider society offer critiques and interrogations that need to be taken up in educational settings (Shakespeare 1999). An exploration of diversity within the category of disability is required, as well as the way that oppression impacts differently on students with disabilities when interconnected with other factors such as gender, ethnicity and sexuality (Meekosha and Jakubowicz 2001). It is necessary to be aware of the variety of strategies employed by different boys to negotiate their masculinities and disabilities for in some ways, men with disabilities 'are never "real men": they don't have access to physical strength or social status in the conventional way' (Shakespeare 1999: 60).

Gilbert and Gilbert summarize the breadth and depth of concerns and issues that boys with physical disabilities must negotiate, and the potential for isolation and marginalization:

> if they are unable to conform to the demands for competence in aggressive and competitive performance or play, or do not match the image of the masculine body, or if they are not accepted as potential participants in the increasingly important arena of sexual relations . . . Disabled boys are subject to the same cultural images of masculinity as others; that it involves a denial of weakness, emotions and frailty. They will often value sport as much as those who are not disabled, and seek the same success and reward. Yet, disabled boys are often stigmatized as weak, pitiful, passive and dependent. They are often perceived as either asexual innocents or animals with little control over their sexual desires. They may also be subject to further marginalization if they differ from the dominant group in terms of 'race', class or sexuality.
>
> (1998: 145)

The following five aspects arose in our research:

1. *Being labelled disabled:* how the use of the label 'disability' evokes differing responses and self-ascriptions in relation to the fashioning and policing of one's masculinity.
2. *The borderland existences of boys with disabilities:* how physical disability interweaves with masculinity, ethnicity and sexuality as boys negotiate their multiple positionings on the borders.

3 *The disability/heterosexuality interface:* how boys with physical disabilities use various strategies of compensation and negotiation to achieve a measure of normalization by the performance or fashioning of a heteronormative masculinity.
4 *Being harassed and harassing:* how boys with physical disabilities are positioned and position themselves within a social hierarchy of 'normal' and 'abnormal' masculinities.
5 *School as a site of the stigmatization of disabilities:* how schools are often complicit in perpetuating harassment and ignorance, and yet recognized by many boys as potential sites for the demystification of physical disabilities.

Being labelled 'disabled'

Our research participants, both able-bodied and with disabilities, tended to perceive schools as sites that reinforce the idealization of the hegemonic embodiment of masculinity. As boys with physical disabilities explain, their bodies' appearances and movements are major signifiers of their lower positioning within the hierarchy of masculinities. In the following, Andrew exemplifies the power of normalizing discourses and practices within which he 'passes' as able-bodied and constructs a hierarchy of disabilities within which he situates himself as closer to 'normal':

> The word 'normal' means to be physically like everybody else. I would say I'm about 95 per cent normal, yes . . . like I had friends who didn't actually know I was disabled until about a year afterwards. I think they thought I'd done something to my wrist because I had it in plaster and expected that I was going through some sort of recovery. They didn't actually know, didn't actually think that I was disabled, so that was a good feeling. I know a lot of people with disabilities, but do I hang out with them, no. A lot of the people I know with disabilities are in wheelchairs, mental impediments. I don't have the patience to put up with that sort of thing, and that's really terrible of me, but that's how I feel. All my friends that I hang out with aren't disabled.
>
> (Andrew, 16 years)

Andrew's attempts to 'pass' as 'normal', and his inferiorization of other boys with more severe physical disabilities, reflects the emphasis by some disability theorists on normalization principles. These discourses of disability are based on instructing people with disabilities on how to conform as much as possible to a socio-culturally prescribed embodied 'norm' rather than encouraging acceptance of embodied diversity (see Morris 1993). This requires the deployment of 'passing', 'covering', 'disavowal' and 'compensatory' strategies as performances of 'normal-bodied' (see Higgins 1992; Taleporos 1999b, 2001; Loeser 2002). There is no recognition of the stigma/normativity dichotomy itself as a social construct. Boys such as Andrew invoke this kind of normalization in order to minimize and invisibilize the realities of bodies with various disabilities (Meissner and Thoreson 1967; Morris 1993; Meekosha and Jakubowicz 1996; Chappell 1997).

Normalizing practices are evoked and upheld by some theorists for people with disabilities in ways similar to assimilationist practices for culturally and sexually 'inferior' groups. Meekosha and Jakubowicz explore how the hetero-normative gaze which 'frames the [normal] space . . . is a male gaze, with male able-bodied points of view, drawn with middle-class and white inflections' (1996: 89). An example of this 'gaze' is provided by Nick who discusses how boys with disabilities are constructed as 'abnormal' and inferiorized by some able-bodied boys: 'They think, "He's got a disability, he's not the same as us and we don't have to listen to him, he doesn't have normal feelings, we can tease him, he's not normal, he doesn't look like he's normal" ' (Nick, 13 years).

For some boys with disabilities, the boundary between able-bodied and disable-bodied was not so demarcated. Bryce, for example, situates himself as living within a borderzone where he is dependent on a technical aid which allows for a fluidity between the hierarchically constructed duality of ability/disability (see Loeser 2002). He is not disabled, he is not abled, but occupies the 'inbetween-space' (Bhabha 1990b; Trinh 1991). He is confused with and dubious of the interviewer's simplistic definition of his hearing ability and attempts to provide her with an insight into the both/and intricacy of his situation:

> Maria: Now some people would say that you have a disability, would you agree or disagree?
> Bryce: Disability? [*looking confused and doubtful*] How do you mean?
> Maria: Well, how would you describe yourself with your hearing aid, would you call that a disability?
> Bryce: No, I can still hear, but if I took my hearing aid off I would say it's pretty much a disability.
>
> (Bryce, 13 years)

People with disabilities such as Bryce contest their identity as deficit, as medical problems, and the dichotomous logics that society neatly comprises those who are able or 'normal' and those who are not. They also challenge the way the disability becomes the prime or sole signifier or identity marker. 'The person becomes "the disabled" . . . rather than being viewed as a complex, multifaceted, fully human person' (Christensen 1996: 65; see also Morris 1991; Higgins 1992).

Pakistani Muslim student Haseeb, who is in a wheelchair, also explained his initial discomfort with the label of 'disability' that was assigned to him in his Australian school, a label that was not used in his rural village home in Pakistan. He then recalls the similarities a teacher in Pakistan pointed out to him in the way different people use different technologies as ways of moving their bodies. His wheelchair is just one system of mechanics. Nevertheless, Haseeb highlights that despite having support, ambition and friendships, it is within his social networks that he feels his disability to the greatest extent:

> In the beginning it was very difficult because, and again it's this cultural thing, in the Pakistani cultures people don't use these words . . . I cannot remember hearing it from friends or from other people living in my village. When I arrived in Australia, I found people using this word for me as part of normal conversation. If you're doing what you want to, then disability is not a problem at all, it's really nothing. Like my teacher in Pakistan says, 'It's like people use motor cycles and cars. Isn't it strange that you're sitting on a seat and you're going and coming? It is because you're disabled that you can run at that speed' . . . this wheelchair is my high speed rollers. Problems and pains in my right leg put me under the category of disability. When I hear it too much, it has one obvious effect. I try to keep to myself away from people, even from those who want me to be with them. I feel I might be a problem for them and they won't tell me about it. I am studying, which I always wanted to do. Pain in my right leg is a problem but it is not a barrier in my education.
>
> (Haseeb, 22 years)

Haseeb's reflections exemplify how the multiple meanings of disability require the interweaving of the embodied with the socially constructed: 'We live with particular social and physical struggles that are partly consequences of the conditions of our bodies and partly consequences of the structures and expectations of our societies' (Wendell 1997: 272).

Boys with disabilities may attempt to use normative performances of masculinity as a way of resisting the disabled label while simultaneously experiencing masculinity as an oppressive social construct (Skord and Schumacher 1982; Asch and Sacks 1983; Morris 1993; Blinde and Taub 1999; Shakespeare 1999). Gerschick and Miller identified three different interwoven patterns which arise as men with disabilities try to come to terms with societal expectations and definitions:

- *'Reformulation':* whereby men with disabilities confront able-bodied standards of masculinity 'by reformulating it, shaping it along the lines of their own abilities, perceptions and strengths' (1994a: 34–7).

- *'Reliance':* whereby men unquestionably adopt particular normalizing practices of masculinity and 'despite their inability to meet many of these ideals, (these men) rely on them heavily' (1994a: 41).
- *'Rejection':* whereby men renounce hegemonic masculinist standards and either construct their own principles or deny the importance of hegemonic masculinity in their lives. 'They have been able to create alternative gender practices' (1994b: 29–30).

Alan displays the tension between reliance and reformulation in relation to his participation in school sport. This example also points to the role played by harassment in the 'passing' and 'covering' strategies deployed by some boys with disabilities:

> I cop all of my peers' abuse because I am not good at sport. This really pisses me off because I don't want to tell them that I am slow and poorly co-ordinated because then they will in turn treat me different again. And now as I get older my problems get worse because my back is starting to go on me, and I will be in a wheelchair by the time I am 25. For now I have found something I can do even when I am older and can't walk. It's computers. I have a gift with them so I am f_____g happy again but still you get dickheads who think it is fun to try to ruin this for me.
>
> (Alan, 16 years)

Indeed, for most of our research participants with physical disabilities, the sporting field became a major site for normalizing one's masculinity, despite medical and other recommendations not to participate in contact sports. Other boys wanted to participate in sport but found the kinds of sports offered do not cater for physical diversity. 'I don't do PE out of fear of embarrassing myself. I just can't get into it, it's just a fear of being laughed at basically. I stuff something up and people laugh at me' (Andrew, 16 years).

Several boys with disabilities such as Marc were able to interrogate their reformulation of dominant masculinity and reflected upon the fact that if it wasn't for the disability, hegemonic masculinity would have remained 'unquestioned and unquestionable' (Schutz 1944) in their lives:

> I would have been either a full sporto, one of those really egotistical pricks. I know me for who I am, and I honestly feel that I'm pretty confident about myself . . . because I sit in a wheelchair and they think, 'Oh my God, he's not normal' and then as soon as I sing and I play music they think, 'Oh, maybe he's not so different after all'. I'm just a larrikin. I've got a disability, and I'm happy with it.
>
> (Marc, 16 years)

Due to his status as 'normal', acquired and secured by his playing in a music band, Marc appeared to be comfortable self-ascribing as disabled. Thus, we can see how the strategic deployment of reformulation negotiations, wherein compensation for physical disability in traditional sports occurs in the form of other normative successes such as playing in a band, allows Marc to make decisions about the use of a wheelchair, otherwise a very visual marker of marginality: 'I chose to go in the wheelchair and everyone accepted it, and it's like being one of the guys.'

For Sam, also in a wheelchair, being disabled meant a rejection of dominant constructs of masculinity such as independence and a broader understanding of and empathy for other social differences:

> Well, [my friend] helps me, he doesn't mind doing things with me in a wheelchair that need doing – which is a lot, because I can't do anything practically myself. I think I do things more seriously. Other boys have more time to muck around. I have more time to think and I'm tolerant of people with differences.
>
> (Sam, 16 years)

Indeed, Sam was very aware of how other boys with disabilities adopted reliance strategies. He said they would 'act crazy' in order to fit in with able-bodied 'cool' boys, 'to be the same as anyone else'.

Able-bodied boys often appeared to be complicit in the need for boys with disabilities to 'be normal', such as participating in sport, for they commented very favourably on those boys with disabilities who participated in sports, despite the risks they knew they were taking: 'He's always having a go at things which I think a lot people really respect in him, he has a go at sport and all those sort of things' (Simon, 16 years).

Another example of reformulating notions of hegemonic masculinity is the way in which a wheelchair becomes incorporated as part of one's male body that can be used to simulate action and speed of a vehicle such as a car or the athletic masculine body itself. Several able-bodied boys commented with admiration on how some boys with physical disabilities utilized their wheelchairs in 'cool' or 'tough' ways: 'He's got a mechanical one [wheelchair], so he drives by himself. He goes very fast . . . he loves driving it, you can tell' (Adam, 13 years). 'Everyone loves him. They just hang around him. They just all want to push him fast' (Josh, 13 years).

Other examples of compensatory or reactive masculinist behaviour, or the reliance upon traditional strategies of asserting one's masculinity among peers, were examples of boys with disabilities becoming involved in aggressive behaviours such as fighting and classroom disruption. While some disabled students resorted to fighting, harassing other students and creating classroom disruptions in an attempt to assert a normative masculinity, they were not disciplined by teachers in the same way that able-bodied boys were for engaging in these behaviours. In this sense, teachers were perceived to be perpetuating the marginalization of these boys by treating their 'normal' disruptive behaviour as 'abnormal' behaviour for boys with disabilities. Several able-bodied and disabled boys commented on how teachers constructed the latter as victims, even when they reclaimed some masculine status through aggressive and attention-seeking behaviour:

> I think that he does things to make people deliberately pay him out. Like he just starts fights with people . . . and just makes people hate him. He tries to act tough. I think they [teachers] are [aware] but they just don't do anything about it. They said they just didn't think it was serious, and they just let it go because he was disabled.
>
> (Andreas, 16 years)

An example of the rejection of traditional hegemonic constructions of masculinity comes from Abdu, who is approximately 70 centimetres in height. Not only has he rejected dominant notions of strength, heroism and independence, he also critiques the label of 'disability' itself and self-ascribes quite differently. He draws a lot of strength from his Turkish family and Muslim religious background, as well as from the Integration Co-ordinator at his school:

> I don't think I've really got a disability. I think that everyone in this world has disadvantages and advantages, so I can say I'm one of the people who have advantages and disadvantages. I'm strong really . . . I think that it's [strength] in your brain and your heart. Like, a strong man to me isn't a person in the *Guinness Book of Records*. They jump down a building, but I don't call that guts because that's not guts, that's being crazy. I've been brought up by people who have taught me, my parents, my family, my religion, people around me, that this is a test. I see myself as normal. Kids all look after each other no matter how you look. I've got an Integration Co-ordinator . . . whenever I need help I go to him, and whenever he needs to know anything from me, or do something about me, he'll come and ask me. And whenever he thinks that something's gonna be good for me, he comes and tells me and we discuss it together, and it's all right.
>
> (Abdu, 16 years)

Abdu has undertaken hierarchical inversion by claiming himself a space of centrality and popularity, possibly based on his marginality. 'I see myself as being the centre of things. I wonder is it because of my height . . . is it because people are fascinated because of what I am? I don't know what the actual thing is . . . but I'm happy with that!'

Rejection of normalization practices and hegemonic masculinity can take the form of proudly self-ascribing as disabled, as Tony explains in the following. This becomes a politicized practice deployed to assert identity and community belonging as a consequence of his 'shame' and 'pain' in failing to measure up to a normative embodied masculinity accentuated for him during puberty. The sense of not being able to live up to 'being a real man' is accompanied by the realization that he could not do 'the whole muscle thing' and fashion his body in such a way as to appear sexually attractive:

> I'm really into now taking on the disabled label because it's been something that I've had a lot of shame about. I remember feeling scared and intimidated of being around people with disabilities, but now I'm claiming that back, that identity. A boy with a physical disability never has the opportunity to have reinforced what they are as a man. I actually entered puberty very early, but what I noticed was that all these guys at my school had big muscles, and were getting taller, and there was so much pain involved in that for me. I felt so ripped off because I wanted to look like that. Here I had these scrawny arms and I wasn't getting bigger, but was getting thinner and thinner. There's that sense of not being a real man and not looking good enough, not being attractive, not doing the whole muscle thing.
>
> (Tony, 24 years)

'I got seven chicks after me'

Crossing and negotiating the disability/heterosexuality interface

Boys with disabilities also find that their disability becomes a signifier of marginal heterosexual masculinity in relation to able-bodied girls. To be male and disabled, such as in a wheelchair, is to be 'impotent, unable to be a (hetero)sexual being, and therefore not a "complete" man' (Morris 1991: 96; Robillard and Fichten 1983; see also Tepper 1997). As Andrew, 16 years, illustrates: 'People think that just because I'm disabled I shouldn't be able to relate with girls, I shouldn't be able to talk to them. It's basically solitary confinement.'

This dominant discourse then constructs a situation in which a boy with a disability may utilize heterosexual relationships and the admiration and affirmation of girls as a measure of his 'normal' masculinity. For example, Kieran, who had a very noticeable speech impediment, believed that the stigma against his self-ascribed 'disability' in the social networks at school had diminished by his being personally affirmed by his girlfriend: 'I'm more confident now . . . I'm not worried anymore. Being in a relationship with a girl, it makes you feel like you're worth something' (Kieran, 16 years).

Regarding the construction of a heterosexual disabled masculinity, there is often tension evident in boys not necessarily wanting to relate to girls who are disabled as this reinforces their own disability. Hence, in negotiating the subordinate disability/dominant heterosexual masculinity interface, both able-bodied girls and disabled girls may become 'props' and signifiers of a disabled boy's location within the hierarchy of masculinities. This may occur even if the boy himself is not consciously aware of the classifying of girls in this way. In the following interview excerpt, Marc moves from a position of self-confidence and successful competition with able-bodied boys as a result of able-bodied girls becoming interested in him. He shifts to interrogating how boys utilize having a girlfriend as a marker of successful heterosexual masculinity, to a realization that he is implicated in the hierarchical classification and use of girls to build his own image. He is taken aback by the question of whether he would consider going out with a girl with a disability. He shifts from a confident, breezy conversational tone in the interview to one of hesitancy and concern. The research interview became a major point of intervention and interrogation into his own social practices of masculinity that had been unquestioned and unquestionable:

> Marc: Oh yes, I've had that [harassment from able-bodied boys], but now who's laughing? [*laughing proudly*] They say, 'If you have sex, will you break?' Because I break bones easy, they go, 'Does your dick break in half?' And then the music and band started, and then the chicks started in Year 9. As soon as I did start going out with girls it didn't matter if they [boys] were paying me out because I was having the last laugh because I actually was with a girl. It is a goal when you're at high school to have your first girlfriend and that's really not good [*disapproving look*].
>
> Maria: Would you ever go out with a girl with a disability?
>
> Marc: I'm not sure. [*Long pause, frowning and looking away from the interviewer.*] I'm not sure. [*Long pause, looking troubled, still looking away from the interviewer.*] I don't know. That's a good question. [*Long pause and sounding very troubled, very uncomfortable and confused.*] I'm not sure about that one.
>
> (Marc, 16 years)

Hearing impaired Bryce was very clear about the kinds of interactions he would have with various differently abled girls and why. His hand gestures on the table, while he discussed the boundaries and hierarchies of these interactions, visibly demarcated the symbolic relational boundaries and hierarchies in place at the school:

> I've had a fair few girlfriends . . . and mostly not deaf or anything. If it was a deaf girl it would be alright. But if it's someone at Integration [with more severe physical disabilities] you don't feel comfortable. When you're going out with that girl you get teased a lot. Sometimes I tease them. I really shouldn't do it, but if you talk to them, then others call you dumb as well. It's like a puzzle. [*extends his arms along the table*]. If a boy here [*indicates a zone with his left hand*] likes a girl, and you want to fit into there [*indicates a zone with his right hand above his left hand zone*], if he went out with her, everyone would tease him because they don't really like her. She's, you know, not right . . . the good girls are the normal ones.
>
> (Bryce, 13 years)

Being a boy with a disability that can be hidden is superior to a boy with a physical disability that is very obvious. This, in turn, is superior to a boy with an intellectual disability. And all of the above masculine variations are superior to being a girl with a disability, albeit with a gradation of disabilities being classifiable within the girls' group as well. 'Boys who have disabilities seek out attractive, caring women. Boys without disabilities seek out attractive, caring women. Girls with disabilities are not usually sought out' (Hastings 1996: 116; see also Asch and Fine 1988, 1997). Thus, it is unsurprising that girls with disabilities evidence lower self-esteem than disabled boys (Deegan 1985; Taleporos 1999, 2001).

Another consequence of heteronormative and gendernormative frameworks is that boys with disabilities are likely to be labelled as gay and experience homophobic harassment (Shakespeare 1996, 1999). This is predominantly based on their embodied appearance and movements which may be constructed as effeminate. For example, Andrew, 16 years, who has cerebral palsy, is often called 'faggot' due to his inability to control the so-called 'limp-wristed' movements of his hand. He believes 'being disabled has probably made me more aware of, probably more sensitive to people's feelings. Like if someone's homosexual, that doesn't bother me in the slightest bit. If someone's black, it doesn't bother me either'. Nevertheless, Andrew finds being called 'gay' or 'faggot' more disturbing than being called 'spastic', again demonstrating the efficacy of hierarchical masculinities where mental disability is constructed as more appropriate and acceptable than homosexual masculinities. 'It's just been a prolonged thing with people calling me names. The traditional one is spastic. I don't take quite as much offence to that as to being called gay and faggot' (Andrew, 16 years).

'We all did it to each other'

Being harassed and harassing

Most boys with disabilities related experiences of being harassed by other students. Harassment can take the form of invisibilizing and ignoring: 'Well, no one really talks to them' (Michael, 13 years). It may be difficult for able-bodied dominant boys to define or perceive certain activities or interactions as harassment: 'Well, they're not actually hassled. Some people embarrass them about what they're like' (Jason, 14 years). For some boys with disabilities, having their wheelchairs and other technical aids touched and played with is a form of harassment manifested in an invasion of privacy or of the body. This is because the wheelchair, hearing aid, laptop and other technologies come to represent or be seen as part of the disabled cyborgian boy's body. This is particularly a concern for boys who have rejected dominant codes of masculinity and do not rely on their wheelchair and other technologies to establish some social popularity or recognition among other boys. Sam explained how the boys' interest and attempts at playing with his wheelchair were harassing intrusions into his personal space. Moreover, he did not understand why his wheelchair should be such a curiosity for them:

> Some kids touch the controls and jump on the back of the chair, which annoys me. I don't know why. They shake my wheelchair. They like pressing the horn too. The boys think wheelchairs are fun machines . . . how fast it can go and what the buttons do. I get angry at them because I don't like noisy kids or kids who muck around and tell jokes and are so silly. Kids do it in the corridor where there are no teachers, they don't do it in class. No one has told them that they shouldn't do it. And sometimes they need telling because they don't think. They don't mean to be mean or anything because they don't understand. I just don't want them to touch the chair because they wouldn't like it if someone touched them or any of their possessions.
>
> (Sam, 16 years)

A reluctance to tell a teacher is commonplace among boys with disabilities, mainly because they do not believe able-bodied teachers understand the embodied symbiotic relationship many boys have with technologies such as wheelchairs. Likewise, they fear drawing more attention to their need and ability to gain special treatment from teachers. Dominant boys may resent certain affirming attitudes and responses being shown to boys with physical disabilities:

> Just little things like, at the end of each class or at the end of the day, the teacher would go 'Oh Marc, you can go out first' and I'd get resentful looks, evil eyes, from everyone in the class. It just made me feel like, why do I have to go out first? I got picked on by people, like, one guy threatened to break my arm . . . only mucking around . . . but you just don't muck around with stuff like that.
>
> (Marc, 16 years)

Several of the boys with disabilities described experiences of harassment which involved physical violence deliberately aimed at the disability, thus risking further injury or fatality. In some cases, this occurred after the school had endeavoured to inform students of the bodily concerns of the boys with disabilities. It appears that within a hegemonic masculinist framework, an admission of physical vulnerability and perceived inferiority warrants an attack on that display or knowledge of vulnerability. Moreover, seeking support from authorities, such as teachers and parents, is also fraught with tensions within this framework. It is further evidence of weakness which, as Marc says, boys with disabilities 'learn' to avoid in order not to be positioned even lower within the hierarchy. Thus, not telling a teacher and displaying an independence and so-called masculine strength in 'sorting out your own problems' can be a strategy to avoid even further harassment for, as many boys tell us, seeking teacher intervention can exacerbate and justify further attacks:

> I didn't want to go to the teachers, I didn't want to tell mum and dad, so I pretty much kept quiet until some guys started actually physically hurting me. The very first day I remember we were in assembly in the library, and the coordinator specifically said, 'You've got to be careful with this boy over here because he breaks very easily, you can't physically touch him or his bones will break.' But they didn't understand. [And teachers] just say [to them] 'Oh, don't do that' and that's it. I don't think it's up to the teachers to fix your problems for you, and I learnt that if you don't handle it yourself you're just going to end up more scared and harassed.
>
> (Marc, 16 years)

A more acceptable strategy to deflect harassment was to seek the protection of peers. Marc clearly admires and aligns himself with the 'toughies', thus gaining status and schoolyard credibility himself. This alignment can become a sanctioned and justified display and performance of hegemonic aggression on the part of able-bodied boys under the platform of heroic mateship:

> I'm just one of the guys, it's just normal. I used to be a bit of a mummy's boy. Then I made a best friend and he was one of these toughie persons.

> I remember I was in the canteen getting some food and this guy goes, 'You shouldn't be eating that' and he goes, whack, straight in my gut. I went out and told my friend who nearly bashed the hell out of him. One time this other guy was giving me the shits, and my friend just went up and pushed him, and the guy pushed him back, so my friend decked him and got suspended for three days.
>
> (Marc, 16 years)

Another normalizing practice was redefining a put-down as humorous, meaningless or 'normal', as Marc would often do. He illustrates the fine line between 'pay-out' and 'nickname' based on his positioning in relation to the dominant boys and his positioning in relation to people with intellectual disabilities:

> The guys used to call me spastic and it used to be a real pay-out. I used to hate it, but as time has gone on people don't say it to pay me out anymore. It's become a nickname. It makes you feel guilty sometimes because of people that are actually mentally disabled and yes, it makes me feel bad sort of . . . but it's just become so commonly used that it's just normal for me.
>
> (Marc, 16 years)

Another student who experienced physical violence that may have had fatal results is Aaron, who wears a pacemaker. As with Marc, teachers' attempts to educate students about Aaron's condition led to a perception of his vulnerability which is seen by some able-bodied boys as warranting a lack of respect, and thus deserving of harassment. It also appears that the bullying is exacerbated due to Aaron's computing skills which he will not use to extricate himself from bullying situations – such as assisting bullies with their homework. And again, Aaron decides not to seek support as he fears that telling teachers about the bullying may have further bullying consequences:

> They call me 'battery boy', 'little heart' or 'dead heart'. If they're all hanging around in the corridor and you need to get to class, they trip you or push you. If I get hit, and the pacemaker gets lodged out of bounds, then I could die. Sometimes they punch me. I get chest pains sometimes. I come to the library a lot. I stick to the computers because I'm really smart with computers – like the library ask me to fix the computers. And this bully comes up and he says, 'I've got this assignment, could you do it on computer for me because I want it to look good.' I said 'No', and he goes, 'It's your fault that I got bad marks'. The teachers tell them [I have a pacemaker], like my health teacher, because they're trying to look out for me, they're warning the

> students. But once they know, they do this. If I tell a teacher, they'll bully me more.
>
> (Aaron, 14 years)

Thus, the onus appears to be on the harassed to find ways of addressing the problem without teacher intervention or structural support. One of these strategies is allowing oneself to be joked about as a means of gaining some popularity and acceptance from other boys. This then allows able-bodied boys to legitimate and justify their bullying, as Glenn does in the following:

> He's got a speaking disorder. People pay him out but he accepts that . . . like we pay him out and everyone cracks up laughing. He'll crack up laughing himself. But he gets treated how he wants to be treated, like if he says, 'No, I don't want to be paid out anymore', we wouldn't. If there's something wrong with what we're doing, he should basically tell us.
>
> (Glenn, 16 years)

Other able-bodied boys, such as Jordan, were very aware of the deliberate harassment and bullying to which boys with disabilities were subjected. For example, he stated that a boy at his school who had a visual impairment was harassed by other boys because his masculinity was constructed as inferior: 'It's not the man to be blind'. Boys like Jordan often experienced major distress and ambivalence over their own failure to intervene when witnessing the harassment. He also illustrates how able-bodied boys can be aware that a major coping strategy of boys with disabilities is pretending the harassment is not affecting them. In so doing, they perform a stoic toughness and resilience in the face of this harassment, and in the way they attempt to deal with the harassment independently of peer and teacher support:

> There was one kid that was blind. It's not the man to be blind. They would trip him, do terrible things, I couldn't believe it. I felt pretty bad not helping him. I really wanted to be his friend and he was really, really nice, a nice guy. But if I helped him, I was going to be in trouble as well, people were going to be mean to me. It was a real attack on my conscience and just thinking about it now I feel bad. He was really tough, he just let it roll off his back. He felt sadness most of the time but then when he would pick himself up he would say something really witty.
>
> (Jordan, 16 years)

Teachers' interventions could simultaneously be both supportive and cause further harassment. Indeed, some teachers were seen as lacking effective communication and other skills in relation to physical disability:

> Most teachers don't take much notice of it [harassment]. Some teachers would just laugh it off, or ignore me completely. Some are very patronizing, as if I was some sort of invalid and that was a bit degrading. Teachers will go, 'Don't do that' [to bullies], but even that's getting a reaction because they'll do it straight away again.
>
> (Andrew, 16 years)

However, Nick indicates that some teachers will provide support if they are told about the harassment, and this highlights the extent to which such practices are often carefully perpetuated outside of the teacher's gaze or surveillance:

> My computer teacher, he really supports me, he really looks out for me. He said to me, 'If anyone starts picking on you, you go to your brother, if they start knocking you and your brother, you come and get me and I'll sort them out.' I found that made me really happy and I felt really safe at school.
>
> (Nick, 13 years)

This was very important to Nick who had experienced a teacher being complicit with harassment from other students when he was younger:

> She used to call me ferret legs. I found that very distressing and one day I was so distressed I just picked up my bag, walked out of class and said to her, 'I don't have to take this', and walked all the way home. I had to have the rest of that entire week off school because I couldn't just go back there. I remember when I went back I had to go to a meeting with her and the principal and the principal was actually on her side. She didn't even let me give my side of the story and they couldn't see how distressed I was that day . . . My mum withdrew me from that school.
>
> (Nick, 13 years)

It is not only teachers who may be complicit with harassment. Normalizing practices and social hierarchies mean that boys with disabilities may also perform discriminatory practices: 'Disabled people exploit each other, as well as being exploited by others' (Shakespeare 1996: 213; see also Vernon 1999; Loeser 2002). 'I think those without social power or those who are insecure prey on other people who they perceive as inferior to them, and replicate their powerlessness and hurt on these lesser victims' (Shakespeare 1996: 208).

Tony discusses this intra-group discrimination and pecking order based on the most 'normal' disabled person to the most multiply marginal person. Some boys with disabilities, including himself, would find boys to harass who were supposedly more 'inferior'. Thus, many of the boys inhabited an oppressed/oppressor borderzone in the struggle for power, status and normalization, a struggle that could be played out in both predominantly able-bodied schools and so-called 'special' schools. For Tony, neither was a safe haven, each came with its particular traumas:

> At the special school I had my chair rammed into and they called me 'Squealer, Squealer'. They called me fag. I was scared of some of those guys. I think on looking back it was their own frustrations . . . you're disabled, you're already sort of not up there in terms of being a man. So how do you reinforce that you're a man? You pick on someone who's a little bit different and that's how you feel better, yeah . . . The irony was that we all did it to each other. Once I was integrated in a normal school, all of a sudden I had a different status. There was a bunch of us that all went to the normal school and we were all special. I was the lowest on the specialness because I was younger and I had the funny voice as well. And I remember there was this girl we used to pick on. I remember her crying and me thinking 'I'm sorry, I didn't mean to upset you', but I'd say something nasty . . . There was no one else there with disabilities as obvious as me and I remember being really traumatized and crying myself asleep at night not wanting to go to school.
>
> (Tony, 24 years)

'To different people I talk differently'

The borderland existences of boys with disabilities

The confusion or conflict that arises in some boys with disabilities of diverse cultures and sexualities can also be traced back to normalization practices and hierarchical dualisms that reinforce constructs of monoculturalism, homogeneity and universality (Meekosha and Jakubowicz 1996, 2001; Vernon 1998, Bryan 1999). Multiple Otherness can be experienced simultaneously and singularly, depending on the context, and oppression may be modified by the presence of some privileged identities, such as being disabled, but also being a male and/or from a higher class status. 'Policies for people who have multiple disabilities, come from non-English speaking backgrounds, live in a remote rural area and are poor have not yet been created. Not to mention being a girl as well!' (Hastings 1996: 115).

In some cases, borderland boys with disabilities may find that other facets of their lives provide points of connection with their peers. For example, in relation to Abdu's dwarfism, other boys from a Turkish Muslim background supported and befriended him due to shared cultural background and understandings: 'He's good to talk to and we know what's going on with him . . . because he's Turkish, that's why it's a bit easier for me to talk to him' (Mustafa, 15 years). In other cases, having a physical disability disrupted hegemonic constructs of masculinity upheld within a particular culture. For example, Tony talks about how being disabled was seen to exclude him from the expectations placed upon able-bodied Greek boys and men:

> The disability totally threw into chaos the whole Greek expectation that your parents will have of you getting married, you know, doing the whole family deal . . . because of my disability those expectations just go away or probably won't be raised.
>
> (Tony, 24 years)

Having a disability may also mean that the boy considers himself to be part of a disability culture that is the Other to the Central able-bodied culture. This was the experience of Bryce, who located himself within 'the deaf culture' with its own language. He was also aware of how he bordered the often conflicting duality of the deaf and hearing cultures. He wanted to belong to both and move fluidly between and within each culture, utilizing the communication skills of both 'signing and talking' rather than having to choose one form of language:

> There's a school that's just for the deaf. I don't feel comfortable with that, you're always hanging around deafies in that school. There are deaf people in the deaf world and the hearing world, I'm in both. I can sign and talk. To different people I talk differently . . . some people in the deaf culture didn't want my brother to teach me English because it's more like a hearing culture and not a deaf culture. My brother knows both cultures – hearing and deaf. I learned that from TV and books and teachers. It's like an Aboriginal culture and a white people culture.
>
> (Bryce, 13 years)

For boys who are disabled and same-sex attracted, they are twice removed from the polarity of 'normal' masculinity and able-bodied 'abnormal' homosexual masculinity. Their physical 'abnormalities' may be seen as compounded and intertwined with sexual 'abnormality' (Rivlin 1980; Rich 1994). The denial or invisibility of homosexuality is greatly exacerbated within education for the disabled. School sex education programmes seldom address homosexuality, let alone in relation to disability, so for young people with disabilities, the articulation of their sexuality with their disability may be especially problematic (Marks 1996; Tepper 1999). Tony discusses the interweaving of his homosexuality and disability within his overall borderland experiences of being on the fringes:

> I see my sexuality as very problematic to me because it's never really been affirmed in any way by any group so that I feel good about it. I am just going back into not identifying as a gay man anymore, you know, because I was rejected by the heterosexual community, and I didn't get accepted by the gay community and so, why did I ever bother coming here?
>
> (Tony, 24 years)

Tony highlights how his disability has resulted in his sexual expression and desire being denied by both the heterosexual and gay communities, thereby forcing him to inhabit an asexual space of limbo in which his alienation and isolation are further accentuated.

'I just keep it a secret at school'

School as a site of stigmatization of disabilities

As boys with disabilities have illustrated, a school is a potentially disabling site due to its lack of flexibility in accommodating a diverse range of student attributes. The source of students' difficulties is seen to reside in their disabilities rather than the limitations of schooling structures and normalized social hierarchies (Robillard and Fichten 1983; Christensen 1996). Indeed, for several boys in our research who were personally involved with people with physical disabilities outside the school site – either with family members or as part of their community – the school was a site of silence about these relationships due to the potentially problematic consequences for the boy in relation to his social status. For example, Darren, 16 years, spoke about his volunteer community work as a personal care attendant with the visually impaired, which he does with his mother. However, he does not talk about his volunteer work at school and indeed avoids people with disabilities at school, even when knowing that some are facing harassment.

Max, 16 years, whose brother has schizophrenia, also expressed his belief that there should be education on physical disabilities and mental health in order to demystify and dispel certain myths, and so that other students could have the understanding he has. He also maintains his worlds of home and school as separate in order to avoid harassment due to the inferiorization of his social status that he believes would eventuate if he told people about his brother: 'They should teach about that [disabilities and mental health issues], I've never heard anything in my whole time at school . . . because even to talk about it is shocking. I just keep it a secret at school' (Max, 16 years).

Most existing literature on education and disability, including the literature which acknowledges and critiques the social construction of disability, is seen as having left intact the disabled/abled dichotomy and rendering students with disabilities as a homogeneous group. Several students believed that schools needed to teach students about the various types of disability, as both teachers and students were ignorant of such diversity. Andrew spoke about preferring to tell people himself about his cerebral palsy as he found that teachers' ignorance only created confusion and mistaken constructions of his disability:

> Some teachers will get it wrong and people will get the assumption that maybe I'm mentally disabled. At school, people could actually educate people not just on disability but different levels of disability, to say you don't need to be in a wheelchair to be disabled, and you don't necessarily have to be any different other than in your physical capabilities than anybody else.
>
> (Andrew, 16 years)

In the following, Abdu describes how students had been educated about his condition before he arrived at the school. This made such a difference to how he felt about being at school and the way other students related to him. His friend, Serdan, confirms this by talking about how the Turkish Muslim boys had phoned each other the night before to discuss 'this Turkish dwarf boy' who was coming to school. The school also had affirming strategies in place such as welcoming and congratulating Abdu for settling well into school via the school newsletter. Thus, a public openness about Abdu, together with education about his condition and how other students could support him, had dispelled any notions of stigma and the need for silence:

> Abdu: When I first came [to the school] I went to my class and straight away everyone knew me. I didn't know anyone but for some reason everyone knew that I was coming. The teacher actually told them.
>
> Serdan: My friend phoned me up and that's what everyone did, about this Turkish dwarf boy coming to this school, so that's how I reckon everyone knew about him. (Serdan, 16 years)
>
> Abdu: The first week in the newsletter there was a message saying congratulations to Abdu for fitting in this school straight away.
>
> (Abdu, 16 years)

It needs to be stated that such openness around disabilities was supported and contextualized by a whole school approach regarding all kinds of diversity. Deconstruction of the stigma of disability and a recognition of its intersection with other socio-cultural factors such as gender, ethnicity and sexuality allows for flexible analysis and policy formulation which is responsive to the multiple, intersecting and constantly shifting interests and allegiances of the student population:

> Just as widespread segregation failed to deliver socially just educational programs to many students with disabilities, the simple wholesale return of those students to regular classrooms without a basic transformation of those classrooms will similarly fail to provide social justice to all students . . . In such a practice students are not seen as disabled, defective or disordered. Rather, all students are seen as different, complex and whole. All students are recognized as reflecting a diversity of cultural, social, racial, physical, [gendered] and intellectual identities.
>
> (Christensen 1996: 76–7; see also Hastings 1996)

Most students with disabilities in our research, however, appreciated having separate spaces within the integrated school wherein they could mix with peers and gain special educational support. Sometimes these spaces were also seen as having intra-hierarchies based on the severity and type of disabilities. Thus, 13-year-old Bryce's construction of a hierarchy of disabilities, with hearing impairment being more 'normal' than other disabilities, was framed by a system whereby disabilities were split into two: 'There's two rooms, one is the Integration Room and then there's a Deaf Room up the top.'

Other students with disabilities, who also appreciated the Integration Room and its support staff, did raise concerns that, although they appreciated the special care of the integration facilitators, at times they were patronized, robbed of independence, or treated as a homogeneous group, as is evident in the words of Sam. He also wants the school to educate able-bodied students about disabilities, although he expresses his embarrassment at being present if they are talking about him:

> Integration Room is good. All the integration kids use it, they have the aides in there and books. I just go there sometimes instead of to class. It's good to be able to come up and do the work. But I had a bit of trouble with the aides. They try and make me get on with the others in the Integration Room, but the problem is that we have different opinions and ideas. Aides should treat us as individuals and old enough to make our own decisions. They should not treat me like a kid. They think it is their job to have a say in my decisions. If it's a physical disability we need physical things done for us and not have our decisions made for us. If the kids don't do work then it's their fault, no one else would be responsible. Teachers patronize you. It's a bit like they talk to little kids sometimes, like I'm stupid or something. They actually don't know how to talk to people in wheelchairs. Maybe schools can get other people to come in and talk, make it part of what they're studying. A visiting teacher came and had a talk to the class. I wasn't there actually. I stayed home.

> It's embarrassing to be there when the class is being taught about my disability.
>
> (Sam, 16 years)

Haseeb was the only student with a disability who preferred the school not to talk about his disability with other students:

> I know what schools do, in kindness, to try to tell other students, 'This person has a problem, do care about him'. But I think this thing isn't helpful in that it makes you feel that you are very different. I don't want to talk about my leg problem too often. Sometimes you don't want to remember that you are actually different in some physical manner. Sometimes I want to forget all about my problem in the leg and want to rather think about things which are positive side of the picture. But when I am suddenly told that I am not the same as the others are, my concentration is lost.
>
> (Haseeb, 22 years)

Conclusion

Overall, it is apparent that boys with physical disabilities are faced with unique conflicts around their masculine identities at school. This is clearly a result of a normative regime of masculinity that affirms and valorizes many of the characteristics that physical disability may take away, including independence, physical strength and (hetero)sexual prowess. The conflict forces boys to rely on, reformulate and/or reject this regime of normalizing practices. In this chapter, therefore, we have drawn attention to the interweaving of masculinity, ethnicity and sexuality for boys who live with disabilities and who are positioned and position themselves within hierarchies informed by a particular sex/gender system.

PART 3
Sites of Intervention

9 'There's no opportunity for guys to get down and think about what they're doing and why they are doing it'

Boys interrogating 'masculinity' in schools

Some people, in reading our work, can't believe that boys would talk about masculinity in this critical way. There is always the implication that it is 'our agenda' driving what the boys say. But some boys told us that they weren't given the opportunity or didn't feel safe to talk about their experiences outside of being policed and regulated by peers and teachers. For example, what is often passed off as boys just joking and having fun is understood differently by some boys who, in the private, safe space of an interview talk about feelings of discomfort and harassment. Some boys even pointed out to us that they wouldn't have been able to talk about these kinds of things if their peers had been present.

We see our research as a dialogue with young people. Of course, our own values and attitudes do play a role in terms of the kinds of questions we ask. However, boys did critically interrogate when we asked general questions relating to school, friends and life. The issue for us is that certain questions are not asked at school and there are so many silences that need to be broken. However, when they are broken in our research, there is a tendency to delegitimate what we say and to essentialize what we say in terms of having a particular kind of agenda!

There is often this question about our focus on homophobia. In evaluations on our presentations we often receive comments indicating that we have placed too much emphasis on homophobia in our discussion about the impact of masculinities on boys' lives at school. In fact, in one presentation that we jointly conducted for teachers from rural and isolated schools, many of the teachers denied that homophobia was a problem. In fact, some male teachers even asserted that the problem of hierarchical masculinities and the 'cool boy' phenomena was not an issue at their school – that high achieving boys and sporty boys were equally valued.

So the problem for us is one of denial, on the one hand, and constructing particular realities, on the other, which negate the impact of sexuality on the policing of masculinities in boys' lives at school. We know that asking certain questions leads to the production of certain knowledges, but the point for us is that important questions are not asked. We are interested in raising issues about why certain questions are not asked, what happens when we do ask them, and whose agenda is driving the kinds of silences which are broken when we ask other kinds of questions.

Introduction

Many of the boys we interviewed were willing to interrogate the impact and effects of normative masculinity on their lives at school (see Martino 2001; Martino and Pallotta-Chiarolli 2001a). In this chapter we are concerned to analyse these boys' attempts to do so and the extent of their understanding of the social practices of masculinity and its implications for teaching boys. While some boys were able to draw on knowledge about 'masculinity' as a socially constructed practice, it will be demonstrated that others still draw on developmental theories of maturity to account for the way boys behave. There were also some boys who were hesitant and reluctant to respond to the question we asked them about their understanding of masculinity, but others were prepared to discuss 'masculinity' and its effects in schools, indicating that opportunities for them to do so had not been provided (Pallotta-Chiarolli 1997). Our research indicates that many boys were willing to discuss their experiences of 'masculinity' and did not resist our attempts to encourage them to reflect on such issues. Hence, in this chapter, we explore:

1. *Hegemonic masculinity as being beyond interrogation:* how boys respond to the invitation to define and interrogate the 'taken-for-grantedness' of hegemonic heterosexual masculinity (Frank 1987; Jackson 1998; Davison 2000).
2. *The binary classification of expressing emotions as either normal or abnormal gendered behaviour for boys:* how boys are aware of heteronormative and gendernormative constructions of emotions such as anger, aggression, grief and sensitivity.
3. *School as a site for interrogating masculinities:* how boys might be encouraged to interrogate and move beyond normative constructions of masculinity (Salisbury and Jackson 1996; Martino and Meyenn 2001; Mills 2001).

'That's just the way it is'

Hegemonic masculinity as beyond interrogation

A number of boys, when asked to explain what they understood masculinity to mean, were stumped. For example, Jarrod, from a single-sex Catholic school, illustrates the difficulties some boys experienced in responding to such a question:

Maria: When you think of the word masculinity, what kind of images come into your head?
Jarrod: I don't know [*laughing*].
Maria: Why are you laughing?
Jarrod: It's just a weird question, I don't know how to answer it.
Maria: I guess another way of putting it would be, what do you think society expects a man to be?
Jarrod: Somebody who loves cars, sort of thing.
Maria: And when you think about yourself, are you being the kind of guy that society expects you to be?
Jarrod: Yes, I reckon I am.
Maria: In what way?
Jarrod: Enjoy the company of girls, talk about cars a lot.
Maria: Why do guys talk about cars a lot?
Jarrod: I don't know, it's just a thing they do.
Maria: Do you know where it's coming from?
Jarrod: No.

(Jarrod, 16 years)

As Connell writes, 'critical autobiography is a key form of pedagogy' in the field of masculinity studies: 'bringing one's own history of gender practices into view is an important step in changing those practices' (1998: iii). Yet, as many of the boys such as Jarrod above experienced in their schooling or in their own reluctance, ignorance or discomfort in addressing hegemonic masculinity, 'there is a resistance to awareness, a motivated unknowing' (in Hickey et al. 1998: iii):

> It is frightening, even dangerous, for one cannot know one's gender practice, in the sense of reflective self-investigation, without becoming aware that it could be otherwise, that other paths were possible. The stability of one's own gendered being is called into question.
>
> (Connell in Hickey et al. 1998: iv)

Chris, also from a single-sex Catholic boys' school, reveals an uncertainty about defining masculinity but then proceeds to identify specific norms that influence the way males behave: 'I'm not sure [what it means to be male] . . . like someone that's really, really tough kind of thing, they think they're the top of everyone' (Chris, 16 years).

The following is a further example of hesitation in responding to the question of interrogating masculinity. Bora, of Turkish Muslim background, talks about a masculinity 'formula':

> Bora: When you say guy, maybe it's equal to hero, for a guy you've got to be a hero, that's their formula in their head [*pauses and shrugs*].
> Maria: And what does it mean to be a hero then?
> Bora: To be tough.
> Maria: Where do you think they're getting these images from?
> Bora: I don't know.
>
> (Bora, 16 years)

Once again, like Jarrod, Bora does not have access to important knowledge about how social attitudes of masculinity are formed. Another Turkish Muslim student, Mustafa, also hesitates in explaining the justification behind a normative construction of gendered relations of power and protection: 'Well, protecting your wife, something like that . . . You got the man thing to do, what can I say, like you have to protect your wife from other people. I just can't explain. It's too hard' (Mustafa, 15 years).

Aaron explores the constructions around masculinity that he is unable to interrogate, although he is aware that they emanate from within his family:

> Well, people think guys are supposed to be wonderful, but they're mainly not that wonderful. For example, like my dad, when I was living with him, when he used to hit my mum, he used to walk into my room and say, 'Oh, stop crying, stop bawling your eyes out, come on be a man.' I'm like four to nine years old, and he's saying 'Come on, be a man!' and I kept on thinking and thinking for years and years. I'm still thinking about it, and what I've been thinking about is how can you be a man without you having to be a boy first.
>
> (Aaron, 14 years)

Here Aaron raises issues about masculinity, violence and power (Mills 2001). He draws attention to the particular role his father has played in trying to enforce a particular version of masculinity built on a rejection of certain forms of emotionality read as weakness.

'I've never thought about it'

Many boys, however, when asked to explain what they understood about 'masculinity', indicated that they had not been encouraged to think about such issues, but were prepared to engage in and to reflect critically on the social expectations of being a boy. One boy, Shaun who attended a Catholic coeducational school, appeared to be stumped by the question. He is asked initially to explain what he thinks life is like as a male:

> Shaun: I've never thought about that type of a question because I've never been confronted with thinking about it . . . I've never had to sit there and go, 'Why did I act this way? Why did I act that way? How am I supposed to act?' I've never thought about what it feels like being a male, because I sure as hell don't know what it feels like being a female, but it's hard to explain what it is.
>
> Wayne: Maybe if I ask you what do you understand about masculinity? Does that make it easier?
>
> Shaun: . . . another reason that I probably won't be able to answer that question is because guys don't talk about their emotions, and I don't like to sit there and think about my emotions. But the things that I can talk about to get the kind of idea of what it is like being a male is my experiences or problems I have with it and the problems I have with other people. And so mostly [*pauses*] hmm, being a male? Umm [*pauses*] I haven't really thought about it, but I have got some sort of idea I suppose of what masculinity would be. It's pretty hard because when people say 'masculinity', straight away I think of the big strong guy who doesn't cry, who will stand up and he will work his guts out. I suppose there's a lot of stuff in the media and the world that has shaped my ideas of being a male.
>
> (Shaun, 16 years)

Here, Shaun emphasizes that he has never been confronted with a question explicitly requiring him to reflect on how masculinity is defined and by whom. However, he is able to articulate what he understands to be the normative ties between certain practices, such as 'guys not talking about their emotions', 'guys not crying', displaying physical strength, working hard, and what constitutes behaving in acceptable or desirable masculine ways (Coleman 1990). Shaun proceeds to use the space of the interview to try to sort through his understandings:

> It's kind of almost a question that I don't know if anyone could be right about and no one could know the answer to. I suppose being a male is just like being a person and the only thing that really makes you male is having your testicles and your penis and being totally different from a female. And I suppose because of that, guys and girls think differently as well, because of our physical shape and other aspects. I suppose I wouldn't be as emotional as another female to a son or a daughter . . . You know, how a mother gives birth to their child and they have that with them and they breastfeed. Like that almost deceives me on what I am

> meant to think about and what I am not meant to think about. It's a very good question, but I just find that it's hard to explain it, if you know what I mean?
>
> (Shaun, 16 years)

Thus, at first, Shaun appears to be appealing to essentialist discourses of biology to explain what he understands about masculinity. On one level, he seems to suggest that the only real differences between males and females are biological, and implies that this should have no impact on the way men and women behave and relate. However, on another level, his confusion stems from an understanding that capacities for nurturing and expressing emotion are somehow grounded in the reproductive differences between males and females. The practices of women giving birth and breastfeeding are linked to what may be interpreted as a 'maternal bond' between mother and child – one, apparently, which a male could never establish in quite the same way.

It is interesting to note that many boys classify expressing emotion in gendered binary terms. For instance, crying, feeling afraid or vulnerable are constructed as unsuitable for males to express, whereas feelings of anger and aggression are interpreted as legitimate expressions of masculinity to the extent that they are not even classified as emotions. This is not dissimilar to the way that whiteness has been naturalized and thereby erased as a category for interrogation (Dyer 1997). There is a splitting of anger and aggression from the category of emotion which is cast and 'othered' as the realm of the feminine.

In the following excerpt, Shaun appears to be indicating that there are social influences that account for the formation of what he understands masculinity to be:

> . . . thoughts of masculinity, or thoughts of being a female, I don't know if people could have figured it out for themselves because there's so much stuff going on in the media. If someone says, 'What's your idea on masculinity?', I could have straight away said, 'Oh, I'm a "snag", I try to deal with my emotions and stuff like that.' I suppose that thinking about being masculine is almost like saying that males and females have differences. They've got obvious differences because of the way the world has led them to think. But on a totally different scale, they think the same and they kind of look out for the same thing, they want to be most successful in life, have kids and they want to have a house, or they want to be famous. When you come to school people are just people, so it means guys and girls are the same, they are just pupils. If you take them out of class and the guys do guys' things and the girls do girls' things, that's where a lot of the differences come out.
>
> (Shaun, 16 years)

Shaun indicates that boys and girls are required to engage in different sets of practices which confer either masculinity or femininity. But, here, such gender differences are linked to the social influences of the media and to enforced institutional practices in schools which lead to girls and boys being separated. However, it is important to note the interweaving discourses of liberal humanism, social construction of gender and essentialist notions of gender duality that inform the rationality deployed by Shaun. In asserting that boys and girls are similar in their aspirations, he asserts a heteronormative and classed subjectivity, while proceeding simultaneously to interrogate the heteronormative and gendernormative separation of boys and girls enforced by schools:

> People [at school] use a lot of the references like, 'If you don't do this, you're a fag'. I remember one teacher . . . on one of those Student Leader camps. They had a fake student council meeting and someone brought up the topic of hair and I said straight away 'You know, instead of making two different rules, why don't we just have one rule like "Tie it up in a ponytail"?' A teacher stood up straightaway – he was a male – and he said, 'If you're going to have long hair in a ponytail, obviously you've got something wrong with your head, obviously you're gay or something like that', [he] said it outright. There's always going to be people [who say] 'You do this, you're gay'. And if a girl does something, 'She's a butch'. So there's this expectation that the guy shouldn't try to delve into the female things and the females shouldn't delve into the male things and they should just stick to their own. And that's the thing that sets us apart and really kind of almost stuffs it up.
>
> (Shaun, 16 years)

Thus, while initially stating that gender differences are grounded in biology, Shaun moves to a position of examining the impact of social and cultural practices in enforcing the oppositional categorization of masculinity and femininity. He draws attention to the role of a teacher's homophobic strategies for policing and patrolling sex/gender boundaries for boys. It is particularly significant that Shaun notes in his interview that the questions posed by the researcher about 'masculinity' had never been addressed at school. He has difficulty at first responding to such questions because pedagogical spaces for interrogating masculinities in these terms have not been made available to him at school.

'Boys become mature as they get older'

Dave, attending the same school as Shaun, also attempts to explain his understanding of the differences between boys and girls and uses certain gender categories to do so. However, tied to his philosophy is the view that as boys get older, they develop more maturity and, hence, a greater capacity for transcending enforced sex/gender boundaries:

> Generally about age 15 or 16, I'd say that boys would share a relationship that would be maturing, definitely noticeably different from say ages 13, 14 . . . they are more mature and more accepting and the boundaries that groups set are less defined. That 'footballer' group, the very masculine attitude group, if they were to expand their boundaries, there would not be so much emphasis put on being physically attractive, sporty, charming, attractive to the opposite sex. They would expand and they might value intelligence more and would add something like the talents of a musician, or someone in the arts who is able to communicate, or good at public speaking . . . they could add that sort of credential to their lists. I think boys' attitudes towards each other in a friendship are not so much influenced by girls but their list of objectives or credentials needed.
>
> (Dave, 16 years)

On one level, it would appear that Dave is mobilizing developmental discourses of maturity to account for changes in the ways that boys learn to relate which, he argues, occurs at ages 15 or 16. Thus, a certain age appears to function as a threshold for developing a wider range of behaviours and an acceptance of themselves outside the limits of a set of credentials for dictating the exclusivity of a particular form of heterosexual masculinity. It is interesting that this observation does not appear to be supported by other boys' comments in terms of their reference to the practices, particularly of the 'footballers'.

Dave's use of the word 'credential' is also significant, demonstrating an understanding of the norms operating within a regime of practices in which the arts are differentiated as sex-inappropriate for boys (Armstrong 1988; Martino 1994, 1997). His comments about boys' policing of masculinity being governed not so much by the surveillance of girls as by the credentials established by other boys, is significant. It illustrates the extent to which masculinity is heavily policed by other boys and not girls (see Hulse 1997). Once again what we see is evidence of a range of interweaving and contradictory discourses which inform Dave's interrogation of social practices of masculinity. While drawing on essentialist discourses to account for age-related differences in boys' interactions with one another, he still appropriates a critical discourse of masculinity to reject what he identifies as the masculine credentials informing the footballers' social relationships.

Dave mentions his own experiences with his best friend, Paul, as a basis for explaining further the social relationships between boys. While he states that there are differences in that he is more 'creative' and his friend more 'mathematical', he suggests that they have a level of maturity which allows them to relate and accept the other's differences:

> We accept each other's faults and weaknesses, and value trust and honesty, and being able to listen to each other when we need to. [These things] are important in a relationship, not credentials, but there are still barriers that were in place when we were 12, 13, 14 years of age, which have not been brought down.
>
> (Dave, 16 years)

Thus, Dave appears to be drawing a distinction between a friendship based on 'masculine' credentials or attitudes – certain requirements such as those needed to publicly validate a heterosexual masculinity – and one based on certain values such as trust, honesty and the capacity to listen and to support one another, which is how he describes his relationship with his best friend. But while he has a close relationship with his friend, he comments that there are still a few barriers that 'have not been broken down'. He talks about still being reserved about 'displaying emotions and putting up a shield' and how these still exist in his relationship with his best friend where there are barriers which he defines as 'sort of invisible emotions that we keep out of view'. Such barriers are tied to Dave's understanding of what he terms 'power plays' with Paul which are linked to a set of norms around which a particular competitive masculinity is established. He claims, for instance, that 'power is not such an issue for girls' in their relationships with one another, as a basis for differentiating what his friendship with Paul is like. It is important to stress that he appears to be talking about a particular kind of power associated with the social practices of competitive masculinity:

> It is not such an issue for girls, to have power is not as important in their friendships. I see it with guys whenever say both students do science and they are friends, and if one does slightly better. I know guys my age go through that type of thing whether it be academic, sporting, even social. 'I've got a girlfriend who may be physically more attractive than your girlfriend, who's more intelligent than your girlfriend', meaning he's got the pick of the crop and you've got the dregs. I expect a more mature attitude from girls. When I see girls communicate with each other,

> the way they do it, it's very non-threatening, there's very little sense of power. They never talk about test scores, 'How did you go in that race? Where did you come?' It's more 'How are you? Is everything all right at home?' – very much more at a personal level, and the barriers are definitely not as high.
>
> (Dave, 16 years)

In drawing attention to the role that competition plays in the way that he relates to his friend, despite the fact that he claims they have a close relationship, Dave confines such practices to boys which he differentiates from the relationships that girls have with one another. His references to power differentials in interpersonal modes of communication that are adopted by girls are noteworthy. He claims that there is 'very little sense of power' in the way that he sees girls relating to one another. At this point in the interview he states outright that such differences are related to differential levels of maturity between boys and girls which are genetically determined or inherited: 'I think the best I could come up with is that they are more mature just genetically, hereditarily, they are more mature. Apparently it's been proven.'

While Dave has acquired highly sophisticated capacities for interrogating the social practices and effects of masculinity in which he and other boys are implicated, there are still some slippages in the interweaving of social and essentialist discourses that inform his understanding of these practices. In light of this, it would appear that making available more knowledge about the social construction of masculinities for adolescent boys might prove to be a useful and necessary undertaking in terms of helping them to understand their own behaviour and ways of relating. This relates to research undertaken by Lingard et al. (2000) who argue that effective or what they term 'productive pedagogies' are dependent upon requisite teacher threshold knowledges about gender. Other dimensions to productive pedagogies include creating a supportive environment, connectedness or relevance of curriculum to students' lives, intellectual demandedness and recognition of difference (see Lingard and Mills 2000).

'You can get angry as long as you punch someone and not cry'

The need to access knowledge about the social construction of masculinity is also highlighted in our interviews with boys who discussed the issue of expressing emotions. At times some of the boys slipped into a problematic binary with the emotions that a 'normal' boy can feel being set in opposition to those which designate a boy as an inappropriate or 'border male'. Many boys, for example, wanted to talk about what could be constructed as the binary debate of 'to cry or not to cry' dilemma. Max articulates his discomfort with the non-emotional performance that boys are expected to maintain. He also discusses how girls are implicated and support this expectation: 'If you like a girl, you've always got to make the first move. And you've got to be sort of non-emotional, not cry and sort of be tough and fearless. I can't really cry in public or can't really cry anywhere because I've never really been able to' (Max, 16 years).

Daniel explains how crying is associated with homosexuality, even when it is a reaction to a painful injury: 'Some people think that if you're a male you got to be real tough, not cry, you're not allowed to be poofy . . . [I think you should be] allowed to cry, that's why God made you cry. I was hit in the head with a golfball and I was crying and everyone reckons I was poofy' (Daniel, 14 years).

Mick discusses the issue of crying on the occasion of the accidental death of a schoolfriend. His comments raise the issue of the legitimacy of crying given tragic circumstances such as those involving the death of a friend:

> Well, because I'm in a boarding house I have a few friends here and they felt pretty bad about it as well. I cried with them a fair bit. I think crying is really important and that you have to do it, I see no problem with it personally. [You] definitely need to talk about it and let yourself think about it, let yourself cry, don't feel ashamed to ask for help because everyone wants to grieve in their own way and they shouldn't be stopped by anything in any way, especially talk to your other close friends and reminisce.
>
> (Mick, 16 years)

Mick's friend, Gavin, also spoke about the need to openly grieve for the friend who had died, but highlights explicitly how the social practices of masculinity are more broadly implicated in boys' rejection of expressivity:

> At the assembly I was crying away and all the boys were sort of whimpering away . . . I don't like it how I can suddenly start crying. But I think it's better to cry at the time than to bottle it in, which I know a lot of my friends have been doing. I suppose they want to seem all strong and like they can handle everything, you know, the old 'I'm a man', sort of thing.
>
> (Gavin, 16 years)

From the same Catholic single-sex school, Alex spoke about a Retreat programme where boys are challenged to express their emotions and engage with each other intimately, such as in a religious ritual of washing and massaging each other's feet as symbolic of what Christ did to his disciples at the 'Last

Supper'. While being seen as transgressing the gendernormative 'comfort zones' of the boys, Alex's comments reveal that it works because it is made clear that the heteronormative 'comfort zones' are not transgressed. It is assumed that these boys are all heterosexual and participating in a ritual of friendship within which there is no possibility of homoerotic desire. And of course, this ritual is occurring outside the normative boundaries of schooling for boys on what is significantly called a 'Retreat'. In his interrogation of boys' engagement in this practice, Alex gives two examples of the tensions which boys experience in transgressing and negotiating the dangerous divide where perceived straight/gay classifications blur on the borders. First, he reconstructs the whole ritual of massaging each other's feet as being about taking on a challenge which has the effect of erasing the embodied and intimate dimensions of touching and its association with homoeroticism. Second, the need to 'trust' someone with massaging the feet involves some tribulation. This is related to the need for boys to maintain a sense of impervious heterosexual masculinity when confronted with not just merely touching the feet of another boy, but with being placed in a vulnerable position of engaging in the sensual practice of massaging:

> I think that the washing of the feet was one example where they tried to break down the sense of 'I'm male, I don't show my feelings'. It's extremely significant, the whole Retreat builds towards that sort of final humiliation . . . not in a bad way, but to show that you need to feel emotion. When you're a boy, because of the masculinity thing, you can't show excess emotion. You find a lot of guys are really affected by that . . . a lot of them are reluctant to do it [wash and massage each other's feet] at first, and some don't. But I think it's a significant step to do that. You've got to admire the guys for doing it because you've got to move outside that sort of comfort zone that you built around yourself – 'I won't do that, and I won't touch another guy'. If you realize that it's not about touching, it's about doing something that you would otherwise not do. You have to trust someone else to massage your feet, it's a big trust. Guys don't acknowledge their friendship and camaraderie with touch. I think so many guys were apprehensive, especially in a school like ours where it's an all boys school. Particularly for a lot of guys who are boarders and in a close environment with a lot of other guys, that's very sensitive. You've got to be very careful . . . the comment of a lot of people was 'I don't want to do that because people might think I'm gay'. There's a big consciousness about not acting in a manner that could be interpreted as being gay. A lot of them thought it was a really worthwhile exercise and they enjoyed it because it's meant to be relaxing as well, when you're getting your feet massaged.
>
> (Alex, 16 years)

Another interesting facet is the use of the word 'humiliation' to define the possibly perceived debasement of pride or descent down the hierarchical ladder of hegemonic rational masculinity in order to experience intimacy between boys. However, this 'humiliation' is seen as having a positive meaning in its breaking of masculinist pride and 'coolness' to reveal the emotional nurturing and intimate self beneath that performance:

> It's a very humiliating experience actually for guys who find it hard to say to other people what they really think of them, and to compliment them and to receive it back is very difficult as well, especially from a male. It's quite powerful and a lot of guys cry, and it's a really sort of emotional time and it's symbolic of a humiliation. You're made to feel special, but also humiliated, not in a bad way. The whole purpose of that is that you come out of that a different person and hopefully a changed person, you just appreciate things more.
>
> (Alex, 16 years)

It is important to note here that homophobia emerges as a major obstacle for boys in developing more nurturing and expressive relationships with one another. What is even more significant is the capacity that Alex has for interrogating these social practices of masculinity. In fact, he goes on to discuss that, despite the positive experience of developing intimate and close relationships with other boys on the Retreat, this did not generally carry on into the boys' lives once they had returned to their everyday existence at school. This, he indicates, is a result of the perceptions and attitudes that many of the boys at school have regarding the ways in which boys are expected to behave and relate:

> Generally, they didn't really discuss what was done on the Retreat. I don't know if they were more comfortable with touching after that, but certainly they appreciated the significance of what happened and they certainly didn't have any remorse or any bad reaction to what had happened on that weekend. There are a lot of guys who still are going to be very conscious about the way they act, what they say, which is why I think the Retreat is good because at least you can try, if you give it a go, you're always going to get at least some who will become more comfortable with who they are.
>
> (Alex, 16 years)

However, while Alex is adamant about the positive effects of the Retreat in helping the boys to get more in touch with their emotions, and to develop more satisfying relationships, he appears to be implying that the kinds of social relationships encouraged within the space of the Retreat need to be developed within the broader whole school context. More specific interrogation at school is needed to break down the 'cool image' that guys feel compelled to establish and maintain. For example, Alex argues that 'it's difficult these days to find out where you stand, especially in this school, everyone is very conscious about acting in the right way, not to be cool just more not to be gay'. In fact, he seems to be indicating that such 'cool' behaviour is either legitimated at school or remains naturalized amongst boys and, hence, is uninterrogated:

> They don't know what they're feeling at the moment, it's like somewhere where they've never been before and it does definitely jolt them out of any sort of self-pride they feel. For a lot of guys the cool image of themselves gets broken down through a humiliation like that. But for a lot of guys it's so hard to describe the change you see in them but they do become a lot more appreciative of everything. You see a lot of the old barriers come up which are almost necessary at school to look after themselves but with their friends some of them are a lot more personal and I think that friendships benefit from that. [But] there's still probably a need to defend yourself, to maintain a certain stance of yourself because some people just aren't ready for what you feel and what you think and who you really are.
>
> (Alex, 16 years)

Alex reiterates how boys' social practices of masculinity are implicated in panopticonic regimes of self-surveillance and how this impacts in significant ways on boys' social relationships and their capacities to develop emotional literacy with other boys.

Ben, straight-identifying, whose passion for drama studies, bouts of depression and attempted suicides also positioned him outside of hegemonic masculinity, was able to clearly discuss normative gendered performances, particularly in situations of violence and harassment:

> Don't get me started. Just the word makes me mad. Masculinity is nothing but a concept. It isn't real, it doesn't really exist. Men are supposed to aspire to it, but are all incapable of doing so. How can males be expected not to hurt or break with all the crap and injustice that goes on in our world? Masculinity is a cruel concept dreamed up by some ancient sadistic psychopath as a way of oppressing men and making them feel inadequate. It must be challenged! What I've come across, so far, in the school situation is for boys to be 'tough'. You can punch someone's head in or have your head punched in, but you can never cry or talk it out. You're expected to swear and be rude, to drink and get involved with drugs and all that crap, that I've never especially been interested in.

> There's a whole big contradiction in society at the moment. Men are now expected to have strength of character, conscience and sensitivity while still having the above 'macho' qualities. If you can't do that then you're not a 'man'. How can you be expected to maintain a balance of such extremes? You can't.
>
> (Ben, 17 years)

He draws attention to how populist discourses of hegemonic masculinity have a major part to play in how males understand what he perceives to be irreconcilable polarities of macho masculinity, on the one hand, and a sensitive masculinity, on the other.

In defining what it means to be a man, John, an Indigenous boy, also rejects biological essentialist notions of gender (Petersen 1998) and associates 'masculinity' with particular moral, ethical attributes of being able to make a stand (see Mangan and Walvin 1987). His analogy of the mother bird taking 'little birds' under her wing, as a means by which to explicate his own definition of a nurturing masculinity, is a powerful statement, indicating that not all boys subscribe to or invest in macho masculinity:

> Well, what I think would be a man is maybe not having the thing between your legs but having a stand. Knowing what to do when situations go wrong to stand up and say 'Yes, I know what to do, I can do it'. Sort of be the big mother bird and take other little birds underneath your wing and show them what to do, show them how to fly, stuff like that.
>
> (John, 17 years)

In the following John highlights how traditional notions of masculinity inform Indigenous boys' definitions of what it means to be male. He also seems to be emphasizing how hierarchical gendered power relations, in the form of a pecking order of masculinities, impinges on Indigenous boys and the ways in which they define and negotiate their masculinities (see Sewell 1998; Davis 2001). This is made clear when John comments that it is probably harder for Indigenous boys because they also have to deal with the racialized context in which Aboriginality is represented and defined (Langton 1993), as well as dealing with the legacy of colonialist logic which persists into the present (Longley 1995; Beresford and Omaji 1996; Aveling 1998):

> Maybe [growing up as a guy] for Indigenous boys is probably harder. It depends on how people react to Indigenous boys. Like I said, you don't really know the true story . . . It's probably like they get a different story from another person, but they're all negative points and they don't really know the true story about it. I think it's hard for boys to express themselves because boys think, 'Oh he's a girl', getting all mushie. But I think

> that boys should express themselves more to get things off their chest because maybe something has happened and they could end up killing themselves, suicide and stuff like that.
>
> (John, 17 years)

John frames the binary categorization of gender, informing the ways in which many boys behave and define their masculinities, as a kind of a trap which can lead to suicide. Because of the pressures and problems that this creates, John advocates an alternative practice of masculinity in his assertion that 'boys should express themselves more to get things off their chest'.

'You see this other version of masculinity'

Interrogating masculinities in schools

As is already evident, a number of boys were willing to engage in discussions about masculinity and its effects on their lives. Shaun, for example, refers to a story called 'Manhood' which he was required to analyse in class by one of the researchers (see Mellor et al. 1991). It is about a father who wants his son to grow up as a man and to be active in sports, despite the latter's lack of interest or desire to engage in such practices:

> Wayne: I wanted to ask you about that story we did in class, 'Manhood', because that talked a bit about the expectations that were placed on this guy by his father to be a man and the pressures involved in that. Do you think more kinds of discussions like that would be useful in getting guys to think about expectations and masculinity? Did the story make you think about maybe some of the pressures about being male in particular?
>
> Shaun: Yes, because I never came across something that talked about being a man or how you are meant to act, or how you are even expected to act. I suppose that in primary school everything's pretty much of a joke, you just go through it. I remember I came here pretty much not knowing anything . . . [right up till now] in Year 11 no one did anything, no one cared and they never said anything like about being guys or being girls or what they are meant to do. I never came across anything that had to do with how to be a man or how to act. I knew that there were expectations around, but I never openly talked about it or came across it. After the last interview I sat down and thought about it for a long time, sitting there talking to maybe anyone, my dad or my brother, my friends and there's no opportunity for guys to get down and think about what they're doing and why they are doing it.
>
> (Shaun, 16 years)

Shaun reiterates that he has not been given the opportunity to interrogate masculinity and appears to be advocating the need for this to be addressed in schools (see Martino 1995a, 2000b; Martino and Mellor 1995). Such strategies, however, need to be developed in accordance with a whole-school approach, committed to creating spaces for students to gain knowledge about masculinities and to assess the effects of social expectations in their lives (see Gilbert and Gilbert 1998). As Shaun indicated, studying a text such as 'Manhood' did appear to be useful in helping him to reflect on his own understanding of masculinity and its impact on his life.

Scott, who attends a Catholic single-sex school, also calls for schooling to encourage boys to think about masculinity as part of the mainstream curriculum and not as part of a Retreat programme, and thus symbolically and physically removed from the normative pedagogical practices of daily schooling. What is interesting about the following interview is the association of normative hegemonic masculinity with a nationalist mythological construction of Australian manhood. This is evident in the way Scott begins to use the Australian colloquial term, 'bloke', as he shifts into a discussion of what 'blokes' do not do while at school, but what Year 12s can do while on Retreat away from school:

> Scott: The Year 12s [Retreat leaders] all gave talks . . . and most of them were talking about the personal aspects of their lives. It was really enlightening to see that they could speak about themselves so freely, I thought that was a pretty admirable thing.
>
> Maria: Do you think that, apart from the Retreat, your school provides enough opportunity for guys to talk about these sorts of things?
>
> Scott: It's only once a year but the [Retreat] lasts a few days and you've got plenty of time, like all day is spent talking to each other. [There's] plenty of time to open up so if that's the sort of thing you want to do, there's plenty of opportunity for you.
>
> Maria: If the Retreats didn't do this, are there other ways? Does the school provide other ways for boys?
>
> Scott: Blokes don't usually talk about things like that. When you do start talking about some things . . . there is no way you would go into such detail as on these Retreats. I think it's just the blokey attitude being Australian . . . all they talk about is sport and cars and women. It's not really Australian to talk about feelings and stuff, especially blokes.
>
> (Scott, 17 years)

As Scott suggests, the school, as a particular institutionalized site of surveillance and regulation with its disciplinary and embodied practices and routines (Foucault 1979), does not appear to be particularly conducive to boys talking 'about themselves freely'. Yet Scott would also like to see his school provide more space to disrupt the 'blokey' masculinity as was successfully undertaken on Retreat:

> Having the same groups that we were in on Retreat, meet every couple of weeks just to talk about things. That could keep the major thing going and try and keep every one remembering what happened on the Retreat . . . not enough people go for that too much.
>
> (Scott, 17 years)

In fact, many boys were able to interrogate normative masculinity and to discuss its power and hierarchical domination in the school. In line with Schutz's (1944) theory of the 'outsider' coming into a community and challenging the 'taken-for-grantedness', Eric, from Hong Kong, was able to define a specific Australian construction of normative masculinity or 'play the whole fantasy' of what it means to be a superior male:

> It's the whole sort of mateship, playing football, being big, being decisive, being protective, being on top of the world . . . you shouldn't express your negative feelings. Ironically the only time that you're allowed to express your feeling is when you lose a football game, or your favourite football team has lost a game, or your favourite bloody football player or cricket player has retired. People cry in front of the bloody camera, in front of the TV screen – which I think is so stupid if you ask me. In Australia, if you're Anglo, male, who sort of fits in all those things, they're obviously seen as really, really masculine. Like drinking beer, and watching football or cricket on TV, play the whole fantasy of what being true masculine means – which I find is really problematic. But what about when they break up with their partner – the pain that they actually would feel, there's no way they can actually show it. Just because they show it, does that mean that they're failures? It's not, it's human emotion.
>
> (Eric, 23 years)

Eric draws attention to the regimes of masculinity in which it is acceptable for men to display emotion within the context of competitive sport and over what he considers to be trivial matters such as that involving a football team losing a game. He draws the comparison with a major crisis such as the break-up of a relationship which leaves the male partner unable to express the pain he is feeling, for fear that he might be perceived to exhibit a failed masculinity. These interrogations are informed by a particular critical discourse or threshold knowledge which enables Eric to undertake particular kinds and levels of problematization. These practices appear to be influenced, to some to degree, by his border or outsider positioning as gay-identifying and Chinese-Australian (Anzaldua 1987; hooks 1994b; Pallotta-Chiarolli 1995c, 1996).

Other boys of non-heterosexual sexualities were also able to define and disrupt normative notions of masculinity due to their outsider status. Luke was able to interrogate the social practices of gender, as well as the 'taken-for-grantedness' and unquestionability of these constructs, pointing out that people are not even aware that they are stereotypes and able to be challenged:

> [You get ideas about gender from] school, media, TV, radio, just conversations. Everyday people, when you sit down and have a conversation with someone they will use these stereotypes without even realizing it. There's the obvious sport stuff, you have male-only teams and the girls play hockey or netball and the guys play basketball or football, there's no flexibility in between that. If you don't fit into those norms then you just don't. I mean there's a lot of construction about how male and female should act within schools and that sort of sets us up for how we live.
>
> (Luke, 19 years)

Rowan, 19 years, a bisexual-identifying young man, explicitly stated: 'I've never felt that I was very traditional, well, I'm not traditionally masculine at all.' When asked to define 'traditional masculinity', he replied: 'To be prejudiced, generally, especially to be sexist, but I do also associate probably most other forms of prejudice with traditional masculinity especially like homophobia.'

He then proceeds to discuss the effects of normative masculinity on him at school, and the intricate push–pull relationship with it. He is both repelled by the narrowness of hegemonic masculinity, while also being attracted to the rewards and ease of living that are bestowed on those boys who perform a hegemonic heterosexual masculinity:

> The problem that I always had was that I felt that I wasn't traditionally masculine at all and at that school a lot of people around me were, and that made life quite difficult for me. But I would think I didn't want to be like that anyway. But then I would just wonder if it was just a case of sour grapes, because I couldn't have it. I would think, 'Well I don't want it anyway'. I'd like to have a more balanced perspective on things, the way I think about the world and the way I react to the world.
>
> (Rowan, 19 years)

Rowan is also able to identify his upbringing as having set him apart and given him the ability to interrogate hegemonic masculinity. Part of the interrogation is the realization that being a dominant male in terms of class, culture and sexuality, as well as gender, means that one has never been on the receiving end of discrimination and thus accepts normative masculinity and the rewards it bestows as 'unquestioned and unquestionable' (Schutz 1944):

> Well, I think having lesbian parents meant that I grew up in an atmosphere that was relatively unprejudiced. I always felt that that set me apart straight away and then being bisexual as well was another issue which gave me a whole different perspective on things generally. Although I'm a white, middle-class male, something that I've always noticed about myself is that I don't have any close friends who are straight men. I thought, 'Well, why could that be the case?' Most of these men or boys – straight Anglo-Saxon, middle-class men – would never have any prejudice directed against them. And I think having prejudice of any sort directed against you, especially when you're growing up, is quite a formative experience and, yes, it forms your personality quite a lot – the way you react to the world and the way you expect the world to react to you. I kind of started to think about the way men and women were treated, because that had always been an issue in my life, because it had always been something that my parents would talk about and would kind of bring up. I've always been taking gender relations into consideration, but just to more of an extent, to a greater extent as I got older.
>
> (Rowan, 19 years)

Rowan exemplifies the learning around gender he has gained from outside school and by deliberately setting up conversations with other 'outsider' boys such as gay friends. The school itself perpetuated a heteronormative and gendernormative model of masculinity that meant Rowan experienced harassment and prejudice, while never having a significant space within which to confront these issues:

Rowan: Well, I talked about it a lot with my friends because it was an issue for us because most of my friends who were boys were gay and I was bisexual myself. So the issues about masculinity confront you a lot more in those circumstances. But I never really noticed it that much discussed amongst most of the boys there. I don't think I was generally very confronting about these things.

Maria: So what makes you a man? What makes you male?

Rowan: I think that it's a lot more of the social construction. I tend to be quite anti considering anything to be biological or genetic. Yes, it obviously starts with what's physical because it's whether you're physically male or physically female that people start treating you in a certain way, but I think that from then on it's all social construction.

Maria: And were you really aware of that at school?

Rowan: Yes, I think so, in the way that boys would talk about girls or women, like in quite objectifying sayings, in the emphasis on physicality, on being masculine physically. But I'm not quite sure, I feel that there was an emphasis on being physically stereotypically masculine.

(Rowan, 19 years)

Another boy, Eric of Arabic background and straight-identifying, also demonstrated a willingness to speak about masculinity and its effects, while at the same time advocating the need for further discussions about such gender-related issues for boys in schools. He talks about how his English teacher attempted to deal with issues of masculinity and what he learnt from those lessons. Eric discusses at length the issue of homophobia and uses language like 'versions of masculinity' to make his point about the impact and effects of normative masculinity on the lives of boys:

Eric: There seems to be a real thing about homophobia around males which I don't think I understand that well. The only explanation I could come up with is that they are insecure about their own feelings, so that's why they're afraid of other people who are different to themselves.

Wayne: How do you think that could change? Could it change?

Eric: It would be hard, it's not going to be easy. It would have to begin with schools, your parents, society, TV, newspapers . . . everything is seen as the one type of male stereotype. It's a particular version of masculinity . . . you have to be at least sort of interested in sports, you have to like girls, and all the rest of it . . . it is fed to you from day one. And you've never actually seen the other version of masculinity which is perfectly normal in the sense that it is just a different way that guys feel about other people, but it's not seen like that as you are growing up. So, when people see that other people are different, then obviously they will want to reject that sort of behaviour or that sort of person because it's something different. Everyone hates change, everyone wants to stick with the things that they know best. All of a sudden you see this other version of masculinity and through your education, you've never been told about it; you never know about that sort of person until you hit high school and that's when people really start calling you names and labelling.

(Eric, 17 years)

If Eric's final comment is read within the context of his opening comment about homophobia in boys' lives, he seems to be suggesting that this form of harassment and policing intensifies once high school starts. Perhaps he is attributing this to the onset of puberty for many adolescent boys. The point is, however, that Eric acknowledges alternative versions of masculinity and has developed quite sophisticated capacities for discussing and interrogating the social practices of masculinity. When asked about the terminology he was using such as 'versions of masculinity', he indicates that he learnt it through studying texts in English (see Martino and Mellor 1995):

> Wayne: You keep using this expression 'version of masculinity'. Where did you pick up this term?
>
> Eric: Well, in English we learnt that society has particular versions of masculinity and particular versions are accepted and others not.

However, Eric has not just taken on the teacher's critical discourse of masculinity, but is able to apply these understandings to his own life and to engage in practices of self-problematization:

> Going through school you need to show people that it is OK to be this other version of masculinity. As you're growing up you show them it's OK to cry, it's all right to be emotional instead of being stand-offish and saying, 'I won't express my emotions, I'll look like a man, if I cry then I'm being a woman.' I coach under-14 and under-12 players in basketball . . . if they fall over on the court and hurt their leg, when I get them back on the bench and make a fuss, the mum and dad go, 'Oh stop going on like a girl', and automatically the guy thinks, 'I'm not supposed to cry'. So, it would be good if we could change the way people treat guys, the way you're not supposed to cry and how you have to be the tough male. The only way that you can change it is by changing some of the values and attitudes of society. Even with newspaper and TV you see it, you always see particular versions of masculinity. Although sometimes, as in studying English, they show you other versions, but it seems that the dominant one is the typical male which also sends a message to young kids that you're not supposed to show your feelings.
>
> (Eric, 17 years)

Thus, Eric talks about the rule of not crying and about 'acting tough' on the occasion of sustaining an injury on the basketball court and points to his role as coach in not requiring boys to behave according to this norm. However, he emphasizes the role of parents and the media in enforcing such practices of normative masculinity for adolescent boys. He also reiterates that other versions of masculinity are not made readily available and implies that English is perhaps the only site in which attempts have been made to place 'masculinity' under a particular kind of investigation. What is significant, though, is that he illuminates the role of the teacher as a crucial factor in determining the extent to which boys will engage in such discussions about masculinity.

In the following excerpt he discusses a short story he studied in English entitled 'The Altar of the Family' (Martino and Mellor 1995), which deals with a father who questions his son's masculinity for playing with dolls:

> Well, I learnt it in English, but I'm not too sure that many other people did because not everyone's interested in the same texts. When we analyse them we see how society is critical of this particular version of masculinity. Then other people read it and they automatically see, say, David in 'Altar of the Family' as very timid and shy and he wants to play with flowers in the forest while his dad says that he has to play cricket or something like that. So I'm saying that people who study it might automatically get turned off, especially males, because they'll go, 'He's a sissy! He's a gay! He's not really male!' So they're already turned off the text, so they don't really understand what it's saying.
>
> (Eric, 17 years)

He continues to elaborate on this point about some students not caring about engaging with the issues and draws attention to the role of pedagogy and the teacher in encouraging boys to do so:

> I've been in all sorts of classes with teachers. [Some] just say, 'Oh, take notes on this. What do you think the issues are? What is this text trying to tell you?', instead of getting people involved in reading especially like in discussion. If people have to write everything down, they already get turned off. But with discussion, I think you bring a lot of issues out and the whole class listens to them. If they are really involved and if you open the discussion between actual boys, then they will be more involved in it. Even if the teacher was just there to make sure it doesn't get out of hand. It depends on the teacher. You have to do something to get the class involved. I know it's hard.
>
> (Eric, 17 years)

Here Eric raises issues about a relevant pedagogy which engages boys and encourages students to debate issues of masculinity. This practice is advocated rather than just providing students with a body of knowledge about certain versions of masculinity through reading selected texts. Eric highlights the supportive and relevant dimensions of a pedagogy outlined by Lingard and Mills (2000) in their longitudinal study on effective teaching. They also indicate that the pedagogy needs to be demanding and to recognize difference in terms of students of social, economic and cultural backgrounds.

Shaun, however, raises the issue that such a productive pedagogy for boys must be informed by a particular threshold knowledge which encourages them to interrogate masculinities and their effects. He makes the point about the need to address issues of masculinity when he claims that in schools 'there's no opportunity for guys to get down and think about what they're doing and why they're doing it'. When asked to explain why he thinks that this is so, he makes the following comment:

> I'm not sure. I think it's almost as if it's a mismanagement of what they teach in schools. They teach algebra and maths and stuff like this that we will never use later on in life, but they won't teach us stuff that is important to us and that we should know and learn. We have to find it out for ourselves and if we don't then we're stuck. There has been stuff about don't 'fall to peer pressure', but that's nothing as deep as going into stuff about how you feel about being masculine or what is masculinity. I'm not sure why we don't have the opportunity. It could be an error on our part but I think it's mostly the people that have to teach stuff that maybe they should turn around and look at what they're teaching us.
>
> (Shaun, 16 years)

Shaun appears to be advocating an approach which both mobilizes boys' existing capacities and also assists them in developing specific capacities for critical thinking about the impact of masculinity in their lives. He also draws attention to the need to develop and to teach a curriculum which is more relevant to the daily lives of students (see Walker 1988; hooks 1994a; Slade and Trent 2000; Martino and Pallotta-Chiarolli 2001a).

Conclusion

In this chapter we have focused on boys' attempts and willingness to interrogate masculinities. While some boys were hesitant or chose not to reflect on the social influences of masculinity and where they came from, others struggled with the limits imposed on them by these expectations. Many boys demonstrated a sophisticated capacity to name problematic social practices of masculinity and called for the need at school to have these issues addressed within the mainstream curriculum. On the basis of what some boys said, it appeared that there was not a commitment at their school to addressing explicitly the social dimensions and effects of certain attitudes and practices of masculinity. These boys, however, advocate the need for such a focus and highlight the beneficial effects of questioning these social expectations about what it means to behave as a 'normal' boy. The implications for schools, as sites of strategic intervention (see hooks 1994a), relate to how boys' existing capacities for self-problematization might be mobilized within a context of a productive pedagogy designed to interrogate masculinities and their deleterious effects.

10 'It's the politics of my school that upsets me'

The rhetoric and realities of school policies, structures and pedagogies

Teachers too can be positioned as borderdwellers, and can also actively use their positions to subvert and challenge those at the Centre. I was one of those border-dwellers both in terms of how I taught and related to students and in terms of how I was perceived. I remember actively resisting, in my own way, the official school culture endorsed at the schools I worked in. There was often a preoccupation with rules, but I always understood this as unhealthy and about a particular kind of power. I remember one senior staff member reproaching me about the fact that I had not reprimanded a student for wearing his cap in class. I also remember standing outside of the staff room talking to a Year 11 boy, only to be approached afterwards by a deputy principal who mentioned, 'Did you realize that that boy's socks were not pulled up?' I replied, 'No, I didn't, I wasn't looking at his legs!'

I saw my classroom as a space where connecting and relating to students were integral to my teaching. Boys would say, 'You never yell at us like the others, why?' and I would reply with a laugh, 'I don't see why I need to yell, and why you'd want to be yelled at anyway?' Or I'd say things like,'OK, look, don't get me wrong, I like your earring and I don't see how wearing an earring has anything to do with how you learn, but you know what will happen if you get caught.' Or in reading the morning's notices regarding the latest rules about hair colours and hair lengths, I'd shake my head, look up at my students and we'd exchange certain looks. Or I'd deliberately question a statement or action in the assembly or news-letter. All of this was not about power tripping or punishing but negotiating and interrogating the boundaries of the system. I remember how many students resisted the authoritarian approaches of many staff members who felt they had to assert their authority to be seen as effective and successful teachers able to 'control' students.

At assemblies the students were required to sing the national anthem. Officially, there was this sense of nationalism being used to create some illusionary sense of community which was quite clearly out of touch with students' own realities and cultural experiences. I remember a group of Year 12 students at one of the final assemblies subversively parodying the national anthem and singing out of tune deliberately. I often wondered too how Indigenous students might have responded if they had been students at this school! It was expected that students would learn the national anthem off by heart during home room time. A copy of the words had to be posted in every classroom. I never enforced such rules. I was more concerned with other kinds of learning and so were the students!

This is the flood of memories that come back to me as I listen to boys talk about teachers and school.

Introduction

In this chapter we focus on boys' constructions of teachers and school as a basis for drawing attention to what might constitute an effective pedagogy for addressing their social and educational needs (see Gilbert and Gilbert 1998; Lingard et al. 2000, 2002). We are interested to illustrate the gaps between the rhetoric and realities of school structures and pedagogies as perceived by many boys. These gaps, contradictions and borders were often considered to be constructed due to the overarching and boundary demarcation framework of hegemonic masculinity. The boys' experiences, perceptions and recommendations highlight the urgent need to evaluate the ways in which power relations and constructs around domination and authority are being played out and systematically legitimated within school structures and classroom practice. The following issues will be explored:

1. *The need for pastoral care and respectful pedagogies:* how boys define and argue for a more effective pedagogy in schools.
2. *The gaps and contradictions between pedagogical policies and teaching practices:* how certain pedagogical practices model a hegemonic masculinist style based on authoritarian, 'discipline and punish' performances which subsequently frame student-student relations and hierarchies of power and domination.
3. *The school assemblies as sites of public performances of dominant and subordinate masculinities, authority and domination:* how school cultural spaces such as assemblies may be sites for reinscribing normative constructs of masculinity and to perform authoritarian methods of domination.
4. *The deployment of school uniforms or dress codes:* how schools use dress codes to fashion and regulate student bodies based on normalization, conformity and rigidity.
5. *The adultcentrism of student leadership policies and initiatives:* how student leadership structures, policies and practices such as student representative councils appear to be carefully controlled and monitored attempts to trivialize students' autonomy and leadership.

Many boys reiterated their lack of understanding of the reasonings and rationale behind school policies and structures, a position accentuated by the way their teachers were often ambiguous or unable to justify certain policies, initiatives and practices. Throughout the research, what becomes apparent is that boys are not resisting school per se, but the way schools are complicit in maintaining and indeed modelling inequitable and normalizing practices, from the way teachers teach to the way public space is allocated to certain 'awards' and recognition (Walker et al. 2000).

'I was like the invisible kid'

The need for pastoral care and respectful pedagogies

Chris was one student who talked at length about how he grappled with the imposition of certain hierarchical power structures legitimated within his school. The problems he was experiencing at school were tied both to the specific ways in which teachers were relating to him and, more broadly, to the legitimation of authoritarianism and hierarchical power relations endorsed by the Catholic, coeducational school he was attending. Many of his problems were also exacerbated by his relationship with his father and previous experiences of bullying in primary school. His interview raises particular issues about the dynamics of hegemonic masculinity operating in his life both at home and school. Chris rejects his father's dictums about 'making it in the real world' and earning a lot of money and identifies with the 'little people'. He asserts:

> how much the real world sucks, and how it's all money oriented, and how someone like me, unless you've got money and power, you can never actually change it. They're all just going to worry about themselves and stuff all the little people.
>
> (Chris, 16 years)

His frustration and sense of powerlessness were also accentuated by the bullying that he was subjected to in primary school, which resulted in him 'stuffing up' his work and feeling that 'no one really cared'. 'I was like the invisible kid . . . no one paid any attention to me.'

Chris draws attention to the pressure he feels to perform at school and how low self-esteem still remains an obstacle for him:

> Everyone's putting all this pressure on me because I'm in the last couple of years of school and they say, 'You're terrible, you're doing bad, you're never going to succeed in life.' It's just they're wondering why I'm a screw-up now – teachers, parents, everyone. They're trying to change me. What took all my primary school life and part of high school life,

> they're trying to change it in one year and it's physically and emotionally impossible. That's why I get so depressed every now and then and I just go way down.
>
> (Chris, 16 years)

Here, Chris reiterates that significant adults in his life are coercing him to conform to particular standards and to perform at school so that he can be successful in life. However, he appears to reject certain 'rules' that are built into a regime of competitive educational practices in which he is incited to achieve in order to reap the long-term benefits of schooling. Moreover, emotionally he feels that he has not developed the capacity to address problems he is facing at school because of his past experiences of bullying. Thus, while rejecting what may be identified as one particular version of masculinity, he establishes another rebel form of masculinity which is enacted against the former in terms of a 'personalised opposition to authority' (Willis 1977: 11).

Chris seems to be calling out for help and for significant adults at school and home to support and understand him which raises the question about the need for pastoral pedagogies:

> They can't understand me, it's impossible. They've only known me for a couple of periods and that's it . . . teachers, parents, they never listen. You try and tell them, but they're too busy to help me properly. Everyone is. If they had absolutely all the time in the world, I'd tell them, 'Help me, help me deal with my problems, help me do better in school, help me mentally, I really need some fine tuning.' That's all I'd say. If I can get that done, I think I can take things from there . . .
>
> (Chris, 16 years)

On the basis of what Chris has indicated about his experiences at home and school, it would appear that he is advocating the need for alternative modes of relating which are organized around a different set of norms such as:

- listening to and respecting young people's point of view;
- granting young people in schools the right to present and to articulate their own point of view;
- avoiding confrontational approaches to dealing with conflict resolution;
- involving young people in decision-making processes (see Collins et al. 1996, 2000; McLean 1997).

Interestingly, Chris specifically mentions that Tai-Kwon-Do provides him with a pressure-free space where the above mentioned norms apply. Here, he documents the positive effects of a particular teacher–student relationship based on non-coercive power and respect (see Hunter 1988, 1994). Consequently, he feels supported and does not fear reprisal for the mistakes he might make:

> It's the only place where you go and you are not judged. It's not like a tournament situation, or like a school scenario, where there will always be a winner and a loser. But with this, there's never one. You never feel the pressure of the other kids, they never laugh at you, they never tease you for what you look like. They encourage you, they say, 'That's a good technique, but you might want to do it this way.' They're always helping, and they're never criticizing. It's just like a free environment. It's my only escape that I can ever get away. It's my little world where I live and can be anything I want and no one cares. In some places they say, 'OK, you can come in only if you do this and this, and if you don't you're terrible, you're an outcast, go away'. They don't say 'You have to'. They say 'You can try if you want to, and if you don't like it, we'll figure out something else for you'. They'll modify for you and it's just great, it's wicked and I love it.
>
> (Chris, 16 years)

In his 'little world' of Tai-Kwon-Do, Chris does not feel pressured in the sense that he is not subjected to coercive and obtrusive pedagogical regimes. He feels understood rather than judged. It is significant that he chooses an alternative Eastern sport rather than a Western competitive team sport. In Tai-Kwon-Do there are no winners and losers and Chris embraces this non-competitive ethic. In contrast, Chris identifies and rejects a corresponding but antithetical system of norms driving the production and regulation of student subjectivities at his own school:

> I see school as encouraging people to be quiet and to conform. I can't stand it. I just reckon the only thing they're worried about is their dignity, their respect in the outside world. The school just tries to churn out a reputation so they can go higher up. You only get a few good teachers that will actually stop and pay attention and actually help instead of worrying about how good it makes them look.
>
> (Chris, 16 years)

In much the same way as Willis's (1977) working-class lads refuse to conform to institutionalized norms of schooling, Chris, despite his middle-class background, also takes up a counter-position (see Martino 1999). This would seem to indicate that such behaviour is not just an instance of what maybe termed an aspect of lower socio-economic status masculinity. Rather, a boy's rejection of school learning is related to broader issues of masculinity, family, teacher imposition of authority and, in particular, the kind of school culture and ethos that prescribes specific relations between students and teachers (see Gilbert and Gilbert 1998; Lingard et al. 2002).

'They're restricting us in a lot of ways'

Boys rejecting power hierarchies at school

What is apparent in our research is that boys are not resisting school per se, but the way schools are complicit in maintaining and indeed modelling inequitable and normalizing practices, from the way teachers teach to the way public space is allocated to certain 'awards' and recognition (Martino and Pallotta-Chiarolli 2001c).

Luc, gay-identifying, for example, was angry at the way schools perpetuated and fostered ignorance in the name of education and educational appropriateness:

> Awareness was the main factor, to combat ignorance. Notice that the calendar says 1999 not 1950. That's what I would have liked my school to have done, progress . . . just be more aware of homophobia. I'm not saying make homophobia the only issue that you deal with, but at least put it right up there with racism and drugs and alcohol and whatever other stuff you were doing. But it was never under that same category.
>
> (Luc, 18 years)

Andrew problematizes schooling as a place that stunts student development and education due to its very stringent moralistic constructs around education and learning, and the normative fashioning of what has been constructed as a 'good citizen':

> They were very restricting in a lot of ways. I guess because they're trying to teach you to be good moral citizens or something. They can overdo that a bit and not let you go your own way, develop properly, or in your own unique way . . . which probably is admirable but it's limiting as well.
>
> (Andrew, 21 years)

School for many boys in our research becomes a place where they are morally and socially regulated in ways that they find restricting their potential for self-development. In fact, they highlight how much of this policing is about projecting a particular image of the 'good moral citizen' which they consider to be at odds with genuine care and concern for the well-being of individual students. This is reiterated by Ben who refers specifically to 'the politics' of his school which restricts students' opportunities for developing their potential and capabilities. In fact, he constructs the school as being 'out of touch with the students' and the principal/deputy principals as being insincere and concerned with appropriating certain forms of oppressive power used to 'big note themselves':

> It's the politics of my school that upsets me. They're all very out of touch with the students at 'St Citizen'. I can't wait to get out. There are too many brick walls created by the administration. It is unfair and the constant contradictions, falseness and hypocrisy in the school's politics – the principals, the vice-principals, the deputies, the coordinators, the directors of curriculum and finance – all these ridiculous titles they invent to big note themselves. Perhaps if the school could provide students with more ways to express themselves and not to feel so oppressed, it would be better.
>
> (Ben, 17 years)

School mottos were also examples of rhetoric that did not translate into reality, nor did schools appear to make them inclusive of all students. The school motto displayed at assemblies in Christian's single-sex Catholic school was a visual metaphor of traditional aggressive and militaristic masculinity and yet was reinscribed with multiple resistant meanings by students. Interestingly, this simplistic and yet multiply inscribed metaphor is the only memory Christian has of the school ever communicating what it really wanted to instil in its students. Its ambiguity allowed students to read into it their own interpretations, often in direct contradiction to the school's meanings:

> 'Fight the good fight' – that was always brought up at assemblies – it became a bit of a joke because of the way I took it. 'Fight the good fight' meant that if it was something that I believed in, then I would fight for it – no matter what the issue was. But I think that what they meant was that if someone is going to attack you, then you defend and go to war. I think they intended it to be like a patriotic motto, whereas I just put my own values to it and my own intentions and used it that way.
>
> (Christian, 23 years)

What these responses indicate is that, despite the imposition of moral and social regulation through school mottos and uses of hierarchical power designed to keep students in their place, these very approaches incite many boys to resistance. The boys expose the basis on which such relations of hierarchical power operate, despite the rhetoric of pastoral care and respect that these schools promote.

'Big teacher up the front and 30 little worker ants'

Teachers policing or teachers teaching?

> Some teachers just teach and just want to get it over and done with. Some of them would be better suited in a police station than a school.
>
> (Simon, 13 years)

While much educational research bemoans the resistance, protestations and apathy of students against learning and against teachers, our research interrogated why students respond in these ways. We found that many students were resistant to rules and policies that they perceived to be in place as symbols of teachers' authority, rather than having rational or functional purposes. Stephen was able to provide several strategies schools could use to deconstruct the teacher–student hierarchical dualism, and reconstruct it into a teacher–student relationship of mutual respect and equity where 'you get treated like a person'. A major facet of this was placing more responsibility onto the students themselves for their work, rather than infantilizing them by turning the issue over to their parents. In striking imagery, he also contrasts the atmosphere of domination and subordination in his previous school to the friendliness of his present school:

> The good things about this school . . . you get treated like a person, and the teachers don't think they're better than you. At my old school it was a lot more that your parents were entirely responsible for you. Here, it's your school work, and if you don't want to do it, fair enough. At my old school if I skipped a class my dad would be contacted straight away and all the teachers are going, 'I think there's going to be some severe disappointment at home about this', and here, if I skip a class it's more that they say to me, 'Look, if you don't make the attendance we're going to fail you'. It's a lot more friendly, it's more like you're on one level – instead of big teacher up the front and 30 little worker ants.
>
> (Stephen, 15 years)

Interestingly, the issue of responsibility is also seen as being a 'two-edge joint' by Stephen. In being treated with maturity and respect, he feels obliged to respond with maturity and respect to his teachers. He soon follows this afterthought with another description of the style of 'teaching' in his previous school that actually incites students to resistance and, hence, is not conducive to effective learning:

> The responsibility thing is a two-edge joint, because they've given the responsibility to me instead of my parents. That forces me to be

responsible. [At my old school] I had this Coordinator in Year 7 and 8, he was always hounding me, he just didn't like me. Whenever I did anything, he would do his best to get me suspended. Once at lunchtime, I just called him dickhead and one of the teachers overheard me and told him. He goes, 'So, you think I'm a dickhead', and I said, 'Yes, I do think you're a dickhead'. So he tells me to write him a 300-word essay on why he is a dickhead. He got me to sit in the general office. This guy is one of the most hated teachers at the school. I ran out of things to say, so I just started polling whoever comes past, 'Hey, why do you think Mr X is a dickhead?' I got the whole essay done and I gave it to him, and he suspended me on the spot for it, and he sent a copy of it home to my dad. He was saying, 'This is a real problem, you're going to have to do something about this.' My dad read it and started laughing. I've still got it around somewhere . . . I was trying to find it last weekend and frame it. [Other teachers] don't take themselves as seriously, they don't have the whole power trip thing happening.

(Stephen, 15 years)

Again, we see that methods of control and domination by using tactics of discipline and punish, rather than engagement and discussion only lead to further student rebellion, and escalate a situation which perpetuates the hierarchical schism between students and teachers. In the above example, it turns a situation where a student has used put-down language against a teacher, overheard by another teacher who – instead of intervening and discussing it with the student – relays it to the teacher himself. Thus, a situation that could have been privately and effectively handled becomes a public contest of who can humiliate whom the most, and who will become the winner. By putting Stephen in the public office space, the centre of school administration and authority, where his reputation is now positioned as both resistant to the Centre around him and accountable to other students walking through, he invites them to become part of the arena of sporting with the teacher, to join in the competition.

Eventually, Stephen considers himself the victor, particularly after his father laughs as well. The essay that began as a punishment and as a humiliation has become a sporting trophy or war medal, an example for himself and for other students on how to resist and use their creativity to defeat the teachers at their own game of making the enemy submit to humiliation and defeat. This example illustrates the need for teachers to use strategies that diffuse and deflect from being constructed as a game or battle of power and wits between the oppressor and the oppressed. Thus, Stephen concludes by saying he would never use such tactics with the teachers at his new school as they refuse to construct or enter into such battles between enemies, but are 'cool' in the way they expect to relate to students in more equitable ways.

Stephen also supports the opinions and experiences of other students in our research that it is mostly the male teachers who embark on what he calls 'the power trip' to see who can humiliate whom, who can dominate whom by performing hegemonic masculinist behaviour, while attempting to emasculate their male students with implications of their femininity or homosexuality, or by positioning them as 'freaks' in relation to 'normal' boys:

> It was more the male teachers who were into the power trip. It was like they were always looking down their nose at you. One time I was doing something and the teacher came up behind and goes, 'Oh, Stephen, that long hair, I thought you were a girl.' When my eyebrow was pierced they told me to take it out or leave. The same thing happened when I dyed my hair green. The vice-principal said these exact words, 'I don't want any freaks or weirdos at this school.'
>
> (Stephen, 15 years)

When Mike was suspended for having green colour in his hair, he interpreted school reactions to this as a power game that served no useful educational purpose. He also articulates his frustration when teachers are unable to provide reasons for punishing him for dying his hair. They construct themselves as merely passively following rules set out by those in higher administrative positions, rather than endeavouring to resist or understand the rules. Thus, schools are often presented as actually performing a mindless following of 'the way things are':

> It just turns you off from the school. It makes you think how ridiculous and pointless do you have to be to try and control people. A lot of people I know have just left the school because they just think it's so pathetic. It was the home room teachers who carry out the bandaid over the ear punishment. If you complained to them, they'd just say, 'Hey I don't write the rules.'
>
> (Mike, 17 years)

Other students talked about the way teachers followed rules in what they encouraged or discouraged students from learning, or what they were too fearful of including in the curriculum, despite student interest (hooks 1994a). Christian distinguished between teachers who actively taught and thought and teachers who passively followed and imparted rules and repressed student learning:

> Some people involved in the hierarchy were a little bit narrow minded. They were very fixed in their ways and didn't want to step outside the nine dots. If I was to challenge a teacher, it didn't really matter what

> subject it was, then we weren't given the opportunity to really back our argument up because I was generally shut off before I was given the chance to really engage in a proper discussion.
>
> (Christian, 23 years)

He recalls choosing a book to review for English, *Someone You Know* (Pallotta-Chiarolli 1991) about a gay teacher with HIV/AIDS, and how his English teacher did not feel comfortable about this:

> My English teacher didn't make me feel comfortable about speaking to him when I wanted advice about reviewing the book. I got the impression that he wasn't himself comfortable talking about the issues that the book raised, being homosexuality, individuality . . . so subsequently I went to a teacher that I saw as being very open minded and very willing to discuss issues that the school would have thought of as taboo. It was quite comforting and it gave me the ability to actually express what I wanted to. Every Tuesday lunchtime I'd spend the whole lunchtime speaking with a particular teacher who had some sort of yard duty. It was like a weekly appointment for me. [It wasn't] necessarily because it was a boys' school as such but because it was a Catholic school.
>
> (Christian, 23 years)

Luc also discusses how the lack of teacher pro-activism in regard to homosexuality and homophobia led to his taking initiatives both inside and outside the school to get these issues on the school agenda. In successfully doing so, he deconstructs existing rules and reconstructs the teaching around homosexuality and homophobia as a new rule that he realizes some teachers will reluctantly obey, because it is a rule officially endorsed and administered by the hierarchy, despite their own discomfort and misgivings. This illustrates the power of having a human rights issue legislated and legitimated through school policy. It is only with this formal coercion then that some teachers will actually shift their professional, if not personal, position on an issue:

> I think a lot of them were too scared to really come out with things because they've just been like that for a hundred years. [They're scared of] their reputations, they've got jobs, and it's a cliché but they don't want to damage their job – which is fair enough. I rang up schools and asked, 'Do you teach units on homosexuality at your school?' and most of them said 'Yes'. So I went to the religion co-ordinator and said, 'You have to do this because it's done everywhere else, and you can't not do it here.' He was angry, he said, 'I don't have to do that if I don't want to.' I just said, 'Look, if you don't do it I'm going to raise these issues with the media.' I threatened . . . and then all the RE classes after about three

> months had sections on homosexuality. I found that the teachers that supported me the most were from the English faculty. That's probably explainable in that it's humanities and it's broad minded sometimes. The kind of ones that didn't were more the sciency ones, and the religion ones were divided.
>
> (Luc, 17 years)

Luc raises some really important issues about the ways in which teachers themselves are fearful of addressing issues such as homosexuality because of the damage that it might do to their reputations and, hence, the perceived risks involved for them personally and professionally (hooks 1994a; Pallotta-Chiarolli 1995b, 1999b). These risks should not be dismissed, given the kind of surveillance that many religious schools undertake of staff, particularly with regards to their sexuality. Male student teachers in research conducted by Martino and Berrill (2002), for example, spoke about their fear of being perceived as sexually deviant for engaging in what might be considered by the wider community to be gender non-conforming behaviours. Those teachers who identified as gay were particularly concerned about any form of self-disclosure for fear of being labelled a pedophile.

Interestingly, just as Luc distinguishes teachers' responses according to masculine/feminine subject areas in the above (see Martino 1997), he also does so according to the gender of the teacher:

> Female teachers [were more supportive] . . . it just goes back to that theory that women are more accepting in a way. [Some of the male teachers] would just ignore me. One of the teachers called me 'faggot' and stuff like that at one stage . . . I don't really know what he taught but I laughed, just went straight to the principal. I said, 'Your teachers aren't allowed to do this, you'd better do something about it.' It's common knowledge that teachers aren't allowed to abuse their students in any way, shape or form. They had a published booklet on discrimination which said absolutely nothing about sexual discrimination, until Year 12 when I changed it.
>
> (Luc, 17 years)

Again we see Luc's strategic manipulation of the power of rules in a school whereby they can be mobilized to legitimate and support a range of issues.

Johnny also used gendernormative imagery and constructs to articulate the perceived differences in the way male and female teachers taught. He compares one female teacher – who was 'a really good teacher' and 'like a second mother to us' – to male teachers who weren't exactly constructed in oppositional terms as 'fathering' the boys, but who were perceived to be more like 'big brothers' or 'mates':

> She'd talk to us and she'd ask us what we were doing on the weekends. It was a lot more comfortable atmosphere to work in, and we all worked a lot better because of that. [Compared with] the female teachers, male teachers don't have a mothering impact or a fathering thing, they're more like big brothers, like mates. Like my physics teacher now, he does pretty much what the graphics teacher did, but because he's a guy I think we just think of him as one of the gang rather than like a mothering sort of figure. Most of my female teachers . . . you really got that impression that they cared about what you were doing and they really wanted you to do well in school and life.
>
> (Johnny, 17 years)

Johnny highlights how certain versions of masculinity and femininity are fashioned through the pedagogical encounter. Gendered modes of relating appear to be built into and inform the ways in which Johnny perceives male and female teachers as relating to students.

Female and male teachers who themselves challenged gendernormative and heteronormative constructions could find themselves recipients of the same harassment and labelling they were teaching against, mainly because they were seen as different from or unsupported by a wider school framework (see Mills 2000; Martino 2001). Christian talks about student resistance and ambivalence to a female teacher in his school:

> [They would say things like] 'She's a prostitute. All she needs is a good hard fuck'. It was just immature because the stupid thing was they were so adamant that she had such a good body. You could see she was making inroads, but with peer group pressure they felt that if they voiced their opinion and actually agreed with her, then they may have been condemned or challenged in a way that they felt they couldn't handle.
>
> (Christian, 23 years)

These comments confirm the research undertaken by Robinson (1996) and Ferfolja (1998) who point out that the main perpetrators of harassment in schools are adolescent boys. Ferfolja also argues that 'sex role appropriate behaviours are expected and condoned' and that 'boys are socialized into valued and socially appropriate masculine roles' and that it is 'such socialization that teaches males to devalue females, oppress effeminacy and thus enhance hegemonic male power' (1998: 402). This is supported by Simon, regarding the way boys at his school respond to 'pretty good looking' and younger female teachers (see Pallotta-Chiarolli 1990b):

> I mean you get some of the younger female teachers who are pretty good looking, they just go along with the [sexist] joke sometimes. I think they

> have to, if they took it too seriously they'd get hassled for about a week. You get your usual bunch of smart ass comments, like, 'Oh, can you come over and help me?', to get them to bend over the table or something like that, and then a guy will make a comment and the teacher will hear him and shake their head and go, 'I can't believe you said that' to the students.
>
> (Simon, 16 years)

'Mates or machos'

Male teachers enacting masculinities

Other boys also talked specifically about the influence and impact of male teachers on their lives, which challenges the simplistic rhetoric about the need for more male teachers in schools without addressing the issue of what kind of male teacher and models of masculinity need to be provided (see Mills 2000; Roulsten and Mills 2000; Lingard et al. 2002). Mike, for example, talked about teachers who did not play the games of power and authority. He mentions two male teachers who treated students in a 'friendly' way and recommends this model to all schools. His example, however, of how certain male teachers could make themselves 'cool' and 'popular' is based on certain sporting and physical behaviours that emulate dominant sporting constructs of masculinity:

> They were both teachers who related to you on a friend level, not like 'I'm overpowering you because I'm the teacher'. They'd talk to you, joke around, but make sure you got all your work done. It was just more of a friend relationship than a teacher–student. Every school should make schooling on a friendship base, not on a 'Right, you threw a piece of paper, five minutes time out' kind of thing because that just discourages people. Maybe this'll sound a bit outrageous, but say you were in a classroom and you see a kid throw a piece of paper across the room, maybe the teacher could run across and catch it and throw it back at him . . . I think as soon as the teacher did that there'd be just a big grin on the student's face, thinking 'Oh my god', and then I think he'd be more inclined to get along with the teacher if they think it's either funny or think he's just laid back and he's a cool person.
>
> (Mike, 17 years)

However, for Wayne, 16 years, male teachers who endeavoured to construct themselves as physically powerful were scorned: 'Just the way he [male teacher] walks around and talks to you, like you're always second best to him. He walks like he's six-foot tall, good build . . . but he's not, he's skinny, about 5 foot 5 inches . . . he'll be really controlling you.'

Glenn illustrates how male teachers may draw upon popular discourses of sport and physical prowess to connect to students (see Roulsten and Mills 2000). What is contradictory here is Glenn's equation with this talk as indicative of treating students 'like adults'. These teachers may not 'smack your fingers every time', but draw upon so-called normalized 'adult' threats of aggression which students interpret as symbols of their being eligible to be situated within the dominant circle of masculine repartee based on aggression and hegemonic sports. The interweaving of three dominant linguistic performances of hegemonic masculinity or 'mateyness' come together for Glenn to enhance the teacher's popularity with male students: humour, references to physical aggression and prowess, and references to football. However, this style of maintaining one's popularity with students plays into and supports dominant and essentialist constructions of masculinity and thus contributes to the marginalization of male students and male teachers who are not located within this 'inner circle' (see Francis and Skelton 2001):

> It's the way they talk to you, they treat you like adults, they have fun, they joke around as well as being serious at times to do your work. When Mr X says, 'Do your work or I'll smash your face in', we all just crack up laughing. It's just funny and it's the way he uses the tone of his voice. If teachers were pretty much all like Mr X it would be really, really good. He treats you like an adult, he doesn't smack your fingers every time, and he lets you talk during lessons, but not too loud. But other teachers, they just won't let you do anything, 'Sit on the chair and do your work'. Mr X doesn't single people out, but if anyone's mucking around in the class he'll pull them aside and say, 'Look, pull your socks up' or 'Come play in the football team' or, 'I'll make you play in the football team'.
>
> (Glenn, 16 years)

Paul believes that the way male teachers relate is also regulated and determined according to the presence or absence of girls in their classes. Again, this is an example of male students drawing upon or inferring what their male adult teachers would do and considering this to be the appropriate 'normal' male behaviour and attitude:

> I think our teachers, seeing as there's males, yell it out . . . whereas if they did that to a bunch of female students, if a male teacher yelled at them, they'd cry. The teacher yells at us, you yell back at him. But men are supposed to be tougher, so the teacher can be tougher, more verbal.
>
> (Paul, 16 years)

'Real bonds'

Teachers connecting with borderland students

In the following, Jonard was aware of how his teacher–student relationship with an Indian teacher was a more equitable relationship of two persons of 'marginal ethnicities' connecting beyond or in subversion to dominant whiteness in the school. From that shared position of marginality, which they consider to be their 'normality', they are able to connect issues of racism to issues of heterosexism within the school and support him in being openly gay:

> I felt this teacher–student relationship between the two of us because she is an Indian, she's not Australian . . . if she were an Australian it would probably feel that she has more status than me . . . so I guess I knew I could act normally with her. She knew that I was gay, I could talk to her about things, about social issues.
>
> (Jonard, 18 years)

Ben, dealing with depression and harassment from other students, also found a teacher who provided a space of comfort, safety and self-expression within the school. His art teacher, who, he claims, 'sensed my unhappiness', allowed him to spend lunchtime in the art room:

> That's why the doors of the art rooms are never locked. Mrs X knows that it is the last place in the school where troubled kids can actually come to escape. She's not there at lunchtimes but there is always paint and paper for you to get everything off your chest with. It's a sort of therapy and I don't know what I would've done this year without the art room.
>
> (Ben, 17 years)

Tony, 24 years, who was in a wheelchair and journeyed to and from the 'special' and 'integrated' schooling system in his early years, remembers the importance of having teachers who were aware of these borderland specificities and could respect and appreciate his achievements, as well as encourage him to do more. He talks about how teachers went out of their way to 'help' and to 'accommodate' him: 'I think my teachers appreciated that it was harder for me.'

Other students also identified features about a teacher that may have been constructed as marginal or subordinate within the hierarchy of teachers at the school. Yet these connections of marginalities led to what Luke below defines as 'real bonds'. He reminisces about a female art teacher who was young and just beginning her teaching career, and yet from her marginal site challenged students when they revealed discriminatory attitudes. He contrasts her deconstructive and connective approaches with students to the controlling and put-down tactics of other teachers. She takes a far more conciliatory approach and invites students to engage in discussions with her, rather than alienating them by returning put-downs with put-downs:

> There were real bonds there between us . . . she was very supportive of any individuality. So if someone put someone else down she would step in and try and make this person realize that maybe they're not taking the right approach. So it wasn't just myself that she supported, it was everyone. It wasn't 'You're making racist comments that really are irrelevant', just 'Okay, why are you making these comments?' She didn't just turn around and go 'Right, you're doing wrong blah, blah, blah', she'd actually make them think about it instead of just snapping down on them. There were plenty of teachers that were very top heavy and had very traditional views, and since it was a selective school with an academic base it was very standardized, very rigid.
>
> (Luke, 19 years)

Boyd, an Indigenous student, mentions a white female teacher at his school who was also outstanding due to her commitment to and interest in the background of her students. She was in fact responsible for teaching Aboriginal and Torres Strait Islander Studies and had gained the respect of many Indigenous boys we interviewed at this school:

> I get along well with mostly teachers who are interested in my background, where I can ask them questions about their background as well. Like Miss Y is a really excellent example for that. She wants to know what's wrong when I'm having a bad day. So I talk to her all the time. She really understands what it's like for a black person. She's white, and she's still learning and she's got a lot to learn I think, but she's really interested. I think she thinks it's a good way of teaching people . . . understanding the way Indigenous people teach and look at things.
>
> (Boyd, 16 years)

For Boyd a 'good' teacher is someone who shows a genuine interest and concern for students. Having an understanding of the students' culture is also important, but he seems to be indicating that taking an active interest in the well-being of students and developing a relationship with them is very important. This issue is raised by Purdie et al. (2000) who claim that teachers 'need to be warm and supportive' and 'culturally aware'. Boyd emphasizes this when asked what makes a good teacher:

> Someone who wants to get to know you more, be more involved with you and who does not just think teaching is a job. Have you ever seen the movie *Lean on Me*? You know how the principal wants to get involved with the students . . . I'd love to go to a school like that where the principal wants to know what's wrong on your bad days. [You could] go talk to him about your problems. But our school is not really like that. I learn better when they become more involved with you, with your background and stuff.
>
> (Boyd, 16 years)

'You don't really see much of it'

The discrepancy between the rhetoric of pastoral care and actual practice

Many students were able to discern the discrepancy between school rhetoric around pastoral care and actual practices. For example, Danny talked about teachers modelling bullying tactics:

> Yes, [the school is] really into that [pastoral care] but you don't really see much of it. All the teachers abuse their power and try to make all the kids scared of them. Once I asked to go to the toilet, and he pulled the desk out and told me to get out . . . he tried to get really aggressive.
>
> (Danny, 16 years)

Jordan points out that the teachers he has disliked 'have been really aggressive' and 'most have been men':

> I've had trouble with getting to know men and actually liking them. They've all expected me to be macho which I've never been able to do. My Year 6 teacher was the worst teacher I've ever had. Before then I didn't know that I was dyslexic, I didn't know that I had a learning disability. I don't know what his problem was. We had maths tests and he used to pick maybe three or four kids out of the class to stand up and tell what their score was. And every time I was always in that group . . . and this particular time I had gotten 1 out of 10 and when it came to me I said, '1', and he said, 'I'm sorry I didn't hear you Jordan, speak up.' I said, '1'. He said, 'What? What was that?' I said '1', and he just laughed. He stood there and he laughed at me and everybody else in the class was laughing at me. I just felt terrible and he didn't tell the other children in the class to stop laughing, he just stood there himself and laughed openly at me. [Male teachers do that kind of thing] to prove that they're on top, that they've got big dicks, that they're the tops, macho.
>
> (Jordan, 16 years)

However, Luc was aware of how the adult educators around him performed politeness and niceness to resist his interventions against homophobia. The schism between rhetoric and reality are highlighted as he juxtaposes the language in his school diary and assembly with the situation in reality. Nevertheless, he persists as a student activist, despite various attempts to silence him. He did research and sought out policies from other schools which addressed homophobia and sexual diversity. He would challenge the principal and teachers at his single-sex boys' Catholic school with its progressive focus on technological education, but lack of commitment to addressing moral and social justice issues:

> [I would say to the principal] 'You can't go ahead in your technological education issues and be back in the 1900s in the way of moral and social issues.' I don't know if he agreed with it but he realized it. They were very nice to me . . . if they're not nice to you it's going to create a lot of trouble . . . it was kind of like a smile and a handshake. A good effort but it was just fake, you could just tell. The school tried to quieten me down, tried to just get me to shut up about it by offering me a free laptop. And I just couldn't help but laugh. I said, 'You can't buy my quietness.' There was once where the Dean of students called my mother up at work and said that it was not acceptable for me to be making them aware about homosexual rights. He was the one that actually said in one of the school assemblies – his exact words were – 'X College is not a place for differences in lifestyles and cultures.' Then I picked up the diary and I read their policies and I just went, 'You're a hypocrite, you're just a damn, fucking hypocrite.' It said, 'We're educating X boys to be men of the future, to go out into the world with experience and knowledge, and to embrace society' . . . blah, blah, blah . . . that really stood out for me, the hypocrisy of the system. They gave students a false perception that they were able to speak their minds freely, but when it came to the bottom line, they weren't allowed.
>
> (Luc, 18 years)

'Religious bigotry posing as religious freedom'

Another area of growing awareness and cynicism among some boys was recognition that despite the rhetoric of 'love, respect for all, care for all', religious schools are not putting these values into action when it comes to students who are non-heterosexual. Catholic schools are using their exemption from anti-discrimination legislation, as well as the protection that democratic legislation gives them in terms of supporting religious freedoms, to practise religious bigotry in relation to homosexuality and bisexuality. Nevertheless, students are increasingly exposing the contradictions and resisting dogmatic traditions:

> It was in RE and [the teacher] was saying how the church teaches equality and I said, 'If it's so equal, then how come women and gay people can't be priests?' And she sort of was a bit stuck. She goes, 'Well, the Bible says that only men can teach the word of God because God was a man and the Bible also says that men and women should be together.' That was pretty much it. Then I said, 'Well, isn't that a bit dated because the Bible was written so long ago?' and she said, 'Oh well, I know it doesn't really answer your question', but she couldn't really give me a straight answer. So I think it might be a real block that Catholic view that gay sex isn't right.
>
> (Max, 16 years)

As Max from a Catholic co-educational school has outlined above, some sexually diverse students in religious schools call for effective challenges of the contradictions and hypocrisy. For many gay-identifying boys who have inherited religious beliefs from their families, such as Rob below, the conflict is constructed as a dual between their religious beliefs and their gay sexuality. It becomes very difficult for many to reconcile or negotiate the two. Usually, religious affiliation is denounced in order to be able to live out their sexuality (Pallotta-Chiarolli 2000):

> There's something about the Catholic system. It kind of closes the door on those kind of issues . . . I don't believe in any God or the teachings of the Christian Church. I think this disbelief stemmed from the whole gay thing. I've read parts of the Bible where homosexuality is practically condemned, so that put me off. When I first discovered that I was gay I felt cheated by God.
>
> (Rob, 16 years)

The contradiction between religious rhetoric of pastoral care for all and the reality of its selective application is poignantly seen in the way Jarrod, 16 years, is able to distinguish between how a school can support a person experiencing racism, but expects the student to just 'stop' being gay rather than seek external support:

Maria: What would you recommend for guys who are getting hassled, say you're being racially harassed, or if you've got a disability and you're being harassed, what would you recommend for them to do?

Jarrod: Tell someone. We've got the Christian youth group with counsellors, talk to them, take advice from them.

Maria: And if you were a gay guy and you were being harassed?

Jarrod: Stop being gay.

However, in some schools, the role of anti-homophobic work was actually handed over to the religious education teachers or school chaplains. While this is significant, it still positions homophobia as an issue of pastoral care detached from the daily curriculum and other workings of the school. Further, by being framed within a discourse of compassion and the need to prevent victimization, it is still constructing homosexuality as the inferior within the hierarchical dualism of heterosexuality/homosexuality, a condition that is not to be celebrated but to be understood and its carriers to be sympathized, tolerated and left alone.

Mills (1996) discusses the presence of 'containment discourses' working to limit or silence any anti-heteronormative disruption. The discourse of teacher 'professionalism' is one of the most powerful educational discourses in its containment of teacher–student challenges to the existing heteronormative order. It regulates and monitors the boundaries between students and teachers so that much remains deliberately unspoken or unconsciously unseen. Teachers who resist the heteronormativity of the school, of one's teaching peers, are liable to be accused of unprofessional activity or have their careers ended. Rowan provides an understanding of why teachers known or perceived to be gay avoided students known or perceived to be gay. Again, we see the panopticonic power of heteronormativity in the way it renders possible points of connection and support useless and vulnerable to further abuse:

> The one thing that I thought was kind of funny at the time was that teachers who were gay . . . and I would be there with my gay friends . . . they always kind of avoided us. I felt they sort of disassociated themselves from us. I guess it would be very, very hard to be a gay teacher, especially at an all boys school, it would be an awful experience so I suppose you would try to make the least of it as an issue as you possibly could.
>
> (Rowan, 19 years)

'Teachers control, students resist'

> I was in class and we're doing a test and someone threw a paper at me . . . I put up my hand and blocked it because it was going to hit me . . . and the teacher turned around and yelled, 'You've failed now.' 'No, let me explain.' 'No, no, 100 lines.' 'No, let me explain.' '200 lines.' And it kept getting worse and worse.
>
> (Jarrod, 16 years)

The above is an example of how the discipline/punish and us/them hierarchical binaries led to an escalation of student resistance to a teacher. Other students distinguished between teachers 'teaching' and teachers 'controlling', and the vicious cycle and interconnections between teachers just 'handing out work' which is not considered 'teaching', and the either aggressive or passive resistance of students:

> Teachers that just hand out work and don't teach you. Lots of my teachers couldn't control my class and just ended by giving up. The teacher tries to make the student do work, the student answers back, and then everyone just talks or doesn't do any work or knocks the teacher . . . Most times I just sit there and draw or something.
>
> (Zach, 14 years)

> It's very much like being in a prison, I suppose, everyone sits there being quiet, doesn't do anything because they daren't. The work gets done but not properly because a lot of the time they don't understand it.
>
> (Matthew, 16 years)

The lack of effective teacher response or engagement with student behaviour also created problems for other students who had to decide whether to resist the dominant disruptive students and thus be liable to harassment and bullying, or whether to pretend to enjoy the goings on:

> [When someone's hassling a teacher] some join in, some just sit back. You don't really want to tell them to stop otherwise you might get paid out. It can be a bit annoying and distracting and you can't get your work done . . . I just feel sorry for the teacher.
>
> (John, 16 years)

Andrew suggests strategies, a meeting on the border, that could avoid these us/them conflicts to the benefit of all students in the classroom and the teacher. He advocates a respectful pedagogy that involves teachers 'listening to the students', being 'flexible' and encouraging student feedback:

> Someone who listens to the students and [takes] input from the students . . . flexible . . . that makes a good teacher. When they realize that the students and the teachers are there working together. There has to be an interaction between the two, it can't be just one way. [Ineffective teachers] get angry pretty easily without thinking 'Why are the kids misbehaving?' If they stop and think about it, there might be a reason. They could talk to their students and ask them why

> they're misbehaving and then the teachers and students could work together more.
>
> (Andrew, 16 years)

Several boys from the same school named the same teacher, a religious brother, who was able to span the us/them divide with students as well as the teacher/friend duality. What needs to be highlighted is the way that neither of the two examples below draws upon hegemonic masculinist criteria in order to ascribe him such a position of popularity and efficacy. Also of note is the way new students learn of this teacher's reputation as it is part of student discursive knowledge and history:

> Everyone looks up to him . . . he's been around for a while. I actually knew him before because he taught my uncle when he was here, so I already knew him from that and just seemed to get passed down through the years. Like when new Year 8s come and they see Brother X and they say, 'Who's that?' 'That's Brother X, one of the biggest legends in the school.' It just gets passed down.
>
> (Matthew, 16 years)

> He's very easygoing, but he's also a very spiritual man. And he knows how to deal with youth. He's got a very good way of putting his point across and he does it in a way that he doesn't impose on you. He's just a very good natured guy and he often comes to say hello and see how things are going. He's just always about, you always notice him, he always makes sure that if he's needed he can be talked to.
>
> (Alex, 16 years)

Brother X acquires an almost iconographic status in these boys' eyes which appears to be related to his capacity to relate in respectful, caring and, most significantly, in non-coercive ways to the students. He is able, as Alex points out, to get his point across in such a way that 'he doesn't impose on you.' Such pedagogies are presented by many boys in our research as being conducive to effectively and productively managing boys' behaviour and engaging them in learning at school.

'Assemblies aren't cool'

Assemblies as public sites of presence and absence, reward and repression

Schools' pastoral ways of relating were often not perceived to be validated at the official level where certain versions of masculinity and competition were endorsed. For example, some boys were unhappy with the hegemonic masculine traits some teachers performed, especially in not affirming student achievements outside the realms of dominant sports. Assemblies were seen to be the domain of those boys who excelled in dominant masculinist capacities. Several students pointed out the contradictions between school rhetoric on inclusivity and the provision of diverse opportunities for student participation and recognition, and the dearth of these opportunities in reality. The response from students was usually a lack of respect and deliberate staging of resistance to those teachers:

> They have the school cricket team, the football team, the swimming team. They get big trophies and medals. For our last school play, the school entered us into this [inter-school] awards night. There were three major prizes of $1,000. Our school won $2,000, which is pretty good. Then a few other people won separate awards for best male vocal, stuff like that. But there was no real praise, 'Let's give them the recognition they deserve', there was none of that. They were like 'Oh, congratulations to the cast of Jesus Christ Superstar because they won this'. But there was no real recognition, that was it. But sporting was up here [*points to the ceiling*]. It was like 'Yeah, they did something, so we'll just put [drama] about here [*points to about halfway between ceiling and floor*].
>
> (Rob, 16 years)

Where schools did put into practice an awards and recognition system that was both broad and inclusive, many students welcomed it and believed it was a very positive facet of schooling:

> The best things would probably be receiving academic and community leadership awards. I try my hardest, we have various speech nights, etc. and they offer awards. It really boosts your confidence because you feel that someone's looking at you, I suppose, seeing how you're going. When you get recognized you feel good about yourself. You do some stuff like community work, and so you get awards for that, and I think that's important in a school. Currently right now we're at a retirement village – it's every Wednesday and we go and help the older people and talk to them and just socialize with them.
>
> (Mario, 16 years)

Other students saw assemblies as outmoded in content and style and could see no other alternative but to not have them at all. The passivity expected of students and the nationalist framework were constructed by many as illustrative of the irrelevance of assemblies and their imposition on students, rather than working with them on incorporating and promoting student involvement and planning:

> Tim: The national anthem, it's really old – that national anthem. No one sings it or anything . . . just stand there like zombies.
> Maria: What could the school do to make the assemblies better?
> Tim: Maybe not have them.
>
> (Tim, 13 years)

> The principal gets up, sings the national anthem, talks. We sit down, talk, get up, and then we go. Usually it's things about how we could improve . . . and he gives us an hour and a half lecture . . . most of it is really boring. The last assembly was really interesting because we had the Japanese students from Oharo. They gave us a gift and one of their students played the piano, and it was really good. Just kind of a different assembly.
>
> (Damien, 14 years)

For many students, the school assembly was another public performance of the authority/subordination and discipline/punish dualities that students resisted as an audience or avoided participating in for fear of being positioned as part of the establishment and thus likely to be recipients of peer ridicule and resistance:

> The deputy talks [at assemblies] . . . you're not allowed to ride your bike at the school . . . chewing gum . . . not spitting . . . other things. They [students] start bullying and mucking around, and then the principal goes up and starts yelling.
>
> (Peter, 14 years)

> Assemblies aren't cool. If you stand up there, it's like, 'I don't want to stand up here'. It's crap. I don't want to stand up in front of all my friends and get some piece of paper that says 'Congratulations'. I hate it, I hate going.
>
> (Glenn, 16 years)

Fear of harassment and strategic decisions on how to perform and where to sit in order to deflect harassing attention from oneself were experienced by both students on stage receiving awards, or participating in some very public capacity, or by students in the audience. Daniel draws attention to both of these:

> I remember feeling that they [assemblies] were quite scary for me. Everyone just went in and sat down with whoever they want and in groups. You

> used to sort of sit in rows, and I was always conscious of watching where I sat because I would be shit scared if someone would sit behind me and something would happen. It was generally academic [awards] which was not something that you really needed – because you were a geek! If you were popular and you got one, then you made out that it was a fluke. Sport [awards] were revered.
>
> (Daniel, 23 years)

Daniel highlights how the assembly functions as a site where he is under increased surveillance and, hence, open to harassment by his peers. Thus, rather than the assembly being a positive and encouraging public ritual, it was a public display of power that only encouraged resistance.

'Uniform' or 'dress code'?

The uniform also functioned in many schools as a means by which to patrol and control student subjectivities through regulatory practices of body fashioning. This is highlighted by Symes and Meadmore who claim:

> In the presentation of self, clothes and the garment systems of which they are a part, are a significant cultural force; they help to frame the body and to inscribe its various anatomical features with social and positionalizing functions. Occupying the border region between the surface of the body and its surrounding space, clothes veil the body, yet unveil, through clues they provide, much about its place in society.
>
> (1996: 171)

The normalizing function of the school uniform and its deployment to regulate students is highlighted by Rowan:

> It's about conformity or teaching you the lesson that everyone should be the same. That's just on a superficial level, but it resounds across lots of levels. Especially with my school uniform, which is basically for boys, you're in training to wear a suit. I think with men it's about issues of masculinity in that it's not seen as masculine to, well, even really pay attention to what you wear, and not to wear anything that's different from a suit and tie. And a tie should really be the only expression of individuality that a man can wear. So I guess in that sense an issue like school uniform is related to issues like masculinity and sexuality.
>
> (Rowan, 19 years)

Most students were not antagonistic to some construction of 'dress code' and many were actually appreciative of reasonable guidelines around attire in order to alleviate competitive and stressful issues around dress and status:

> Yes, I was happy with the school uniform. I can remember being happy that I had something to wear every day because coming from a lower to middle-class background, the whole clothes thing was an issue. We had a casual dress day, and that was a problem for me. I always knew that was just another thing that I would get teased for, so I was quite glad to have the uniform.
>
> (Daniel, 23 years)

However, students were able to discern a fine line or border between traditional notions of 'uniform' as 'both a privileging and punitive device' (Symes and Meadmore 1996: 185) and its deliberate attempts at erasing any individuality, and more inclusive and flexible notions of a 'dress code' within which students could negotiate and fashion a style of school clothing. Where schools insisted on a 'uniform', and used discipline/punish rhetoric to enforce the wearing of a rigid style, the school uniform became a visual marker of resistance to school authority for many boys:

> Minimal commitment to the uniform is a way of gauging rebelliousness and intransigence. Hence laxity of appearance, even in areas of quite minor dishevelment like a shirt hanging out or a shoelace undone, even hands in pockets, is an area of constant exhortation . . . in a discourse of reprimand.
>
> (Symes and Meadmore 1996: 187)

Rowan talks about the use of the uniform by his state school to construct itself as on par with local private schools. He also discusses the gaps constructed between school uniform rules and shifting student strategies of resistance that then require the rules to be rewritten or revised:

> Well, it was a public school that was in this sports competition in an organization of schools which were all private, and my school was the only public school. It really wanted to be a private school . . . so it wanted to be able to strictly enforce uniform. I think it just wanted as much control over students as it possibly could . . . if you see a teacher coming, put your tie on, and tuck your shirt in. One incident I remember was that everyone started dyeing their hair in various colours, and the school didn't have any rules about that, simply because it hadn't occurred to them that anyone would do that.

> So they brought in the rule that you could only dye your hair natural colours.
>
> (Rowan, 19 years)

Stephen, 15 years, discusses how he found a way of subverting school uniform rules at his previous school by using border tactics that he claims are actually supporting the school colours: 'The uniform was horrible, so ugly – grey trousers, green jumper with a little yellow emblem – it was really ugly. When I dyed my hair green they got really pissed off, but [I said] 'Oh, you're getting pissed off, it's school colours!'

'Student leaders or the principal's puppets?'

Many schools have policies concerning the need to promote and honour student leadership in the school. Student leadership is often institutionalized and structured as a student representative council which is meant to work alongside administration in improving the school. Students in our research were highly critical of student representative councils and other student leadership structures in which students were not actually able to effectively lead the school and take on significant responsibilities (Pallotta-Chiarolli 2000). As Tim, 13 years, says: 'School leaders . . . you don't really take much notice of them . . . it's not something that you take seriously. They don't really make an impact in the school. The school's made a decision . . . they just go through with it. They don't really care.'

A student leader himself, Andrew, believed student leadership was an underused and undervalued resource:

> Student leaders could do anything, I think, whatever the teachers want them to do. It could be a sort of monitor to look for bullying, to see what's going on, maybe with the younger kids to see how they're getting along together . . . because they often have little fights, and they [student leaders] could take some of the onus off of the teachers on duty . . . just to help out.
>
> (Andrew, 16 years)

Luke discusses the lack of power which student leadership groups had in his school, and their adultcentric domination by the 'higher powers'. Indeed, their performance of leadership, 'around a nice big table', emulates the style of their adult leaders and yet it is rendered powerless and passive. He is also aware that his categorization as 'school queer' has positioned him outside the boundary of eligibility for student leader membership:

> We had our little student bodies who would get together. They'd all sit around a nice big table and talk about what would be nice to happen, and sometimes those things did happen. But really, strictly, no they had no say. I mean they can put suggestions forward on what they would like to happen, but ultimately it was up to the higher powers that be to say Yea or Nay, so I don't see them as having any real power. You had to be voted in by so many people or get this approval and that approval. As the school queer it just wasn't going to happen.
>
> (Luke, 19 years)

Similarly, Daniel recalls wanting to be part of the Student Representative Council, and yet staying away from it as it would draw too much dangerous attention to himself. Making himself as invisible as possible was his daily strategy to avoid being labelled gay and consequently being subjected to harassment:

> In terms of SRC there was no way that I was going to be anywhere where I would have to speak up or be in the front of the class or push anything. I remember I actually got asked by a lot of people to be school captain in Year 12 and I remember thinking, 'Yes, I would really like that.' Then I thought, 'There is no way that I am going to get up there in front of all these other people.' It's only going to draw attention to myself and it was absolutely the last thing I would ever want.
>
> (Daniel, 23 years)

Many students were highly critical of the processes of electing and nominating students for leadership positions. It appears that 'popularity' and 'passivity' were two criteria, the former leading to hegemonic masculinist boys as leaders, the latter leading to minimal resistance and challenging of taken-for-granted school policies and practices:

> I was actually elected but I wasn't given my position because the teachers had a meeting to discuss whether they thought I was worthy, and apparently I wasn't. They said to me they thought that I wasn't quite mature enough. But I think it was more the fact that they they were worried about allowing a student who was going to challenge them in a lot of things that they were teaching. Being a student councillor you would have this status over the other students and therefore some sort of influence. So if Christian was wearing this badge and he was to challenge the teachers, then it would be a ticket for the others to jump on the bandwagon and challenge as well.
>
> (Christian, 23 years)

In other cases, students identified student leaders as 'squares', unpopular with other students as they did not participate in dominant performances of physically aggressive masculinity. This 'outsiderhood' rendered them powerless to deal with the bullying in their schools, as they were seen as not understanding or participating in this aspect of male student culture:

> Most student leaders are squares, like they're not people who go out and party all the time. They've got a good reputation on school work, and if you've got a good reputation you become a student leader. But if you've got a bad reputation – like fighting all the time – you don't. But if a student leader walked up to someone and said, 'Oh, stop picking on this kid', probably they'd turn around and hit him one. They haven't got enough power to stop fights.
>
> (Glenn, 16 years)

A school catering for diversity

This chapter has explored boys' understandings of the limitations of school structures, as well as the possibilities. In the course of our research, we inadvertently came across a school wherein the students that we interviewed unanimously agreed that the school offered a positive experience in all ways. We offer the voices of four Turkish Muslim students and one Pakistani Muslim student, two of whom had physical disabilities, from an inner city state co-educational school as they describe and demonstrate the potential for schools to be borderzone sites of both learning and pastoral care.

First, all five students agreed that the principal set the tone of the school in the way he established a rapport with students that was devoid of traditional hegemonic masculinist performances, and there was an expectation for teachers to follow suit. He is also constructed as having devised 'his own policies and procedures', rather than following educational rules and regulations that perpetuate unequal power relations. Abdu, 16 years, for example, constructs the principal as 'personable': 'I mean, you know the schools where the principal won't actually talk to the students at all . . . not even when they bump in to them, they wouldn't say "Hello, how are you?" But our principal will, when he sees us, he'll say "Hello, how are you?".'

Second, the teachers were seen as both friendly and effective:

> Abdu: They act like they're friends, not just teachers.
> Serdan: Yeah. They call to students, they don't yell at them.

Haseeb, in particular, was over-awed at the care and attention provided by the school. A recent arrival from Pakistan, disabled and in a wheelchair, and experiencing difficulties at home, he found himself homeless while attempting to complete his secondary schooling. He believes the support and flexibility shown to him by his teachers is responsible for his successful completion of secondary schooling and achieving a position in a university's engineering course:

> The teachers, from inside them, they were willing to help, they wanted to know your problems and they wanted to support you. Whenever I told them I'm having trouble, I found that, for example, when I didn't have any place to live the teacher, Miss X, the counsellor, she started calling different places. It took her an entire day but finally she found some place for me to live. The school wanted to help. It's not the teacher's duty to help with my problems, they did it by themselves. For example, Mr X said, 'I heard that you were having trouble with getting furniture, I have a lot of furniture and I can get it for you.' They were doing the things they were not supposed to in terms of helping me.
>
> (Haseeb, 22 years)

Third, the school rarely had whole school assemblies, but gave out awards and conducted sessions on a smaller and more intimate scale. Thus, rather than a principal at the top of a hierarchical ladder, leadership was distributed and this distribution was evident in the way school leaders and specific teachers took responsibility for the smaller group meetings:

> There's a meeting once a week. They just ask the students if you've got anything to tell them, and they [student leaders] just go and say what the class wants. Or if there's graffiti on the walls, they will talk about it and try to get students to do something.
>
> (Bora, 15 years)

Fourth, the wearing of a school uniform was more along the lines of a 'dress code' which allowed for flexibility and individuality, such as the wearing of earrings and various hairstyles and colours, while minimizing student stress over attire that may symbolize unequal socio-economic and cultural statuses. According to the students, the focus was not on what students wore, but on how they treated each other:

> We've got a rule that you don't have to wear strict uniform . . . you can dress it up however you like. The only thing is you gotta just stick to each other and be able to do whatever you want. We all believe that if you don't want someone else to do something to you, you wouldn't do it to them.
>
> (Abdu, 16 years)

Conclusion

In this chapter we have highlighted students' perspectives on school, and have demonstrated that an official rhetoric of pastoral care is often at odds with the realities described by the boys of their relationships with teachers, and more broadly of the school culture. There was often the sense that many teachers either failed to listen to or were not interested in understanding the opinions of their students. Many boys reiterated that effective teachers were those who listened, who related respectfully, and in unobtrusive ways to their students. What many boys had to say about male teachers also raised questions about the simplistic solution of merely providing more male teachers as role models for boys in schools, without necessarily considering the models of masculinity conducive to facilitating effective learning and social development for boys (Lingard and Douglas 1999; Mills 2000). The issue that needs to be addressed is not so much the gender of the teacher, but the kinds of pedagogical practices considered to be conducive to effective learning in schools (Slade and Trent 2000). Based on what the boys said about their problems, schools need to create spaces to involve students, in productive ways, in the decision-making practices that impact on their everyday lives at school. If the problems that boys are experiencing are to be effectively addressed, schools must address the discrepancy between official and public discourses of pastoral care that they espouse, and the actual practice and reality of how they position and construct students within an oppressive hierarchy of domination and subordination (hooks 1994a).

11 'I don't like reading . . . I like playing sport or being outside'

Interrogating masculinities in English and physical education

As I walk into schools to do interviews, the school culture looks down at me from the walls, encircles me, as it did when I was a teacher.

In the main hallways and reception areas where the public may enter and approve of the school and the boys it produces, I see rows of framed photos of sports teams, cricket bats and footballs held by captains, boys' arms folded across chests to boost the biceps, shoulders squared, faces grim. The recent colour photos stretch down the corridors into the black and white images of the school's history.

I see my reflection shadowed in glass cabinets of shiny gold and silver trophies, medals, and shields – years and years of names of winners engraved eternally into them. This is a school for winners. The school's glory has been established on the sports field.

Above my head, waving slightly like flags, are sports banners ablaze with school colours.

As I sit in reception areas, I browse through collections of school annuals and newsletters displayed on coffee tables: pages and pages of sports photos, pages and pages of sports results. A few pages of art, drama, music, debating and creative writing in the school annuals, very little in the newsletters, just announcements of forthcoming drama and music performances where it is 'hoped' families can spare some time to attend and, despite how busy life is, will 'try' to get their sons to some rehearsals. Meanwhile, newsletters remind parents that it is 'compulsory' for boys to play sport on Saturdays and it is 'assumed' that parents will 'support their sons in attending each practice or detentions will be issued'. The school annuals also include some examples of student writing tucked in there. But nowhere do I see photos or read about dance.

Now and again, I do see a 'literary' newsletter, proudly pronouncing that it is compiled occasionally by a small group of students and a passionate English teacher. It is 'voluntary' and students pay if they want to buy one. This provides funds so that the next one can be produced. But who pays for the weekly news-letters of sport results and sport commentaries? Why are they handed out freely, weekly and compulsorily to each student? I ask some English teachers if the literary newsletter sells. Not very well, it seems. Some teachers buy them.

And where are the boys who are not in the photos in the hallways and annuals, and whose names do not shine at me from glass cabinets? I do find them in sanctuary spaces deep within the school, in art rooms, libraries, drama spaces and music rooms. Yes, I have been there when they've been occasionally brought out for display at an assembly, to be given their few minutes before being quietly tucked away again, while the audience snickers and shuffles, and then falls silent as the sports captains and coaches take the stage to deliver their scores.

Why is it that I had to leave Australia, visit a school in a small town in New Zealand, Invercargill, to find a school where the public space where students congregate at lunchtimes has walls filled with dazzling photos of sport people intermingled with photos of debaters, artists, musicians, actors and writers, each with their own biography and name proudly proclaiming their equally treasured talent?

Introduction

School subjects are constructed as hierarchically oppositional and polarized in their gendernormative and heteronormative articulations and manifestations of masculinity/femininity, activity/passivity, physicality/emotionality, heterosexuality/homosexuality, toughness/softness (Martino 1994, 1997). Physical education and English are crucial sites in which certain forms of masculinity are valorized and endorsed, or denigrated and invalidated. They are two subject areas often perceived by boys as oppositional. For example, boys from Martino's earlier study (1994) claimed that they would rather be outside playing sport than inside studying English or reading (see also Martino 2001). We explore the effects of such gender dualisms and hierarchies in relation to subjects English and physical education. We are interested in exploring boys' varying experiences of sport and English at school and what the possibilities and implications might be for undertaking some critical sociological gender work in sport as a site where dominant masculinities are often reinscribed and reinforced (see Parker 1996) and in English as a site where alternative masculinities are policed.

The following themes emerged in our research with boys in regard to English and physical education:

1 *English and physical education as hierarchical and oppositional sites:* how performances of masculinity are validated or invalidated, rewarded or harassed.

2 *The need for critical literacy interrogations in English and a critical sociology of sport in physical education:* how critical perspectives on normative and heteronormative masculinities can be incorporated into the pedagogical repertoires of teachers.
3 *The influence of socio-cultural factors:* how issues of ethnicity, sexuality, disability and socio-economic status impact on students' participation in English and physical education.

'English is most suited to girls because it's not the way guys think'

The boys we interviewed highlighted the extent to which subject English was a gendered space. Some talked about enjoying English, but others commented on how English was often constructed by boys as boring or discussed in disparaging terms as a sex-inappropriate subject. In fact, this confirms earlier research which highlighted the pivotal role of masculinity and sexuality in the way that many boys perceive and engage in English (see Martino 1994, 1997): 'English is most suited to girls because it's not the way guys think . . . this subject is the biggest load of bullshit I have ever done . . . most guys who like English are faggots' (Shaun, 15 years). This highlights the extent to which English is somehow linked to normative practices that conflict with some boys' notion of what constitutes desirable heterosexual masculinity (Millard 1997). While it is important to note that not all boys reject English, we need to understand that institutional structures, policy, as well as other socio-cultural discourses such as socio-economic status, Indigeneity, ethnicity and sexuality interweave with gender to impact in significant ways on boys' individual literacy practices. Wilhelm and Smith (2001), for example, claim that some boys in their study engaged positively with literacy but did not necessarily embrace the official literacy practices sanctioned by the school (see Alloway and Gilbert 1998). They also suggest that boys' engagement with literacy is not always linked directly to the social practices of masculinity in the ways that Martino (1994, 1995a) has explicated. However, other researchers have continued to draw attention to the gendered patterns of boys' literacy and other social practices and we argue for the need in the English classroom to make the links between boys' private and public lives in relation to how they engage with literacy both inside and outside of schools (Murphy and Elwood 1998; Hall and Coles 2001).

Through their involvement in sport and other leisure activities, many boys learn to establish a desirable normative masculinity. These social practices of masculinity inform their participation in the school curriculum in which certain subjects get framed in terms of public/private polarities involving gendered ascriptions of activity and passivity:

> 'I don't like reading. I think it's because I'm an active person and can't sit down doing nothing. I like playing sports or being outside.'
>
> (Jeremy, 14 years)

> I am not someone who is able to sit still and read for a while. I would rather be outside with friends, or working on my bike, or watching a video, or listening to music and playing on my 'gameboy'. I find these activities more amusing and more worthwhile.
>
> (Craig, 14 years)

> When a book comes up against TV, or computer, or kicking the footy with friends, mate! It has no chance. I read computer, surf, porn, footy and fishing mags because they're quick and interesting to me.
>
> (Damian, 14 years)

Boys appear to define their experience of reading against other practices which they find more enjoyable. For instance, Jeremy, Craig and Damian associate reading with passivity, and would rather be engaging in other activities which may entail 'sitting down', but which are clearly not framed as passive.

In focusing on 'how' these boys are making sense of reading, it would appear that their resistance or lack of motivation is tied to a wider set of social practices in which a particular hierarchical system of gender operates (Connell 1994, 1987). In other words, the above boys' involvement in reading is limited by a gender regime in which masculinity and femininity are defined as opposites understood in terms of the following dualisms – active/passive, public/private, outside/inside, and so on. They construct reading as a passive activity which is set in opposition to other practices such as sport which they consider to be more appropriate or enjoyable (see Millard 1997; Alloway and Gilbert 1998). In this sense these other social practices confer a particular credentialed status of masculinity which account for boys' investment. At the basis of some boys' rejection of and resistance to reading is the idea that it is perceived to be a feminized practice; thus, the construction of the literate subject in schools may be at odds with boys' investment in a particular kind of masculinity which is defined in opposition to femininity and its associated practices (Millard 1997; Alloway and Gilbert 1997b, 1998). In light of this, attempts need to be made in the English classroom to interrogate gender regimes and provide boys with an opportunity to critically evaluate the effects and impact of masculinities in their own lives and in the lives of others.

However, this can hardly be achieved if the texts selected for boys do not somehow accommodate their existing cultural experiences and knowledges. But the dilemma is that this may run the risk of reproducing the very forms of masculinity that need to be challenged. Moreover, it may lead to homogenizing boys and framing their interests in narrow and essentialist terms. In addition, it may result in merely catering for dominant boys' interests in the literacy classroom as a means of enhancing their motivation to read. For example, some boys indicated that the problem was those texts officially sanctioned by English teachers. The material that they were required to read at school for English, they claimed, was irrelevant to them and their everyday lives. This highlights the point that Alloway and Gilbert (1997a, 1997b, 1998) make about the students being disenfranchized in the English classroom through the selection of texts offered to them for study. Many of the boys mentioned that they wanted to read books which dealt realistically with relationships and the problems they experienced in their daily lives (see Martino 1998; Martino and Pallotta-Chiarolli 2001b). While such texts may not be entirely unproblematic in their representation of masculinities, the point is that the boys appeared to be calling out for more contemporary and culturally relevant reading material to be provided for study in the English classroom. This is reflected in the following responses:

> I like the kind of stories which involve things like love themes/relationships, suicide, drugs, alcohol, adolescence, peer pressure, abortion, depression, pregnancy and other issues that relate to us and that we are interested in at this time in our lives.
>
> (Dion, 14 years)

> The kinds of texts I enjoy reading are normally texts which concern issues that affect me. For example issues such as adolescence and relationships (not soppy style relationships though), sex, death, rape, murder, green jelly, underpants and sports.
>
> (Steve, 15 years)

In light of what these boys had to say, it would seem imperative to make accessible culturally relevant texts which present characters and situations that both girls and boys can relate to in their everyday lives (see also Pallotta-Chiarolli 1998a). The fact that these boys were also interested in learning more about relationships through their engagement in reading challenged stereotypes about boys' literacy practices. They were not merely asking to be fed the traditional action-packed and science fiction sub-genres. This has real implications for how we might actively engage boys in reading in the literacy classroom.

The issue for some teachers and researchers is how texts, which cater for boys' stereotypical interests, may be strategically deployed in the English classroom, while simultaneously taking boys forward to critically examine their reading habits and practices (see Hall and Coles 1997). So a tension arises between involving boys while at the same time engaging them critically. For example, several boys in a particular school enjoyed studying the film, *Mad Max*, indicating that it related to them and that it was appealing because of the violence and action:

> *Mad Max* was good . . . I liked that . . . probably because of the violence, I guess. I don't know, it just related to me more. 'Cause it's sort of the same movie that I'd probably watch most of the time. Just a lot of action, a lot of things happening.
>
> (Josh, 15 years)

What is important about boys' identification with this text in these terms is that it is situated within a normalizing regime for fashioning a particular version of masculinity that has appeal for many boys. This practice of identification, as Moon (1998: 23) argues, constitutes 'a component of specific literacy' which is an effect of trainings that these boys receive in fashioning for themselves culturally validated versions of masculinity. In other words, through their viewing or reading of *Mad Max*, many boys like Josh are able to reinscribe a version of masculinity that they find desirable. Thus, they are caught up in certain social practices of masculinity which influence both their involvement in and how they engage with texts in subject English:

> It [*Mad Max*] fits my category of things I enjoy. I enjoy the action 'cause I like thrills and stuff. I like violence. I don't know why but I do . . . all that death and gore and all blood things. [Other people] like soppy books. They like people who use smart thinking. I like that as well but they find other ways besides violence to solve things, and I don't like that kind of stuff.
>
> (Chris, 15 years)

Through his use of the word 'soppy', which has pejorative overtones, Chris appears to be rejecting those texts that he perceives to be dealing with emotion and from which any form of violence, blood or gore is absent. However, he indicates that while he embraces 'smart thinking', he gains far more pleasure from seeing violence being used 'to solve things'. It is in this sense that he engages in a literacy practice in which a dominant form of masculinity is being asserted. Interestingly, Chris is unable to critically reflect on why he embraces and invests in violent representations.

Greg's comments below also indicate how regimes of masculinity impact on boys' engagement with particular texts. This in turn highlights how specific trainings, through which particular understandings about masculinity are acquired, operate in terms of how he responds to *Mad Max* and other texts:

> I did just as much work on *Mad Max* as I did on anything that we read. More of the film things – that documentary *Guns*, stuff like that is good. And analysing movies, I enjoyed that. I prefer not reading . . . I'm too slow at reading . . . I can't really visualize what's going on, which helps you more. Like I just read a page and go 'What's going on? What the hell was I reading?' I don't like thick novels and stuff like that . . . small print and heaps of pages . . . I couldn't get through it. I just like reading magazines, surf magazines, *Playboy* – nah! [*laughs*] Well, I look at *Playboy* – nah! Just surfing magazines, music magazines, but mainly look at the pictures in those [*laughs*]. Otherwise I just watch telly.
>
> (Greg, 15 years)

Greg is willing to engage in a literacy practice only if he finds the text relevant to him. His lack of engagement with certain print texts is related to his inability to 'visualize what is going on'. Later, he makes the point that he enjoys reading surf magazines, but only in the sense of looking at the pictures. And if he is not reading his magazines, or alluding to reading *Playboy*, a magazine constructed as acceptable reading as it validates his heterosexual masculinity, he prefers to watch TV. What emerges here is this boy's exposure to reading a range of texts that are tied to his interests and gender-specific trainings into which he has been inducted from a very young age (see Moon 1993, 1998). Through his familiarity with specific genres it appears that he acquires 'a practical facility' with reading certain kinds of texts, while simultaneously learning about culturally sanctioned versions of hegemonic masculinity. In this sense, it is possible to understand why he may not have developed similar sets of capacities and skills for reading print texts. The cultural norms governing what constitutes desirable masculinity, and around which particular heteronormative desires are organized, do not encourage him to engage with different kinds of genres or print-based fiction texts to the same extent. Informing Greg's responses to reading are particular attitudes to print literacy which cannot be reduced merely to categorizing him as an 'inadequate reader'. Wider regimes of masculinity and the kinds of gendered trainings he has received from a very young age need to be investigated in exploring his resistance to print-based literacy. Several researchers have highlighted the extent to which regimes of hegemonic masculinity have had a major part to play in influencing boys' engagement with particular genres, texts and various kinds of literacy practices involving multi-media and computer technologies (see Martino 1994, 1998; Alloway and Gilbert 1997a; Hall and Coles 1997; Millard 1997; Gilbert and Gilbert 1998; Rowan et al. 2002).

The effects of such outside of school trainings (Murphy and Elwood 1998) emerge with another boy, Robert, 15 years, where the opposition of sport and study comes into play when we ask him what he really likes about school: 'Ah, probably the sport. I enjoy that more than the academic side . . . football.' Later when we ask him to tell us about what he thinks of English, another opposition is worked into the way he sees his involvement in the literacy practices associated with this subject:

> Robert: When I think of English I think of reading, and . . . I've never really enjoyed it 'cause when I was younger, I never really enjoyed any of the books I got and it just turned me off books completely. My mum used to buy thick novels, and I thought 'I'm not gonna waste my time reading that thick book. It's gonna take me ages to read it.'
>
> Wayne: So is there anything about English that you like?
>
> Robert: Oh, I enjoy it. It's a good subject. I like analysing. I don't like writing that much, but when I have to, I do. I don't mind analysing movies . . . that's good. I prefer analysing movies to print . . . sort of visual, like the movie has the camera angle and that makes me interested.

Like other boys in our research, viewing or analysing film for Robert is set in opposition to reading print texts. Writing is also included in this opposition as a devalued practice. Robert has clearly developed a set of capacities for reading film because he willingly and actively engages with these texts outside of school (see Alloway 1995; Davies 1995; Jordan 1995). What is also interesting is Robert's reference to his mother's buying books for him, which raises questions about the gendered nature of literacy practices within his family (see Nichols 1994).

'I can read but I can't read'

Performances of literacy versus performances of masculinity in the English classroom

Many boys said that while they were able to perform the techniques of literacy ('I can read'), performing an 'appropriate' masculinity often prevented or deterred them from displaying their literacy abilities ('I can't read'). Some boys spoke of the fear of reading aloud, of inciting ridicule and harassment in English for engaging in the learning practices established and sanctioned in that subject by teachers and which contravened hegemonic performances of masculinity:

> I didn't think I could not do it [reading] but I hated reading out aloud. Whenever the class was reading a novel, taking it in turns, I'd just be

> dreading it when it's my turn . . . I just started getting nervous for some reason, just all the attention on me.
>
> (Mike, 17 years)

Students who enjoyed creative writing and reading would often do so in the privacy of the home. Peter talked about his discomfort at reading out his poems at school for fear of harassment, while regularly reading them at home to his mother:

> I read them to my mum when I get home . . . [At school] they'd start yelling, like 'Why don't you get out of the class'. Some of them are laughing . . . some of them come up and read their stories and everyone starts shouting at them . . . [the teacher] can't send out the whole class, so she does nothing. The [other boys] probably don't like their story or it's something wussy . . . if you've got cats in the story . . . if someone doesn't want to fight . . . if they talk about friendship . . . then 'Why didn't you put a fight in the story?'
>
> (Peter, 14 years)

Peter's use of the word 'wussy', as a category for judging and harassing boys on the basis of what they consider to be 'unmasculine' content, highlights how masculinity is policed in this English classroom. The power of such gender regimes and how they operate is also foregrounded by Peter when he mentions the collective investment of other students in validating and legitimating this particular version of masculinity to the extent that the teacher is unable to send the whole class out of the room as a disciplinary tactic.

Mark, 14 years, also mentions that he was nervous reading in front of the class: 'I just feel really nervous that if I make a mistake, you feel you're going to get bagged out and more harassed from the other kids.' But Mark also acknowledges he may get teased less than other students because he is good at sport, again illustrating the influence of these binarily and hierarchically constructed subject areas: 'I think it might be they can see that I'm all right at sport, and that's what they like, so as long as I'm doing good at what they like they won't worry about teasing me as much.'

Several boys indicated that they not only enjoyed English but excelled in literacy tasks. However, they were afraid to show their ability and interest in case they were targeted for not being a 'cool' boy:

> If I showed that I could do it easier I would get paid out, like if I ask lots of questions or if I answer a lot of questions, which I probably could, I might get paid out a bit more. You just sit back and don't really try and act like you're real smart . . . it's cool to be stupider than be smarter.
>
> (Max, 16 years)

Ben described how he was harassed and unrecognized for his literary and artistic achievements by his peers, and yet this reflects the broader school structures whereby a hierarchical opposition was in place regarding what achievements were recognized and rewarded:

> I'm very passionate about visual, performing and literary arts. In an ideal school, I could be appreciated for what I'd like to offer instead of being judged. Football is more what we expect from male students. I think that's wrong and very outdated. There is so much pressure within the school to be good at the sciences, maths and other academic subjects. Students who do excel at these subjects are continuously celebrated at my school with awards, scholarships, and certificates. There are no art awards or drama awards. It's just a typical example of the oppression of students' originality at my school.
>
> (Ben, 17 years)

Several boys spoke passionately about the opportunities English provided: 'You can express yourself in any way you like and there is really no wrong or right answer' (Jason, 14 years). Jarrod also mentioned that he enjoys English as he has grown older: 'You start reading and thinking about issues' (Jarrod, 16 years). Younger boys, like Eddie, however, enjoyed English and wanted space to write and read widely in ways beyond the narrowness of the school curriculum, and indeed refuted the stereotype of boys not wanting to read and write:

> Eddie: I've always liked spending time in the library, like reading and writing. Just quiet things you do at school which lets you daydream and do your work. I like books, just books themselves, like all the pages and the writing. It lets me learn about stuff they don't teach me in school.
>
> Maria: Some people say that a lot of boys don't like reading and writing. Do you think that's the case?
>
> Eddie: I think that's probably the stereotype of boys. Like people consider boys to be strong, tough, love sport, hate school.
>
> (Eddie, 11 years)

Thus, the expectation from peers, and reinforced by school structures, is for boys to demonstrate their masculinity through sport, and their academic abilities through traditional masculinist subjects. The harassment some boys receive from other students for enjoying and/or excelling in English is framed by school structures and curriculum hierarchies, clearly illustrating the link between structural hierarchies and inequities, and student–student hierarchies and inequities.

'Physical education or sport?'

An ideal site for health promotion and the reality of harassment

When examining what boys in our research say about sport and its role in their lives, it becomes very apparent that, like the subject English, physical education and sport is a site for policing, regulating and reinforcing certain versions of masculinity by peers and school structures. This reflects broader cultural trainings and understandings of 'normal' masculinity: '[Sport] tends to be idealized as a special realm . . . fostering leadership, discipline and responsibility; ideally it promotes participation, equality and fairness' (Fielder 1998: 31; see also Messner 1992). However, in reality, sport also plays a major role in reinforcing the dominance of certain masculinities and the manipulation of Other masculinities, such as those regarding disabilities, non-heterosexual sexualities, ethnicities, Indigeneity and low socio-economic status (see Walker 1988; Poynting et al. 1999). For example, in relation to ethnicity, Mathew, 16 years, states: 'You're expected to be into sport if you're a wog, you're into soccer, and there's even clothing expectations.'

Several boys in our research supported Plummer's finding that schools 'were not above exploiting the masculine status associated with football to enhance their own public profiles' (1999: 226). The men in his research expressed similar frustrations to many boys in our research that academic success was not as prestigious as football, and that school authorities often contributed to the subordination of other forms of success. Sport competition is deployed as a form of inter-school status and hierarchy, which in turn is reflected in the internal competition and hierarchies formed among boys (Skelton 2000). Thus, a school's commitment to and investment in the 'football narrative' has implications for other aspects of schooling for boys and teachers such as classroom management (Martino 1999).

School sports are intended to be part of a broader curriculum fostering physical fitness, health and well-being. Physical education is idealized as transcending inequalities among students, definitely not constructing them. For many boys, the parameters of fitness and health implied in the physical education curriculum are reduced to sport as the sole focus. This perpetuates and is consequent upon the wider socio-cultural discourses around sport that frame its deployment in the school site (Parker 1996; Swain 2000). Many boys were very aware of the impact of the media's centralization of men's sport and idolization of male sporting figures on the place of sport in their own school lives: 'I think they all want to become superstars in the end. My dad follows football. It's the only game that they pretty much televise on TV today' (Chris, 16 years). Several boys considered the prominence of football in schools to be directly linked to upholding nationalist constructs of Australian identity:

> The school I would have to say is obsessed with it [football]. They are pretty much a typical Aussie school. Well, the typically Aussie person is a person who loves their sport. I mean, like at an assembly you go in there and you have a 15-minute talk on sport.
>
> (Josh, 15 years)

This view was particularly in evidence among migrant or refugee boys who challenged the taken-for-grantedness of the pre-eminence of sport and identified it in terms of nationalist symbolism and identity marking:

> This school is a very sport oriented environment. In my Philippines school we would have academic awards . . . here in Australia I know this guy who is a Nobel Prize Laureate, he complains that the Australian government gives more awards to sports people rather than scientists. I think what he said is really true. In Australia they give more importance to sports people rather than scientists.
>
> (Jonard, 18 years)

Discrimination in sport or the deployment of a racialized hierarchy of masculinities can be codified as appropriate or 'unquestioned and unquestionable' (Schutz 1944) in a sporting context (Fielder 1998):

> I was doing softball, because it was like a new sort of game for me [coming from Hong Kong]. But this guy, he was holding a helmet and he forced it onto my head when he was running past me. It was quite painful and then I complained to the teachers and said 'Why are people so racist and discriminative?' The teachers' response was, 'Oh you just can't go to any country that there's no racism', which was quite shocking. But then I thought, 'Oh well, there's nothing I can really do' . . . so stopped playing that game altogether.
>
> (Eric, 22 years)

Thus, within a sport site, 'violence and harassment' take on an 'ambiguous function' (Fielder 1998: 33) and ambiguous meanings (see also Messner 1992; Connell 1998).

> I know for a fact that boys at school who are strong always seem to show off. When we're playing football they're always bumping the smaller guys trying to prove that they're bigger and stronger than everyone else. They're sort of like animals really, they just go up to these particular

> people and start bumping them to see who can dominate the pack. They don't do it in an abusive or offensive way so the teachers can't really get you into trouble for it.
>
> (Michael, 13 years)

The boys within our research confirm the ambiguity of violence and harassment within physical education with sport being manipulated by dominant boys for the purposes of extending their power and privilege.

This is highlighted by the experiences of same-sex attracted young men, or young men homophobically harassed, where school sport was a site of fear and lack of safety. As Daniel explains in the following, it was not sport itself that was problematic. Indeed, after he left school, he refound his passion for sport. It was the 'culture' surrounding sport and the way both teachers and students colluded and conspired to inferiorize and marginalize anyone who was not participating to some ascribed measurement of ability. Students would use the greater freedom of sports lessons, such as less teacher surveillance, to harass their peers and it was the anxiety over harassment that affected student participation:

> The [physical education] boundaries were a lot looser and the teachers were a lot more laid back. There was more freedom for people to do the more negative things. It was blokey, and I really felt that because I couldn't perform at sport, the 'phys ed' teachers thought I was wasting their time. There was that blatant disregard for you if you didn't excel or if you didn't look the part. I mean, I did love sport but I just always associated sport with something bad is going to happen . . . I'm not going to be able to get away without being harassed or potentially harmed. It was the culture, it wasn't sport itself. I'm really passionate about sport and it's really important to me in my life at this point.
>
> (Daniel, 23 years)

Leon talks about how he was targeted as gay because he wasn't into sport. He also mentions sport as a space where violence was perpetrated due to the lack of surveillance by teachers. However, he and some friends performed subversive strategies of resistance against the dominant culture of competitive sport:

> I wasn't acting like them [other boys], and that's probably why I got called a faggot. We'd just be out there having a hell of a good time . . . it was just fun. But you have to act macho, that way other kids won't pick on you. 'Cause if you're tougher than them, then they know that you'll pound them one. They definitely established that with me in Year 8 because they just beat me up . . . a good punch in the guts and that was

> during sport. Sport's a brilliant time just to target people . . . there was just no reason . . . they're just trying to establish a pecking order. And particular types of sports draw a particular type of people . . . so those kids who are into competition and winning would be the ultimate. The goal is not to have a good time or socialize, it's to win. I suppose that's one of the reasons why they always got pissed off with us in sport, 'cause we weren't interested in winning.
>
> (Leon, 17 years)

Some research shows that boys identify sport as the ideal site for fitness, fun and friendship (Gilbert and Gilbert 1998). Many boys in our research either identified these features or saw sport as having this potential if the negative, unhealthily competitive and exclusionary practices were dealt with. For example, Eddie, 11 years, described how becoming a circus performer had had a positive impact on his schooling and friendships. Becoming a part of a group of young people enjoying a range of physical activities after school in a collaborative rather than competitive manner also led to the cessation of his involvement in petty crimes such as shoplifting and other 'mucking around'. Playing football at school had not achieved any of this, and had indeed alienated him. He rejected its emphasis on competition and perpetuation of aggressive and rebellious masculinist traits – which he and his friends then performed in other ways such as shoplifting and vandalism. The most important attractions of sport were clearly the social aspects, 'but many of these young people also valued the possibility of pursuing their own standards of excellence in ways they felt they had some control over' (Gilbert and Gilbert 1998: 60). It is also a site for legitimate and unproblematic bonding and emotional expression for many boys. The pleasure to be gained from it warrants continued support for participation in sport but that 'the infusion of sport with the ideology of hegemonic masculinity is an important factor militating against positive and continuing participation in and enjoyment of sport for young people' (1998: 64).

> I think sport is a great way of meeting people, making friends. Also sport can keep you clean, healthy and get you away from drugs, cigarettes, etc. I mean, if you're talented you're talented; if you're not, you play for fun.
>
> (Ven, 17 years)

Several boys spoke about 'alternatives' to hegemonic sports such as various outdoor education activities and drama where bonding, emotional expression and enjoyment of body and participation were achieved by boys without the detrimental inhibitors of hegemonic masculinist competition and aggression (see Gard and Meyenn 2000). 'I always remember my camps.

You go on it with a group of guys and we all hiked together. It's a good experience' (Andrew, 16 years).

'All the important students were sports people'

School sport has a normalizing function in many affluent and/or religious single sex boys schools where it is entrenched as not only 'normal' and 'natural', but institutionalized as 'tradition' and 'ritual' (Connell 1998; Davison 2000). Many boys in our research who attended single-sex Catholic schools in Australia discussed the pre-eminence given to masculinist sports both structurally and socially in their school:

> My school is pretty much one of the biggest sporting schools around. Basically all the prefects were sport people, all the school captains, the vice captains, all the important students were sports people. You could never be school captain if you didn't play rugby or something like that . . . A lot of teachers [supported this]. They used to cut off half a school day to have a three-hour assembly to present sports awards. I mean that's all very well. Present your sports awards, but I never heard of a music assembly or a drama assembly . . . [they] would be devoted ten minutes. But they take out chunks of school days to talk about sport . . . [and] a big lift-out section in the newsletter. Yes, sport was seen as being as important as your education . . . and sport was compulsory on Saturday morning, and you had to front up to Saturday sport otherwise you'd get detention.
>
> (Luc, 18 years)

Luc emphasizes the investment of his affluent Catholic single-sex school in sporting success as part of its culture and development of a competitive, hegemonic masculinist structure. This contrasts with the approach taken by the state co-educational school at which 'non-sporting' Johnny was school captain:

> Well I think our school mainly focuses on academic achievement, and then sport . . . we don't have big cheerleaders and major house sports. But the sports that we do have, it's their sort of goal in life – they don't get picked on at all. I'm not one of them. We've got art, drama, music, all sorts of things. There are so many other things you can do, so if you weren't involved with that [sport], you wouldn't be victimized. I also play in a rock band at school. All the different educating focuses – art, drama, sport – have major activities in the year, so no one is singled out as the best or most popular.
>
> (Johnny, 17 years)

Within institutional or structural hierarchies, which legitimate a pecking order of masculinities, students who had some kind of physical impairment often spoke about how teachers publicly pressured them to participate in sport. This fuelled a situation where harassment by their peers was perpetuated and condoned, as Jason illustrates:

> I wear glasses and it's really hard for me to play full-on contact sport. They [teachers] just said, 'You should just take them off.' But I can't really see well without them, so it's pretty pointless. I usually wanted to stay out of sports, and they [the teachers] always used to push me, and if I didn't do well they would get quite angry . . . they'd tell me off in front of the whole class. Our school is concentrating a lot more on sport and less on academic . . . want to succeed well and win, win, win. Maybe they haven't had a lot of academic achievers here before and they just thought the best strong point would be sport. I try my hardest and then I always get a low score in an activity. They wouldn't really talk to me about it, they would just give me low marks for it.
>
> (Jason, 14 years)

School coaches and physical education teachers undertake a role within a framework of the wider sporting culture that controls what is do-able and thinkable, and is 'vested with the responsibility to produce a certain (hegemonic) type of masculine identity' (Fitzclarence and Hickey 1998: 74). Thus, the 'naturalization' and thereby normalization of sport-playing for boys, as promulgated through schools and sporting organizations, needs to be addressed and deconstructed: 'there is certainly nothing "natural" about throwing a ball through a hoop, hitting a ball with a bat, or jumping over hurdles' (Messner 1992: 163; Mauss 1973). Davison queries whether physical education courses actually teach students certain skills or whether they are assumed to have certain skills by their very being male: 'I do not ever remember being specifically taught to play any sports. It was just assumed that, as a boy, you inherently knew the rules of baseball, hockey, volleyball, rugby, etc. PE was just a place/space to "play" the games' (2000: 258): 'It's like you don't learn much [in PE]. They assume that you know how to play a certain game already' (Max, 16 years).

Physically demanding activities such as dance and gymnastics, where both men and women excel, are not as esteemed as those sports which serve to provide an arena for the expression of traditional forms of hegemonic masculinity (Lingard and Douglas 1999). Gard and Meyenn also argue that movement forms favoured by girls such as dance and gymnastics have effectively been marginalized in the official curriculum. Some male students and teachers 'resist certain movement forms such as dance, and actively construct sport as a "naturally male" pursuit' (2000: 21). Other physical education activities make sporadic or marginal appearances in schools, but are not regulated and routinized on a daily basis, as Mike explained when asked what other sports were offered apart from football:

> Every year there'd be a day where you choose [a sport]. There's just a list on a page of these activities and you just choose one and you just do it for the day. Like there might be a surfathon, or a rideathon, or a walkathon, or fishathon, those sorts of things.
>
> (Mike, 17 years)

Boys who were involved in physical fitness or sporting activities that were outside the norm of schoolboy sports such as football, soccer and cricket often found that their skills were publicly unrecognized or unacknowledged in school assemblies and newsletters alongside the dominant masculinizing sports: 'They don't really mention it [circus performances]' (Eddie, 11 years). They stated that teachers, especially physical education teachers, treated them differently compared to how the footballers were treated and revered. Some students often decided not to let their teachers know of their outside physical fitness involvements. Thus, we have students deliberately splitting their 'sporting worlds' into two distinct sites due to a school's inability to expand its construction of 'sport':

> If you don't play football or aren't in any of the school teams, they [PE teachers] just don't really like you that much. They've mainly got school notices about football. He [PE teacher] doesn't really know that I do circus.
>
> (Danny, 16 years)

The polarity of 'sporty' and 'non-sporty' constructs a dilemma for border boys. They choose not to locate themselves as 'normal' popular 'sporty' boys at the top of a social hierarchy, but rather may find themselves resisting by enacting an opposing stereotype of a 'normal' boy, that of a 'yobbo' – the dominant image of a spectator sportsperson:

> Sport people seem to be elevated above the rest of us, and I think that's crap. The closest I get to physical exercise is the [TV] remote control or lift a beer can. Oh yes, I'm proud of being a yobbo. You've got to like beer and football.
>
> (Stephen, 15)

Another performative arena regarding hegemonic masculinities and sport image is in relation to body image. The focus on a hegemonic ideal masculine body leaves little room for what Davison labels 'alternative bodies': 'If you cannot shape yourself to the masculine standard demanded in PE class, you risk being shamed by the PE teacher and by other students' (2000: 262; see also Wienke 1998; Pope et al. 2000). A school's focus on hegemonic masculinist participation in sports can be very restrictive and problematic for boys with 'alternative bodies' or physical disabilities that may lead them to being subjected to harassment: 'If they're going to tease me about sport well it just shows that they're mindless people who are careless about other people's disabilities . . . usually I just walk away [when] the kids start teasing me and laughing. And I find that very depressing' (Nick, 13 years).

Tony found that, even within a 'special school' for students with disabilities, there were hierarchies of popularity based on sporting ability. This is an example of the power of normalizing practices at work within so-called marginal spaces (Freire 1972; Anzaldua 1987). Upon going to an 'integrated school', Tony finds that the actual integration of students into physical fitness activities is limited. For teachers, it appeared easier to exclude Tony completely due to his disability rather than challenging a system that disables him:

> At special school the hockey is big, and I was so bad in it . . . that's why I had few friends. I remember I was always the last person to be picked on the team. [In the integrated school] I think that it was too easy to say 'Tony is disabled and can't do PE'. PE could've been made better for me to be in it. But they'd just run around the oval and I couldn't do that.
>
> (Tony, 24 years)

'A critical sociology of sport'

Given the prevalence and implication of hierarchical hegemonic masculinities in physical education, Fitzclarence calls for the introduction of 'a critical sociology of sport' in schools (in Fitzclarence et al., 1997; Hickey et al., 1998). In ways similar to implementing critical literacy pedagogies (Muspratt et al. 1997), a critical sociology of sport also requires the interrogation of masculinities in this curriculum site. This would involve delving into the 'whys and wherefores' and taken-for-grantedness of physical education and sporting cultures (see Fitzclarence et al. 1997). In the following, Mark reveals his confusion over the issue of violence in football. On the one hand, he is determined to play and emulate the heroes he sees on television; on the other hand, he sees the game as violent and potentially injurious to him. Yet he is prepared to risk injury and pain in order to play. Throughout the interview, he appeared to be confused and was unable to critically analyse the construction of football as promulgated within professional clubs, within the media, and the links between hegemonic masculinity, violence, pain and injury. The gaps in his understandings of the 'whys and wherefores' behind and within what he is able to describe is where a critical sociology of sport is needed to make the connections and interrogations:

> I see it on TV and I see how they're good, and I just really love doing all those things. I like football, yes, because I like just getting them down and pushing people around . . . like just tackling them and bumping them. I can see how it's violent. I don't know how I feel. It's too many feelings. People get hurt so many times, like the AFL they get hurt a lot. But I'm just really into taking the chance because I like sport so much.
>
> (Mark, 12 years)

Simon attends a school where some deconstructing of masculinity and sports has been undertaken. However, his very analysis of where and how this critical interrogation of sport has occurred – and where it is not occurring – reveals the perpetuation of certain hierarchies. For example, the chaplain, and not the sports teachers, challenges machoism in sport; he feels powerless to control those boys who want to pursue a macho sporting construction of the self. Second, the differences between media representations of men's and women's sports and the powerful structures behind them lack a critical understanding and have not been addressed at school. Without a framework of a critical sociology of sport, Simon's arguments remain contradictory, essentialist and gendernormative:

> Our chaplain spent a lot of time trying to dispel the macho theory that because you're a guy you have to be good at sport and interested in things like violence. You've got so much bias in the [media] coverage of sport. Women's sport, I have to say, it's pretty much boring . . . it's just that male sport is generally a lot quicker and the skill levels quite often are higher. It's generally that society wants to see the best of everything, they don't want to see this other sex which just aren't playing as good because they're not as physically strong as men. Guys in Australia are brought up in a sporting sort of society, but they are now being brought up to think about themselves and be in touch with their feelings, and to be able to talk about that sort of thing. But it's still very much a stereotype set by the media – 'You have to be good at sport' thing.
>
> (Simon, 16 years)

A critical sociology of sport calls for schools to engage with the question: 'How can physical education be planned for and taught so the centrality of traditional team sports in the curriculum is dislodged and so that it provides opportunities for all boys and girls to explore a variety of more equitable and empowering movement possibilities?' (Wright 1998: 24). In the following, Abdu lacks a critical analysis regarding the socio-cultural and gendered histories of sport which requires the kind of interventionist pedagogy outlined by Wright:

> There are of course females who like football, but generally it's males because it's just one of the things that they are brought up with. It's like a female would like knitting, but not a male. I don't actually know where it comes from, but it just comes, it's just there.
>
> (Abdu, 16 years)

Physical education classes have a great potential to broaden the way boys and men think about their bodies in relation to everyday gender practices (Davison 2000). The creation of a discursive space where young men can speak of 'possible contradictions inherent to masculine performances' may allow for a better understanding of body health and encourage more respect for their bodies and other boys' bodies. Ultimately this may lead to a greater enjoyment of physical education classes where there is not an investment in maintaining hierarchical masculinities (Davison 2000: 264; see also Gard and Meyenn 2000).

Coaches and teachers need to 'become self-conscious of their own subjective investments in practices such as football and to critically review their own practices and what they seek to reproduce' (Fitzclarence et al. 1997: 72; see also Kenway 1998). Max, 16 years, talked about the way physical education teachers did not appreciate his talents and achievements in drama and art and considered themselves to represent the pinnacle of success: '[PE teachers] just love all the sportos and they don't have time for anyone else. They just think they're all quite hot shots . . . the way they act, the way they walk, they way they talk.' Schools need to establish research into what boys and girls value about sport, what kinds of programmes they want, and how these might be offered in ways that are non-sexist so that students experience sport as a site for developing self-reliance, enjoying 'social networks and a sense of belonging, recognition and approval from others' (Gilbert and Gilbert 1998: 71). Schools need to shift their focus to 'encourage personal challenge rather than overcoming opponents, thereby catering for a wider range of boys' abilities and interests and avoiding the need for boys to "prove their manhood" on the sport field' (Lingard and Douglas 1999: 138). These could include dance, gymnastics, swimming, climbing, running and sailing.

In the following, Simon positions such activities undertaken through outdoor education as in-between the polarity of sports and academics and as his most significant learning experiences of schooling. This is because rather than emphasize the physical or intellectual rewards of the two polarized curriculum areas, outdoor education offers opportunities to acquire and experiment with social and interpersonal skills. Simon says that these skills can be used to avoid a more traditionally masculinist, competitive and aggressive way of working with people, as he dramatizes with his fist punching the air:

> I've found that the things I've gained the most from [my school] hasn't been the academic programme or the sporting programme. It's probably been the outdoor ed programme – not for the actual physical skills and knowledge, but for the attitudes you get from working as part of a small group, understanding how different people react in different situations, respecting others' opinions. Things like that aren't pushed enough and definitely you see it in a lot of the guys who have done all the outdoor ed stuff . . . you can understand something about people instead of just going in there and [*makes a fist and does a gesture of boxing someone*].
>
> (Simon, 16 years)

However, in schools where the extra-curricular activities were being broadened, it appears that the broadening of activities made available to boys was still being hierarchically categorized. Those subjects and activities that more closely could be assimilated and modified to emulate normative notions of masculinity were considered more appropriate than those that were less able to do so and were more likely to be constructed as feminine: 'The school has actually got a very strong music thing because there's quite a few jocks that do it. But drama, you can tell that quite a few people are homosexual' (Matthew, 16 years).

Thus, there was the development of the marginal within the marginal categories that illustrate the power of normalizing practices and the centrality of hegemonic, heterosexual masculinity that has still not been challenged (Gard 2001). For example, Peter explained that at his school, it was 'more okay' for boys to do music than drama because in music boys could make lots of loud noises and perform simulated aggressive acts with musical instruments such as drums, whereas drama was being taught in a 'softer, quieter' manner:

> Guys want to get into the music and jump around and go crash, bang [*gestures wildly with hands as if hitting drums*]. Most kids don't like drama, that's something that girls like. Like gymnastics, that's kind of like a girl's sport. They reckon it's girly and they don't want to do it.
>
> (Peter, 13 years)

As Gard writes, the introduction of dance into a school physical education curriculum whereby it becomes 'yet another "reflection-free zone" in which the unexamined, self-defined "normality" and "superiority" of certain kinds of male is given free reign' is perpetuating gendernormative and heteronormative hierarchies (2001: 222).

A critical sociology of sport interrogates essentialist understandings and justifications such as contact sports being 'an outlet for men's naturally aggressive tendencies' (Lingard and Douglas 1999: 138; see also Flintoff 1991; Crawford 1994; Mills 1997). Similarly, it problematizes the socio-cultural, gendered and homophobic assumptions that may underlie the belief that sport participation provides 'a safe place' for boys 'to seek intimate attachment with others' (Messner 1992: 168). Several boys discussed sport as an appropriate site for the display of bonding and emotional connection between boys. Proving oneself physically in a sport made the more effeminized 'talking' appropriate and beyond harassment:

> Sport is the only way that boys tend to get together and share with each other. It seems to be an easy environment because you're all mates and you're all playing in the same footy team, so it's easier to talk. [Those boys who don't play sport] don't develop the mateships. They tend not to socialize as much. Guys say, 'Oh, he's a bit of a loser, he doesn't play sport.'
>
> (Scott, 17 years)

In the following, Michael is able to link the lack of interrogation and intervention by teachers to the perpetuation of student subordination and harassment. Teacher-directed and initiated 'scare tactics' create anxiety and fear of failure for some boys and prevent them 'having a go':

> If a student is scared of doing a sport, they [teachers] usually pick on them by making them go first. They'll put them with a group of really good sports people that are able to do it quite easily. I think the boys are shit scared that they're going to be teased, that they'll make complete and utter fools of themselves.
>
> (Michael, 13 years)

The non-interventionist approach of teachers is seen to give violence within or related to sport permission to continue: 'They get in fights in football. The students think, "Oh yes, he [the coach] thinks it's all right" so I may as well keep doing it' (Damien, 14 years). 'Some teachers . . . it's obvious they don't care. If they're very sporty teachers themselves, they side with [aggressive students]' (Matthew, 16 years). The professional responsibility of physical education teachers should be 'the provision of opportunities for *all* children to experience enjoyment and achievement in physical contexts, and to gain skills, knowledge and understanding that will be a basis for them to lead active and healthy lives' (Penney and Chandler 2000: 76).

> Most of the time [sports teachers] pressured me to feeling like I was going to throw up at the point of exhaustion. I ended up talking to one of them [teachers] and I just yelled, 'What in the fuck do you think you are? How dare you treat me like this!' In the end, I was the one that was the bad person by the principal. I just thought that's very unfair. Our PE teacher was a big sport fan, he expected everybody else to be as well.
>
> (Jordan, 16 years)

Thus, a critical sociology of sport requires acknowledging and catering for the psychological and sociological dimensions of physical development, and its connection to mental health. Hence, framing physical education and school sport within a critical sociology of sport means:

> seeking curricula and pedagogical practices that are directed towards the development of critically informed citizens who are committed to playing a part in establishing more equitable societies in which all individuals are valued; in which individual, social and cultural differences are celebrated collaboratively and creatively advanced, rather than pre-defined and 'delivered'... the realization of such visions demands radical changes in and of physical education in all arenas, and specifically, in policy, in curriculum design and in lesson contexts.
>
> (Penney and Chandler 2000: 73).

Conclusion

In this chapter we have highlighted what boys think are some of the issues with regards to the role that masculinity plays in influencing their involvement in the construction, teaching and study of English and physical education. In focusing on boys' gendered perceptions of English and physical education, it is not difficult to see the impact that hierarchical masculinities have on their learning and social interactions with each other, and how these relate to wider cultural practices and relations of power. We have explored possibilities for engaging boys in a critical literacy agenda and what Fitzclarence calls a critical sociology of sport, organized around addressing issues of masculinity (Fitzclarence *et al* 1997; Hickey *et al* 1998; see also Mellor and Paterson 1991; MacLean 1995, 1997; Martino 1995b, 1998; Martino and Mellor 1995; Alloway and Gilbert 1997a). The curriculum 'is a register of social and historical values and beliefs, just like any other aspect of social and cultural life' (Fielder 1998: 31; Light and Kirk 2000). This was also highlighted by boys who spoke about the impact and effect of teachers' pedagogical practices in English and sport as sites for both reproducing and interrogating normalizing regimes of masculinity. On the basis of our research, we need to consider how boys' experiences and insights can inform the development of a critical interventionist pedagogy in schools. This would involve:

- the need for teachers to interrogate their own perceptions of and investments in the curriculum;
- the effects of pedagogical practices and school structures and traditions in perpetuating hierarchical divisions and marginalities among boys;
- the need to find ways of challenging social practices of masculinity in schools that are built around the valorization of a competitive sports ethic and femiphobia, which also regulates many boys' participation in English.

12 'So what's a healthy boy?'
Health education as a site of risk, conformity and resistance

As a teacher, I remember students rejecting and resisting health education. They saw it as a waste of time, in much the same way as they responded to religious education. Some of my students told me that they saw teachers as just giving them the facts about drug use but never really discussing the realities. This was also the case with sex education. The facts about contraception were discussed, but not relationships and desire.

I remember hearing boys talking about having a joint at a party. It was 'cool' to do drugs and to talk about it with your mates. They would also ask me whether I smoked 'mull' and I would tell them I didn't and why I didn't. I remember one time talking to a group of boys during the lunch break who were trying to convince me that there was no problem with smoking marijuana. I just told them that they needed to be informed about the possible side effects, that they should speak to their doctors and seek out information, rather than just stating that it wasn't a problem. I remember after one of these chats, one of the students approached me quietly and asked me where he could get further information about marijuana and its effects. I always found these informal spaces where we could chat about these issues really significant. It was like the boys felt that they could be honest – I don't think it felt like I was telling them it was wrong and that they shouldn't do it.

The interviews also became safe spaces for honesty and critical reflection. Sometimes boys asked questions such as, 'So what do you do when your friends take drugs around you?' and 'Have you ever taken drugs?' I thought about how I could share my stories in honest and thoughtful ways because I had never taken drugs. I could easily talk to them about how I made decisions about drugs, alcohol and smoking despite peer pressure when I was growing up. At 15, two of my friends had died from 'bad drugs'. I wonder if I did take drugs, binge drink or smoke, how I would have been able to answer these questions.

I teach students who are going to be health educators in schools. Some come into tutorials complaining or joking about 'hangovers' or experiencing 'Eccy Tuesdays' when the emotional slumps of weekend drug-taking and binge drinking are felt during the week. So I ask them to think about what this means, given that they are going to be health educators. How will they answer students' questions? How will they border and straddle the professional and the personal?

Introduction

The need for effective health education for boys is increasingly being acknowledged. Research has highlighted the impact of hegemonic constructions of masculinity on boys' physical, mental, emotional and sexual health and wellbeing (Connell 1997; Pease 1997; Mills 2001). Boys often begin smoking and drinking as symbolic of adult male status; motor vehicles are often used as an extension of male power; and heterosexual intercourse without a condom may be a signifier of sexual prowess and power (Harrison et al. 1992; Huggins 1999). Certain juxtapositions and paradoxes are evident in how boys negotiate and adhere to some dominant oppositions between hegemonic masculinity and healthy masculinity. There is a confluence between hegemonic masculinity and healthy masculinity when the latter is constructed as physical fitness and playing sport (Gard 2001). The divergence occurs when the way to signal one's conformity to dominant masculinity is by resistance to health education and healthy behaviours in relation to drugs, alcohol, smoking, unsafe sex and other risk-taking behaviours.

However, there are multiple and interwoven dimensions of resistance and reinforcement in both how students respond to health/sexuality education and in terms of how health/sexuality curriculum and pedagogy are enacted. For example, sexual health education may reinforce heterosexist constructions of sexuality by not engaging with issues of sexual diversity. This may reinforce some students' already existing homophobic attitudes. On the other hand, sexual health education that does engage with sexual diversity, and which therefore resists heteronormative sexuality, may be met with homophobic resistance from some students. Likewise, drugs, alcohol and smoking education may resist normative constructions of masculinity by challenging the 'it's cool to do drugs, drink and smoke' behaviour often associated with normative masculinity. This may then be met with resistance from students in order to reinforce the 'cool' masculinities in which they invest. However, drug, alcohol and smoking education, as well as sexuality education, may often be undertaken within a pedagogical regime that is in the business of moral regulation, invigilation and control. This is a means by which hierarchical power relationships between teachers as expert and disciplinarian, and students as ignorant and needing to be policed, are reinforced. This approach may fuel boys' resistance and disruption as a means of reinforcing a normative masculinity that is anti-authoritarian and rebellious. In light of these complexities, this chapter will explore the following:

1 *The gendered dimensions of boys' risk-taking behaviours:* how boys are often compelled to undertake risk-taking behaviours in order to reinforce normative constructions of 'cool' masculinity.
2 *Boys' responses to drug, smoking and alcohol education:* how health education functions as a multiple site of reinforcement/resistance in relation to normative masculinity;
3 *Boys' responses to sex and sexuality education:* how sexual health education functions as a multiple site of reinforcement/resistance in relation to heteronormative masculinity.

Throughout, we will also explore how some boys endeavour to extricate themselves from this hegemonic masculinity versus healthy masculinity bind. The kinds of health discourses and individual discourses that inform boys' resistance to substance abuse and call for sexual diversity in education will also be examined.

'Just wanting to be cool'

Risk-taking behaviours as strategies of conformity

Boys often undertake risk-taking behaviours and practices in order to gain the approval of their peers and acquire a 'cool' status in the pecking order of masculinities: 'I reckon it was just wanting to be cool all these little kids doing it [drugs and smoking]' (Mike, 17 years). This is also reflected by Luc, who talks about drug use as a compulsory social practice to enhance one's image and hence 'cool' status amongst peers:

> It's image. I don't think half of them ever wanted to do drugs. Because their friends were doing it, they felt obliged to. I mean I've done it as well. I started smoking because it was a social thing and then you just realize that you made a mistake. But that's how it kind of starts, 'I'm cool, I've got a joint hanging out of my mouth, look at me'.
>
> (Luc, 18 years)

However, other boys undertake risk-taking behaviours in times of vulnerability or need, having been discouraged by the codes of 'cool' masculinity from engaging in help-seeking behaviours. Conforming to a normative masculinity requires silence and denial when emotional or physical pain is being experienced. Pollack (1998) reports on studies that show that by the time boys reach high school, one in ten of them has been kicked in the groin, and though 25 per cent of these boys actually suffer injuries to their groin area, the majority never tell an adult. One year after the trauma, 25 per cent show signs of depression and 12 per cent manifest post-traumatic syndromes (1998: 46–7). The symptoms of depression in boys often remain untraced to experiences and expectations that have been constructed as 'normal' rituals, activities and attitudes for growing boys, such as undertaking dangerous contact sports and other risk-taking practices which require boys to demonstrate that they are tough and able to endure pain. Thus, the interrogation of unhealthy and risk-taking gendered behaviours in boys needs to take account of the very hyper-masculinist culture within which these young men grow up: 'our media promote risk-taking for young people almost as sport' (Ponton 1996: 2). This widespread socio-cultural acceptance and normalization of boys' risk-taking behaviours frame, complicate and decrease the efficacy of health education and promotion efforts as 'our culture has come to believe that adolescence is naturally a tumultuous time', as well as constructing a 'romanticized perception of risky behavior as sexy and exciting' (Ponton 1996: 3–4).

In this sense, injury can be seen as a status symbol among many boys, especially if those injuries have been acquired on the sports field (Moller 1997). Many boys in our research were critical of the way coaches ignored or were ill-prepared to deal with sports injuries and expected boys to adopt a stoic attitude: 'Injuries? Well, just deal with them. They [sports coaches] weren't really prepared for those sorts of events' (Christian, 23 years). In the following, Jarrod constructs the acquiring of injuries within an essentialist gendered framework of boys 'mucking around' that involves performing a range of status-enhancing risky behaviours undertaken at school with a group of friends:

> I was stuffing around with my mates swinging on this big gate, and I fell off it and my ankle and collarbone broke. I limped into class . . . and I came the next day with the cast and crutches. Girls are obviously more cautious. We tend to muck around in front of our mates not worrying about consequences. It can't be helped.
>
> (Jarrod, 16 years)

Another example is some boys' participation in 'car culture' wherein motor vehicle use 'is a performance and demonstration, a process of making masculinity that causes young working-class men's higher incidence of death and injury on the road' (Walker 1998: 24). Christian, 23 years, talks about how boys used cars to establish and compete for positions in the hierarchy of masculinities: 'it was definitely a big issue to do the biggest burn outs, or have the loudest car, or the fastest car, and there was definitely a lot of challenges to a drag race flying around.' It follows then that a priority is to possess a car that peers admire, with speed and performance being the most important elements (Connell 1997): 'The only status around here is having a better car' (Paul, 16 years).

Likewise, there are clear links between smoking, alcohol consumption 'and being male in this society . . . substances are differentially functional in maintaining or enhancing gendered identities' (Beckwith 1992: 19–20). While for girls, binge drinking is perceived as both being and permitting behaviour that transgressed dominant feminine constructions, binge drinking for boys can be seen as perpetuating and entrenching dominant constructions of masculinity (Sheehan and Ridge 2001).

In the following, Michael's peer group connects smoking with other 'normal' status-enhancing performances of masculinity such as having sex with many girls, indeed using the latter to entice Michael to undertake the former: 'I was faced with some peer pressure about smoking. They said I could get with four girls if I had a smoke. But I didn't take up the offer and they just started teasing me because I was chicken . . . I was uncool' (Michael, 13 years).

For some boys, smoking and substance use are ways of compensating for supposed flaws in their masculinity or for trying to minimize the bullying they might receive if they did not conform to these normalizing practices. Jordan discusses smoking and substance abuse as ways to disguise his feelings of unpopularity, minimize harassment, and conceal signs of nervousness and vulnerability through the embodied practice of holding a cigarette:

> It was about being accepted. I had to do something for people to like me. I was always alone. I actually got addicted to cigarettes and it took a lot for me to stop. It sounds really weird, but it made me feel good. I thought I was cool, I was doing something with my hands. I thought I wasn't fiddling around and I wasn't looking really stupid, you know, twisting my fingers. I had a cigarette in my hand. It make me look like I was wasn't nervous.
>
> (Jordan, 16 years)

The compensatory strategy is deployed because images of power and invulnerability are socio-culturally associated with the substance itself: 'the macho, beer-drinking male is affirmed and validated. He is portrayed as strong, dominant, individualistic, ambitious, competitive, and self-reliant, all the so-called positive aspects of the male stereotype' (Beckwith 1992: 20). However, some students in our research also spoke about smoking and drug use as a release from the stress of performing an invulnerable powerful masculinity. For Daniel, substance abuse assists in dealing with threats of violence he receives from rival gangs:

> Sometimes you're stressed out at school, like people saying, 'You're dead, I'm going to kill you'. I keep getting cranks on my mobile, and when I go out I'm worried about them, getting into fights, and I don't want to get

> my phone stolen. I came home really stoned and I was throwing up everywhere.
>
> (Daniel, 15 years)

For Paul, drinking was a way of impressing peers at school by having a 'story' to tell about shared social practices of masculinity. It is also a way of relinquishing responsibility, having a good time and avoiding feelings of anxiety, loneliness and boredom. His words illustrate his border position as being both complicit in and interrogating substance abuse. While he does not have a problem with wanting to fit in with peers by getting drunk, peers who need to smoke are constructed as having addictions and ridiculed for attempting to fit in and conform:

> Every time we come back to school, you get the story 'I was drunk on the weekend, I got drunk every night'. But I never drink to the extent that I would throw up. I mean I've been drunk a few times, but that's just normal. You're just with a group of friends. You feel bored and you just need to make it exciting. You ask some of them, 'Do you smoke?' 'Only socially.' They think that's a good answer, but really I think it's pathetic because they want to fit in by smoking with their friends.
>
> (Paul, 16 years)

Other students point to depression or trauma as a reason for 'doing drugs', which again can be linked to boys feeling they have fewer ways of expressing and dealing with emotions or seeking support without being constructed as vulnerable and weak: 'I think I may have started to feel better about myself really, because I was quite depressed. I was confused about life and I didn't know whether I wanted to live or not' (Kieran, 16 years). In the following, Rob's cigarettes and alcohol became ways of dealing with depression at the realization that within a heteronormative society being gay would position him as an outsider, and that he would have to maintain a facade of heterosexual 'coolness' at school:

> I'd be depressed. I'd sit outside, smoking four cigarettes in a row because I was just so upset. I thought that it [being gay] was something which was going to totally ruin my life. My parents were going to hate me, everyone was going to turn against me. Even when I was depressed, I wouldn't show it. I'd think, 'I can't act like this at school. I have to put up a front. I can't be depressed because they're going to ask me what's wrong and I don't want them to know.' Guys can't walk around moping and whingeing because guys just don't do that. It's one of those unspoken laws.
>
> (Rob, 15 years)

Some boys in our research were able to resist undertaking risk-taking behaviours. Neil, an Indigenous boy, highlights how taking drugs and 'getting wrecked' are so much tied to wider social practices of masculinity which he and his friendship group reject:

> I want to be healthy and strong. A lot of kids at school drink at parties and smoke . . . but I have the mind power not to do any of that stuff. I can still have fun without any of that stuff. People say to me, 'You want a drink or a smoke?' I say, 'No I don't do any of that stuff', and they look at me and they're thinking, 'Bullshit, you do so, I know you've tried it.' I can just imagine if I was an undercover cop I would catch so many boys and girls. I just look at them and they look like shit, their eyes are closed and they're looking around. They see it as cool. If your eyes are red and really glassy, you're cool. They are going around like this because they want the attention, they want to get recognized. I just see it as uncool people trying to be cool. I can honestly say that in our group, none of our boys drink, we don't smoke cigarettes, gunge or anything like that. It's something we don't do.
>
> (Neil, 16 years)

Neil discusses the peer group practices of masculinity which involve taking drugs, drinking and smoking to act 'cool'. He also highlights how, through such risk-taking practices, many boys feel compelled to prove or assert their masculinities. However, he stresses that he wants to be 'healthy and strong' and moreover, that his friends reject this kind of behaviour.

The reasons other boys gave for resisting were often framed within familial discourses, such as having witnessed illnesses and deaths due to risk-taking behaviours and injuries, or within a discourse of staying physically fit and sporty. Thus, without negating the significance of these boys' resistance, it is interesting to note how this resistance could be legitimated through acceptable or appropriate discourses such as Christian, 23 years, refusing to binge drink in order to be able to perform at his optimum as a sports person: 'I think I was just very concerned about my sporting future and I developed my own idea that if I drank alcohol it may be detrimental to my performance . . . and I tried to stop others from doing it.' Thus some boys, who had achieved some 'cool' boy status in the arenas of sport, physical fitness and muscularity, were able to be critical of substance abuse and indeed police their peers about it without being targeted themselves.

Another form of legitimation by some students was differentiating between levels or categories of substance abuse. The category of recreational drug use was constructed by some as legitimate and controlled within certain social spaces, while addiction was the problematic or illegitimate form of drug use:

> I know a lot of kids who want to go binge drinking at parties. It's like an extra kick to the party and the kids who do drugs as well, it is. But I think the kids who get more into the drugs and are doing it after school, it isn't so much like a thing to get a bonus in the party, it's like there's some other problem.
>
> (Johnny, 17 years)

Thus, drugs and alcohol in different social contexts are given different meanings: 'I don't think it was anything to do with being traumatized and that I needed to escape or anything like that. I think that it was just recreational' (Rowan, 19 years).

Some boys had decided not to use drugs or cigarettes due to a realization that the very acts of drug-taking were abhorrent to them. This was a difficult reason to admit to as it could lead to these boys being labelled as effeminate or weak. Usually, these boys had already publicly rejected dominant masculinist practices, or had been labelled as 'not real men' by others. Matthew strongly rejected drug-taking as an abhorrent activity; he identified as gay, and had already come to terms with external ascriptions at school regarding his 'abnormal' or 'effeminate' masculinity. This simultaneously made him vulnerable to harassment and allowed him space to reject substance abuse practices as he did not have to try and conform to a masculinity that others had already decided he did not adequately perform:

> It's macho building, proving to others that they can hold their liquor and do all of this stuff on the weekend and be fine on Monday. I wouldn't smoke marijuana because I can't stand cigarettes, I wouldn't do heroin because I hate needles, I wouldn't snort anything because I don't like things going up my nose, I'm definitely an anti-drugs person.
>
> (Matthew, 16 years)

Likewise, boys with chronic illness or physical disability concerns, which prohibited drug use, were legitimately positioned as beyond having to participate in masculinist peer behaviours, as they were already to some extent not considered to be 'real men': 'I've been sick for 17 years of my life, I have the worst immune system, I've spent lots of time in hospitals. But I can remain healthy because I don't smoke, I don't drink. Just want to keep excelling, excelling. Drugs would decell me' (Jason, 17 years).

In the following, due to chronic illness, Lance has reformulated his construction of acceptable 'macho' masculinity to not have to include drug use as long as other 'props' or signifiers of masculinity are available. Again we see the significance of role models and significant others outside of school:

> My one kidney – if I drink, I lose it. You can still be macho and not do drugs, you can still do stuff like ride bikes. Like my brother, he's got his car, his system and all that. But he has a drink every now and then but he doesn't get drunk. He doesn't smoke, doesn't do drugs.
>
> (Lance, 15 years)

'Oh cool, you got detention for doing drugs'

Health education as the site of resistance and reinforcement

Having explored the links between boys' risk-taking behaviours and social practices of masculinity, as well as their various rationalizations for conforming or not conforming to these practices, we now turn to exploring health education as a specific site of intervention. All the boys in our research believed schools should have drug and other substance abuse education. However, they often spoke about health education as a site of resistance by some boys in order to publicly display and reinforce their positioning within hegemonic codes of masculinity at school. Thus, they were often aware of the limited efficacy of drug and alcohol education when it is competing with social acceptance and belonging issues being felt by some of the boys, and their compliance with group norms around drinking and drug use: '[Drug and alcohol education] would have gone over some people's heads probably because they're just too set on being popular' (Andrew, 16 years). This is also highlighted by Lance, 15 years: 'They teach us in health ed about that [drugs, alcohol, smoking], what it does. They talk about peer pressure . . . but I hear them [the other guys] talk . . . they go, "I don't care" . . . and they go, "Oh, it's good, you feel high."

Many boys were able to draw the link between risk-taking substance abuse or drug use as strategies of conformity to a hegemonic construction of 'cool' masculinity played out as rebellion to societal conformity and school authority in regard to anti-drug education: 'Well [you play up in health education] to be a rebel. Or to act cool in class' (Ven, 17 years).

Several boys spoke about the normalization of drug-taking as part of a successful initiation into a new school and the links with the normalization of drug-taking and alcohol use within the home, where fathers were often given as examples of having used drugs, alcohol and cigarettes. With this congruence of home/peer group as the site for experiential and detailed knowledge about substances, the school health education programme is positioned as peripheral and irrelevant. In the following comment by Tim, the decision to stop substance abuse was not related to health education. Having already established his resistant conformity among peers by being familiar with drugs from home and having used them as well, he no longer had to fit in:

> Everyone does smoking and drinks and it's just what you do at a new school . . . with all new people you start to hang around from different schools . . . to impress other people. I'm over it now. My dad used to grow it in the backyard, he doesn't anymore. I just knew what it all looked like and knew how to smoke it and stuff like that . . . Schools are falling a bit behind with all that stuff.
>
> (Tim, 15 years)

Most boys were quite critical of health education approaches they considered 'soft' and trivial which would then be met with student responses that also trivialized and undermined health education: 'In the drugs seminar they say, "Don't mix drinks", but it's not going to stop you mixing drinks. It makes absolutely no difference at all' (Simon, 16 years). In the following, Mike calls for a particular approach which moves away from teachers 'just saying general things' to a more informed pedagogy about the consequences and realities of drug-taking/substance abuse:

> If there's going to be any education it should be warning, like saying 'this will happen if you keep doing this'. Have a video full of statistics saying how many mental breakdowns or things like that. So then that can maybe scare people out of it. Because if teachers are just talking about it, saying just general things about it, they [students] just kind of laugh. They won't listen.
>
> (Mike, 17 years)

The failure to provide relevant education such as harm minimization strategies in regard to drugs and alcohol in the younger years means that some boys construct themselves and their peers as being superior and more knowledgeable than their educators, thus feeling affirmed in their dominance and resistance. In the following, Eddie attended school in a coastal regional area that is well known for its thriving drug culture. Yet the school adhered to traditional 'Just Say No to Drugs' abstinence education with students who were being raised in a community where harm minimization education would have been considered far more useful and respected by the students:

> If you're street wise, you actually know what to do when drugs actually happens, not just 'Don't do drugs'. School hasn't taught me anything about drugs. It's usually just what you learn being in society or being out there with other people. Instead of trying to make kids sit through something absolutely ridiculous . . . no, they don't teach us at all.
>
> (Eddie, 11 years)

Some schools were seen as not providing drug, alcohol and smoking health education, but had strict disciplinary codes regarding the infringement of an anti-drug school policy:

> Drug policies come in like 'No smoking in school uniform or on school property', but people go out at lunch, have a smoke on the oval or go to the toilets and have a smoke and they get busted. Oh yeah, they'll do it again. It's like 'Oh cool, you got detention'. I don't agree with out of school suspension because they just go home and then go out with pals. I've had one suspension for smoking and that's what I did . . . I went out and had fun.
>
> (Glenn, 16 years)

Thus, substance use being reduced to a 'discipline and punish' model only perpetuated and reinforced resistant anti-authoritarian performances of masculinity which, of course, reproduced dominant constructions of masculinity in the school:

> They could talk about it in a way that makes it easier for us to relate to, instead of just having what the government gives them to do . . . just saying 'There's the curriculum'. They should actually talk to us about it like individuals, or [ask] if anybody has any stories. No one should get a detention if they bring something up about it. If somebody smoked inside the school, the teacher will keep us all back and say 'Who was it?' and then if you don't want to tell, they give a detention.
>
> (Michael, 13 years)

However, there were boys who identified themselves as resisting dominant notions of drinking, smoking and taking drugs, as a result of the realistic and relevant health education they had received at school: 'We learned a lot of things. It's scary to know that your lungs are rotten and you could die with most of the stuff that's going around these days' (Jason, 14 years).

A few of the boys actively and enthusiastically participated in drug and alcohol education if the hierarchical model of teacher as authority and student as passive recipient was disrupted, thereby reducing the likelihood of student resistance and a reinforcement of dominant masculinist responses to health education. In the following, Mark is active in two student initiatives: an official school programme based on a peer education and leadership model; and unofficial student-driven learning in a science class that deconstructs the authoritarian model of impartial teacher as non-drug user and expert. In its place is a teacher who answers students' questions honestly, admits to smoking, and provides his class with a cigarette to conduct an experiment on the effect of smoking on the lungs:

> We did a special training course on tobacco, and then went and taught primary school students in the area. I felt good about passing on the information about smoking, what the effects are and what it's like at high school, and how easy it is [to get involved in smoking]. It made me feel good that they were actually paying attention and learning something from us. In science class we asked one of the teachers if he smoked and got a cigarette off him, and we set up an experiment that smoked the cigarette and it turned the water into black. I could tell that's what my lungs would be like.
>
> (Mark, 14 years)

Another example of a health education strategy in some schools was the setting up of a 'health room' or 'youth information room' with a youth worker. Instead of classroom lessons in health being given, students could go to this room during breaks, before and after school, and in free lessons, and independently access any health information they required. They could also initiate private discussions with the youth worker and school counsellor who have private rooms off the main room. Thus, it was perceived by boys to be an effective, private, independent and non-coercive strategy that does not demand a public admission and surveillance of health concerns:

> They have a lot of information on drugs . . . and you can read any of that stuff on drug complications. It's full of pamphlets in there. People just go in there. I mean you've got this room with information material. They also have this other room with curtains all the way around it for the youth worker and you've got the school counsellor's room which is in the back, soundproof, so you can't hear anything.
>
> (Paul, 16 years)

Reinscribing dominant meanings of words such as strength, courage, resilience and 'risk' could also be a way of doing health education as some boys such as Haseeb, 22 years, resisted drugs as a sign of their strength and resilience: 'For me drugs is not an option. Although I have problems, I have frustrations. I've had a hard time. I have a very high resistance against problems, and I just don't think that drugs would help.'

For other boys, such as the Muslim boys, cultural and religious prohibitions either acted as convenient justifications for why they did not engage in drug-taking, or were systems and regulations that needed to be negotiated. Thus, an effective multicultural framework within the school can also be conducive in health education and promotion programmes around substance abuse: 'Actually in my religion you are not supposed to drink alcohol and do drugs. That's why I don't . . . other boys don't stir because they already know that about me' (Mustafa, 15 years).

Serdan: Mostly I don't drink, but if I do drink I just take a tiny bit.
Abdu: I've never drank in my life because in my religion it's not allowed . . . I mean a little bit of it would help you, but there are so many that can't stop.
Serdan: That's what I think too but it's up to you as well.
Abdu: No one can say 'You have to believe in this'.
Serdan: Yeah, some people are made to those rules, like some people don't drink, some people do drink but they pray at the same time.
Abdu: You know, there's all different types of Muslims.

(Abdu and Serdan, both 16 years)

'The teacher glossed over it and moved on'

Sexuality education as a site of reinforcement and resistance

Sexuality education is a technique of governance (Foucault 1979). It is 'the most formal expression of the training and disciplining of bodies' and 'both constructs and confirms the categories of "normal" and "deviant" that are central to the regulation of social life' (Thorogood 2000: 428–9): 'They just try and teach marriage, like not having sex before marriage' (Danny, 16 years). This is interconnected with the dominant socio-cultural construction of adolescence as 'dangerous moral territory' between the polarities of 'childhood' and 'adulthood', 'the space most in need of policing'. Adolescent sexuality is thought to be 'emergent but as yet not conclusively fixed', and therefore subject to both 'desirable' and 'undesirable' influences (Thorogood 2000: 429). In this sense, boys in our research reflected upon sexuality and sexual health education as a site of moral intervention and policing that was overwhelmingly heteronormative and gendernormative: 'they taught us about puberty but different sexuality like being gay was one thing they didn't mention at all' (Simon, 13 years).

Our research shows that the exclusions and narrow parameters of sexual health education undermine the curriculum's status among students and thus leads to resistance as a way of reinforcing a 'cool' and normative masculinity through disruptive behaviours. Resistance to and silencing of sexual diversity by both teachers and official curriculum reinforce the notion among students that health education is a major site in which gender and sexuality are scrutinized and regulated: 'The boys just giggle, make all sexist comments about it, don't pay any attention. They go "We all know it" and then start laughing about it and joking around . . . but the teachers never talk about gay stuff here, I've never done anything on it' (Mark, 14 years).

Boys tend to use sex education lessons as a place for 'the particularly strident exercise of hyper-heterosexual performance, for the sex education class is the place . . . where uncertainties and fears about heterosexuality might (inadvertently) surface' (Fromme and Emihovich 1998: 181–2; Forrest 2000; Hilton 2001).

Reproductive anatomical heterosexuality is learned and normalized within the context of science and health education. This focus on anatomy perpetuates the separation of physical bodies from feelings such as pleasure, desire and hurt; and the construction of a social sexual identity (Levinson et al. 1995; Fromme and Emihovich 1998). Some boys reported no formal sex education, while others reported that the usual approach was to position sex education in the heteronormative and gendernormative curricula of biology, sports, or religious studies. Boys' accounts of school sex education portray it as 'clumsy, biased, and not addressing the needs most pressing for students grappling with difficult issues' (Plummer 1999: 116). The reproductive and biological focus reinforces the dominant heterosexist hegemony of the school environment, sustaining silence about possible alternative identities and privileging the normalization of heterosexuality, a privileging that is then taken by students into their lives outside the health classroom and used to police each other in other school settings. As gay-identifying Byron recalls:

> It [sexuality] was defined: this is what heterosexuality is, this is what homosexuality is and this is what bisexuality is. The teacher basically glossed over it and moved on. Boys would start making fun of it [homosexuality], not taking it seriously, grossing out about it . . . I don't think anyone could really have the courage to take it on board or talk openly about it.
>
> (Byron, 21 years)

Where sexual diversity education had been implemented, some boys did report on its effectiveness and necessity: 'We watch videos on homosexuality and how they get hassled for it . . . It has opened people's eyes in that gays are normal people as well' (Murray, 15 years).

The implementation of HIV/AIDS education within the curriculum as often the only space where non-heterosexual sexuality may be discussed further perpetuates certain values and dominant discourses regarding same-sex attraction as deviant and diseased. Teaching about HIV/AIDS within a minoritizing discourse inadvertently results in the disease being aligned with a minority group rather than as a result of sexual practices. Andrew provides an example of this problematic link between HIV and homosexuality so that even while students feel that they are getting 'progressive' sex education, their discussion reveals the heteronormative framework within which this 'progressive' education is located:

Andrew: We actually had a guy who had AIDS come and talk to us. That was quite memorable. They were pretty thorough about sex education. I felt it was quite progressive actually when I look back, which you might not think of in a country school.

Wayne: So what was particularly progressive about the sex education?

Andrew: Well it was your usual sort of diagrams, but it was quite frank about condoms and sex. I think it was the people doing it, these sport teachers mainly. They were quite funny about it and relaxed about it. They weren't a couple of stuck-up old people who weren't used to doing it, they were quite progressive in their attitudes.

Wayne: Was homosexuality spoken about as part of the course?

Andrew: No, maybe very briefly once. Except I guess when this guy came, but he didn't come as part of a broader thing, he just turned up one day and they fitted it in. But again he tended to talk more about AIDS rather than being gay. Certainly mentioned it, but not in detail . . . I think in the end they wanted us to shake hands with him as he left and a lot of the guys didn't. And afterwards there was sort of talk, 'Oh what a poofter' and stuff like that.

(Andrew, 21 years)

This heteronormativity and the association of homosexuality with disease was particularly problematic for boys like Eric who were identifying as non-heterosexual, and wanting some affirmation and guidance from these classes:

> Basically they were sort of saying what a condom is and how to use it with lubricant . . . and blah, blah, blah . . . and hand out a banana that you can practise on. They just skipped the whole homosexuality thing, whether there were maybe students who might realize they were gay.
>
> (Eric, 23 years)

When asked whether his school addressed same-sex sexualities, Eddie provided the following discussion of pedophilia as the only piece of learning, and the way students resisted this learning – not because of its homophobic stereotyping but because it was common knowledge to the 'street smart' and only required by the 'other kids'. Thus, the course content reinforces dominant constructs around homosexuality that remain uncontested and unresisted in the classroom:

> Like they might in sex education say, 'This is one of the things that happens: if you're walking down a street and a man pushes you over and forces you to touch his penis, is that good or bad?' Obviously we know that's not good. That's why I find it pretty annoying how we have to sit

> through stuff like that. That's why I think they should single out some of the other kids, the kind of not street smart.
>
> (Eddie, 11 years)

Same-sex attracted students, such as Luc, were also critical of school counsellors who constructed his sexuality as necessarily the problem, and espoused homophobic views:

> There was a school counsellor, a very, very right wing, conservative sort of woman. I once went to see her about something that was happening at home . . . I mentioned in passing that I was gay and she goes, 'This is what you've come to see me about.' I'm like, 'No, no, I've come to see you about something else.' She was like, 'Are you sure you're gay? I recommend you go and see this man and he'll do something about it.' She recommended me going to see priests and confessing my sins. Her words were, 'You really should go to confession.' I cracked up laughing when I walked out of there.
>
> (Luc, 18 years)

Same-sex attracted students reported turning to outside support groups and health services in the light of ineffectual and heterosexist school counselling:

> I did consider suicide, and X (gay activist) is a really good person and I rang him. He is such a motivator . . . and with that conversation I told myself I should learn more about being assertive, about positive thinking. It's unfair I'm going to kill myself just because of others, some losers who want to make my life difficult. But thank God there was X – who told me life is important, you are important.
>
> (Jonard, 18 years)

Not only is sexuality education found to be heteronormative, but many students also pointed to its inherent gendernormativity as well (see Meyer 1991; Kalof 1995; Fromme and Emihovich 1998). The reduction of sexuality education to anatomy was often met with sexist responses and performances by the boys, particularly to biological information about menstruation and wet dreams, even if it was delivered in single-sex classes meant to alleviate the level of embarrassment and performances of ridicule:

> You learn all about girls' periods. For guys it's just this major joke. It's hysterical watching these videos, and for girls it's really uncomfortable. And I think guys tend to pick on girls. Like when girls go aggro over something, they say 'Oh she's got her period' and laugh.
>
> (Johnny, 17 years)

Thus, teaching about menstruation may provide an officially sanctioned discourse which 'offers boys opportunities to practise male power by ridiculing women' (Diorio and Munro 2000: 351). In a comparison of how menstruation and wet dreams are presented in education, Diorio and Munro found major differences that are complicit with and reinforce dominant heteronormative masculinist codes regarding the body and sexuality:

> Menarche introduces girls to their social position through the interpretation of their bodily processes as problematic. First ejaculation carries no parallel interpretation, nor does it mark a boy's subsumption under a system of control . . . Boys learn to use menstrual put-downs against girls as socially gendered expressions of gender conflict, as structural exercises of power, and as implicit protections against 'letting the male side down' through susceptibility to female desirability.
>
> (2000: 360).

However, teachers indicate their own discomfort by being unable to successfully intervene when boys disrupt learning with laughter and trivialization:

> I think a lot of them just took it [learning about menstruation] as something funny, because we split up, it was all boys and all girls. A lot of laughs . . . They also talked about things like wet dreams. I remember everyone just started laughing and wouldn't take the teacher seriously. I think the teachers found it more uncomfortable than we did sitting there listening to them.
>
> (Mike, 17 years)

Single-sex classes for boys have often been advocated as a suitable strategy for addressing sexuality education and more broadly boys' education issues (Martino and Meyenn, 2002). In the following, while discussing a teaching approach that was resisted due to its alienating and patronizing content, Simon suggests a greater focus on desire and feelings is required, but is unsure whether single sex or co-educational classes would be less likely to be embarrassing or harassing. Indeed, many boys had mixed feelings about single-sex and co-educational groupings in health education as both were seen as leading to gendered forms of harassment or silencing:

> We did technical sex ed in science. You get two mice . . . and then you have about 50 mice about 3 weeks later . . . and you have to look after the mice, that type of thing. We also did 'This is how humans reproduce' [with] these really really bad '70s videos, just cartoons. And you're sitting there going, 'This is stupid, I already know this, it's not

> telling me anything.' But it's the emotional side they don't really deal enough with. I think it would probably be better, like a male teacher with a bunch of guys, and a female teacher with a bunch of girls, then they can come together and talk about it because I think it's very awkward if you've got a bunch of guys and a bunch of girls in there together. But it's uncomfortable with all your friends and peers of the same sex.
>
> (Simon, 16 years)

Thus, sexuality education needs to move beyond 'factual' reproductive and bodily mechanics to incorporate social, cultural and emotional discussions that include gendered relations (Fine 1988: 33; Lupton and Tullock, 1996).

Many students, particularly those from Catholic schools, found sexuality education problematic and a site of student resistance if teachers' religious values constrained the openness and groundedness of the discussion:

> The teachers have their point of view only so you can't argue against it. If we brought up about abortion, he's against it, and we would say, 'What about if you got your girlfriend pregnant, and you haven't got enough money, you don't think you can handle having a child, why can't you have an abortion?' He goes, 'There's no buts about it, abortion shouldn't be legal.' He's a true Catholic and he's fully against everything basically. But it's our choice if we want to be who we are . . . it was difficult getting along with him.
>
> (Glenn, 16 years)

Here, Glenn constructs the male teacher in critical terms, highlighting his inflexible pedagogy in terms of acknowledging the diverse opinions of students. Given the populist discourse that boys prefer and need more male teachers in schools (Lingard and Douglas 1999), it is interesting that Glenn indicates his preference for female teachers and their associative gendered pedagogies which he believes will provide the perspectives of women that would otherwise be silenced: 'I would say we need more female sex ed teachers because males can only give their point of view and tell us about their knowledge. But when females come in they can tell us what it's like, you know, like how females like to be treated and stuff like that.'

Using religious education as a site for sexuality education also led to resistance as well as critical deconstruction of religious rhetoric:

> I think it [sexual diversity] should be taught, but if they did teach it, it would go against what they teach in RE. So they're not really going to do it, which is pretty sad . . . they're probably just scared to because of the Catholic line. They say the Catholic Church is equal for everyone but they

> don't mention homosexuals. If you dig deeper into the equality thing, you actually find out that the church isn't really equal.
>
> (Max, 16 years)

Students also talked about a transmission model of sexuality education which involved teachers providing knowledge detached from any meaningful interactive engagement or discussion (see Fromme and Emihovich 1998):

> A lot of them were science teachers who were just roped in, regardless of training or experience, and they just think, 'OK, there's a lesson plan, I'm going to follow it', you know – even if something doesn't fit in those black and white lines.
>
> (Daniel, 23 years)

> [Sexuality] was taught by PE teachers who had no interest in it whatsoever. Every lesson they would put overheads on an overhead projector and we were supposed to copy them down, and no one took the subject seriously at all. And so I just think it's not necessarily the policy itself, or the actual ideas themselves that are being taught about, so much as the method of teaching and the level of involvement and education of the people who are teaching them.
>
> (Rowan, 19 years)

Rob, 15 years, discussed his teacher's discomfort, conservatism and homophobic views which he claimed led certain students to deliberately raise issues they knew the teacher would find contentious. He saw this as an attempt to create disruption in the class: 'I remember my RE teacher said something about marriage and someone mentioned something about gays getting married. There were a few derogatory comments made but nothing was really done about it by the teacher.'

However, Paul, attending a single-sex Catholic school indicated that, even though boys may hold similar views to the teacher, they strategically bait the teacher in order to destabilize his power base. They are conscious of the potential effects of their actions in their capacity to create disruption in the class. Their behaviour was motivated by the fact that the teacher had not created an adequate open space for them to discuss such issues:

> He's a very church point of view person. We never really do any work because if you don't want to work you just go 'You should be able to have an abortion' and he'll go, 'You're mental' and that's it . . . the whole argument will be about abortion for the rest of the lesson, so it's good. I think the whole class gangs up against him. Even if someone believes 'Oh, gays should be locked up' and he's saying the same thing,

> we'll still argue with him just for the fun of it. Yeah, the class really gives it to him.
>
> (Paul, 16 years)

Another issue that many boys raised was the incongruence between sex education framed within an abstinence discourse and a discourse constructed by students that many of them were already sexually active by the time they receive sexuality education in school (Fromme and Emihovich 1998): 'You need to get taught at a younger age because a lot of the time by the time they actually get taught about it, a lot of people have already experienced it all' (Josh, 15 years).

The need for sexuality education that moves beyond the abstinence discourse is highlighted by Boyd, an Indigenous boy, who discusses how boys tend to think it's 'cool' to have unprotected sex. He draws attention to how the fashioning of heterosexual masculinities for some boys are also grounded in the 'risky business' (Mills 2001) of unsafe sexual practices:

> Some boys think they're cool because they get to have sex, and they have sex without a condom. They think it's cool, you're taking a chance. Like if a boy talks to his mate, first question they usually ask was, 'Did you do it with a condom?' And if the person says 'Yes', they'll say, 'Oh you should have done it without a condom, it feels better.' But stuff they get from teachers, they just sort of ignore it. They [teachers] usually just give out pamphlets, that's about it.
>
> (Boyd, 16 years)

Boyd also points to the limits of a sexuality education that fails to address the realities and pressures involved in young people engaging in sexual practices.

Schools may use the presence of multicultural or migrant and religious parent populations as a justification for undertaking minimal sexuality education. This justification was not supported by several students such as Ven who are from migrant and refugee backgrounds. They were able to articulate their borderzone positions in relation to home and school cultures, religion and sexuality education:

> First time I learned it [sexuality education] I felt uncomfortable . . . I'm Muslim. Now that I'm in Australia, it's a free country, so people do whatever they want to do. In my country there are some restrictions, people kind of hesitate or are reluctant to do it. My parents are happy I'm doing sex education. They don't make a big deal.
>
> (Ven, 17 years)

Conclusion

In this chapter we have explored boys' risk-taking behaviours within the context of health education as a site of performing, reinforcing and resisting heteronormative and gendernormative codes of masculinity. This has involved using boys' perspectives to investigate possible strategies for making health education in schools a site of interrogating these constructions and hierarchies (Beckwith 1992; see also Connell 1997; Epstein and Johnson 1998). Our research has highlighted the need to find productive ways of talking realistically, sensitively and within a broader socio-cultural framework about health issues in classrooms. Such a pedagogical approach must not be dissociated from the real-life experiences and worlds of young people and the issues they are facing. Boys also indicated that some teachers felt uncomfortable to broach such issues in less dispassionate ways. The very institution and culture of the school itself prevents healthy discussions about maintaining emotional, psychological and physical well-being of students. In light of this, policy directives and the development of health/sexuality curriculum need to address the following questions:

1. How does health education both reinforce and resist societal messages regarding gender and sexuality?
2. What are the gaps and silences in the health education curriculum?
3. How is the content of the health education courses policed and selected, and by whom?
4. What is considered to be acceptable and unacceptable content and teaching methodology?
5. What are the responses and reactions of boys and girls to the health education curriculum and teaching methodology?

Conclusion

In this book our aim has been to provide access to complex ways in which the boys and young men we interviewed made sense of their experiences of schooling and the role that normative constructions of masculinity played in their lives at school. We accessed the voices of certain boys inhabiting borderland spaces and who are not often heard in the literature on boys, schooling and masculinities, particularly in the Australian context. But we have not excluded the 'cool' boys and the Anglo-Australian boys who are positioned and position themselves at the top of the social hierarchy of masculinities in their respective schools. Our interest has been to provide some insight into the classifications and dualistic categories that inform these boys' social relations and modes of thinking, both in terms of intra- and inter-group hierarchical peer relations. We have drawn attention to how many of the boys problematize and inhabit in-between spaces in their negotiations and fashioning of the social practices of masculinity. Some boys deployed dualistic categories in their thinking, while simultaneously resisting and problematizing them. We see our research as contributing significantly to understanding better the ways in which boys come to understand what it means to be a boy, and what the implications of this are for their learning and social relationships at school. In light of this research, there are practical implications for schools which we will detail and outline below:

1. *Whole-school approach.* There needs to be a whole-school approach to addressing masculinities developed within the context of an understanding of the role that gender plays in the lives of both staff and students at school. This needs to be informed by an understanding of the social and cultural influences of gender and how these impact on the social and educational dimensions of schooling which we believe are intertwined (Gender Equity Taskforce 1997).
2. *Provision of professional development for staff.* Professional development needs to provide staff with particular understandings about gender and how it intersects with a range of other variables such as socio-economic status, sexuality, Indigeneity, geographical location and disability. The question of 'Which girls?/Which boys?' needs to frame any further developments in policy, curriculum and pedagogical practice around gender reform (Collins *et al.* 2000; Lingard *et al.*, 2002).

3 *Student voice as pedagogical text.* Using the voices of students can be a powerful way of initiating and planning for discussions about a range of issues such as bullying and harassment, homophobia, heterosexism, taking risks, emotional and physical health, attitudes to school and more broadly the effects of masculinity and gender on their lives. Students are more likely to be involved and interested if they can read about what other people their age really think and feel about what matters to them (see Pallota-Chiarolli 1998a; Martino and Pallotta-Chiarolli 2001a).

4 *Undertaking a gender audit.* The first step in involving students and actually listening to what they have to say is to undertake a particular gender audit through administering anonymous surveys. This can be a powerful way of finding out what is actually going on for students in localized and specific school populations. Open-ended questions such as the following can be used to achieve this objective:

- What is school like for you?
- Do you experience any problems at school?
- How do you think the school can help address these problems?
- As a girl/boy, do you experience particular problems at school?
- What can the school do to address these problems?
- What are some of the positive influences at school that help you to learn more effectively?
- What are some of the negative influences that stop you from achieving your best at school?

5 *Student involvement in the decision-making processes and school management.* The gender audit is the first step to involving students actively in the daily management practices of the school which impact directly on their lives. As Collins *et al.* argue, it is important to encourage 'all students to accept responsibility for their behaviour and to take initiatives for change' (2000: 101). Moreover, they indicate that those schools which were not amenable to gender reform and, hence, developing more effective teacher/student relationships 'were repressive in their teacher/student relations and did not offer their students opportunities to develop wise judgements or to exercise their autonomy in responsible ways' (2000: 101).

6 *Teacher/student relations.* There needs to be further reflection on approaches to disciplining and relating to students in schools. On the basis of what many boys reported in our research, top-down authoritarian approaches are not effective and actually have the adverse effect of inciting rebellion and resistance. Once again what students

say about ineffective teaching approaches needs to be incorporated into professional development sessions for teachers.

7 *Relevant curriculum.* Many boys mentioned that school or school learning in terms of curriculum content was not interesting or relevant to them. There needs to be specific attempts made to choose relevant and culturally inclusive material to engage students in active learning and reflection.

On this last point, many boys reiterated the importance of teachers 'getting real', 'getting informed', 'getting comfortable' and 'getting honest' about issues such as drugs, sex and sexualities, and socio-cultural and religious values (Martino and Pallotta-Chiarolli 2001c). As Christian, 22 years, reflected on his experiences at school: 'I got the impression that teachers weren't comfortable talking about these things and therefore weren't capable of giving me any direction.'

In fact, many of the boys we interviewed pointed the way forward to formulating what could serve as a useful framework for effective 'exploration' and talking about 'what matters' in schools. For example, they reiterated the importance of schools and teachers addressing the multiple and diverse realities of being a boy in Australia; listening to and creating spaces for boys from Indigenous communities, from culturally diverse and refugee backgrounds to talk about issues such as families, sex, sport, friendship, racism and risk-taking behaviours. These voices could then be used to initiate and facilitate discussions, writing and research activities on their own cultural and familial histories, as well as encouraging all boys to think about the impact of various factors – such as family and teacher expectations, peer group, outside of school influences – on their lives (see Martino and Pallotta-Chiarolli 2001a).

It is clear that schools need to be able to negotiate the supposedly dichotomous positions of 'school culture' and 'social culture', and to be 'up-front' with students about why certain issues cannot be discussed in more open ways. Even the acknowledgement that at this point in time and place certain religious frameworks make certain classroom discussions difficult for teachers; how laws, belief systems and what is constructed as 'normal' and 'abnormal' shift over time; and follow this engagement with information about where students can access more open and useful texts and discussion. As we have illustrated in this book, our research points to the need to find ways of engaging with students within neo-liberal, conservative frameworks (Epstein and Johnson 1998) in far more realistic and respectful ways as opposed to denying, dismissing, trivializing or ignoring student questions and concerns (hooks 1994a).

However, in order to conduct such discussions in classrooms, students need to feel safe and teachers also need to be supported. This kind of work or approach needs to be developed within the context of a school culture, curriculum and pedagogical practices that:

- model equity and break down the hierarchies of masculinity among staff and students;
- assist all boys in building their self-esteem so that they can have the courage to stand up to the peer group influences which can often place them at risk or put them in compromising situations;
- recognize that public school displays or responses to the kinds of interrogations and personal discussion boys are calling for may need to take place in private journal writing, private reading, or through texts that do not expect boys to discuss their own situations.

Boys tell us that there is an expectation for girls and boys in schools to adhere to certain constructs of success, achievement, competitiveness such as in educational and sporting achievement, being heterosexual, performing the 'correct' ways of being male and female, and that often teachers label boys as 'inappropriate' or 'failures' according to heteronormative and gendered constructs. In light of this we need to ask:

1 What is the role of the school culture and curriculum in perpetuating or providing alternatives to the limited notions of masculinity?
2 How do teachers build a relationship which equitably fosters and affirms a diversity of ways of being a boy, rather than perpetuating the stereotypes that boys should behave, look and act only in certain ways in order to be validated?

In terms of its practical implications, we see this book as providing an opportunity to listen to boys' voices and to move to a greater understanding of the negotiation of power relations in their lives. This is pertinent given that many boys may not feel comfortable and safe discussing the issues they talked about in the interview in the public space of the classroom where they are under a particular surveillance from their peers. We believe that it is by listening to these boys that teachers might be able to understand more about what are the influences and issues in boys' lives at school which may not have been spoken about before.

Listening and understanding is a first step in developing a school culture that affirms the diversity of young men. We hope that this book will be a catalyst for those working in schools to undertake and initiate this kind of work. As the boys themselves tell us, they want teachers who provide spaces where all students can have fun without that fun being at someone's expense, who negotiate rather than impose boundaries, and who treat all students respectfully as young adults who come with so much understanding, experience and savvy from within the worlds they travel.

References

Alloway, N. (1995) *Foundation Stones: The Construction of Gender in Early Childhood*. Carlton, Victoria: Curriculum Corporation.

Alloway, N. (2000) *Just Kidding: Sex-Based Harassment at School*. Sydney: New South Wales Department of Education and Training, Student Services and Equity Programs.

Alloway, N. and Gilbert, P. (1997a) *Boys and Literacy*. Melbourne: Curriculum Corporation.

Alloway, N. and Gilbert, P. (1997b) Boys and literacy: lessons from Australia, *Gender and Education*, 9(1): 49–58.

Alloway, N. and Gilbert, P. (1998) Reading literacy test data: benchmarking success, *Australian Journal of Language and Literacy*, 21(3): 249–61.

Anzaldua, G. (1987) *Borderlands/LA Frontera: The New Mestiza*. San Francisco: Spinsters/Aunt Lute.

Anzaldua, G. (ed.) (1990) *Making Face, Making Soul/Haciendo Caras*. San Francisco: Aunt Lute.

Armstrong, N. (1988) The gender bind: women and the disciplines, *Genders*, 3, Fall, 1–23.

Arnot, M., David, M. and Weiner, G. (1999) *Closing the Gap: Postwar Education and Social Change*. London: Polity Press.

Asch, A. and Fine, M. (1988) Introduction: beyond pedestals, in M. Fine and A. Asch (eds) *Women with Disabilities: Essays in Psychology, Culture, and Politics*. Philadelphia: Temple University Press.

Asch, A. and Fine, M. (1997) Nurturance, sexuality and women with disabilities, in L.J. Davis (ed.) *The Disability Studies Reader*. New York: Routledge.

Asch, A. and Sacks, L. (1983) Lives without, lives within: autobiographies of blind men and women, *Journal of Visual Impairment and Blindness*, 77(6): 242–7.

Aveling, R. (1998) Aboriginal studies: for whom and to what ends?, *Discourse*, 19(3): 301–14.

Bakhtin, M. (1965) *Rabelais and his World*. Bloomington: Indiana University Press.

Bakhtin, M. (1981) *The Dialogic Imagination*. Austin: University of Texas Press.

Beckett, L. (ed.) (1998) *Everyone is Special! A Handbook For Teachers on Sexuality Education*. Brisbane: Association of Women Educators.

Beckett, L. (2001) Challenging boys; addressing issues of masculinity within a gender equity framework, in W. Martino and B. Meyenn (eds) *What about the Boys? Issues of Masculinity in Schools*. Buckingham: Open University Press.

Beckwith, J.B. (1992) Substance abuse, responsible use, and gender, *Drugs in Society*. 1: 18–23.

Beresford, Q. and Omaji, P. (1996) *Rites of Passage: Aboriginal Youth, Crime and Justice*. Fremantle: Fremantle Arts Centre Press.

Bergling, T. (2001) *Sissyphobia: Gay Men and Effeminate Behaviour*. New York: Harrington Park Press.

Bhabha, H. (1988) The commitment to theory, *New Formations*, 5: 5–23.

Bhabha, H. (1990a) The other question: difference, discrimination and the discourse of colonialism, in R. Ferguson, M. Gever, M.T. Trinh and C. West (eds) *Out There: Marginalization and Contemporary Cultures*. Cambridge, MA: MIT Press.

Bhabha, H. (1990b) The third space, in J. Rutherford (ed.) *Identity: Community, Culture, Difference*. London: Lawrence & Wishart.

Bhabha, H. (1990c) DissemiNation: time, narrative, and the margins of the modern nation, in H.K. Bhabha (ed.) *Nation and Narration*. London: Routledge.

Bhabha, H. (1994) *The Location of Culture*. London: Routledge.

Blinde, E. and Taub, D. (1999) Personal empowerment through sport and physical fitness activity: perspectives from male college students with physical and sensory disabilities, *Journal of Sport Behavior*, 22(2): 181–2.

Bottomley, G. (1992) *From Another Place: Migration and the Politics of Culture*. Melbourne: Cambridge University Press.

Bourke, C., Bourke, E. and Edwards, B. (2000) *Aboriginal Australia: An Introductory Reader in Aboriginal Studies*. Brisbane: University of Queensland Press.

Brah, A. (1996) *Cartographies of Diaspora*. London: Routledge.

Britzman, D. (1995) Is there a queer pedagogy? Or stop reading straight, *Educational Theory*, 45: 151–65.

Bryan, W. (1999) *Multicultural Aspects of Disabilities: A Guide to Understanding Minorities in the Rehabilitation Process*. Springfield, IL: Charles C. Thomas.

Burbules, N.C. (1997) A grammar of difference: some ways of rethinking difference and diversity as educational topics, *Australian Educational Researcher*, 24(1): 97–116.

Burfit, J. (1998) Straight acting, *Outrage Magazine*, 187: 36–8.

Burke, J.F (1999) Reconciling cultural diversity with a democratic community: *Mestizaje* as opposed to the usual suspects, *Citizenship Studies*, 3(1): 119–40.

Butler, J. (1990) *Gender Trouble: Feminism and the Subversion of Identity*. London: Routledge.

Chappell, A. (1997) From normalisation to where?, in L. Barton and M. Oliver (eds) *Disability Studies: Past, Present and Future*. Leeds: Disability Press.

Cheng, C. (1999) Marginalized masculinities and hegemonic masculinity: an introduction, *Journal of Men's Studies*, 7(3): 295–315.

Child, I. (1970) *Italian or American? The Second Generation in Conflict*. New York: Russell and Russell.

Christensen, C. (1996) Disabled, handicapped or disordered: what's in a name?, in C. Christensen and F. Rizvi (eds) *Disability and Dilemmas of Education and Justice*. Buckingham: Open University Press.

Chua, P. and Fujino, D. (1999) Negotiating new Asian–American masculinities: attitudes and gender expectations, *Journal of Men's Studies*, 7(3): 391–413.

Coates, S. (1987) Extreme femininity in boys, *Medical Aspects of Human Sexuality*, August: 104–10.

Coleman, W. (1990) Doing masculinity/doing theory, in J. Hearn and D. Morgan (eds) *Men, Masculinities and Social Theory*. London: Unwin Hyman.

Collins C., Batten, M., Ainley, J. and Getty, C. (1996) *Gender and School Education*. Canberra: Australian Council for Educational Research.

Collins, C., Kenway, J. and McLeod, J. (2000) *Factors Influencing the Educational Performance of Males and Females in School and their Initial Destinations after Leaving School*, Canberra: Department of Education, Training and Youth Affairs.

Connell, R. (1987) *Gender and Power*. Cambridge: Polity Press.

Connell, R. W. (1989) Cool guys, swots and wimps: the interplay of masculinity and education, *Oxford Review of Education*, 15(3): 291–303.

Connell R. (1992) A very straight gay: masculinity, homosexual experience, and the dynamics of gender, *American Sociological Review*, 57: 735–51.

Connell, R. (1994) Knowing about masculinity, teaching boys and men. Paper presented to the Pacific Sociological Association Conference, San Diego, April.

Connell, R. (1995) *Masculinities*. Sydney: Allen & Unwin.

Connell, R. (1997) Australian masculinities, health and social change. *Proceedings of the Second National Men's Health Conference*, Fremantle, Western Australia, 29–31 October, 14–21.

Connell, B. (1998) 'Foreword' in C. Hickey, L. Fitzclarence and R. Matthews (eds) *Where the Boys Are: Masculinity, Sport and Education*. Geelong: Deakin University Centre for Education and Change.

Connelly, F.M. and Clandinin, D.J. (1990) Stories of experience and narrative inquiry, *Teacher Education Quarterly*, 21(1): 145–58.

Cope, B. and Kalantzis, M. (1995) Why literacy pedagogy has to change, *Education Australia*, 30: 8–11.

Crawford, J. (1994) Encouraging male participation in dance, *Journal of Physical Education, Recreation and Dance*, 65(2): 40–3.

Crowley, V. (1993) Teachers and contradictions of culturalism, in G. Verma (ed.) *Inequality and Teacher Education: An International Perspective*. London: Falmer.

Davies, B. (1993) *Shards of Glass: Children Reading and Writing Beyond Gender Identities*. Sydney: Allen & Unwin.

Davies, B. (1995) What about the boys? The parable of the bear and the rabbit, *Interpretations*, 28(2): 1–17.

Davies, B. (2000) *A Body of Writing 1990–1999*. New York: AltaMira Press.

Davis, J. (2001) Transgressing the masculine: African American boys and the failure of schools, in W. Martino and B. Meyenn (eds) *What about the Boys? Issues of Masculinity in Schools*. Buckingham: Open University Press.

Davison, K. (2000) Boys' bodies in school: physical education, *Journal of Men's Studies*, 8(2): 255–66.

Deegan, M. (1985) Multiple minority groups: a case study of physically disabled women, in M.J. Deegan and N.A. Brooks (eds) *Women and Disability: The Double Handicap*. New Brunswick: Transaction Books.

Diorio, J. and Munro, J. (2000) Doing harm in the name of protection: menstruation as a topic for sex education, *Gender and Education*, 12(3): 347–65.

Dodson, M. (1994) The end in the beginning: re(de)fining Aboriginality, *Australian Aboriginal Studies*, 1: 2–13.

Douglas, M. (1966) *Purity and Danger: An Analysis of Concepts of Pollution and Taboo*. New York: Ark.

Duruz, A. (1999) Sister outsider, or 'just another thing I am': intersections of cultural and sexual identities in Australia, in P. Jackson and G. Sullivan (eds) *Multicultural Queer: Australian Narratives*. New York: Haworth Press.

Dutton, K. (1995) *The Perfectible Body: The Western Ideal of Physical Development*. London: Cassell.

Dyer, R. (1997) *White*. London: Routledge.

Ely, M., Anzul, M., Downing, M. and Vinz, R. (1997) *On Writing Qualitative Research: Living By Words*. London: Falmer Press.

Epstein, D. (ed.) (1994) *Challenging Lesbian and Gay Inequalities in Education*. Buckingham: Open University Press.

Epstein, D. (1997) Boyz' own stories: masculinities and sexualities in schools, *Gender and Education*, 9(1): 105–15.

Epstein, D. (1998) Real boys don't work: 'underachievement', masculinity and the harassment of 'sissies', in D. Epstein, J. Elwood, V. Hey and J. Maw (eds) *Failing Boys?* Buckingham: Open University Press.

Epstein, D. and Johnson, R. (1998) *Schooling Sexualities*. Buckingham: Open University Press.

Epstein, D., Elwood, J., Hey, V. and Maw, J. (eds) (1998) *Failing Boys? Issues in Gender and Achievement*. Buckingham: Open University Press.

Fanon, F. (1967) *Black Skin, White Masks*. New York: Grove Weidenfeld.

Ferfolja, T. (1998) Australian lesbian teachers: a reflection of homophobic harassment of high school teachers in New South Wales government schools, *Gender and Education*, 10(4), 401–15.

Fielder, J. (1998) Stereotyping Aboriginal footballers: postcolonial reading strategies, *Interpretations*, 31(1): 30–4.

Fine, M. (1988) Sexuality, schooling, and adolescent females: the missing discourse of desire, *Harvard Educational Review*, 58: 29–53.

Fine, M. (1997) Whitnessing whiteness, in M. Fine, L. Weis, L.C. Powell and L.M. Wong (eds) *Off White: Readings on Race, Power and Society*. New York: Routledge.

Fisher, S. (1997) Who's doing the bullying? Responding to hegemonic masculinity within secondary schools. Submitted in part requirement for the degree of Master of Arts, Department of Social Sciences, RMIT.

Fitzclarence, L. and Hickey, C. (1998) Learning to rationalise abusive behaviour through football in C. Hickey, L. Fitzclarence and R. Matthews (eds) *Where the Boys Are: Masculinity, Sport and Education*. Geelong: Deakin University Centre for Education and Change.

Fitzclarence, L., Hickey, C. and Matthews, R. (1997) Getting changed for football: challenging communities of practice, *Curriculum Perspectives*, 17(1): 69–73.

Flintoff, A. (1991) Dance, masculinity and teacher education, *British Journal of Physical Education*, 22(4): 31–5.

Forrest, S. (2000). 'Big and tough': boys learning about sexuality and manhood, *Sexual and Relationship Therapy* 15(3): 247–61.

Foster, V., Kimmel, M. and Skelton, C. (2001) What about the boys?: an overview of the debates, in W. Martino and B. Meyenn (eds) *What about the Boys? Issues of Masculinity in Schools*. Buckingham: Open University Press.

Foucault, M. (1978) *The History of Sexuality*, Vol. 1. Trans. R. Hurley. New York: Vintage.

Foucault, M. (1979) Studies in governmentality, *Ideology and Consciousness*, 6: 5–22.

Foucault, M. (1980) *Michel Foucault: Power/Knowledge: Selected Interviews and Other Writings 1972–1977*, C. Gordon (ed.). Sussex: Harvester.

Foucault, M. (1982) The subject and power: Afterword, in H. Dreyfus and P. Rabinow *Michel Foucault: Beyond Structuralism and Hermeneutics*. Sussex: Harvester.

Foucault, M. (1984a) Preface to *The History of Sexuality*, Vol. 2, in P. Rabinow (ed.) *The Foucault Reader*. London: Penguin.

Foucault, M. (1984b) Truth and power, in P. Rabinow (ed.) *The Foucault Reader*. London: Penguin.

Foucault, M. (1985) *The History of Sexuality*, Vol. 2. Trans. R. Hurley. New York: Vintage.

Foucault, M. (1986) *The History of Sexuality*, Vol. 3. Trans. R. Hurley. New York: Vintage.

Foucault, M. (1987) The ethic of care for the self as a practice of freedom, *Philosophy and Social Criticism*, 12: 113–31.

Foucault, M. (1988) Technologies of the self, in L. Martin, H. Gutman and P. Hutton (eds) *Technologies of the Self*. Massachusetts: University of Massachusetts Press.

Francis, S. (1995) Pacific Islander young people: issues of juvenile justice and cultural dislocation, in C. Guerra and R. White (eds) *Ethnic Minority Youth in Australia: Challenges and Myths*. Hobart: National Clearinghouse for Youth Studies.

Francis, B. and Skelton, C. (2001) Men teachers and the construction of heterosexual masculinity in the classroom. *Sex Education* 1(1): 9–21.

Frank, B. (1987) Hegemonic heterosexual masculinity, *Studies in Political Economy*, 24: 159–70.

Frank, B. (1993) Straight/strait jackets for masculinity: educating for real men, *Atlantis*, 18(1,2): 47–59.

Freire, P. (1972) *Pedagogy of the Oppressed*. Harmondsworth: Penguin.

Fromme, R.A. and Emihovich, C. (1998) Boys will be boys: young males' perception of women, sexuality, and prevention, *Education and Urban Society*, 30(2): 172–88.

Game, A. and Metcalfe, A. (1996) *Passionate Sociology*. London: Sage.

Gard, M. (2001) Dancing around the 'problem' of boys and dance, *Discourse: Studies in the Cultural Politics of Education*, 22(2): 213–25.

Gard, M. and Meyenn, R. (2000) Boys, bodies, pleasure and pain: interrogating contact sports in schools, *Sport, Education and Society*, 5(1): 19–34.

Garton, S. (1998) War and masculinity in twentieth century Australia, *Journal of Australian Studies*, 56: 86–95.

Gender Equity Taskforce (1997) *Gender Equity: A Framework for Australian Schools*. Canberra: Ministerial Council for Employment, Education, Training and Youth Affairs.

Gerschick, T.J. and Miller, A.S. (1994a) Manhood and physical disability, *Changing Men*, 27: 25–30.

Gerschick, T.J. and Miller, A.S. (1994b) Gender identities at the crossroads of masculinity and disability, *Masculinities*, 2(1): 34–55.

Gilbert, P. and Gilbert, R. (1998) *Masculinity Goes to School*. Sydney: Allen & Unwin.

Giroux, H. (1992a) Post-colonial ruptures and democratic possibilities: multiculturalism as anti-racist pedagogy, *Cultural Critique*, 21: 5–39.

Giroux, H. (1992b) *Border Crossings: Cultural Workers and the Politics of Education*. New York: Routledge.

Giroux, H. (1992c) Resisting difference: cultural studies and the discourse of critical pedagogy, in L. Grossberg, C. Nelson, and P.A. Treichler (eds) *Cultural Studies*. New York: Routledge.

Glassner, B. (1992) Men and muscles, in M.S. Kimmel and M.A. Messner (eds) *Men's Lives*. New York: Macmillan

Goldflam, A., Chadwick, R. and Brown, G. (1999) *Here for Life Youth Sexuality Project*. Perth: WA AIDS Council and Gay and Lesbian Counselling Service.

Graham, D. (1989) *Dying Inside*. Sydney: Allen & Unwin.

Green, R. (1987) *The 'Sissy Boy Syndrome' and the Development of Homosexuality*. Binghamton, NY: Vail-Ballou Press.

Groome, H. (1995) Towards improved understandings of Aboriginal young people, *Youth Studies Australia*, 14: 17–21.

Gucciardo, T. (1987) The best of both worlds: a study of second-generation Italo-Australians, Catholic Intercultural Resource Centre papers no. 51.

Guerra, C. and White, R. (eds) (1995) *Ethnic Minority Youth in Australia: Challenges and Myths*. Hobart: National Clearinghouse on Youth Studies.

Hall, S. (1990) Cultural identity and diaspora, in J. Rutherford (ed.) *Identity, Community, Cultural Difference*. London: Lawrence & Wishart.

Hall, C. and Coles, M. (1997) Gendered readings: helping boys to develop as critical readers, *Gender and Education*, 9(1): 61–8.

Hall, C. and Coles, M. (2001) Boys, books and breaking boundaries: developing literacy in and out of school, in W. Martino and B. Meyenn (eds) *What about the Boys? Issues of Masculinity in Schools*. Buckingham: Open University Press.

Harp, R. (1994). Native by nature?, in E.M. Godway and G. Finn (eds) *Who is this We? Absence of Community*. Montreal: Black Rose Books.

Harris, M.B. (ed.) (1997) *School Experiences of Gay and Lesbian Youth: The Invisible Minority*. New York: Harrington Park Press.

Harrison, J., Chin, J. and Ficarotto, T. (1992) Warning: masculinity may be dangerous to your health, in M.S. Kimmel and M.A. Messner (eds) *Men's Lives*. New York: Macmillan.

Hastings, E. (1996) Assumption, expectation and discrimination: gender issues for girls with disabilities in Gender Equity Taskforce, *Gender Equity: A Framework for Australian Schools*. Canberra: Ministerial Council for Employment, Education, Training and Youth Affairs.

Haynes, F. and McKenna, T. (eds) (2001) *Unseen Genders: Beyond the Binaries*. New York: Peter Lang.

Herbert, J. (1995) Gender issues for Aboriginal and Torres Strait Islander girls – exploring issues for Aboriginal and Torres Strait Islander boys, *The Aboriginal Child at School*, 23(2): 9–16.

Hesse, B. (ed.) (2000) *Un/Settled Multiculturalisms: Diasporas, Entanglements, 'Transruptions'*. London: Zed Books.

Hey, V. (1997) *The Company She Keeps: An Ethnography of Girls' Friendship*. Buckingham: Open University Press.

Hickey, C., Fitzclarence, L. and Matthews, R. (eds) (1998) *Where the Boys Are: Masculinity, Sport and Education*. Geelong: Deakin University Centre for Education and Change.

Higgins, P.C. (1992) *Making Disability: Exploring the Social Transformation of Human Variation*. Springfield, IL: Charles C. Thomas.

Hilton, G.L.S. (2001) Sex education – the issues when working with boys, *Sex Education* 1(1): 31–41.

Holland, W. (1996) Mis/taken identity, in E. Vasta and S. Castles (eds) *The Teeth are Smiling: the Persistence of Racism in Multicultural Australia*. St Leonards, NSW: Allen & Unwin.

Holland, J., Ramazangolu, C. and Sharpe, S. (1993) *Wimp or Gladiator: Contradictions in Acquiring Masculine Sexuality*. London: Tufnell Press.

hooks, b. (1990) *Yearning: Race, Gender and Cultural Politics*. Boston: South End Press.

hooks, b. (1994a) *Teaching to Transgress: Education as the Practice of Freedom*. New York: Routledge.

hooks, b. (1994b) *Outlaw Culture: Resisting Representations*. New York: Routledge.

Huggins, A.K. (1999) The Australian Male: Illness, Injury and Death by Socialisation. Unpublished paper provided by Allan Huggins to the authors.

Hughson, J. (1997) Football, folk dancing and fascism: diversity and difference in multicultural Australia, *ANZJS*, 33(2): 167–86.

Hulse, D. (1997) *Brad and Cory: A Study of Middle School Boys*. Hunting Valley, OH: University School Press.

Hunter, I. (1988) *Culture and Government: The Emergence of Literary Education*. London: Macmillan.

Hunter, I. (1994) *Rethinking the School: Subjectivity, Bureaucracy, Criticism*. Sydney: Allen & Unwin.

Jackson, D. (1998) Breaking out of the binary trap: boys' underachievement, schooling and gender relations, in D. Epstein, J. Elwood, V. Hey and J. Maw (eds) *Failing Boys?: Issues in Gender and Achievement*. Buckingham: Open University Press.

Jackson, P. and Sullivan, G. (eds) (1999) *Multicultural Queer: Australian Narratives*. New York: Haworth Press.

Johnson, P. (1993) Anti-racist education and Aboriginal studies in the primary school, in K. Riddiford, E. Wilson and B. Wright (eds) *Contemporary Issues in Aboriginal and Torres Strait Islander Studies*. Proceedings of the 4th National Conference, Cairns College of Technical and Further Education, Queensland, pp. 1–13.

Jordan, E. (1995) Fighting boys and fantasy play: the construction of masculinity in the early years of school, *Gender and Education*, 7(1): 69–86.

Kalof, L. (1995) Sex, power and dependency: the politics of adolescent sexuality, *Journal of Youth and Adolescence*, 24(2): 229–49.

Kehily, M. and Nayak, A. (1997) Lads and laughter: humour and the production of heterosexual hierarchies, *Gender and Education*, 9(1): 69–87.

Kendall, C. (1998) Combating lesbian and gay youth suicide and HIV/AIDS transmission rates: an examination of possible education strategies in Western Australian high schools in light of prevailing state statutes, *E Law – Murdoch University Electronic Journal of Law*, 5(4).

Kendall, C. (2001) *Gay male pornography: an issue of sex discrimination*. Doctoral thesis, Law School, University of Michigan, Ann Arbor.

Kenway, J. (1998) Masculinity studies, sport and feminisms: fair play or foul? in C. Hickey, L. Fitzclarence, and R. Matthews (eds) *Where the Boys Are: Masculinity, Sport and Education*. Geelong: Deakin University Centre for Education and Change.

Kenway, J. and Willis, S. with Blackmore, J. and Rennie, L. (1997) *Answering Back: Girls, Boys and Feminism in Schools*. Sydney: Allen & Unwin.

Kessler, S., Ashenden, D.J., Connell, R.W. and Dowsett, G.W. (1985) Gender relations in secondary schooling, *Sociology of Education*, 58: 34–48.

Kimmel, M. (1994) Masculinity as homophobia: fear, shame and silence in the construction of gender identity, in H. Brod and M. Kaufman (eds) *Theorising Masculinities*. Thousand Oaks: Sage.

Langton, M. (1993) 'Well, I heard it on the radio and I saw it on the television': an essay for the Australian Film Commission on the politics and aesthetics of filmmaking. North Sydney: Australian Film Commission.

Laskey, L. and Beavis, C. (1996) *Schooling & Sexualities*. Geelong: Deakin University Centre for Education and Change.

Lather, P. (1991) *Feminist Research in Education: Within/Against*. Geelong: Deakin University.

Letts, W. and Sears, J. (eds) (1999) *Queering Elementary Education*. Colorado: Rowman & Littlefield.

Levine-Raskey, C. (1998) Framing whiteness: working through the tensions in introducing whiteness to educators, *Race, Ethnicity and Education*, 3(3): 271–92.

Levinson, R.A., Jaccard, J. and Beamer, L. (1995) Older adolescents' engagement in casual sex: impact of risk perception and psychosocial motivations, *Journal of Youth and Adolescence*, 24: 349–64.

Light, R. and Kirk, D. (2000) High school rugby, the body and the reproduction of hegemonic masculinity, *Sport, Education and Society*, 5(2): 163–76.

Lingard, R. and Douglas, P. (1999) *Men Engaging Feminisms: Pro-feminism, Backlashes and Schooling*. Buckingham: Open University Press.

Lingard, B. and Mills, M. (2000) Productive pedagogies, *Education Links*, 60: 10–13.

Lingard, R., Mills, M. and Hayes, D. (2000) Teachers, school reform and social justice: challenging research and practice, *Australian Educational Researcher*, 27(3): 99–115.

Lingard, B., Martino, W. and Mills, M. (2002) *Addressing the Educational Needs of Boys (Research Report)*, Canberra: Department of Education, Science & Training.

Lionnet, F. (1989) *Autobiographical Voices: Race, Gender, Self-Portaiture*. Ithaca: Cornell University Press.

Loeser, C.J. (2002) Bounded bodies, mobile selves: the significance of the muscular body in young hearing-impaired men's constructions of masculinity in S. Pearce and V. Muller (eds) *Manning the Millennium: Studies in Masculinities*. Curtin University of Technology, WA: Black Swan Press.

Longley, K. (1995) Postcolonial reading, *Interpretations*, 28 (1): 1–13.

Lugones, M. (1990) Playfulness, world-travelling, and loving perception, in G. Anzaldua (ed.) *Making Face, Making Soul/Haciendo Caras*. San Francisco: Aunt Lute.

Lugones, M. (1994) Purity, impurity, and separation, *Signs: Journal of Women in Culture & Society*, 19(2): 458–79.

Lupton, D. and Tulloch, J. (1996) All red in the face?: Students' views on school-based HIV/AIDS and sexuality education, *Sociological Review*, 44(2): 252–71.

Mac an Ghaill, M. (1994a) (In)visibility: sexuality, race and masculinity in the school context, in D. Epstein (ed.) *Challenging Lesbian and Gay Inequalities in Education*. Buckingham: Open University Press.

Mac an Ghaill, M. (1994b) *The Making of Men: Masculinities, Sexualities and Schooling*. Buckingham: Open University Press.

Mac an Ghaill, M. (1996) Sociology of education, state schooling and social class: beyond critiques of the New Right hegemony, *British Journal of the Sociology of Education*, 17(2): 163–75.

Mac an Ghaill, M. (2000) Rethinking (male) gendered sexualities in education: what about the British heteros?, *Journal of Men's Studies*, 8(2): 195–212.

McLaren, P. (1993a) Multiculturalism and the postmodern critique: towards a pedagogy of resistance and transformation, *Cultural Studies*, 7(1): 118–46.

McLaren, P. (1993b) White terror and oppositional agency: towards a critical multiculturalism, *Strategies*, 7: 119–33.

McLean, C. (1995) What about 'What about the boys?', *South Australian Education of Girls and Female Students' Association Inc. Journal*, 4(3): 15–25.

McLean, C. (1997) Engaging with boys' experiences of masculinity: implications for gender reform in schools, *Curriculum Perspectives*, 17: 61–5.

McMahon, A. (1998) Blokus domesticus: the sensitive New Age Guy in Australia, *Journal of Australian Studies*, 56: 147–57.

Mangan, J. and Walvin, J. (1987) *Manliness and Morality: Middle-Class Masculinity in Britain and America 1800–1940*. Manchester: Manchester University Press.

Marks, G. (1996) Coming out as gendered adults: gender, sexuality and disability, in C. Christensen and F. Rizvi (eds) *Disability and Dilemmas of Education and Justice*. Buckingham: Open University Press.

Martino, W. (1994) Masculinity and learning: exploring boys' underachievement and under-representation in subject English, *Interpretations*, 27(2): 22–57.

Martino, W. (1995a) Gendered learning practices: exploring the costs of hegemonic masculinity for girls and boys in schools. Paper presented to the Gender Equity Task Force Conference, 22–24 February.

Martino, W. (1995b) Deconstructing masculinity in the English classroom: a site for reconstituting gendered subjectivity, *Gender and Education*, 7(2): 205–20.

Martino, W. (1997) 'A bunch of arseholes': exploring the politics of masculinity for adolescent boys in schools, *Social Alternatives*, 16(3): 39–43.

Martino, W. (1998) 'Dickheads', 'poofs', 'try hards' and 'losers': critical literacy for boys in the English classroom, *English in Aotearoa* (New Zealand Association for the Teaching of English), 25 September: 31–57.

Martino, W. (1999) Cool boys, party animals, squids and poofters: interrogating the dynamics and politics of adolescent masculinities in school, *British Journal of the Sociology of Education*, 20: 239–63.

Martino, W. (2000a) Policing masculinities: investigating the role of homophobia and heteronormativity in the lives of adolescent boys at school, *Journal of Men's Studies*, 8(2): 213–36.

Martino, W. (2000b) 'The boys at the back': challenging masculinities and homophobia in the English classroom, *English in Australia*, 127–8: 35–50.

Martino, W. (2001) Powerful people aren't usually real kind, friendly, open people! Boys interrogating masculinities at school, in W. Martino and B. Meyenn (eds) *What About the Boys? Issues of Masculinity in Schools*. Buckingham: Open University Press.

Martino, W. and Berrill, D. (2002) Dangerous pedagogies: addressing issues of sexuality, masculinity and schooling with male pre-service teacher education students, in K. Davison and B. Frank (eds) *Masculinity and Schooling: International Practices and Perspectives*. Nova Scotia: Fernwood.

Martino, W. and Mellor, B. (1995) *Gendered Fictions*. Cottesloe, WA: Chalkface Press.

Martino, W. and Meyenn, B. (eds) (2001) *What About the Boys? Issues of Masculinity in Schools*. Buckingham: Open University Press.

Martino, W. and Meyenn, B. (2002) 'War, guns and cool, tough things': interrogating single-sex classes as a strategy for engaging boys in English, *Cambridge Journal of Education*, 32(3): 303–24.

Martino, W. and Pallotta-Chiarolli, M. (eds) (2001a) *Boys' Stuff: Boys Talking about What Matters*. Sydney: Allen & Unwin.

Martino, W. and Pallotta-Chiarolli, M. (2001b) Gender performativity and normalising practices: exploring heteronormativity, heterosexism and transgenderism in the lives of young people at school, in F. Haynes and T. McKenna (eds) *Unseen Genders: Beyond the Binaries*. New York: Peter Lang.

Martino, W. and Pallotta-Chiarolli, M. (2001c) 'The chance to explore': boys wanting to talk about what matters, *Teacher Learning Network*, 8(3): 32–35.

Mason, G. and Tomsen, S. (1997) *Homophobic Violence*. Sydney: Hawkins Press.

Mauss, M. (1973) Techniques of the body (Trans. B. Brewster), *Economy and Society*, 2: 70–87.

Mauss, M. (1985) A category of the human mind: the notion of person; the notion of self, in M. Carrithers, S. Collins and S. Lukes (eds) *The Category of the Person: Anthropology, Philosophy, History*. Cambridge: Cambridge University Press.

Meekosha, H. and Jakubowicz, A. (1996) Disability, participation, representation and social justice, in C. Christensen and F. Rizvi (eds) *Disability and Dilemmas of Education and Justice*. Buckingham: Open University Press.

Meekosha, H. and Jakubowicz, A. (2001) Disability studies dis/engages with multicultural studies. Paper for the Disability with Attitude Conference, UWS, 16 February.

Meigs, M. (1983) *The Medusa Head*. Vancouver: Talon Books.

Meissner, A.L. and Thoreson, R.W. (1967) Relation of self-concept to impact and obviousness of disability among male and female adolescents, *Perceptual and Motor Skills*, 24: 1099–1105.

Mellor, B. and Paterson, A. (1991) Reading character: reading gender, *English in Australia*, 95: 4–23.

Mellor, B., O'Neill, M. and Patterson, A. (1991) *Reading Fictions*. Cottesloe, WA: Chalkface Press.

Memmi, A. (1965) *The Colonizer and the Colonized*. Boston: Beacon Press.

Messner, M. (1992) *Power at Play: Sports and the Problem of Masculinity*. Boston: Beacon Press.

Meyer, V.F. (1991) A critique of adolescent pregnancy prevention research: the invisible white male, *Adolescence*, 26(101): 217–22.

Millard, E. (1997) Differently literate: gender identity and the construction of the developing reader, *Gender and Education*, 9(1): 31–48.

Mills, M. (1996) 'Homophobia kills': a disruptive moment in the educational politics of legitimation, *British Journal of Sociology of Education*, 17(3): 315–26.

Mills, M. (1997) Football, desire and the social organisation of masculinity, *Social Alternatives*, 16(1): 10–13.

Mills, M. (2000) Issues in implementing boys' programmes in schools: male teachers and empowerment, *Gender and Education*, 12(2): 221–38.

Mills, M. (2001) *Challenging Violence in Schools: An Issue of Masculinities*. Buckingham: Open University Press.

Minter, S. (1999) Diagnosis and treatment of gender identity disorder in children, in M. Rottnek (ed.) *Sissies and Tomboys: Gender Nonconformity and Homosexual Childhood*. New York: New York University Press.

Moller, J. (1997) Young men and injury, in *Proceedings of Second National Men's Health Conference*, Fremantle, Western Australia, 29–31 October, 325–30.

Moon, B. (1993) Reading and Gender: From Discourse and Subject to Regimes of Practice. Unpublished thesis submitted for the award of the Degree of Doctor of Philosophy, School of Communication and Cultural Studies, Curtin University of Technology.

Moon, B. (1998) Reading gender, in W. Martino and C. Cook (eds) *Gender and Texts: A Professional Development Package for English Teachers*. Adelaide: Australian Association for the Teaching of English (AATE).

Moraga, C. and Anzaldua, G. (eds) (1981) *This Bridge Called My Back: Writings by Radical Women of Color*. Watertown, MA: Persephone Press.

Morris, B. (1990) Racism, egalitarianism and Aborigines, *Journal for Social Justice Studies*, 3: 61–73.

Morris, J. (1991) *Pride against Prejudice: Transforming Attitudes to Disability*. London: Women's Press.

Morris, J. (1993) Prejudice, in J. Swain, V. Finkelstein, S. French and M. Oliver (eds) *Disabling Barriers – Enabling Environments*. London: Sage.

Murphy, P. and Elwood, J. (1998) Gendered learning outside and inside school: influences on achievement, in D. Epstein, J. Elwood, V. Hey and J. Maw (eds) *Failing Boys? Issues in Gender and Achievement*. Buckingham: Open University Press.

Murrie, L. (1998) The Australian legend: writing Australian masculinity/writing Australia masculine, *Journal of Australian Studies*, 56: 68–77.

Muspratt, S., Luke, A. and Freebody, P. (1997) *Constructing Critical Literacies*. Sydney: Allen & Unwin.

Nagel, J. (1994) Constructing ethnicity: creating and recreating ethnic identity and culture, *Social Problems*, 41(1): 152–76.

Neisen, J. (1992) Gender identity disorder of childhood: by whose standard and for what purpose? A response to Rekers and Morey, *Journal of Psychology and Human Sexuality*, 5(3): 65–7.

Nichols, S. (1994) Fathers and literacy, *Australian Journal of Language and Literacy*, 17(4): 301–12.

Nickson, A. (1996) Keeping a straight face: schools and homosexuality, Part 1, in L. Laskey and C. Beavis (eds) *Schooling and Sexualities*. Geelong: Deakin University Centre for Education and Change.

Owens, R.E. (1998) *Queer Kids: The Challenges and Promises for Lesbian, Gay, and Bisexual Youth*. New York: Harrington Park Press.

Pallotta-Chiarolli, M. (1989) From coercion to choice: second-generation women seeking a personal identity in the Italo-Australian setting, *Journal of Intercultural Studies*, 10(1): 49–61.

Pallotta-Chiarolli, M. (1990a) From coercion to choice: the personal identity of the second-generation Italo-Australian adolescent girl, Multicultural Australia Papers no. 68. Collingwood, Victoria: Ecumenical Migration Centre.

Pallotta-Chiarolli, M. (1990b) The female stranger in a boys' school, *Gender and Education*, 2(2): 169–83.

Pallotta-Chiarolli, M. (1991) *Someone You Know: A Friend's Farewell*. Adelaide: Wakefield Press. (New edition, 2002).

Pallotta-Chiarolli, M. (1992) What about me? A study of Italian lesbians, in K. Herne, J. Travaglia and E. Weiss (eds) *Who Do You Think You Are? Second Generation Immigrant Women in Australia*. Sydney: Women's Redress Press.

Pallotta-Chiarolli, M. (1995a) 'A rainbow in my heart': negotiating sexuality and ethnicity, in C. Guerra and R. White (eds) *Ethnic Minority Youth In Australia: Challenges and Myths*. Hobart: National Clearinghouse on Youth Studies.

Pallotta-Chiarolli, M. (1995b) 'Can I write the word GAY in my essay?', in R. Browne and R. Fletcher (eds) *Boys in Schools: Addressing the Issues*. Lane Cove, Sydney: Finch.

Pallotta-Chiarolli, M. (1995c) 'Only your labels split me': interweaving ethnicity and sexuality studies, *English in Australia*, 112: 33–44.

Pallotta-Chiarolli, M. (1996) A rainbow in my heart: interweaving ethnicity and sexuality studies, in L. Laskey and C. Beavis (eds) *Schooling and Sexualities: Teaching for a Positive Sexuality*. Geelong: Deakin University Centre for Education and Change.

Pallotta-Chiarolli, M. (1997) We want to address boys' education but . . ., *Curriculum Perspectives*, 17(1): 65–8.

Pallotta-Chiarolli, M. (ed.) (1998a) *Girls Talk: Young Women Speak their Hearts and Minds*. Lane Cove, Sydney: Finch.

Pallotta-Chiarolli, M. (1998b) Cultural diversity and men who have sex with men. Sydney: National Centre in HIV Social Research, University of New South Wales.

Pallotta-Chiarolli, M. (1999a) *Tapestry: Italian Lives Over Five Generations*. Milson's Point, Sydney: Random House.

Pallotta-Chiarolli, M. (1999b) Diary entries from the 'Teachers' Professional Development Playground': multiculturalism meets multisexualities in education, in G. Sullivan and P. Jackson (eds) *Multicultural Queer: Australian Narratives*. New York: Haworth Press.

Pallotta-Chiarolli, M. (1999c) 'Multicultural does not mean multisexual': social justice and the interweaving of ethnicity and sexuality in Australian schooling, in D. Epstein and J.T. Sears (eds) *A Dangerous Knowing: Sexual Pedagogies and the Master Narrative*. London: Cassell.

Pallotta-Chiarolli, M. (1999d) 'My moving days': a child's negotiation of multiple lifeworlds in relation to gender, ethnicity and sexuality, in J.T. Sears and W. Letts (eds) *Queering Elementary Education: Advancing the Dialogue about Sexualities and Schooling*. New York: Rowman & Littlefield.

Pallotta-Chiarolli, M. (1999e) Review of *Masculinity Goes to School* (P. Gilbert and R. Gilbert) and *Schooling Sexualities* (D. Epstein and R. Johnson), *Australian Educational Researcher*, 26(1): 98–103.

Pallotta-Chiarolli, M. (2000) What do they think? Queerly raised and queer friendly students, *Youth Studies Australia*, 19(4): 34–40.

Pallotta-Chiarolli, M. and Skrbis, Z. (1994) Authority, compliance and rebellion in second-generation individuals from cultural minorities, *Australia and New Zealand Journal of Sociology*, 30(3): 259–72.

Pallotta-Chiarolli, M., Van De Ven, P., Prestage, G. and Kippax, S. (1999) Too busy studying to have sex? Homosexually active Asian male international students and sexual health. Sydney: National Centre in HIV Social Research, University of New South Wales.

Palmer, D. and Collard, L. (1993) Aboriginal young people and youth subcultures, in R. White (ed.) *Youth Subcultures: Theory, History and the Australian Experience*. Hobart, Tasmania: National Clearing House for Youth Studies.

Parker, A. (1996) The construction of masculinity within boys' physical education, *Gender and Education*, 8(2): 141–57.

Partington, G. (1998) *Perspectives on Aboriginal and Torres Strait Islander Education*. Katoomba, NSW: Social Science Press.

Patterson, O. (1983) The nature, causes, and implications of ethnic identification, in C. Fried (ed.) *Minorities: Community and Identity*. Berlin: Springer-Verlag.

Pease, B. (1997) The sexual politics of men's health, in *Proceedings of Second National Men's Health Conference*, Fremantle, Western Australia, 29–31 October, 371–8.

Penney, D. and Chandler, T. (2000) Physical education: what future(s)?, *Sport, Education and Society*, 5(1): 71–7.

Perrotti, J. and Westheimer, K. (2001) *When the Drama Club is not Enough: Lessons from the Safe Schools Program for Gay and Lesbian Students*. Boston: Beacon Press.

Petersen, A. (1998) *Unmasking the Masculine: 'Men' and 'Identity' in a Sceptical Age*. London: Sage.

Pettman, J. (1992) *Living in the Margins*. Sydney: Allen & Unwin.

Plummer, D. (1999) *One of the Boys: Masculinity, Homophobia, and Modern Manhood*. New York: Harrington Park Press.

Pollack, W. (1998) *Real Boys: Rescuing our Sons from the Myths of Boyhood*. New York: Random House.

Ponton, L.E. (1997) *The Romance of Risk: Why Teenagers Do the Things They Do*. New York: Basic Books.

Pope, H., Phillips, K. and Olivardia, R. (2000) *The Adonis Complex*. New York: Touchstone.

Poynting, S., Noble, G. and Tabar, P. (1998) If anyone called me a wog, they wouldn't be speaking to me alone: protest masculinity and Lebanese youth in western Sydney, *Journal of Interdisciplinary Gender Studies*, 3(2): 76–94.

Poynting, S., Noble, G. and Tabar, P. (1999) Intersections of masculinity and ethnicity: a study of male Lebanese immigrant youth in western Sydney, *Race, Ethnicity and Education*, 2(1): 59–77.

Price, B. and Price, D. (1998) Unheard voices, *Journal of Australian Indigenous Issues*, 1: 15–23.

Purdie, N., Tripcony, P., Boulton-Lewis, G., Fanshaw, J. and Gunstone, A. (2000) *Positive Self-identity for Indigenous Students and its Relationship to School Outcomes*. Canberra: DETYA.

Ratti, R. (ed.) (1993) *A Lotus of Another Color: An Unfolding of South Asian Gay and Lesbian Experience*. Boston: Alyson.

Redman, P. (1996) Curtis loves Ranjit: heterosexual masculinities, schooling and pupils' sexual cultures, *Educational Review*, 48(2): 175–82.

Rich, A. (1980) Compulsory heterosexuality and lesbian experience, *Signs*, 54: 631–60

Rich, P. (1994) Coming out blind and gay: how I survived the straight and sighted, *Changing Men*, 27: 33–6.

Rigby, K. (1996) *Bullying in Schools: And What To Do About It*. Melbourne: Australian Council for Educational Research (ACER).

Rickard, J. (1998) Lovable larrikins and awful ockers, *Journal of Australian Studies*, 56: 78–85.

Rivlin, M. (1980) The disabled gay – an appraisal, *Sexuality and Disability*, 3(3): 221–2.

Robillard, K. and Fichten, C. (1983) Attributions about sexuality and romantic involvement of physically disabled college students: an empirical study, *Sexuality and Disability*, 6(3/4): 197–212.

Robinson, K. (1996) 'Great tits, miss!' The silencing of male students' sexual harassment of female teachers in secondary schools: a focus on gendered authority, *Discourse*, 21(1): 75–90.

Rottnek, M. (ed.) (1999) *Sissies and Tomboys: Gender Nonconformity and Homosexual Childhood*. New York: New York University Press.

Roulsten, K. and Mills, M. (2000) Male teachers in feminised teaching areas: marching to the men's movement drums, *Oxford Review of Education*, 26(1): 221–37.

Rowan, L., Knobel, M., Bigum, C. and Lankshear, C. (2002) *Boys, Literacies and Schooling: The Dangerous Territories of Gender-based Literacy Reform*. Buckingham: Open University Press.

Safran, W. (1991) Diasporas in modern societies: myths of homeland and return, *Diaspora*, 1(1): 83–99.

Said, E. (1979) *Orientalism*. New York: Random House.

Said, E. (1986) Orientalism reconsidered, in F. Barker, P. Hulme, M. Iversen and D. Loxley (eds) *Literature, Politics and Theory*. London: Methuen.

Said, E. (1990) Reflections on exile, in R. Ferguson, M. Gever, M. T. Trinh and C. West (eds) *Out There: Marginalization and Contemporary Cultures*. Cambridge, MA. MIT Press.

Salisbury, J. and Jackson, D. (1996) *Challenging Macho Values: Practical Ways of Working with Adolescent Boys*. London: Falmer Press.

Schutz, A. (1944) The stranger: an essay in social psychology, *American Journal of Sociology*, 49(6): 499–507.

Sewell, T. (1997) *Black Masculinity and Schooling: How Black Boys Survive Modern Schooling*. Stoke-on-Trent: Trentham Books.

Sewell, T. (1998) Loose canons: exploding the myth of the 'black macho' lad, in D. Epstein, J. Elwood, V. Hey and J. Maw (eds) *Failing Boys? Issues in Gender and Achievement*. Buckingham: Open University Press.

Shakespeare, T. (1996) Power and prejudice: issues of gender, sexuality and disability, in L. Barton (ed.) *Disability and Society: Emerging Issues and Insights*. London: Longman.

Shakespeare, T. (1999) The sexual politics of disabled masculinity, *Sexuality and Disability*, 17(1): 53–64.

Sheehan, M. and Ridge, D. (2001) 'You become really close ... you talk about the silly things you did, and we laugh: the role of binge drinking in female secondary students' lives, *Substance Use and Misuse*, 36(3): 347–72.

Shofield, A.T. and Vaughan-Jackson, P. (1913) *What A Boy Should Know*. London, Cassell.

Signorile, M. (1997) *Life Outside: The Signorile Report on Gay Men: Sex, Drugs, Muscles, and The Passages of Life*. New York, NY: HarperPerennial.

Simpson, L., McFadden, M. and Munns, G. (2001) 'Someone has to go through': indigenous boys, staying on at school and negotiating masculinities, in W. Martino and B. Meyenn (eds) *What about the Boys? Issues of Masculinity in Schools*. Buckingham: Open University Press.

Skelton, C. (2000) 'A passion for football': dominant masculinities and primary schooling, *Sport, Education and Society*, 5(1): 5–18.

Skelton, C. (2001) *Schooling the Boys: Masculinities and Primary Education*. Buckingham: Open University Press.

Skord, K. and Schumacher, B. (1982) Masculinity as a handicapping condition, *Rehabilitation Literature*, 43(9–10): 284–8.

Skrbis, Z. (1999) *Long-distance Nationalism: Diasporas, Homelands and Identities*. Aldershot: Ashgate.

Slade, M. and Trent, F. (2000) What are the boys saying: an examination of the views of boys about declining rates of achievement and retention, *International Journal of Education* 1(3): 201–29.

Spickard, P.R. (1992) The illogic of American racial categorization, in M.P. Root (ed.) *Racially Mixed People in America*. Newbury Park: Sage.

Steinberg, D.L., Epstein, D. and Johnson, R. (1997) *Border Patrols: Policing the Boundaries of Heterosexuality*. London: Cassell.

Swain, J. (2000) The money's good, the fame's good, the girls are good: the role of playground football in the construction of young boys' masculinity in a junior school, *British Journal of Sociology of Education*, 21(1): 95–109.

Symes, C. and Meadmore, D. (1996) Force of habit: the school uniform as a body of knowledge, in E. McWilliam and P.G. Taylor (eds) *Pedagogy, Technology, and the Body*. New York: Peter Lang.

Synott, J. and Whatman, S. (1998) United to the sea and land: cultures, histories and education in the Torres Strait, in G. Partington (ed.) *Perspectives on Aboriginal and Torres Strait Islander Education*. Katoomba, NSW: Social Sciences Press.

Taleporos, G. (1999) The inaccessible orgasm: sexual recreation for people with disabilities, *NICAN Network News*, 8(4): 7–8.

Taleporos, G. (2001) Sexuality and physical disability – healing the wounds of a flesh focused society, in C. Wood (ed.) *Sexual Positions: An Australian View*. Melbourne: Hill of Content.

Tepper, M.S. (1997) Living with a disability: a man's perspective, in M.L. Sipski and C.J. Alexander (eds) *Sexual Function in People with Disability and Chronic Illness: A Health Professional's Guide*. Maryland: Aspen Publishers.

Tepper, M. (1999) Letting go of restrictive notions of manhood: male sexuality, disability and chronic illness, *Sexuality and Disability*, 17(1): 37–52.

Thorogood, N. (2000) Sex education as disciplinary technique: policy and practice in England and Wales, *Sexualities*, 3(4): 425–38.

Tizard, B. and Phoenix, A. (1993) *Black, White or Mixed Race? Race and Racism in the Lives of Young People of Mixed Parentage*. London: Routledge.

Tran Binh Dong (1999) Foreword, in P. Jackson and G. Sullivan (eds) *Multicultural Queer: Australian Narratives*. New York: Haworth Press.

Trinh, M.T. (1989) *Woman, Native, Other*. Bloomington: Indiana University Press.

Trinh, M.T. (1990a) Cotton and iron, in R. Ferguson, M. Gever, M.T. Trinh and C. West (eds) *Out There: Marginalization and Contemporary Cultures*. Cambridge, MA: MIT Press.

Trinh, M.T. (1990b). Not you/like you: post-colonial women and the interlocking questions of identity and difference, in G. Anzaldua (ed.) *Making Faces, Making Soul/Haciendo Caras*. San Francisco: Aunt Lute.

Trinh, M.T. (1991) *When the Moon Waxes Red*. New York: Routledge.

Trinh, M.T. (1992) *Framer Framed*. New York: Routledge.

Tsolidis, G. (1986) *Educating Voula – A Report on Non-English-Speaking Background Girls and Education*. Melbourne: Ministry of Education, Victoria.

Tsolidis, G. (2001a) *Schooling, Diaspora and Gender: Being Feminist and Being Different*. Buckingham: Open University Press.

Tsolidis, G. (2001b) New cultures, new classrooms: international education and the possibility of radical pedagogies, *Pedagogy, Culture and Society*, 9(1): 97–110.

Udis-Kessler, A. (1990). Bisexuality in an essentialist world: toward an understanding of biphobia, in T. Geller (ed.) *Bisexuality: A Reader and Sourcebook*. Ojai, CA: Times Change Press.

Vasta, E. (1975) Adolescents in conflict: a sociological study of the personal and social adjustment of second-generation Italian immigrants. Thesis presented for Honours in Sociology, University of Queensland.

Vasta, E. (1993) Multiculturalism and ethnic identity: the relationship between racism and resistance, *Australia New Zealand Journal of Sociology*, 29(2): 209–25.

Vernon, A. (1998) Multiple oppression and the disabled people's movement, in T. Shakespeare (ed.) *The Disability Reader: Social Science Perspectives*. London: Cassell.

Vernon, A. (1999) The dialectics of multiple identities and the disabled people's movement, *Disability and Society*, 14(3): 385–98.

Walker, J.C. (1988) *Louts and Legends*. Sydney: Allen & Unwin.

Walker, L. (1998) Under the bonnet: car culture, technological dominance and young men of the working class, *Journal of Interdisciplinary Gender Studies*, 3(2): 23–43.

Walker, L., Butland, D. and Connell, R.W. (2000) Boys on the road: masculinities, car culture, and road safety education, *Journal of Men's Studies*, 8(2): 153–69.

Ward, R. (1985) *The Australian Legend*. Melbourne: Oxford University Press.

Ward, N. (1995) 'Pooftah', 'wanker', 'girl': homophobic harassment and violence in schools, in *Girls & Boys: Challenging Perspective, Building Partnerships: Proceedings of the Third Conference of the Ministerial Advisory Committee on Gender Equity*. Brisbane: Ministerial Advisory Committee on Gender Equity.

Wendell, S. (1997) Toward a feminist theory of disability, in Lennard J. Davis (ed.) *The Disability Studies Reader*. New York: Routledge.

Wienke, C. (1998) Negotiating the male body: men, masculinity, and cultural ideals, *Journal of Men's Studies*, 6(3): 255–83.

Wilhelm, J. and Smith, M. (2001) Literacy in the lives of young men: findings from an American study, *English in Australia*, 132, 17–28.

Williams, W. (1997) Multicultural perspectives on reducing heterosexism: looking for strategies that work, in J.T. Sears and Walter L. Williams (eds) *Overcoming Heterosexism and Homophobia: Strategies that Work*. New York: Columbia University Press.

Willis, P. (1977) *Learning to Labour: How Working Class Kids Get Working Class Jobs*. Westmead: Saxon House.

Wilson, A. (1987) *Mixed Race Children: A Study of Identity*. London: Allen & Unwin.

Wright, J. (1998) Reconstructing gender in sport and physical education, in C. Hickey, L. Fitzclarence and R. Matthews (eds) *Where the Boys Are: Masculinity, Sport and Education*. Geelong: Deakin University Centre for Education and Change.

Zerubavel, E. (1991) *The Fine Line: Making Distinctions in Everyday Life*. Chicago: University of Chicago Press.

Zucker, K.J. and Bradley, S.J. (1995) *Gender Identity Disorder and Psychosexual Problems in Children and Adolescents*. New York: Guilford Press.

Index

INVESTIGATING GENDER
CONTEMPORARY PERSPECTIVES IN EDUCATION

Becky Francis and Christine Skelton (eds)

> This is an excellent account of the dilemmas and opportunities facing contemporary theories of gender and education. The book brings together some of the most sophisticated researchers in the field to demonstrate the power, the mysteries and the complexities of the concept of identity. The case for a new approach to gender theory is convincing and exciting. Teachers, academics and policy makers need to recognise the value of such contemporary concerns.
>
> Madeleine Arnot, University of Cambridge.

Investigating Gender maps the contemporary and developing theoretical debates in the field of gender and education, and provides an overview of the diverse areas of research within gender and education. Contributions have been commissioned from recognized experts in the field in order to provide a comprehensive reader on gender and education for undergraduate students. The book will also provide stimulating reading for postgraduate students and academics.

Recent changes, developments and challenges in the field are outlined in the first section of the book. It also catalogues the influence of research in this area on policy in the UK context. The second section focuses on recent innovations in theoretical debates in gender and education. Overviews of research developments in particular subject areas (such as sexuality, social class, masculinity etc) are provided in the third section, where contributors draw on their own research findings to illustrate the discussion.

Contents

Contributors

Stephen Baron, Jo-Anne Dillabough, Becky Francis, Martyn Hammersley, Wendy Cealey Harrison, Mary Jane Kehily, Helen Lucey, Anoop Nayak, Carrie Paechter, Ann Phoenix, Diane Reay, Lynn Raphael Reed, Sheila Riddell, Christine Skelton, Alastair Wilson.

240pp   0 335 20787 1 (Paperback)   0 335 20788 X (Hardback)

BOYS, LITERACIES AND SCHOOLING

THE DANGEROUS TERRITORIES OF GENDER-BASED LITERACY REFORM

Leonie Rowan, Michele Knobel, Chris Bigum, Colin Lankshear

Current debates about boys and schooling in many Western nations are increasingly characterized by a sense of crisis as government reports, academic research and the day to day experience of teachers combine to indicate that:

- boys are consistently underperforming in literacy
- boys are continuing to opt out of English and humanities
- boys represent the majority of behaviour problems and counselling referrals
- boys receive a disproportionate amount of special education support.

This book responds to the complexity of the current debates associated with boys, gender reform, literacy and schooling by offering a clear map of the current context, highlighting the strengths and weaknesses of the various competing solutions put forward, and outlining a range of practical classroom interventions designed for dealing with the boys/literacy crisis. The authors consider the ways in which particular views of masculinity, gender reform, literacy, technology and popular culture can either open up or close down new conceptualizations of what it means to be a boy and what it means to be literate.

Contents

Introduction – Dangerous places: debates about boys, girls, schooling and gender-based literacy reform – What about the boys? The rhetoric and realities of the new gender crisis – How, who, where, when, why and what way? Mindsets on gender reform in schools – Some really useful theoretical company for transforming and transformative literacy education – Mindsets matter: an overview of major literacy worldviews – Making it not so: transformative literacy practices for girls and boys – Exorcizing digital demons: information technology, new literacies and the de/reconstruction of gendered subjectivities – From Pacman to Pokemon: cross-generational perspectives on gender and reform in a 'post-feminist' age – Conclusions – Bibliography – Index.

256pp 0 335 20756 1 (Paperback) 0 335 20757 X (Hardback)